New Orleans
FOR
DUMMIES®
4TH EDITION

by Julia Kamysz Lane

BICENTENNIAL
1807
WILEY
2007
BICENTENNIAL

Wiley Publishing, Inc.

New Orleans For Dummies®, 4th Edition

Published by
Wiley Publishing, Inc.
111 River St.
Hoboken, NJ 07030-5774
www.wiley.com

WILEY

About the Author

Julia Kamysz Lane is a freelance writer and book reviewer whose work has appeared in numerous newspapers and magazines. She and her husband are dividing their time between Chicago and New Orleans while they restore their 1940s bungalow after severe flooding from Hurricane Katrina in 2005. They care for a small zoo of pets, comprised of four dogs — Catahoula Desoto, Dalmatians Darby and Jolie, and All-American Shelby — and two cats, Cricket and Bruiser Bear.

Dedication

This book is again dedicated to my parents, Rich and Ellen Kamysz, for hosting us and our many pets in their home for eight months after the storm. Mom and Dad, we can never repay you for your love, patience, and generosity during that difficult time.

Author's Acknowledgments

I would first and foremost like to thank my editor, Stephen Bassman, for his enthusiasm, guidance, and excellent listening skills when I was eager to share my New Orleans experiences.

And grateful thanks to the following for factual and emotional support during the revision of this book: my wonderful New Orleans friends Becky Anderson; Esther Carlisle; Victoria Cooke; Mark and Bonnie Suckow (congrats on twins William and Robin!); Angela Portera and Dayna Dufrene, for hosting us countless times while we salvaged flooded possessions and gutted our house; and Michael Depp and Darleen Mipro, for initiating a long overdue reunion and hosting at the very last minute (congrats on baby Jude!).

Thank you WWOZ (www.wwoz.org) for playing such awesome, funky music over the Web so I could be inspired by New Orleans culture and attitude no matter where I was, and especially while working on this book.

I also want to thank my new Illinois friends Dave and Shasta Newton; Ralph and Barb Scalise; and Grant and Whitney Rupp (aka "Whant").

Of course, I must thank my family, especially my parents Rich and Ellen Kamysz, my father- and mother-in-law Rich and Barb Lane, and my brother Marty Kamysz and sister-in-law Renee Kamysz, all of whom helped us get back on our feet again. I am grateful to my young nieces, toddler Lauren and baby Megan Kamysz, for making me laugh, smile, and look forward to the future.

Many compassionate people offered us money, clothes, and a shoulder to cry on in the months after the storm, plus food, crates, toys, and more for our pets. I will never forget your kindness.

Lastly, thank you to my husband and best friend, Brian Lane, who never gave up looking for those antique salters among the wreckage of our New Orleans home. Ultimately, the salters didn't matter as much as having you by my side as we rebuild our life together. TBIL!

Publisher's Acknowledgments

We're proud of this book; please send us your comments through our Dummies online registration form located at www.dummies.com/register/.

Some of the people who helped bring this book to market include the following:

Editorial

Editors: Stephen Bassman, Development Editor; Lindsay Conner, Production Editor

Copy Editor: Melissa S. Bennett

Cartographer: Tim Lohnes

Editorial Assistant: Melinda Quintero

Senior Photo Editor: Richard Fox

Cover Photos
Front: © Cosmo Condina/ Getty Images
Back: © Richard Cummins/Corbis

Photo Credits: "Portrait of a Katrina survivor" © Thomas Neff

Cartoons: Rich Tennant, www.the5thwave.com

Composition

Project Coordinator: Kristie Rees

Layout and Graphics: Stephanie D. Jumper, Amanda Spagnuolo

Proofreaders: David Faust, Techbooks

Indexer: Techbooks

Publishing and Editorial for Consumer Dummies

Diane Graves Steele, Vice President and Publisher, Consumer Dummies

Joyce Pepple, Acquisitions Director, Consumer Dummies

Kristin A. Cocks, Product Development Director, Consumer Dummies

Michael Spring, Vice President and Publisher, Travel

Kelly Regan, Editorial Director, Travel

Publishing for Technology Dummies

Andy Cummings, Vice President and Publisher, Dummies Technology/ General User

Composition Services

Gerry Fahey, Vice President of Production Services

Debbie Stailey, Director of Composition Services

Contents at a Glance

Maps at a Glance

Table of Contents

Introduction

. . . .

*N*ormally, revising this guide and finding new ways to help you plan and enjoy your visit to this unique city is fun and straightforward. I tell you about the many new hotels, restaurants and shops and bring you up to date on old favorites. I also offer travel tips and advice that only a local would know. But after Hurricane Katrina devastated New Orleans and the surrounding Gulf Coast in 2005, this revision has proven more difficult — both logistically and emotionally — to write than I expected. For although many of the neighborhoods, places and historic landmarks you will want to visit have been mercifully spared, much more of the city (that perhaps visitors would not typically tour) was not.

When Hurricane Katrina first threatened the Crescent City, my husband and I chose to evacuate our Lakeview home with our many beloved pets. It was a wise decision, as our home and neighborhood were devastated by flooding from the breached levees. For days, even weeks after Katrina, we spent hours on the phone trying to find out if our friends and neighbors were safe. Some had stayed and some had evacuated like us. Thankfully, everyone we knew was okay, but we knew that many others lost loved ones or couldn't find someone dear to them.

During those first weeks after the storm, the city itself seemed lost. When I first saw video footage of the flooding, I didn't recognize my own neighborhood. I feared the worst. But as time passed, and people began to recover and rebuild, it became clear that the city would survive. Old traditions and places that were once taken for granted are now revered and honored. Communities that had fallen by the wayside due to poverty and inadequate education are finding support from around the world. And everyone is coming together to help one another like never before.

So when you visit New Orleans, don't be surprised if you get caught up in the spirit of the locals. Once easy and carefree, they are now fiercely determined to make "The City That Care Forgot" one that you will always remember. I hope that you find this book to be both practical and inspirational as you discover New Orleans's many pleasures.

About This Book

New Orleans For Dummies, 4th Edition is a reference book, not an exhaustive, voluminous guide that requires hours of reading. The information is laid out in the logical order of a step-by-step manual — from planning your trip to arriving to seeing attractions to checking out the nightlife and so forth — but you don't need to read the book in order from front to back. Scan the table of contents or the index to find what you need.

Dummies Post-it® Flags

As you're reading this book, you'll find information that you'll want to reference as you plan or enjoy your trip — whether it be a new hotel, a must-see attraction, or a must-try walking tour. Mark these pages with the handy Post-it® Flags included in this book to help make your trip planning easier.

Travel information can and does change at any given time, and this is doubly true in the wake of Hurricane Katrina. Businesses are still repairing property damage. Prices and hours of operation are subject to change as businesses adapt to fluctuating crowds. I therefore suggest that you call ahead for confirmation when making your travel plans. The author, editors, and publisher can't be held responsible for the experiences of readers while traveling. Your safety is important to us, however, so I encourage you to stay alert and be aware of your surroundings. Keep a close eye on cameras, purses, and wallets — all favorite targets of thieves and pickpockets.

Conventions Used in This Book

This book includes reviews of hotels, restaurants, attractions, bars, and other businesses and often uses abbreviations for the following commonly accepted credit cards:

AE: American Express

CB: Carte Blanche

DC: Diners Club

DISC: Discover

MC: MasterCard

V: Visa

This book also includes some general pricing information to help you as you decide where to unpack your bags or dine on the local cuisine. I use a system of dollar signs to show a range of costs for one night in a hotel or a meal at a restaurant (including entree, drinks, and tip). Check out the following table to decipher the dollar signs:

Cost	Hotel	Restaurant
$	Less than $100	Less than $15
$$	$100–$200	$15–$30
$$$	$201–$300	$31–$45
$$$$	$301 and up	$46 or more

A note about maps in this edition

Conventional travel-guide wisdom says that when a business closes, delete it from the map. However, the state of New Orleans after Hurricane Katrina is anything but conventional. Though some businesses we once recommended are closed as we go to print, many are pushing to reopen in 2007. We're optimistically keeping these businesses on the maps in this edition, listed under **"Closed, May Reopen"** in the map keys and marked on the maps with white bullets instead of black ones. We encourage you to call for updates. Businesses we listed in the previous edition of this guide that will not reopen are labeled **"Closed Permanently"** and are mapped with a shaded gray bullet. We hope this notation gives you a sense of how Katrina affected this book in between updates. It is not meant to give a comprehensive view of affected properties; many, many other businesses that we don't map were damaged or destroyed.

For those hotels, restaurants, and attractions that are plotted on a map, a page reference is provided in the listing information. If a hotel, restaurant, or attraction is outside the city limits or in an out-of-the-way area, it may not be mapped.

Foolish Assumptions

In this book I make some of the following assumptions about you and what your needs may be as a traveler:

- ✔ You may be an inexperienced traveler looking for guidance on whether to take a trip to New Orleans and how to plan for it.

- ✔ You may be an experienced traveler who hasn't had much time to explore New Orleans and wants expert advice when you finally do get a chance to enjoy what the city has to offer.

- ✔ You may be an experienced traveler who has visited New Orleans before Katrina hit and you want updates on some of your favorite hotels, restaurants and attractions and suggestions on how to make the most of your first post-Katrina visit.

- ✔ You're not looking for a book that provides all the information available about New Orleans or that lists every hotel, restaurant, or attraction. Instead, you're looking for a book that focuses on the best places to give you that uniquely New Orleans experience.

If you fit any of these criteria, this book gives you the information you need.

How This Book Is Organized

New Orleans For Dummies, 4th Edition is designed to serve as two books in one: It's both a trip-planning guide and a savvy reference book, boiling off the excessive minutiae of other, more conventional travel guides, leaving you with the essential information you need to enjoy New Orleans without getting fleeced or disappointed — and without looking like an obvious tourist.

Part 1: Introducing New Orleans

Part I introduces you to the city of New Orleans, and I include the somber but essential topic of Hurricane Katrina. I describe why this disaster occurred and how the city is coping. This part also gives you some historical background, plus a fine-tuned list of the city's best, with tips on what time of year to visit.

Part 11: Planning Your Trip to New Orleans

In this part, you get your hands dirty with the details of planning your trip, from dealing with money to getting to the Crescent City, plus tips for travelers with special needs.

Part 111: Settling into New Orleans

This part helps you get the lay of the land before you arrive, describes your lodging options, introduces you to New Orleans's neighborhoods — including those that flooded — and leads you to the best spots to sample the city's culinary delights, from beignets to jambalaya. By eating out during your stay, you are supporting a New Orleans tradition: great food you can't get anywhere else.

Part 1V: Exploring New Orleans

How often do you get a chance to shop *and* make a difference? Please feel free to eat out and buy souvenirs galore — from antiques to pralines to T-shirts — and help New Orleans's economy grow. Here I tell you what you need to know to enjoy the many sights and shopping delights of New Orleans. Plus, I provide you with optional itineraries to manage your time, and finish with a list of day trips if you'd like to stray from the city for a day or two.

Part V: Living It Up After Dark: New Orleans Nightlife

If you were concerned that locals are too tired from rebuilding to party, you are happily mistaken. If anything, we need some fun to recharge our batteries. So please, try not to retire to your hotel room after the sun goes down, because you may miss out on at least half of what New Orleans is all about. This part starts with a rundown of the city's varied and exciting cultural scene and goes on to the best bars and clubs in the French Quarter and beyond.

Part VI: The Part of Tens

Part VI gives you handy information in list form. I take this opportunity to outline ten classic experiences you can still have in New Orleans, the top ten issues the city faces at this crucial juncture, and I give you a reminder of ten things we lost in the hurricane.

Post-Katrina Information

You'll find a compendium of information — including a timeline and a list of notable figures — in the brand new Chapter 2, "Hurricane Katrina and Its Aftermath." Elsewhere, I've done my best to include the latest closings and openings as we go to print, but you'll need to call ahead to confirm before you visit (especially for restaurants). Throughout this guide, I assess Katrina's impact on each industry (in sections called "Assessing Katrina's Affect On . . ." at the beginning of relevant chapters), and I've also updated every single listing to give its post-hurricane status. If a business is closed but looks poised to reopen, I've optimistically kept its review in the book, with a note about its limbo status and details of the damage done. If a business looks closed for good, I've removed the listing and made a note in the "Assessing Katrina's Affect On . . ." section. I've also kept the defunct businesses listed on the map (with a special notation by the bullets). This allows you to glance at the maps and get a sense of the hurricane's impact. See "A note about maps in this edition" in this section. Finally, look for hurricane emergency hotline numbers and other pertinent safety information in the Appendix.

Icons Used in This Book

In the margins of this book, you will find a number of helpful little icons designed to draw your attention to particularly useful bits of information.

This icon highlights money-saving tips and/or great deals.

This icon highlights the best the destination has to offer in all categories — hotels, restaurants, attractions, activities, shopping, and nightlife.

This icon gives you a heads-up on annoying or potentially dangerous situations such as tourist traps, unsafe neighborhoods, rip-offs, and other things to beware of.

This icon highlights attractions, hotels, restaurants, or activities that are particularly hospitable to children or people traveling with kids.

This icon points out useful advice on things to do and ways to schedule your time.

Where to Go from Here

Because I break up this book into easily digestible parts and chapters, turn right to the section that interests you. If you're anxious to read about Hurricane Katrina, turn to Chapter 2. If you already know when you're going to New Orleans and where you're staying, for example, skip to Part IV (though you may want to make a pit stop at Chapters 5 and 8). If you've been to New Orleans before and know your way around, jump straight to Parts IV and V to look for the latest information on attractions, sights, and clubs affected by Katrina, plus places that may be new to you.

Part I
Introducing New Orleans

WHY PILOTS DON'T DRESS FOR MARDI GRAS BEFORE FLIGHTS

"That was a nasty patch of turbulence. I'd better go back and reassure the passengers."

In this part . . .

So you want to visit New Orleans, eh? Well, good, because the city can use your tourist dollars in the wake of Hurricane Katrina. Hotels are eager to host you, restaurants are eager to serve you, and locals in general are eager to host visitors and resume life in this beloved American city.

This part of the book introduces you to New Orleans: You'll find an overview of the city's best (Chapter 1) , a necessary discussion of Katrina and its aftermath (Chapter 2), a brief rundown of the city's history and culture (Chapter 3), and seasonal information to help you decide when to visit (Chapter 4).

Chapter 1

Discovering the Best of Post-Katrina New Orleans

. . . .

In This Chapter

▶ The best hotels

▶ The best restaurants

▶ The best museums

▶ The best clubs

▶ The best romantic experiences

. . . .

*W*hen revising my "Best Of" list for this edition, I was pleasantly surprised to find that most of my favorites survived or returned after rebuilding, though there were a few that didn't make it. The hip Hotel Monaco — which gave my Catahoula dog, Desoto, the V.I. P(uppy) treatment a couple years back — closed its doors for good. French Quarter restaurant Bella Luna, with its lovely view of the Mississippi, is no more. Long-time family-owned seafood restaurants Sid-Mar's, Weaver's, and Bruning's — all in my neighborhood — were flooded beyond repair. And one of my favorite hangouts, Plantation Coffeehouse, is likely not coming back because the landlord isn't cooperating with the owner (who knows his customers would give anything for just one more sip of their famous iced coffees). Of course, if you travel beyond the usual tourist areas of the city, you'll find that every flooded neighborhood lost many favorite and popular places. But locals (myself included) are focused on what survived and what is to come.

For more information on the hotels, restaurants, clubs, museums, and romantic spots noted in this chapter, look for the Best of the Best icon throughout the book.

The Best Hotels

  ✔ For historic charm, the **Hotel Monteleone** boasts quite a history as the oldest and largest hotel in the French Quarter. **Maison Dupuy** carries the distinction of once being home to the world's first cotton press. See Chapter 10.

✔ For guaranteed pampering, you have two great options in the Central Business District. Old-line **Le Pavillon** offers everything from complimentary hors d'oeuvres to shoeshines. **International House** (built in 1906 to accommodate the world's first trade center) exemplifies New Orleans's talent for adapting older buildings from their original use (or a state of outright neglect) into unique lodging. See Chapter 10.

✔ **The Ritz-Carlton** is happily slated to reopen just as we go to print. The hotel is an ambitious renovation of a one-time New Orleans institution, the Maison Blanche department store, and signifies a return to Canal Street's glory days. See Chapter 10.

✔ Smaller but equally impressive is the recently renovated **Block-Keller House,** which gives a taste of how Mid-City will look as the Canal streetcar works its restoration magic down the line. See Chapter 10.

The Best Restaurants

✔ For Cajun and Creole, try Emeril Lagasse's flagship restaurant, **Emeril's,** where you can taste what he calls *"new* New Orleans cuisine." Or if you're a traditionalist, try **Antoine's, Arnaud's,** or Paul Prudhomme's **K-Paul's Louisiana Kitchen.** See Chapter 11.

✔ Dine at one of first-rate restaurants from the city's dining dynasty, the Brennan Family, including **Bacco** and **Brennan's,** both located in the French Quarter. Their Garden District jewel, **Commander's Palace,** reopened in 2006 to great fanfare. See Chapter 11.

✔ Stroll and nosh: Eat a greasy, roast-beef po' boy from **Elizabeth's,** an overstuffed muffuletta from **Central Grocery,** a plateful of shucked oysters from **Acme Oyster House,** a hamburger from **Port of Call** or **Clover Grill,** and a breakfast of *beignets* — a tasty fried doughnut — at **Café du Monde.** See Chapter 11.

The Best Museums

✔ To discover more about its New Orleans's origins, and the city's storied (and often sordid) past, visit the **Cabildo,** an entertaining museum focusing on life in early Louisiana and the site where the Louisiana Purchase was sold to the United States in 1803. See Chapter 12.

✔ Go to the **Chalmette Battlefield National Park,** which marks the site of the Battle of New Orleans, part of the War of 1812. The park also contains a cemetery for Civil War soldiers. See Chapter 12.

✔ Ride the **Canal Streetcar** to Mid-City's **New Orleans Museum of Art,** which boasts beauty inside and out with its extraordinary **Besthoff Sculpture Garden.** Both attractions have rebounded from the storm thanks to the support of art lovers worldwide. See Chapter 12.

The Best Clubs

✔ Get a taste of modern-day brass bands getting funky at down-and-dirty hangouts **Donna's Bar & Grill** and **Funky Butt.** See Chapter 17.

✔ Catch live jazz at local clubs **Snug Harbor** and **Sweet Lorraine's.** Enjoy R&B at hallowed halls such as **Tipitina's** and the **Maple Leaf.** See Chapter 17.

✔ Jam to cajun and *zydeco* tunes (popular music of southern Louisiana that combines French, Caribbean, and blues music — with guitar, washboard, and accordion) at the **Maple Leaf** or at the world's most musical bowling alley and celebrity haunt, **Mid City Lanes Rock 'n' Bowl.** See Chapter 17.

The Best Romantic Experiences

✔ Stroll along the lush scenery of the **Garden District** and the rolling expanse of water and parkway at the **Moonwalk.** See Chapter 12.

✔ Take your love on a **carriage ride** through the French Quarter or a relaxing **riverboat cruise** along the gently rolling Mississippi. See Chapter 12.

✔ Reserve a dinner for two at always cozy **Court of Two Sisters** and **Feelings Café.** For details, see Chapter 11.

Chapter 2

Examining Hurricane Katrina and Its Aftermath

● ●

In This Chapter

▶ Understanding pre-Katrina conditions and why the levees failed
▶ Examining a timeline of the storm, both during and after
▶ Seeing post-Katrina New Orleans through an insider's eyes
▶ Finding more information about the city's recovery
▶ Donating money

● ●

*O*n August 29, 2005, Hurricane Katrina changed the city of New Orleans forever. Its impact will be felt for years, perhaps even generations, to come.

More than 80 percent of the city flooded and the brackish water lingered for weeks. When Hurricane Rita followed soon thereafter, neighborhoods that had finally drained and dried out flooded yet again because the levee repairs were not complete. Despite such widespread devastation, the people of New Orleans are working hard to make it better than ever.

The purpose of this chapter is to give you some much-needed context using timelines, maps, and more. Most likely, your knowledge of Katrina's effect on the city stems from the near-constant mainstream television and newspaper coverage during the weeks immediately after the storm. Some media outlets did a more thorough job of reporting the facts than others. I hope this chapter will help you better understand these facts by presenting the events as they unfolded. I offer my own opinion in a separate box called "My two cents: The author sounds off," on p. 32.

Before the Storm

It was a well-known fact that New Orleans could drown under the right circumstances. Considering its geography, aged levee protection system, and past close calls with other storms, most locals feared it was inevitable — yet warnings were never taken seriously by the proper authorities.

A city below sea level

You may be surprised to learn that New Orleans is older than the United States of America. You can locate it just upriver from the mouth of the Mississippi and the Gulf of Mexico, with Lake Pontchartrain to the north; it was founded by Jean-Baptiste Le Moyne de Bienville, in 1718. The city was an ideal port. Decades before that, Sieur de la Salle had explored the Mississippi River and claimed all lands drained by the river for the French. (He named this territory Louisiana after his king, Louis XIV.) Bienville named his new city *La Nouvelle Orléans* (New Orleans) after Philippe, Duc d'Orléans.

The original footprint of the city was quite small, encompassing the area now known as the French Quarter. Part of the attraction of this location was the high ground found along a crescent-shaped bend on the East bank of the Mississippi. As the population grew, however, the surrounding swamps and wetlands were drained and natural waterways and bayous were filled in to make way for new developments. So in general, older neighborhoods that hugged the river, such as the French Quarter, Faubourg Marigny, Bywater and parts of Uptown, stayed dry during Katrina. Newer sections of the city, such as Gentilly, Lakeview, and New Orleans East, tended to be one to six feet (or more) below sea level and were at risk of minor street-flooding during even a typical thunderstorm.

Despite this "soup bowl effect," the city has survived for nearly 300 years thanks to a natural defense of barrier islands, a buffer zone of wetlands and swamp, natural levees, and more recently, manmade levees.

A look at the levees

The word *levee* is French for "raised," and it originated in colonial Louisiana to describe the steep mounds of dirt, buffered by vegetation to prevent erosion, that border a body of water. This is one of the oldest and most common forms of flood control in the world.

By the late 19th century (before the levees were built), wealthier people tended to live on higher ground by the river, and poorer people were clustered in lower lying areas. For the latter, occasional flooding in their neighborhoods was a part of life. Around this time, the City of New Orleans created a drainage plan and the Sewerage and Water Board was in charge of instituting it in the early 20th century.

The massive flood of 1927 (see "The City's Disaster History," below), during which the Mississippi breached its natural levees in many places upriver, changed everything. In the past, a city had created a levee around its borders but no one had constructed a connected levee protection system down the length of the river. The Army Corps of Engineers was given responsibility for flood control for the entire Mississippi River Valley. As a result, the Mississippi River boasts one of the most extensive levee systems in the United States.

Cross-section of New Orleans

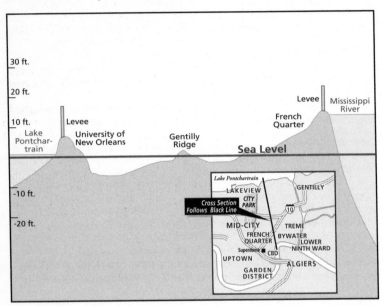

Lake Pontchartrain is the second-largest saltwater lake in the United States after the Great Salt Lake in Utah. It was formed from part of the Gulf, trapped by the Mississippi River Delta as deposits of silt piled up over thousands of years. The lake did not have natural levees per se, but the south shore — which is the New Orleans side — was probably the result of a river tributary. During the Great Depression of the 1930s, the Works Progress Administration made numerous improvements to the city, including a massive lake reclamation project. A seawall was built hundreds of yards away from the natural shore, and sand was pumped to fill it in. This area was 10 feet above sea level and served two purposes; it offered levee-like protection from hurricane storm surge and it allowed the city to expand and build additional residential neighborhoods. Subdivisions built in this area did not flood during Katrina; however, they were an island amid total destruction.

In the decades before Katrina, New Orleans grew increasingly dependent on manmade levees for a number of reasons. For one, the Louisiana coastline is steadily eroding due to previous storms and saltwater intrusion. Also, the manmade levees prevent the Mississippi River from naturally overflowing its banks and depositing silt to rebuild the coastline. Instead, the silt drains down into the Gulf of Mexico.

The levees controlled flooding from both the Mississippi River (to the south) and Lake Pontchartrain (to the north). Popular bike and running paths follow the top of many of the levees for miles, allowing for one of the most scenic routes in and around New Orleans. When Hurricane Betsy hit in 1965 (see "The city's disaster history" below), flooding much of the city, the Corps was instructed by Congress to build an official line of defense: the Lake Pontchartrain and Vicinity Hurricane Protection Levee. However, for the past 40 years, the project has remained incomplete because Congress never appropriated the necessary funds. It's hard not to imagine how many lives could've been saved during Katrina if this had been finished years ago as originally intended.

Of course, that is assuming that the Corps of Engineers properly designed and implemented the Lake Pontchartrain and Vicinity Hurricane Protection Levee. On June 1, 2006, the Corps publicly admitted faulty levee design and construction led to the unprecedented flooding throughout the Greater New Orleans area. This confession came as a much-needed salve to New Orleanians, especially in the face of criticism from some people around the country for choosing to live in a flood-risk area. It also allowed locals to move past the blame and plan for a better future, one that should include solid levee protection.

The city's disaster history

New Orleans has experienced its share of natural and manmade disasters, from fires to hurricanes to yellow fever epidemics. Below are the major events that tested its citizens' survival skills:

- **1788 and 1794:** Fire destroyed 80 percent of the city, including much of the French Quarter and its French Colonial buildings. The ruling Spanish rebuilt it, hence the tiled flat roofs, pastel-hued stucco and ironwork balconies that are hallmarks of the Quarter even today.

- **1853–1855:** In three years' time, an acute viral disease commonly known as yellow fever claimed 12,944 victims. At the time, no one knew what caused it; later it was discovered that infected female mosquitoes passed it on to humans. Today, a 10-year vaccine is available, although yellow fever epidemics continue to occur in Africa, South and Central America and the Caribbean.

- **1858:** Yellow fever killed 4,845 people.

- **1867:** Yellow fever claimed 3,107 lives.

- **1878:** Yellow fever victims numbered 4,046.

- **1905:** The last major yellow fever epidemic occurred, during which 437 people died.

- **1927:** Swollen with water from heavy rains up north, the Mississippi River broke through levees all along its route. In a misguided attempt to save New Orleans, dynamite was used to blow up a levee north of the city which consequently flooded St. Bernard Parish and stranded thousands of poor residents. Later, it was determined that the dynamite was unnecessary as breaches further north drained much of the excess water flow. Given this incident in 1927, many locals in 2005 questioned whether levees had been purposely weakened again after Katrina.

✔ **1965:** Hurricane Betsy was a strong Category 3 storm known as "Billion-Dollar Betsy" as it was the first hurricane to cause more than $1 billion dollars in damage (which would be $10–$12 billion today). Storm surge forced water from Lake Pontchartrain into neighborhoods such as Gentilly, the Upper Ninth Ward, and the Lower Ninth Ward, and parts of St. Bernard Parish. Some residents drowned in the attics of their one-story homes because they-couldn't get to the roof. Later, locals were encouraged to keep an axe in the attic.

✔ **1969:** Hurricane Camille made initial landfall near the mouth of the Mississippi as a Category 5 storm, which made it the second most intense landfall by a U.S. hurricane (Katrina is third). The Mississippi coastline suffered the most damage thanks to a 24-foot storm surge. In total, Camille killed 259 people and caused $1.4 billion in damage. Before Katrina, this hurricane was the benchmark by which all other storms were measured.

✔ **1998:** At its strongest, Hurricane Georges was a Category 5 storm that was barreling toward New Orleans, but it veered off toward Mississippi at the last moment.

Repeated warnings

In 2001, the Federal Emergency Management Agency (FEMA) predicted that one of the three "likeliest, most catastrophic disasters facing this country" would be a major hurricane targeting New Orleans. And yet, this same agency proved to be woefully under-prepared when faced with the real thing, when Katrina slammed into the Gulf Coast in 2005.

In June 2002, the *Times-Picayune* published a five-part series called "Washing Away" that warned of the city's vulnerability. "It's only a matter of time before South Louisiana takes a direct hit from a major hurricane. Billions have been spent to protect us, but we grow more vulnerable every day," the paper reported, predicting details of the hurricane and the aftermath with chilling accuracy. You can read the report at www.nola.com/hurricane/?/washingaway.

During the Storm: A Timeline of Events

This section is designed to give you the facts about the disaster as it unfolded. I've organized the events by date, categorized into four main time periods; each section contains a brief description of the main events for that time period, followed by a few other specific dates and events.

August 23–25: Hurricane formation and initial landfall

August 23: Hurricane Katrina began innocuously enough, like so many storms before it. A tropical depression developed over the southeastern Bahamas, labeled Tropical Depression Twelve.

August 24: The tropical depression strengthens and was designated Tropical Storm Katrina.

Katrina in context: An interview with tour guide Rebecca Sell

Rebecca Sell gives walking tours of the French Quarter through the Friends of the Cabildo. She gave the editor of this guide a tour in June 2006 and was extremely knowledgeable and engaging. We followed up with her to ask about Katrina and the future of the city.

How would you characterize Hurricane Katrina's devastation in historical terms? Is this the greatest challenge the city has ever faced?

Rebecca Sell: Historically, no I don't think this is the greatest challenge the city has ever faced. The two devastating fires of the 1700s were only six years apart. The first one was in 1788, and it burned 80 percent of the city to the ground in a day. That is similar to what happened after the levees broke last summer, and 80 percent of the city was inundated with water. The yellow fever plagues of the 1800s were horrible as well. In our worst year, 1853, we lost 10,000 to the disease. That was one in ten people living in the city. I can't imagine how devastating and frightening that must have been. I do think that Hurricane Katrina, or rather the failure of the levees, will be considered the greatest catastrophe of the century.

Why was the city built on sinking marsh land? Did early settlers realize the potential for future floods?

RS: I can only speculate that yes, they realized the potential for disaster, but the value of a port near the mouth of the Mississippi River far outweighed any risk. I think that many people forget that New Orleans is more than great food, music, and culture. Its greatest asset is the port. The Mississippi River and the Gulf of Mexico are the two reasons that the city was founded in the first place, and it has been a love-hate relationship ever since. The Quarter sits on the highest land in the city, so the French did attempt to protect the population somewhat. I should add that most of the neighborhoods that flooded during Katrina were our 20th-century neighborhoods. I have seen maps of the flooding and maps of early New Orleans; the dry areas were the oldest neighborhoods.

(continued)

(continued)

What are your predictions for the future of New Orleans? Will rising rent be a major factor in determining who repopulates the area?

RS: I think that New Orleans has a long way to go in terms of recovery. It really is a tale of two cities. As far as tourists are concerned, the Quarter and any place they would like to visit are fine. We encourage them to come down and enjoy the city. We then encourage them to seek out the surrounding devastation and get a firsthand look at the challenges facing us today.

Rising rent is definitely a problem. In most neighborhoods they have doubled or tripled in a matter of months. That's a staggering blow to someone who may have lost their job and everything they own because of the storm. Part of what makes New Orleans unique is her bohemian population. Unfortunately, rising rents are forcing many of these creative people — as well as the middle class — to settle elsewhere. It's not just the renters though; lack of insurance is another issue. Some homeowners are finding that they can no longer get, or afford, insurance for their property. This is a major problem that must be dealt with if the city hopes to make any kind of a comeback.

What was your personal experience with Hurricane Katrina? Did you get out of the city, and was your living space damaged?

RS: No, I did not get out of the city. My husband and I evacuated to a three-story building in the Quarter. It was absolutely terrifying. Imagine sitting in darkness for hours, listening to the storm rage outside, not knowing if the building was about to be ripped to pieces, or if rising floodwaters were about to chase us into the attic. When the levees broke, it was total chaos. We managed to get out the Wednesday after and eventually found ourselves staying with family in the Midwest for six weeks. That entire time, we didn't know where our friends were, if we had a home or any possessions . . . if there was anything for us to return to. We were in total limbo. The anxiety was terrible.

Our living space was damaged, but not so badly that we could not return. We made the place livable again and tried to make a go of it. A few months later, I lost my source of income due to the crippled post-storm economy. That is how I came to work for the Friends of the Cabildo, and I feel very fortunate for that opportunity. Now, a year later, we have found that we are being priced out of our neighborhood. This disaster is an ongoing source of stress for everyone affected.

How often do you give tours, and where can a visitor book one?

RS: The **Friends of the Cabildo**, which is the organization I work for, offer French Quarter walking tours Thursday through Sunday at 10:00 a.m. and 1:30 p.m. These tours meet at the 1850 House Museum Store located at 523 St. Ann Street on Jackson Square. We do not take reservations and ask guests to arrive 15 minutes prior to departure to purchase tickets. For more information, visitors may call ☎ **504-523-3939**. I also highly recommend **Gray Line's Hurricane Katrina Tour**, which runs daily. Gray Line's number is ☎ **504-569-1401**.

August 25: Katrina was upgraded to a Category 1 hurricane and made landfall near Hallandale Beach, Florida. Though expected to travel west, it moved south along the coastline to Miami, taking six lives and causing major tree damage.

August 26–28: Crossing the Gulf

As Katrina approached, many locals didn't pay much attention to it. Once it made landfall in southern Florida, meteorologists and talking heads predicted it would curl up and hit the Florida panhandle.

August 26: The National Hurricane Center (NHC) announced a shift in the possible path, which headed toward the Louisiana/Mississippi coast. Late that evening, the NHC predicted it would hit Buras, Louisiana, only 66 miles southeast of New Orleans. After traveling across Florida, Katrina had weakened and was downgraded to a tropical storm.

August 27: Katrina again strengthened to a Category 3 hurricane at 5am. Later that day, Louisiana Gov. Kathleen Blanco asked President Bush to declare a federal state of emergency for the state of Louisiana, which he did, putting FEMA in charge of relief efforts. New Orleans Mayor Ray Nagin called for a "voluntary evacuation" and announced that the Superdome would be opened as a shelter of last resort. (The Superdome had previously served as a shelter during Hurricane Georges, with mixed results; people were detained there for days, even though the hurricane narrowly missed the city, and many grew frustrated and vandalized the property.)

August 28: Hurricane Katrina reached Category 4 intensity, with winds up to 145 mph, just after midnight. At a 10 a.m. press conference, Nagin announced the first mandatory evacuation in New Orleans' history, which was heeded by thousands of people, some of whom were already in the process of leaving.

August 29–September 1: Louisiana and Mississippi landfalls, breach of levees and flooding

August 29: Early in the morning, Katrina made its second landfall in Buras, Louisiana, as predicted by the National Hurricane Center the previous day. Though the hurricane was downgraded to a Category 3, this slim finger of land was decimated by sustained winds up to 125 mph and storm surge from the Gulf. A few hours later, Katrina crossed Breton sound and made its third and final landfall in Pearlington, Mississippi.

In the meantime, around 8 a.m., the first evidence of levee breaches in New Orleans was reported as water rose on either side of the Industrial Canal. By 9 a.m., the Lower Ninth Ward was inundated by 6 to 8 feet of water and New Orleans East was submerged as well. Two hours later, St. Bernard Parish, to the east of New Orleans, was under 10 feet of water. At 11 a.m., local authorities announced the breach at the 17th Street Canal, which flooded (my neighborhood) Lakeview, and combined

Path of Hurricane Katrina

Map legend:
- —— Storm Path
- Hurricane-force Winds
- Tropical Storm-force Winds

Map labels: DOWNGRADED TO TROPICAL DEPRESSION ON AUG. 30, TN, OK, AR, SC, MS, AL, GA, Jackson, TX, LA, ATLANTIC OCEAN, Baton Rouge, Mobile, Pensacola, New Orleans, Biloxi, AUG. 29, Houston, AUG. 28, FL, CENTER OF KATRINA ON AUG. 24, 2005, Gulf of Mexico, Ft. Lauderdale, AUG. 25, Miami, AUG. 27, AUG. 26, BAHAMAS, CUBA

with breaches at the London Street Canal, completely drowning Mid-City to the southeast and Gentilly to the east. All three residential areas received up to 12 feet of water.

August 30: By this time, it was clear that the city's drainage pumps were quickly overwhelmed as water continued to pour in from the lake. The focus turned in earnest to rescuing stranded survivors. For days thereafter, thousands of people were saved from flooded homes and buildings by both civilians and the U.S. Coast Guard. Looting also became widespread and Gov. Blanco requested federal troops to help bring law and order back to the city. She also ordered hundreds of buses to the area; they eventually evacuated more than 15,000 people by September 1.

August 31: Sandbagging efforts at the breaches had failed and an unprecedented 80 percent of the City of New Orleans was under water. President George W. Bush left his ranch in Crawford, Texas, and flew directly to Washington; he was criticized after widely published photos showed him looking down at the devastation from the air.

Mayor Nagin ordered the New Orleans Police Department to stop search and rescue efforts in order to prevent further looting and uphold a curfew. At this point, 8,300 National Guardsmen were on duty in the Gulf Coast.

September 1: The country's attention turned to the thousands of citizens who went to the Superdome as a shelter of last resort. Living conditions had deteriorated considerably, there was no longer any food or water, and some instances of violence were reported.

(The *Times-Picayune* later noted that these stories of violence and death in the Superdome were greatly exaggerated; some in the media referred to up to 200 dead bodies, though only 4 were found in the vicinity. "As the fog of war-like conditions in Hurricane Katrina's aftermath has cleared, the vast majority of reported atrocities committed by evacuees have turned out to be false, or at least unsupported by any evidence, according to key military, law enforcement, medical and civilian officials in positions to know," *Times-Picayune*, 9/26/06.)

Facts at a glance: Katrina

Dates: Formed August 23, 2005 and dissipated August 31, 2005

Highest winds: 175 mph, sustained for 1 minute

Damages: $81.2 billion (Source: US Department of Commerce)

Fatalities: An estimated 1836, with an additional 705 missing

Deaths by state: Alabama (2), Florida (14), Georgia (2), Kentucky (1), Louisiana (1,577; includes out of state evacuees), Mississippi (238), Ohio (2)

Number who lost power in Louisiana: 900,000

Money raised by American Red Cross, Salvation Army, and other organizations: $4.25 billion

New Orleans population, pre-Katrina: 437,186 (Source: Brookings Institute)

Post-Katrina population in September 2006: 187,525 (Source: Brookings Institute)

Post-Katrina rent increase through September 2006: 45 percent (Source: Greater New Orleans Community Data Center, www.gnocdc.com)

Breakdown of fatalities by race*: Black (53 percent), White (39 percent), Hispanic (2 percent), Other (2 percent), Unknown (4 percent)

Breakdown of fatalities by gender*: Male (53 percent), Female (47 percent)

Breakdown of fatalities by age*: Older than 75 (46 percent), 61–75 (23 percent), 51–60 (14 percent), 41–50 (8 percent), 31–40 (3 percent), 21–30 (1.5 percent), under 20 (1.5 percent), unknown (3 percent)

Sources: All data is from the *Times-Picayune* unless otherwise noted. *The breakdown of fatalities by race, gender, and age is based on reports from the morgues of St. Gabriel and Carville, as reported in the *Times-Picayune*.

Timeline of the Flooding in New Orleans

Lake Pontchartrain

L. Pontchartrain
Causeway

University of
New Orleans

UNO

Leon C. Simon Dr.

LAKEVIEW

Robert E. Lee Blvd.

BUCKTOWN
West Esplanade Ave.

CITY
PARK

METAIRIE

Veterans Mem. Blvd.

Canal Blvd.

West End Blvd.

17th St. Canal

St. Bernard Ave.

Paris Ave.

London Ave. Canal

Elysian Fields Ave.

Franklin Ave.

Press Dr.

Gentilly Blvd.

GENTILLY

OLD
METAIRIE

Metairie Rd.

Airline Dr.

City Park Ave.

Bayou St. John

Fair Grounds
Racetrack
(Jazz Fest)

TREME

Esplanade Ave.

FAUBOURG
MARIGNY

JEFFERSON

Earhart Expwy.

MID-CITY

Tulane Ave.

Canal St.

St. Louis
Cemeteries

Washington Ave.

St. Claude Ave.

BYWATER

Carrollton Ave.

FRENCH
QUARTER

Superdome

CBD

ALGIERS

CARROLLTON

Broadway

Tulane
University

Crescent City
Connection

UPTOWN

St. Charles Ave.

Louisiana Ave.

AUDUBON
PARK

Napoleon Ave.

GARDEN
DISTRICT

GRETNA

Magazine St.

Audubon Zoo

WESTWEGO

HARVEY

Flooding occurred August 29 through
September 1, 2005. Please see the
accompanying box in this section.

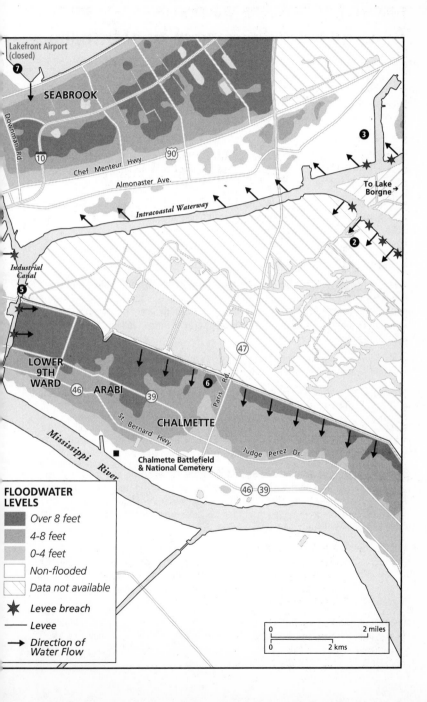

Lakefront Airport (closed)

SEABROOK

Downman Rd.

Chef Menteur Hwy.

Almonaster Ave.

Intracoastal Waterway

To Lake Borgne →

Industrial Canal

LOWER 9TH WARD

ARABI

CHALMETTE

St. Bernard Hwy.

Paris Rd.

Judge Perez Dr.

Chalmette Battlefield & National Cemetery

Mississippi River

FLOODWATER LEVELS

Over 8 feet
4-8 feet
0-4 feet
Non-flooded
Data not available
★ Levee breach
— Levee
→ Direction of Water Flow

0 — 2 miles
0 — 2 kms

Timeline of the flooding in New Orleans

The following text is taken from the "Flash Flood" interactive graphic at www.nola. com/katrina/graphics/flashflood.swf, *reprinted with permission from the* Times-Picayune. *All events occurred between August 29 and September 1, 2005. You'll find a map illustrating these events on p. 22, with bullets that correspond to the ones mentioned below.*

August 29, 2005

4:30 a.m.: Rising water in the Industrial Canal leaks through damaged gates into neighborhoods on both sides of the I-10 High Rise. The flow is minor compared to what is in store for these areas. See ❶.

5:00 a.m.: Katrina's storm surge begins pounding the MR-GO levee. By dawn, levee sections crumble and Lake Borgne advances into wetlands toward St. Bernard Parish. See ❷.

6:10 a.m.: Katrina makes landfall at Buras. A wall of water 21 feet high crosses the Mississippi River and its levees, inundating most of Plaquemines Parish.

6:30 am: Surge builds in the Intracoastal Waterway's "funnel," and levees protecting Eastern New Orleans are overtopped and breached. Soon, the area is under water. See ❸. To the west, witnesses report sections of the 17th Street Canal levee wall are leaning toward Lakeview. Water leaks through cracks in the wall into the neighborhood. See ❹.

6:50 a.m.: Storm surge from the "funnel" reaches the Industrial Canal. Water overtops floodwalls and levels on both sides, but the worst is still ahead. See ❺.

7:30 a.m.: Levee wall panels on the west side of the Industrial Canal breach, flooding the Upper Ninth Ward, Bywater and Treme. See ❺.

7:45 a.m.: Two floodwall sections on the east side of the Industrial Canal fall, releasing a wall of water into the Lower Ninth Ward, tossing homes and cars around like toys. The water also pours into Arabi and Chalmette. See ❺.

8:30 a.m.: Lake Borgne advances to St. Bernard Parish's second line of defense, easily topping the 7-foot to 9-foot 40-Arpent Canal levee and filling neighborhoods from Poydras to Chalmette. See ❻. To the north, a one mile stretch of floodwall on the south side of Lakefront Airport is topped by surge from Lake Pontchartrain, adding to already severe flooding in eastern New Orleans. See ❼.

9 a.m.: Surge rises to 10 feet in the London Avenue Canal and levee wall panels on both sides start bending. Water leaks into yards, but the flow is still minor. See ❽. About two miles west, surge reaches an embankment at the foot of the Orleans Avenue Canal that is 6 feet lower than the floodwalls. Water tops the embankment and pours into City Park.

9:30 a.m.: I-wall panels on the east side of the London Avenue Canal fail, releasing a wall of water and sand into homes and expanding the flooding of Gentilly. See ❽.

9:45 a.m.: Several 17th Street Canal levee wall panels fail, releasing a roaring torrent of water into Lakeview. Water from this breach eventually fills much of midtown New Orleans and parts of Metarie. See **8**. On the north shore, Katrina makes landfall near Slidell. Storm surge is 15 feet at the Lake Pontchartrain shoreline and reaches more than five miles inland at some points. St. Tammany Parish neighborhoods from the Rigolets all the way to Madisonville are flooded.

10:30 a.m.: I-wall panels on the west side of the London Avenue Canal are pushed over, adding 8 feet of water to flooded Gentilly and contributing to rising water across the city. See **8**. Parts of Jefferson Parish also flood as rainwater leaks through an unstaffed pumping system. See **9**.

August 29–September 1, 2005

With Katrina's eye north of the city and moving away quickly, surge levels drop and levee overtopping ceases. But Lake Pontchartrain remains swollen, and water continues bleeding into the city until the lake level equalizes with the floodwaters at midday on September 1.

Homeland Security Secretary Michael Chertoff was widely criticized for not knowing about the thousands of people who had flocked to the Ernest N. Convention Center and who were without any provisions.

National Guardsmen and much-needed supplies arrived at the Superdome.

People desperate to get out of the city attempted to cross the Crescent City Connection over the Mississippi River, but police with the City of Gretna on the West Bank closed off access. Evacuees charged it was an act of racism, but police chief claimed Gretna could not handle an influx of storm victims from New Orleans.

September–October 2005: Dealing with immediate crisis

September 2: President Bush signed a $10.5-billion relief package and discussed the possibility of a federal takeover of the New Orleans evacuation.

Later that night, during a live "Concert for Hurricane Relief" on NBC, rapper Kanye West departed from the teleprompter script and said, "George Bush doesn't care about black people," which prompted a national debate about race and Katrina.

September 4: The last people were evacuated from the Superdome by bus to the Reliant Astrodome in Houston, Texas. Other survivors were transported from the Convention Center and along the raised highways to the Cajundome in Lafayette, Louisiana, and other in-state shelters. But there were still more storm victims, including pets, in flooded homes and buildings throughout the area. By this time much of the media, including the city's two newspaper offices, had been forced to go to higher ground. National reporters embedded themselves where they could and showed images of a drowning city and its desperate citizens.

Sean Penn was seen in a small boat with several friends and journalists, rescuing locals. Though initial reports claimed his boat sprung a leak, historian Douglas Brinkley later told Larry King on CNN that the boat was merely overloaded and taking in water, and that he and Penn saved up to 40 people.

September 6: Despite the mandatory evacuation still being in effect, many people on dry land had refused to leave, so Nagin ordered a forced evacuation of any holdouts for public safety reasons. Many of these people stayed anyway, determined to thwart possible looters, or protect pets because they didn't realize how bad the damage was throughout the city.

As rescue efforts continued, the levee breaches were gradually addressed; the canals were sealed off from the lake with sheet pilings, and sandbags were piled up on the breaches themselves.

September 9: Secretary Chertoff removed FEMA Director Michael Brown from overseeing any further Katrina relief efforts.

September 12: Brown officially resigned.

One week later, Nagin had tentatively begun allowing residents to return to one area of the city, Algiers, on the nonflooded West Bank. However, Hurricane Rita threatened the city and he again ordered another mandatory evacuation. This storm made landfall further west, near the Louisiana-Texas border, but its storm surge caused flooding in parts of southeast Louisiana that had remained dry during Katrina and reflooded other areas where the levee breaches were incomplete.

A music lounge owner returns and rebuilds

The following is from the exhibit "Come Hell and High Water: Portraits of Hurricane Katrina Survivors," first shown at the at the Ogden Museum of Southern Art (925 Camp St.; ☎ 504-539-9600) in the summer of 2006. Thomas Neff, a Professor of Art at LSU's School of Art, photographed nearly 200 hurricane survivors with a 5x7 inch view camera. He spent 45 days in the city and slept in his van for 21 nights.

Photo © Thomas Neff, 2005.

Figure 2-1: Antoinette K-Doe, Mother-in-Law Lounge.

Although Antoinette was determined to protect the lounge and care for her disabled niece, seven days of fear and isolation were enough. After flagging the National Guard from an upstairs window, they were taken by boat to an I-10 on-ramp, bussed to the airport, and flown out of state. When her dear friends, Savannah-Rose I and II, DJs by trade, discovered that Antoinette had been taken to parts unknown, they launched a frantic search. One month passed before she was found—living in a Boy Scout camp near Atlanta. Antoinette had been gone about five weeks, but when she returned to the lounge, saw the damage, and smelled the rankness and mold, she totally lost it.

As she reflected to me on her life with Ernie, author of the famous song "Mother-in-Law," and recalled her part in resurrecting his career a decade before he died—reclaiming his honorable title, "Emperor of the World"—she began to feel renewed hope. Together they had transformed the lounge, with its brightly painted murals, into a New Orleans cultural treasure, as evidenced by a bronze plaque from the city mounted on the front door. She also realized that she could bring the lounge back again, even if she had to do it alone. With renewed strength and confidence about her own future, as well as the future of New Orleans and its musical heritage, she began the arduous task of gutting the ruined interior.

Antoinette's effort to rebuild gained force when the lounge became the first project undertaken by the Hands On network; a group of sixty national and international volunteer organizations whose role focuses on entrepreneurial civic action. When the project was less than half complete, Hands On partner and Hip-Hop superstar Usher visited the site one Sunday in May and asked the team leader to finish the project at his expense, including the second-floor apartment. Antoinette was overwhelmed by this outpouring of support and reverence the world was showing for Ernie's legacy and his music.

On August 29, 2006, a gala event took place to reopen the newly restored Mother-in-Law Lounge. In typical New Orleans style, an open casket was on hand for guests to deposit a written memory of Hurricane Katrina. Once filled with *memento mori*, it was then buried right next to the lounge, on a site previously occupied by Ernie's Pink Cadillac Limo.

October 5: Most flooded neighborhoods were finally reopened to residents; some returned, anxious to see the damage inflicted on their homes and belongings. Many others remained in shelters for months afterward throughout the country as they awaited news of friends and relatives, the fate of their homes and employers, and the city itself. By this point, it was estimated that 1.5 million people had evacuated for Katrina.

After the Storm: New Orleans Post-Katrina

November 2005–present: Cleanup, recovery, and long-term planning

November 21: A group of homeowners whose properties flooded appear at the state capitol in Baton Rouge to support new legislation calling for a single unified levee district (instead of seven) in hopes of removing perceived corruption and complacency.

November 30: Residents from the most devastated neighborhoods are outraged when the Urban Land Institute's report recommends that post-Katrina rebuilding efforts focus on nonflooded areas of the city and abandon low lying neighborhoods altogether.

December 22: The watchdog group Bureau of Governmental Research criticizes Mayor Nagin's Bring New Orleans Back Commission for considering a Catch-22 proposal. The report, still being drafted and yet to be released, eventually recommends that everyone be given the opportunity to rebuild regardless of location. The draft notes that neighborhoods have one year to prove sustainability or properties will be bought out by the city. Needless to say, this recommendation proves as unpopular as the Urban Land Institute's plan.

January 16, 2006: In response to concerns that New Orleans would permanently lose many of its African-American citizens who evacuated, Nagin stated in a Martin Luther King Day speech that it would be a "chocolate city" again. Though the phrase was a reference to a 1975 album of the same name by Parliament and has positive connotations, the reaction to the mayor's speech was overwhelmingly negative.

February 28: The city celebrated Mardi Gras Day on a smaller scale. Many floats had politically charged names and themes, including "The Headless State," "Homeland Insecurity," and "The Pigs of Patronage." "The Inferno" depicted President Bush as a horned devil, and showed Blanco, Nagin, and Brown as cooks brewing a giant pot of human gumbo in the Superdome.

March 25: Charity Hospital, the city's only Level 1 trauma center, was permanently closed.

April 27: The Louisiana Recovery Authority approved a $7.5 billion "Road Home" plan that allows homeowners to rebuild their storm-damaged homes.

May 20: Despite criticism and opposition, Nagin was re-elected Mayor for a second term.

June 1: The Army Corps of Engineers published a 6,113-page report admitting flaws in the design and implementation of the levee system, which resulted in most of the flooding during Katrina. "The hurricane protection system in New Orleans and southeast Louisiana was a system in name only," the report stated. The report noted that, in some cases, floodwalls that should have contained the water instead tilted enough to shift the grounds, and this allowed water to rush underneath. Thus the water breached the levees from below, not from above. Chief engineer of the Army Corps, Lt. Gen. Carl A. Strock told the *New York Times,* "[The report] is what it is. Call it a mea culpa, or call it a dry recognition, or admission, or whatever — but we're not ducking our accountability and responsibility in this."

June 20: Gov. Blanco called in the Louisiana National Guard to patrol flooded neighborhoods where looting and squatting run rampant, and ordered the NOPD to focus on nonflooded areas.

July 15: Actor Brad Pitt toured the devastated Lower Ninth Ward to help raise awareness of the neighborhood's plight.

August 8: The Society of American Military Engineers, primarily comprised of Corps of Engineers employees, presented the Wheeler Medal to Walter Baumy for overseeing the "restoration of more than 169 miles of ravaged hurricane protection systems, 68 pumping stations and 4 water control structures" between August 29, 2005, and June 1, 2006. Many New Orleanians complained that the Corps was rewarding itself for work that was caused by its own past levee blunders.

August 11: Lt. Gen. Carl Strock, commander and chief engineer of the Army Corps of Engineers, announced his retirement "based on family and personal reasons."

August 22: Nonprofit New Orleans-based organization LEVEES.org observed the "Anniversary of the Worst Engineering Disaster in U.S. History" and released a report on the Corps' performance.

September 25: Saints beat the Falcons in football season opener, which received national attention. President Bush flipped the coin to open the game, and U2 and Green Day performed at half time. Even Falcons coach Jim Mora acknowledged the significance of the Saints' win: "As tough as it is to lose a game, I'd be lying if I said there isn't a little, little, little piece of me that didn't appreciate what this game meant to this city. It meant a lot."

Names in the News

Here are just a few of the people who played a part in New Orleans' welfare during and immediately after the storm. Other folks are currently contributing in some way to the recovery and rebuilding efforts.

Vice Admiral Thad W. Allen: Chief of Staff of the U.S. Coast Guard, Allen replaced former FEMA director Michael Brown on Sept. 11, 2005, after Brown resigned amid criticism for FEMA's response to Katrina victims.

Marty Bahamonde: He is the FEMA regional director whose urgent first-hand accounts of the Katrina devastation to New Orleans were reportedly ignored by his boss, Michael Brown (who sent him there), and higher ups. A T-shirt, "Marty for Mayor," was created in his honor during the mayoral campaign of 2006.

Kathleen Babineaux Blanco: She is the current Governor of Louisiana and the first woman to hold this post. After former FEMA Director Michael Brown stepped down, he was quoted as saying, "Blanco reminded me of an aunt I have whom I love to pieces. But I would never trust this aunt to run a state . . . I just see Blanco as this really nice woman who is just way beyond her level of ability" (*Times-Picayune, 5/3/06*). Blanco clashed with President Bush several times during the height of the Katrina crisis (as detailed in Douglas Brinkley's book, *The Great Deluge*). As we go to print, she is not backing down from her demand that the state receive offshore oil and gas-drilling revenue for much-needed coastal rebuilding.

Douglas Brinkley: This Tulane professor of history was a prolific television commentator in the months after Katrina. He is also the author of *The Great Deluge: Hurricane Katrina, New Orleans, and the Mississippi Gulf Coast.* In the week after the storm, he joined actor Sean Penn and several others in a boat to rescue locals.

Michael Brown: The FEMA Director during the hurricane, he was forced to resign soon thereafter amidst heavy criticism. President Bush infamously told him, "You're doing a heck of a job, Brownie!"

George W. Bush: President Bush was widely criticized in the wake of Hurricane Katrina. Though he declared a state of emergency in the Gulf Coast two days before the hurricane made landfall, later mobilized the National Guard and Coast Guard, and signed a bill appropriating $10.5 billion for relief efforts, many criticized his administration for not responding fast enough. Bush was also criticized for selecting and supporting Michael Brown as FEMA Director, for flying Air Force One over the region and not stopping to visit on August 31, 2005, and for giving what many felt were inappropriately upbeat speeches when he first visited the area on September 2. (Search for the text of his speeches at www.whitehouse.gov/news.) In a February 2006 ABC News interview, Bush admitted some mistakes: "I agree that we didn't do as good a job as we could have done on Katrina . . . There was no situational awareness, and that means that we weren't getting good, solid information from people who were on the ground, and we need to do a better job . . . There's no question we've got more work to do, and our report on Katrina outlined the work that needs to be done . . . The chaotic scenes were very troubling. It was very unsettling for me to realize our fellow citizens were in near panic wondering where the help was." (Full text at: http://abcnews.go.com/WNT/story?id=1671087&page=1.)

Joseph Canizaro: The real estate and banking mogul — and friend of President Bush — was tapped to serve on Mayor Nagin's Bring New Orleans Back Commission.

Michael Chertoff: Secretary of Department of Homeland Security, which oversees FEMA, he developed a bad reputation during the hurricane. He publicly stated that the Convention Center situation was just a rumor, and at a press conference, commented that no one could have predicted such a catastrophic event.

Citizens for 1 Greater New Orleans: Founded by Uptown realtor Ruthie Frierson in response to what she saw as a lack of clear leadership, this is a "non-partisan, non-sectarian grassroots initiative formed to be a voice for reform and renewal for Greater New Orleans and a better Louisiana." Visit www.citizensfor1greaterneworleans.com.

Eddie Compass: After 26 years of police service, New Orleans Police Department superintendent Compass "retired" four weeks after Katrina, a key time during which officers were criticized for everything from being disorganized to deserting their positions to looting. He also made alarming claims about conditions at the Superdome and the Convention Center that were later found to be untrue.

Anderson Cooper: Host of the CNN show "360°" and author of *Dispatches From the Edge,* Cooper kept New Orleans and the Mississippi coasts' recovery efforts in the national spotlight months after the hurricane came ashore.

Lt. Gen. Russel Honoré: A Louisiana native, Honoré was sent to New Orleans by President Bush to coordinate military relief efforts as commander of the Joint Task Force Katrina. Mayor Nagin described him as a "John Wayne dude" who got the job done.

Jed Horne: *Times-Picayune* editor and author of *Breach of Faith.*

Rep. William Jefferson: He is the U.S. Representative of Louisiana (D–New Orleans) and the first African-American in this position since Reconstruction. Jefferson is the subject of a federal investigation for accepting legislative bribes that predates Katrina and is still ongoing as of the time of this writing. Immediately after the storm, he was criticized for inappropriate use of a government vehicle and personnel to check on his Uptown home after Katrina. In December 2006, he defeated Karen Carter in a runoff election and held his seat for a ninth term in what the *New York Times* called "an astonishing act of political survival" (12/10/06).

Sen. Mary Landrieu: She is a U.S. Senator (D–Louisiana), daughter of former Mayor Maurice Edwin "Moon" Landrieu, and sister to Louisiana Lt. Governor and 2006 mayoral candidate Mitch Landrieu. Her New Orleans home was destroyed by Katrina, and she was a vocal supporter of the nonprofit organization, Women of the Storm (www.womenofthe storm.net).

Laura Maloney: Executive Director of the Louisiana SPCA, she efficiently evacuated animals in the shelter's care to Texas days before the storm. She then oversaw an unprecedented animal rescue effort with the help of staff — many of whom had lost their own homes to flooding — and hundreds of volunteers around the country, even after the shelter building was a total loss.

Mayor C. Ray Nagin: Once an executive with Cox Cable, he was elected to his first political office because voters were tired of experienced politicians' corruption and patronage. His lack of political experience was later seen by many as a shortcoming during Katrina. Gov. Blanco described him as "a total void" during Katrina. He astounded and angered many locals with his comment that New Orleans be a "chocolate city" again and that Katrina was God's punishment for the U.S. invading Iraq. Most recently, he came under fire for suggesting that an event commemorating the one-year anniversary of Katrina feature fireworks and a comedy show. He was narrowly elected to a second term in 2006.

My two cents: The author sounds off

As I write this, one year later, the shock has worn off, allowing anger and sadness to more readily surface. When my husband and I went to sleep on the evening of Friday, August 26, 2005, we did not know that our lives and the city we loved would be forever changed in just a few days' time. That Friday afternoon, we missed hearing an important announcement by the National Hurricane Center that Hurricane Katrina would most likely not go to the Florida Panhandle and was instead headed toward the Louisiana/Mississippi coast. We also missed NHC's late-night update that the storm was indeed heading right for us.

The next morning, my husband went to his computer and refreshed the Web page he had left open the night before, showing the predicted path of the hurricane. He watched in horror as the latest map indicated the path leading directly to New Orleans. He rushed into the bedroom and woke me up with these words, "Honey, we have to get out of here."

For me, Saturday, August 27, alternated between a blur of packing activity and frozen moments of disbelief and denial. We had evacuated the year before for Hurricane Ivan without worry, but for some reason, I felt differently this time. I was nervous and uneasy. In speaking with friends and neighbors, though, it seemed that I might be over-reacting. Some of them didn't plan to evacuate, dismissing the media's projections as the usual melodrama or saying they remembered being kids in New Orleans during Betsy or Camille and our neighborhood hadn't flooded then. We would be safe.

Nevertheless, we didn't relish the idea of holing up in our house with four large dogs and two cats for a few days (at most) without electricity. If there was flooding, we wouldn't be able to exercise the dogs, either. Evacuation was our best option and we decided to drive to my parents' house in the Chicago area and make a mini-vacation out of it, just as we had the previous year.

We left very early the morning of Sunday, August 28, and took part in what would be the most successful evacuation in U.S. history thanks to "contraflow" in which expressways heading into the city were closed off from inbound drivers and instead diverted to allow outbound traffic. Contraflow was first tested in 2004 and did not go well because it was implemented far too late; in 2005, the state learned its lesson and contraflow allowed one million people to smoothly and quickly evacuate prior to the storm.

We arrived at my parents' house late that night and settled in for what we thought would be a nice surprise visit. On Monday, August 29, initial news reports said New Orleans was lucky once again as the storm had veered to the Mississippi coast. It wasn't until later in the day that word spread about the rising water in the city and the breached levees throughout the city.

When I heard that the 17th Street Canal levee had breached, I found a map and located 17th Street in Metairie. I remember thinking, "Oh, those poor people." Then I realized that the canal bordering the west side of my neighborhood, Lakeview, was called the 17th Street Canal and I was in fact one of those poor people whose house was flooding. And what about my friends and neighbors who had stayed behind? Were they in danger? I began crying and stayed glued to CNN for the next two weeks when I wasn't on the phone trying to reach people in hopes that they had made it out.

The images of stranded storm victims looked like something from a movie. How could the backdrop for these desperate moments — the Superdome, Canal Street, I-10 — be New Orleans, where I had lived for 12 years and which I knew more intimately than my hometown up north? Why weren't these people getting the help they needed? The lack of local, regional and federal government coordination and assistance absolutely infuriated me.

Months later, we learned that this "natural" disaster was largely manmade. The Army Corps of Engineers' flawed levee design and construction caused this unprecedented tragedy, in which thousands of people lost their lives and tens of thousands more lost their homes or livelihoods or beloved family and friends. One year later, New Orleanians are still waiting for a long overdue apology from the Corps, which is the next (albeit belated) step after admitting its role in this catastrophe.

Right now, the rebuilding process lacks a strong leader whom the people trust and respect. You can't blame us for being skeptical of government at any level. Mayor Nagin appears to be well intentioned, but I wonder if someone with more experience could've been a more aggressive leader and helped us embrace his or her vision for a new New Orleans. Between the Bring New Orleans Back Commission, the Urban Land Institute and other recovery committees, residents are in limbo, unsure which rebuilding plan will take hold and what exactly our role should be to ensure the future of the city.

I am impressed with the growing collectives of civic-minded individuals since the storm. Their grassroots efforts are paying off in getting straight answers from the government about everything from base flood elevation changes and levee protection to medical care and schools. This experience has changed us, and as long as we remember the lessons from Katrina, I think New Orleans will not only survive, it will thrive.

Anna Pou, M.D.: This LSU Health Sciences Center staff physician was arrested along with two nurses for allegedly killing critically ill patients at Memorial Hospital at the height of the Katrina crisis, which set off a controversy about mercy killings.

Garland Robinette: A popular WWL radio host, he is best known for his interview with Mayor Nagin on September 2, 2005, in which an emotional Nagin told the federal government, "Get off your asses."

Chris Rose: *Times-Picayune* columnist and author of one of the most personal and compelling Katrina books, *1 Dead in Attic*. His columns continue to give voice to locals' concerns, frustrations and tiny victories as the city recovers.

Sandy Rosenthal: She is the founder of Levees.org, a nonprofit grassroots organization designed to keep the Army Corps of Engineers on its toes.

Lt. Gen. Carl A. Strock: Chief of the Army Corps of Engineers, he retired in August 2006, citing the failure of the levees in New Orleans as one of the reasons. In June 2006, the Corps admitted that its faulty levee design and construction caused the widespread flooding in New Orleans, not the "overtopping" of the levees that was initially publicized in the weeks after the storm.

Ivor Von Heerden: He is director of LSU's Hurricane Center and author of *The Storm.*

Anne Milling: She is the founder of Women of the Storm (www.womenofthe storm.net), a nonprofit grassroots organization comprised of 150 south Louisiana women. The group extended personal invitations to federal officials to travel to the state to see Katrina and Hurricane Rita damage first-hand, and the group paid all expenses. The women are asking Congress to allow 50 percent of offshore oil and gas revenues generated in Louisiana to go toward the state's funds for coastal restoration and protection.

Resources for Further Information

Communication and information proved critical during and after the storm. Flooding destroyed most of the city's radio and television stations, and the *Times-Picayune* was unable to publish a traditional newspaper for three days (though it did put out a cyber-edition on the Web). The Internet allowed the rest of the world to find out what was happening in the city and keep up with its massive rebuilding efforts even today. If you would like to learn more about Katrina's effect on New Orleans, try the following resources.

Books

Even if you only read one or two books before your trip, I guarantee the extra insight will make your visit all the more meaningful. If I had to recommend just one book to you, I'd choose *Breach of Faith* (Random House, 2006), by *Times-Picayune* staffer Jed Horne. He offers a local's perspective and a journalist's storytelling talent. The editor of this guide picks the excellent *1 Dead in Attic* (Chris Rose Books, 2006), by Chris Rose, another *Times-Picayune* writer. This small, widely available book of short, eloquent essays truly captures the city's outrage and heartbreak.

- *Bayou Farewell: The Rich Life and Tragic Death of Louisiana's Cajun Coast* (Vintage, 2004), by Mike Tidwell

- *Breach of Faith: Hurricane Katrina and the Near Death of a Great American City* (Random House, 2006), by Jed Horne

- *Come Hell or High Water: Hurricane Katrina and the Color of Disaster* (Basic Books, 2006), by Michael Eric Dyson

- *Control of Nature* (Farrar, Straus & Girou, 1990), by John McPhee

- *Dispatches From the Edge: A Memoir of War, Disasters, and Survival* (HarperCollins, 2006), by Anderson Cooper

- *The Great Deluge: Hurricane Katrina, New Orleans, and the Mississippi Gulf Coast* (William Morrow, 2006), by Douglas Brinkley

- *Disaster: Hurricane Katrina and the Failure of Homeland Security* (Times Books, 2006), by Christopher Cooper and Robert Block

- *1 Dead in Attic* (Chris Rose Books, 2006), by Chris Rose

- *Path of Destruction: The Devastation of New Orleans and the Coming Age of Superstorms* (Little, Brown, & Co., 2006), by John McQuaid and Mark Schleifstein

- *The Ravaging Tide: Strange Weather, Future Katrinas, and the Coming Death of America's Coastal Cities* (Free Press, 2006), by Mike Tidwell

- *The Storm: What Went Wrong and Why During Hurricane Katrina — The Inside Story from One Louisiana Scientist* (Viking Adult, 2006), by Ivor von Heerden

Online Articles

If you're looking for news coverage of New Orleans online, you can't do better than the *Times-Picayune*, at www.nola.com, and you'll find all of their Katrina-related coverage gathered at the Pulitzer-Prize winning www.nola.com/katrina. As we go to print, they're still displaying their 9-part anniversary series "Katrina: One Year Later," which offers before-and-after videos and slideshows, profiles of rescuers and survivors, and updates on rebuilding efforts.

Many other excellent articles and in-depth profiles are available online. Here are some that I recommend for further reading:

- **"Leaving Desire: The Ninth Ward After the Hurricane,"** by Jon Lee Anderson, *The New Yorker,* September 19, 2005. "Eight days had

Two perspectives on "Devastation Tours"

Author Julia Kamysz Lane: When I first learned of the Katrina disaster tours, I was horrified and angry. Would tourists take pictures of me standing on what was left of my porch, my dust mask hanging around my neck and mold and dirt all over my donated clothes after a day of gutting? I did not want complete strangers to see my family photos, letters, and journals drying out on the muddy ground that used to be our lush green yard. I also did not want them to stare at the towering trash pile in front of our house, filled with everything we once had.

But a fellow Lakeview resident changed my mind. She thought it could only help if the public saw firsthand what we were going through. Only then would they begin to understand how many people were affected by the devastation. In turn, they would recognize how hard we were working to make New Orleans whole again. We hoped they would be inspired to help us rebuild.

Each tourist who has passed through my neighborhood has been polite and respectful of property. I personally have preferred not to talk to them if I'm working on my house as it's too emotional for me, but I appreciate their ongoing concern for us and the city we love.

If you're looking to take a bus tour, **Gray Line** offers the popular 3-hour "Hurricane Katrina — America's Worst Catastrophe," which tours Lakeview, Gentilly, Eastern New Orleans, and the Ninth Ward, at 9 a.m. and 1 p.m. daily. Tickets are $35 per adult, $28 for children, and $29 per person for groups of 10 or more. Book at least a day in advance at ☎ **800-535-7786**, or visit www.graylineneworleans.com.

Editor Stephen Bassman: I visited New Orleans in the summer of 2006 (shortly before editing this guide) as part of a tightly scheduled media tour, so I had no time to book an official "devastation tour." Instead, I hailed a taxi outside my French Quarter hotel early one morning. I asked the driver — Jean, a Haitian man — if he would drive me around the Lower Ninth Ward. He said he toured the area several times a day and would take me for $40 an hour.

The images I'd seen on television did not prepare me for the up-close reality. We passed hundreds of decimated cars piled up under Interstate-10, awaiting impounding. Once in the Lower Ninth Ward, we saw more abandoned cars and the remains of houses. Some were missing fronts, offering views of their moldy, ruined interiors. One house had been rocked off its foundation and had landed, unceremoniously, on top of a car. A few workers were clearing debris from some areas, and patches of this once crowded — mostly poor, black — neighborhood now resembled barren fields. Jean drove right up to the levees to point out the breach (now repaired), before driving me back to the hotel. I asked him if these tours depressed him, and he chuckled nervously and didn't respond.

It is difficult to "recommend" these tours, but you won't get a sense of the storm's impact if you stay in the French Quarter. A taxi is easy to hail at any time and less intrusive than a large bus. Drivers charge $25 to $60 an hour (feel free to negotiate). Note that while the Ninth Ward is almost completely destroyed, Lakeview, Gentilly, and others are rebuilding and offer a few more signs of hope, as Julia communicates.

Websites at a glance

Architecture Preservation

Preservation Resource Center:

www.prcno.org

Civic Activism

Citizens for One Greater New Orleans:

www.citizensfor1greater
neworleans.com

Levees.org:

www.levees.org

Women of the Storm:

www.womenofthestorm.org

Katrina

Hurricane Katrina Information:

www.hurricanekatrina
information.com

Times-Picayune Katrina coverage:

www.nola.com/katrina

Media

The Dead Pelican:

www.thedeadpelican.com

Gambit Weekly:

www.bestofneworleans.com

The Times-Picayune:

www.nola.com

Nature Preservation

Coalition to Restore Coastal Louisiana:

www.crcl.org

Rebuilding

NOLA Rises:

www.nolarises.com

Rejazz New Orleans:

www.rejazzneworleans.org

passed since Hurricane Katrina made landfall, and [Shawn] Alladio was out on a search for trapped survivors and for what rescuers were calling 'holdouts' — residents who didn't want to leave their homes — in one of the poorest and worst-hit parts of the city, the Ninth Ward ... " Log onto: www.newyorker.com/fact/content/articles/050919fa_fact

✔ **"The Long, Strange Resurrection of New Orleans,"** by Charles C. Mann, CNNMoney.com, August 29, 2006. "Hurricane Katrina was the biggest natural disaster in US history — and its aftermath became the biggest management disaster in history as well. Fortune lays bare this surreal tale of incompetence, political cowardice ... and rebirth." Log onto: http://money.cnn.com/magazines/fortune/fortune_archive/2006/08/21/8383661

✔ **"The Lost Year: Behind the Failure to Rebuild,"** by Dan Baum, the *New Yorker,* August 21, 2006. "More than just New Orleans was at stake. A third of the world's population lives in coastal zones, many of them in delta cities that may flood as the climate changes and seas rise." Log onto: www.newyorker.com/fact/content/articles/060821fa_fact2

✔ **"Apocalypse There,"** by Matt Taibbi, *Rolling Stone,* September 2005. "I'm in the lounge of the Four Seasons with Sean Penn and other assorted media creatures, debating the merits of rescuing animals instead of humans in a disaster area." Log onto: www.rollingstone.com/politics/story/7661196/apocalypse_there

Charitable Organizations

The city of New Orleans and its citizenry still need help, even if we won't always admit it out of stubborn pride. Please consider donating to the following local charities:

✔ The **United Way of Greater New Orleans** (☎ 504-822-5540; www.unitedwaynola.org) continues to provide varied assistance to victims of the storm.

✔ **New Orleans Area Habitat for Humanity** (☎ 504-861-2077; www.habitat-nola.org) works with volunteers to build new homes throughout the region.

✔ **Tipitina's Foundation** (www.tipitinasfoundation.org) provides services and sometimes instruments for both professional musicians and students.

✔ The **New Orleans Musician's Clinic** (☎ 504-568-3712; www.neworleansmusiciansclinic.org) provides health care and assistance to the city's musicians, including those who left during Katrina and are trying to return.

✔ The **Louisiana SPCA** (☎ 504-368-5191, www.la-spca.org) lost its building and all of its contents in the flood. They need money to build a new shelter.

Chapter 3

Digging Deeper into Local Traditions and History

*A*wareness of New Orleans' history is more crucial than ever in the wake of Hurricane Katrina, as the city attempts to hold onto its core identity even as it rebuilds and transitions. In this chapter, I introduce you to New Orleans' culture and how it came to be, and I recommend some of the books and movies that best evoke its quirky spirit.

History 101: The Main Events

Considering that New Orleans is surrounded by water and was once mainly swamp, it's amazing that anyone found any use for it at all. Its story begins in 1682, when the Sieur de la Salle explored the Mississippi River and claimed all lands drained by the river for the French. He named this territory Louisiana after his king, Louis XIV. Nearly 40 years later, in 1718, Jean-Baptiste Le Moyne, Sieur d'Iberville, founded New Orleans as a strategic port city. He named it *La Nouvelle Orléans* (New Orleans) after Philippe, Duc d'Orléans.

The French community that settled along this bend in the river — in a town 15 feet below sea level — flourished. So it came as a surprise when in 1762 Louis XIV handed over the Louisiana territory to his Spanish cousin, King Charles III. It didn't last long — only until 1800 — but in that time the French Quarter went up in flames twice and was rebuilt while under Spanish rule. Much of the French architecture was replaced by Spanish styles, leaving permanent reminders (such as courtyards and wrought-iron balconies) of that brief regime. The territory returned to

A New Orleans timeline

1682 Sieur de la Salle stops near what is now New Orleans while traveling down the Mississippi River and claims the territory for Louis XIV.

1699 Pierre Le Moyne, Sieur d'Iberville, rediscovers and secures the mouth of the Mississippi on Mardi Gras day.

1718 The first governor of Louisiana, Iberville's brother, Jean-Baptiste Le Moyne, Sieur de Bienville, founds New Orleans.

1723 New Orleans replaces Biloxi as the capital of Louisiana.

1752 Ursuline Convent completed.

1762 Louis XV secretly cedes Louisiana west of the Mississippi to Spain.

1788 and 1794 Fires destroy much of the city; Spanish-style buildings replace much of the French architecture.

1794 Planter Etienne de Boré granulates sugar from cane for the first time.

1803 France officially takes possession of the Louisiana Territory and sells it to the United States, the famous "Louisiana Purchase".

1805 New Orleans incorporates as a city.

1812 Louisiana admitted as a U.S. state.

1815 Battle of New Orleans resolves the War of 1812.

1832–33 Yellow fever and cholera epidemics kill 10,000 people in two years.

1837 First newspaper covers a Mardi Gras parade.

1840 New Orleans is the fourth-largest city in the United States and is second only to New York as a port.

1850 City becomes largest slave market in the country.

1861–62 Louisiana secedes from the Union.

1865–77 Reconstruction and carpetbaggers flood the city.

1890 Homer Plessy is arrested riding a train recently segregated by Jim Crow laws; he sues the state, leading to the landmark U.S. Supreme Court decision *Plessy v. Ferguson*.

1892 First electric streetcar operates along St. Charles Avenue.

1900 Louis Armstrong is born.

1928 Huey P. "Kingfish" Long elected governor of Louisiana; four years later, he is elected to the U.S. Senate.

1935 Long is assassinated.

1938 Tennessee Williams arrives in New Orleans.

1956 Lake Pontchartrain Causeway, the world's longest bridge, is completed.

1960 Public schools are integrated.

1964 Canal Streetcar makes last run; riders pelt new buses with tomatoes.

1975 Superdome opens.

1977 Ernest N. "Dutch" Morial becomes the first African-American mayor.

1984 Louisiana World Expo spurs redevelopment of riverside area between Canal and Poydras streets.

1988 Anne Rice moves back to New Orleans.

2000 National D-Day Museum opens.

2004 Anne Rice sells her New Orleans properties and moves to the suburbs. Canal streetcar returns with great fanfare.

2005 Hurricane Katrina causes levees to breach, flooding 80 percent of the city. An unprecedented rebuilding effort begins.

2006 In June, Governor Blanco calls in the Louisiana National Guard to patrol flooded neighborhoods where looting and squatting runs rampant. The Superdome holds first football game post-Katrina on September 25.

France, but in 1803 Napoleon secretly sold it to the United States, marking the historical Louisiana Purchase. By that time, the Caribbean *gens de couleur libre* (free people of color) were immigrating to New Orleans in droves after the Haitian Revolution, adding to the city's mix of food, music, and architecture.

As the cotton and tobacco industries grew, New Orleans prospered, making it the second-wealthiest city in the nation after New York City. The War of 1812 was resolved in 1815 in the Battle of Orleans. The infamous pirate Jean Lafitte and General Andrew Jackson joined forces at Chalmette Battlefield (see Chapter 12) to claim victory over the British. Success, sophistication, and society reigned, making New Orleans an attractive destination. By the mid-1800s, Louisiana had seceded from the Union and was the fourth-largest city in the United States. After the end of the Civil War, carpetbaggers brought even more cultural influences to the Crescent City.

Those years of prosperity slowly faded away as river transportation became less important and other industries overtook cotton and tobacco in profitability. A century after the War Between the States, New Orleans's leaders actually considered constructing an expressway along the Mississippi River and French Quarter. Fortunately, that never happened, but it reflected the city's desperation to regain what it had lost.

The oil bust of the 1980s negatively impacted the New Orleans economy, and Fortune 500 companies began to flee. Only the hospitality industry continued to thrive, encouraging the talent of musicians, chefs, and other creative entrepreneurs. In the late 1990s and early 2000s, the local community enjoyed a cultural renaissance. After hurricane Katrina's devastating impact in 2005, New Orleanians show a renewed appreciation for their art, food, language, music, and the many diverse peoples whose long-ago influences remain.

Tracing the Mardi Gras Tradition

It's fitting that Pierre Le Moyne, Sieur d'Iberville, rediscovered and secured the mouth of the Mississippi in 1699 on Mardi Gras day, a holiday cherished by New Orleanians for nearly 175 years. Although Creole societies per European custom already celebrated the holiday, it wasn't until 1837 that a newspaper gave the first official account of a public Mardi Gras parade, complete with masked revelers. Some people deplore the debauchery seen today, but in the mid-1840s, the debauchery was far more extreme and risked being banned.

Thankfully, a group of men formed the first Mardi Gras organization, the Mistick Krewe of Comus, named after the god of mirth and revelry. In 1857, they paraded by torchlight on two mule-drawn floats — so very quaint and quite different compared to today's standards where you see a monstrously large, two-story, tractor-pulled Bacchusaurus float zoom past as part of the superkrewe Bacchus. Comus also invented the "secret society" and issued 3,000 coveted invitations to a ball that would become *the* event for New Orleans's upper class. In time, other krewes joined in on the fun, hosting their own parades and balls.

Most krewes are hierarchies, with one member ruling as king and several others serving as the royal court. (Some krewes, such as Endymion and Bacchus, recruit celebrities from film, television, music, and sports to act as their kings.) Many krewes have roots in private, exclusive organizations, with agendas ranging from the socially aware to purely pleasurable.

Mardi Gras is the culmination of Carnival (please don't confuse the two terms). *Mardi Gras* is French for "Fat Tuesday," though the term generally applies to the final two weeks of *Carnival* (from *carnisvale,* or "farewell to flesh," which begins on January 6, the 12th night of Christmas). The idea of Mardi Gras is to cram as much sin and decadence as you can into this final frenzied fortnight. On Ash Wednesday, the Christian season of Lent begins, which consists of 40 days of fasting and repentance. Of course, not all celebrants on the streets during Mardi Gras are strict religious adherents; most come for the party.

I hope you can come for the next Mardi Gras, which always falls 46 days before Easter. Dates for the next four years are February 20, 2007, February 5, 2008, February 24, 2009, and February 16, 2010. See the "Mardi Gras Parade Routes" map (see p. 209) in Chapter 12 for the major parades that take place during the last days of Carnival.

All hail Rex (not the dog)

The identity of *Rex* (the King of Carnival) is kept secret until the day before Mardi Gras. To be named King of Carnival is the ultimate honor for a New Orleanian, usually signifying his prominent standing and work in the community. The king is almost always an older man; his queen is usually of college age and always a young debutante as well as the daughter of a prominent member of society. The krewe of Rex parade always ends in an elaborate tradition: The parade stops at Gallier Hall for a toast from the mayor before moving to Canal Street, where Rex gives a speech, toasts his queen, and presents her with a big bouquet of roses.

Building Blocks: Local Architecture

One of the big reasons why I choose to live in New Orleans is the extraordinarily beautiful, old architecture. The delicate gingerbread on an Eastlake Victorian home or the cast-iron railing of an Italianate shotgun house starkly contrast with plain, nearly identical suburban homes across the country. And the sheer number and variety of architectural styles — from the early 1800s Creole cottage to the 1940s bungalow — are breathtaking compared to the cookie-cutter developments found elsewhere.

The most common form of architecture is the classic shotgun. Raised on brick piers, it's a narrow, long structure, where one room lines up behind another. Many natives hated growing up in one because of the lack of privacy; you have to go through the bedrooms before you get to the kitchen, which was typically added on to the back. (Some were lucky and lived in a camelback shotgun, where the bedrooms were on the second floor.) If you open the front and back doors and look down the hall, it gives the appearance of a shotgun barrel. Or, some say it got its name because you could shoot a shotgun through the doors and not hit anything. The breezeway provided a form of air conditioning, as did the brick piers because air flowed underneath the floorboards. You can find this practical yet attractive style throughout New Orleans and especially in what were working-class neighborhoods, such as the Irish Channel (see Chapter 8).

You can find photos of other popular architecture styles — such as the Creole Cottage and the Double Gallery House — at www.prcno.org, the Web site for the nonprofit Preservation Resource Center of New Orleans.

If you want to find out more about New Orleans architecture, page through Lloyd Vogt's illustrated *New Orleans Houses: A House Watcher's Guide* (Pelican Publishing Co.). Or start collecting the *New Orleans Architecture* series (Pelican); each book is devoted to one particular neighborhood, such as the French Quarter, the American Sector, or the Garden District. My favorite feature of the series is the inclusion of past and present photos of the same house, when possible. Too often, the listing abruptly ends with the word "demolished."

Thankfully, the largest collections of historic properties, such as in the French Quarter and along St. Charles Avenue, were spared Katrina's wrath. The shotguns and Creole cottages of the Ninth Ward, the arts-and-crafts bungalows and cottages of Lakeview, and the contemporary ranches and colonial-style homes of New Orleans East were not so lucky. Time will tell what new architecture will pop up as the city rebuilds these neighborhoods. Several design projects and competitions to create low-income housing are in the works, including Global Green USA's "Sustainable Design Competition for New Orleans" (see www.globalgreen.org for the finalists' designs).

Taste of New Orleans: Local Cuisine

Cajun versus Creole

Much of New Orleans's cuisine rests on two regional foundations: Cajun and Creole cooking. **Cajun cooking** brought New Orleans to national attention in the early 1980s thanks to the popularity of chef Paul Prudhomme. Cajun descends from the households of the Acadian country folk who came from Nova Scotia to settle in rural Louisiana. In their new home, economy often dictated that these folks throw all available foods into a single pot — a tradition that created jambalaya, étouffée, and red beans and rice (which many locals eat every Mon like clockwork).

Most people assume that Cajun food is always prepared spicy and served piping hot. Although Cajun cuisine certainly relies on spice a great deal, its foundation is a combination of regional ingredients. Even though serving Cajun food steaming hot is wise, neither the physical heat nor the spice should overwhelm the flavor.

Creole cooking is more varied and urban than Cajun food. Creole originated in the kitchens of New Orleans proper as a mix of French and Spanish cuisines. It relies heavily on high-quality ingredients smothered in rich, delicate sauces, with African and Caribbean spices providing an extra kick.

Muffuletta versus po' boy

Italian cold cuts and cheese stuffed into round Italian bread and slathered with olive salad dressing: This is a *muffuletta* (say muff-ah-*lot*-ah). That description may not do it justice. Trust me; this savory local fixture is worth every salty bite. Half of a muffuletta makes a great meal, and a quarter makes a nice, filling snack. Few people can eat a whole one. As with many foods in New Orleans, arguments abound as to who makes the best. Check out Chapter 11 to see my picks.

The other signature sandwich of New Orleans, the ***po' boy,*** proved cheap and filling during the streetcar strike of the late 1920s, with the idea that it's the only food a poor boy or "po' boy" can afford. Though not much different in structure from a hero or a sub, it's fixed in the minds of many locals as *the* premier New Orleans sandwich. The sandwich isn't all that complicated; take a crusty loaf of French bread, slice it open lengthwise, and stuff it with just about anything you can imagine. Roast-beef po' boys are great, especially if you have a little *debris* (gravy) dripping down the sides. Ham and cheese is a standard combo, and hot smoked sausage is also good. Seafood is a reliable standby; fried fish, soft-shell crab, oysters, and shrimp are all popular ingredients. Weird as it may sound, many people enjoy french-fry po' boys; that's right, a sandwich of french fries between two slices of French bread — and hopefully some of that rich, brown gravy. It's in keeping with New Orleans's "anything goes" attitude. (Just skip the french fry po' boy if you're on a low-carb diet!)

Obviously, po' boys aren't exactly health food. The best sandwiches have fried fixings or thick sauces (or both). They are also a *teensy* bit messy; you're just not getting the proper New Orleans experience if your shrimp or roast beef isn't spilling out of the sides of your overstuffed sandwich.

Is your mouth watering yet? See Chapter 11 for more food listings.

Word to the Wise: The Local Lingo

Surprisingly, many native New Orleanians sound like they're from Brooklyn. Perhaps the dialect can be traced back to the enormous influx of Italian and Irish immigrants from New York City in the decades after 1803, when New Orleans became an American city as part of the famous Louisiana Purchase from France. Some locals don't appear to have an accent at all until you hear them pronounce a word like "trout" or "about," which sounds just like a Canadian would say it — must be that Acadian influence. And don't be scared if someone wants to "ax" you a question. For a glossary of New Orleans terms, check out the Cheat Sheet in the front of this book; for terms specific to Mardi Gras, see Chapter 12.

Background Check: Recommended Books and Movies

Turning the pages

Please don't limit your fiction about New Orleans to Anne Rice. As much as many people adore her, I invite you to explore authors whose works also serve as portals to New Orleans. Pulitzer Prize winners John Kennedy Toole's *A Confederacy of Dunces* (Louisiana State University Press) and Shirley Ann Grau's *The Keepers of the House* (Vintage) are classics — as is Walker Percy's *The Moviegoer* (Vintage).

More recent writings that caught my eye include John Biguenet's *Oyster* (Ecco), which is a must-read if you plan a day-trip to bayou country, such as Lafitte (see Chapter 15). Valerie Martin's *The Great Divorce* (Vintage) is about a veterinarian at the New Orleans (read Audubon) Zoo whose marriage is falling apart. Nancy Lemann's *Lives of the Saints* (New American Library) offers frank insight into New Orleans high society. Other authors whose work I admire include Sheila Bosworth, Robert Olen Butler, and Patty Friedmann.

If, after all these suggestions, you still want something by Rice, read *The Feast of All Saints* (Ballantine), a historical novel about *les gens de couleur libre* (free people of color) in 19th-century New Orleans. Christine Wiltz's excellent *Glass House* (Louisiana State University) examines the current state of racial tension.

A short list of nonfiction is near impossible, but forced to pick, I choose *Fabulous New Orleans* (Pelican), by Lyle Saxon; *The Last Madam: A Life in the New Orleans Underworld* (DaCapo Press), by Christine Wiltz; *Frenchmen, Desire, Good Children and Other Streets of New Orleans* (Touchstone), by John Churchill Chase; and any essay collection by the witty, worldly Andrei Codrescu.

Arthur Hardy's Mardi Gras Guide is an annual magazine and my personal Mardi Gras bible come Twelfth Night. It contains the all-important parade schedule, calendar of related events, and informative articles on Carnival history. You can buy one almost anywhere in the city (it usually comes out right after Christmas), order a copy by phone ☎ **504-838-6111,** or purchase one on the Web www.mardigrasneworleans.com/arthur/index.html).

Of course, I have been reading anything and everything related to Katrina. The most dramatic and passionate narrative of the storm and its immediate aftermath can be found in *The Great Deluge: Hurricane Katrina, New Orleans, and the Mississippi Gulf Coast* (Morrow), by Tulane historian and best-selling author Douglas Brinkley. *Times-Picayune* columnist Chris Rose has become an invaluable voice of the people post-Katrina, and his self-published *1 Dead in Attic* is a harrowing must-read (it's widely available, even in gift shops); I also recommend *Breach of Faith: Hurricane Katrina and the Near Death of a Great American City* (Random House), by *Times-Picayune* editor Jed Horne. He shares shocking individual stories without resorting to melodrama or cheap sentimentality. For more Katrina-related book recommendations, see Chapter 2.

For more reading ideas, I strongly recommend *The Booklover's Guide to New Orleans* (Louisiana State University Press), by *Times-Picayune* book editor Susan Larson.

Screening The Big Easy

Hollywood loves to make movies in and about New Orleans because of its odd combination of eccentricity and timelessness. Tennessee

Williams's *A Streetcar Named Desire,* starring Marlon Brando and Vivien Leigh, perfectly captures New Orleans and is a must-see. Another classic is Louis Malle's *Pretty Baby,* which was somewhat scandalous at the time of its release for his portrayal of Brooke Shields as a child prostitute. (Susan Sarandon stars as her mother.) The bordello scenes were shot inside The Columns Hotel on St. Charles Avenue (see Chapter 10). Before you head over to Harrah's New Orleans Casino (see Chapter 12), rent *The Cincinnati Kid,* in which Steve McQueen stars as a New Orleans card shark.

Locals laugh at the put-on accents but still love Dennis Quaid as a semi-corrupt cop and Ellen Barkin as an assistant district attorney in the sexy crime caper *The Big Easy.* Julia Roberts plays a law student in John Grisham's legal drama *The Pelican Brief.* Lastly, if you're planning to go to bayou country for a day-trip (see Chapter 15), try to see *Eve's Bayou* before you go. The scenery is breathtaking, and the actors (including Samuel L. Jackson) are heartbreaking.

In 2002, Louisiana lawmakers approved tax incentives for studios that film in the state and hire local workers, which spawned a slew of productions in New Orleans and earned it the nickname "Hollywood South." Jamie Foxx came to town for his Oscar-winning turn in *Ray,* and Kate Hudson filmed the haunting thriller *The Skeleton Key.*

Post-Katrina, filmmakers are slowly returning to the city. *All the King's Men* (starring Sean Penn, Jude Law, and Kate Winslet) was filmed here before the storm hit, but the stars returned for the film's premiere in September 2006. Several other films are shooting as we go to print, including *The Curious Case of Benjamin Button*, starring Brad Pitt.

Chapter 4

Deciding When to Go

● ●

In This Chapter

▶ Planning your trip around the seasons

▶ Perusing a calendar of festivals in and near New Orleans

● ●

Compared to the rest of the country, New Orleans is slow to change. Locals always favor tradition over trends. Nevertheless, the timing of your trip should be a crucial consideration. If you don't like hot weather, don't spend too much time here during the summer months, when the humidity sticks to you like cotton candy. If you don't like crowds (especially rowdy, drunken ones), the charms of Mardi Gras or Jazz Fest may be lost on you.

Keeping Hurricane Season in Mind

After Katrina, it goes without saying that you should take hurricane season — June 1 through November 30 — into consideration when planning your trip. Most tropical storm and hurricane activity occurs August through October. If you decide to go during this time, please plan ahead for what you will need to do in case of an evacuation. See www.nola.com/hurricane for a comprehensive "Hurricane Center" of news reports, evacuation tips, and lots of links.

Planning Your Trip Around the Seasons

New Orleans has three seasons: Hot, Cold, and In Between. (Though locals will tell you there are four seasons: crawfish, shrimp, crab and "erster," or oyster.) Except for late spring through early summer (when temperatures are just uniformly hot), the seasons tend to run together. That's because this port city, a natural drop-off point for various cultures, also seems to be a way station for nearly every weather pattern on the North American continent. A butterfly beating its wings in Kansas City seems to affect the weather in New Orleans. As a result, bundling up under layers of clothing in the morning and then stripping down to a tank top and shorts by mid-afternoon isn't uncommon. Unless you're coming in the dog days of summer, prepare for a little bit of everything.

Table 3-1		Average Monthly Temperatures for Metropolitan New Orleans									
	Jan	*Feb*	*Mar*	*Apr*	*May*	*June*	*July*	*Aug*	*Sept*	*Oct*	*Nov*	*Dec*
High °F	61	64	72	79	84	89	91	90	87	79	71	64
High °C	16	18	22	26	29	32	33	32	31	26	22	18
Low °F	42	44	52	58	66	71	74	73	70	60	51	46
Low °C	6	7	11	14	19	22	23	23	21	16	11	8

Spring

Pros:

- The weather is perfect for visiting plantation homes or Audubon Park.
- Wear shorts: Average highs are in the 70s and 80s.
- Jazz Fest, held the last weekend of April and the first weekend of May, turns the city into one giant musical mecca.
- Other events, including the rapidly growing French Quarter Festival, make the spring a "festive" time to visit.

Cons:

- The mercury can climb into the 90s with frightful speed.
- At the same time, average lows can dip into the 60s and even the 50s. Bring a light sweater or jacket, just in case.
- In New Orleans, April *and* May bring showers, so bring an umbrella, and be prepared to use it.

Summer

Pros:

- Tourism in New Orleans generally lags in the summer, so it's a great time to beat the crowds and snag a bargain or two.
- The season brings pleasant breezes, plenty of sunshine, and colorful vegetation.

Cons:

- It's *hot*. Average highs are in the 80s and 90s, with temperatures often soaring into the 100s. You may want to limit your sightseeing to cooler hours in the early morning and evening; the afternoons can be unbearable. Drink plenty of fluids, seek shade and air-conditioned buildings, and don't skimp on the sunscreen.

✔ It's not just hot; it's humid. In New Orleans, humidity can often be as high as 100 percent, resulting in an atmosphere you can practically drink through a straw. With all that moisture in the air, rain can — and does — fall at the drop of a hat. Keep that umbrella handy, especially if you venture out in the afternoon.

✔ School's out. Teen foot traffic makes for crowded shopping destinations, and attendance at museums, parks, and other kid-friendly attractions rises.

Fall

Pros:

✔ Fall means a respite from the grisly heat of July and August, making for cool breezes.

✔ The cool breezes also carry romantic properties that shouldn't be discounted. A lazy evening watching the pale sunset over the river is a beautiful experience.

✔ Fall means Halloween, which offers a basketful of revelry options in a city known for playing dress-up. (See "Perusing a Calendar of Events" later in this chapter.)

Cons:

✔ October and November are the driest months of the year (which isn't necessarily a guarantee against sudden downpours).

✔ It's the tail end (and the most active part) of hurricane season, which begins June 1 and ends in November. Most storms come knocking between August and November, so don't discount the possibility of a sudden and abrupt change of location should a big storm hit.

Winter

Pros:

✔ Compared with much of the country, New Orleans gets away easy. The weather is often mild to middling cold, and you'll never get snowed in. Plan to bring a lightweight coat or jacket.

✔ The first three weeks of December are traditionally slow for tourism, so finding a good room at a good rate is much easier.

✔ Crowds aren't a big problem in the early part of December, so waiting in line doesn't take as long.

✔ After December, New Orleans has a lot going on. Don't miss New Year's Eve in the French Quarter, or the Sugar Bowl each January.

- ✔ You can't forget Mardi Gras. Depending on the year, Carnival can fall almost anywhere in February or early March.

- ✔ New Orleans is made for romance, making it the perfect spot for a Valentine's Day getaway.

Cons:

- ✔ Although winter is a cakewalk compared to, say, winter in Chicago, cold weather can catch you unawares if you don't plan (and pack) for the possibility. Occasional cold snaps bring the temperature down to freezing and below.

- ✔ You may want to make room for a larger coat, as well. The wind-chill factor, which can knock another 10 or 20 degrees off the thermometer, exacerbates the cold weather. (You'll still likely experience topsy-turvy weather, so pack lighter wear, too.)

- ✔ If you don't like large crowds and snarled traffic, you'd do better to avoid New Year's and Mardi Gras.

Perusing a Calendar of Events

New Orleans truly deserves its reputation as a party capital. No matter what time of year you visit, you can find an excuse to *laissez le bon temps rouler* (let the good times roll). The local newspapers' calendars of events are bursting with things to do, from casual celebrations to full-out festivals.

If you're coming to New Orleans for a specific event, especially Mardi Gras or Jazz Fest, you need to do a bit more advance planning than you would otherwise. I can't stress this point enough: Make reservations for these two events (as well as for the Sugar Bowl and the French Quarter Festival) as early as possible. As their dates draw closer, hotel rooms become scarcer than honest politicians (the latter are infamously rare in Louisiana). I recommend that you begin calling 8 to 10 months ahead.

Don't assume you're off the hook if you come for a smaller event such as, say, the Rayne Frog Festival (hop to the end of this chapter for details). Even during the less popular (and populous) festivals and events, finding a place to stay can become a Herculean exercise if you wait too long. Plan ahead to avoid a headache of scrambling for a room.

The following sections present the city's best festivals and events, listed under the months in which they occur. For more-detailed information, visit the **Times-Picayune** and **Gambit Weekly** Web sites (www.nola.com and www.bestofneworleans.com, respectively), **New Orleans Citysearch** (www.neworleans.citysearch.com), or **Inside New Orleans** (www. insideneworleans.com). **Huli's Calendar of Louisiana Festivals and Events** is an indispensable, comprehensive resource for festivals throughout the state. You can find this publication at bookstores and newsstands throughout the city; go to www.louisiana-festivals.com or call ☎ 504-488-5993 for a copy or for specific information.

January

The **Allstate Sugar Bowl Football Classic** (☎ 504-828-2440; www. allstatesugarbowl.com). Crowds begin pouring into the city around late December. If you're a football fanatic and can afford to spend the money, the Sugar Bowl is perfect. Getting tickets can be difficult, especially when the Sugar Bowl hosts the national college football championship. If you want to go, check a ticket service such as **Ticketmaster** (www.ticketmaster.com). January 1.

Carnival (☎ 800-672-6124 or 504-566-5011; www.neworleanscvb.com) runs from January 6 to Mardi Gras day, but only the last two weeks leading up to Mardi Gras see a huge increase in tourism. You'll be lucky to find a vacant hotel room within 100 miles of the city if you don't make your reservations well ahead of time. Call for specific dates.

Mardi Gras (☎ 800-672-6124 or 504-566-5011; www.mardigrasday.com). On this day and most of the two weeks preceding it, life in New Orleans is hectic, to put it mildly. (See Chapters 3 and 12 for more information on Mardi Gras.) Can be as early as February 3 or as late as March 9, but it always falls on the Tuesday 46 days before Easter.

February

The **Black Heritage Festival** (☎ 504-827-0112). This two-day celebration features craft exhibits, soul food (such as jambalaya, fried chicken, and gumbo), and live music in Armstrong Park. You can find related activities along the Riverwalk, in Audubon Park, and at various Louisiana State Museum buildings. Late February or early March.

March

On **St. Patrick's Day,** celebrations and parades overtake the city. The Downtown Irish Club sponsors a parade the Friday before St. Patrick's Day. Call local tavern Molly's on the Market, where the parade kicks off, at ☎ 504-525-5169 for more information. March 17.

The Tennessee Williams/New Orleans Literary Festival (☎ 504-581-1144; www.tennesseewilliams.net) celebrates the life of this famous playwright with performances, lectures, and walking tours. Held over a four-day period in March.

April

The **French Quarter Festival** (☎ 800-673-5725 or 504-522-5730; www. frenchquarterfestivals.org) serves as the unofficial start of the city's prime festival season because it leads directly into Jazz Fest. Hailed as the state's largest free music festival (and the world's largest jazz brunch), it gets bigger every year, offering plenty of free entertainment (unlike Jazz Fest, which is by ticket only), with an emphasis on local and regional music and food. Check on room availability well in advance. Second weekend in April. (*Note:* If it conflicts with Easter, it's held the first or third weekend in Apr).

Jazz Fest, the **New Orleans Jazz & Heritage Festival, (☎ 504-522-4786** or 504-558-6100; www.nojazzfest.com). A diverse lineup of hundreds of musicians (from big-ticket names to local acts, representing just about every genre under the sun) perform on various stages at the New Orleans Fair Grounds, and many more turn up after hours in the city's music clubs and concert halls as venues capitalize on the eager, music-hungry traffic. The city is crowded, prices are higher, and hotel and restaurant reservations are hard to come by — so plan ahead. Many attendees begin making reservations for the following year's festival even before the current one ends. Last weekend in April (Fri–Sun) and first weekend in May (Thurs–Sun).

May

The **Greek Festival (☎ 504-282-0259;** www.greekfestnola.com) features Greek food, crafts, music, and dancing. Last weekend in May.

June

The **International Arts Festival (☎ 888-767-1317** or 504-367-1313 is another popular music festival, with a decidedly Caribbean feel. The city's third oldest festival focuses on calypso, reggae, and regional food, and takes place during the second weekend in June.

July

The popular **Essence Festival (☎ 800-725-5652** or 504-523-5652; www.essence.com) is both a music festival and a series of seminars on topics of importance to the African American community. The festival has featured appearances by Prince, Gladys Knight, Patti LaBelle, Lauryn Hill, The Isley Brothers, Mary J. Blige, Sinbad, Kenny G, Maya Angelou, Missy Elliott, Clarence Carter, and Irma Thomas, among many others. Held during the weekend closest to the Fourth of July.

Tales of the Cocktail (☎ 800-299-0404; www.talesofthecocktail.com) is one more excuse to drink alcohol in the Big Easy (as if this city needs another). The annual festival features mixologist demos, walking tours/bar crawls, pairing menus at top restaurants, and more. Most events are $25; dinner rates vary. Held at various locations for five days the last week of July.

Enjoying festivals off the beaten path

Not everything worth doing in Louisiana happens inside the corporate limits of New Orleans. Check out these noteworthy festivals that take place just outside the city.

Festival International de Louisiane (☎ 337-232-8086; www.festival international.com) is a mammoth celebration of the cultural heritage of southern Louisiana (primarily a mix of French, Hispanic, and African-Caribbean cultures). It usually takes place during the last weekend of April in downtown Lafayette, about a two-hour drive from New Orleans.

Lafayette also plays host to **Festivals Acadiens** (☎ 337-233-7060), a celebration of Cajun culture. Cajun food and music are the main attractions, with workshops and other activities sprinkled throughout. Third weekend of September.

The **Original Southwest Louisiana Zydeco Music Festival** (☎ 337-942-2392; www.zydeco.org) in Plaisance (roughly a three-hour drive north of New Orleans) celebrates the unique joys of *zydeco,* the popular accordion-driven music of the Creoles of southern Louisiana. Aside from the event itself, an all-day fair is held on Saturday with music, food, and crafts. The celebration extends to the surrounding areas of Lafayette, Opelousas, and Lake Charles. Labor Day weekend.

I'd be remiss if I didn't at least mention the **Rayne Frog Festival,** in Cajun Country, about a two-hour drive from New Orleans in an area west of Lafayette. Cajuns can turn just about anything into an excuse for a festival, as evidenced by this event's frog races and frog-jumping contests. (Didn't bring a frog? Don't worry; you can rent one. Seriously.) On the culinary side, you can also participate in a lively frog-eating contest. Held every September. For exact dates and full details, contact the **Rayne Chamber of Commerce** (☎ 337-334-3121; www.rayne.org).

September

Southern Decadence (☎ 800-876-1484 or 504-522-8047; www.southern decadence.net), which promises just that — decadence, and lots of it. Thousands of gays and lesbians converge upon the city during this festival. They assemble on Sunday in the 1200 block of Royal Street and then head off on a secret parade route known only to the grand marshal. Expect drag queens galore and lots of drinking. The celebration is wild and, like Mardi Gras, not all the street celebrations are appropriate for young children. Labor Day weekend.

September marks the start of football season, with another year of gridiron action for the New Orleans Saints (☎ 504-733-0255; www.neworleanssaints.com). The team struggles, giving credence to a supposed curse. An entire cemetery had to be relocated in order to build the Superdome; some locals suggest the disturbed spirits haunt the team.

October

The **Gumbo Festival** (☎ 504-436-4712) offers attendees every type of gumbo you can imagine — and many that you can't. The festival features games and carnival rides as well as jazz, blues, and Cajun music to put you in the mood for food — and work off what you eat. Generally held during the second weekend in October.

With the locals' penchant for masking, it's a given that New Orleans loves Halloween. Children can attend **Boo at the Zoo** (held on and around Halloween; ☎ 866-ITS-AZOO or 504-866-4872; www.audubon institute.org) and a yearly program at the **Louisiana Children's Museum** (☎ 504-586-0725; www.lcm.org). Meanwhile, events such as the **French Market Pumpkin Carving and Decorating Contest** (☎ 504-522-2621) and the **Moonlight Witches Run** offer more adult-oriented fun.

Speaking of adult-oriented, the annual **M.O.M.'s Ball,** thrown by a debauched group known as the Krewe of Mystic Orphans and Misfits, is one of the season's hot-ticket events, a notoriously raucous bash. It's an invitation-only event, so you won't find any public ticket information, but keep an eye out for it if you're in town in October.

November

The **State Farm Bayou Classic** (☎ 225-771-3170) is a college football rivalry between a pair of Louisiana institutions: Grambling University and Southern University. The annual event is one of the major social events of the year, so make your reservations early if you plan to attend — around 75,000 people turn out for the game. Thanksgiving weekend.

The **Celebration in the Oaks** (☎ 504-483-9415). During this festival, sections of City Park's lovely old oaks are draped with lights and holiday-themed figures delight kids of all ages. You can visit the park on foot, by car, or by carriage. Late November to early January.

December

You won't see Dick Clark or Ryan Seacrest there, but the **Jackson Square New Year's Eve** celebration is beginning to resemble New York City's — right down to the lighted ball dropping from the top of Jackson Brewery and dramatic fireworks over the Mississippi River.

Part II

Planning Your Trip to New Orleans

"I think we should arrange to be there for Cayenne pepper-Garlic-Andouille sausage week, and then shoot over to the Breathmint-Antacid Festival."

In this part . . .

This section helps you create a workable budget, points out some money-saving tips about cutting costs and avoiding hidden expenses (Chapter 5), and lists some invaluable resources for travelers with specific needs — whether you're bringing a large family, needing a wheelchair-accessible hotel, searching for a gay-friendly spot, or hoping to take advantage of senior-citizen discounts (Chapter 7). You uncover the diverse options available to you, including using a travel agent, booking a package tour, and finding secret airfare deals (Chapter 6).

You also get the opportunity to tie up the loose ends of buying travel insurance, renting a car, making reservations, and packing for your trip (Chapter 8).

Chapter 5

Managing Your Money

. . . .

In This Chapter

▶ Budgeting your trip
▶ Uncovering hidden costs
▶ Getting the lowdown on cash, credit cards, and traveler's checks
▶ Handling a lost or stolen wallet

. . . .

*I*n a city as tempting as New Orleans, traveling without a budget is
the surest path to financial disaster. Thanks to numerous historical
attractions, French Quarter souvenir shops, and fabulous restaurants
and bars, you don't need to set foot inside Harrah's Casino to break your
bank. In fact, you can easily max out your credit card just by sampling
the city's many culinary delights. In this chapter, I give you tips on how
to exercise willpower and fiscal responsibility without sacrificing self-
indulgences.

If you do go over budget, remember that you're contributing to an economy that desperately needs tourist dollars. (You can also contribute
directly to the city's rebuilding efforts by giving to a local charity; see p.
38 for a list of organizations.)

Planning Your Budget

The best way to get a handle on your budget is to walk yourself through
your trip, starting with transportation to your nearest airport (or, if
you're driving, how much gas you expect to use per day). If you're flying,
first add up the costs of your transportation to the airport, your flight,
and the ride to your hotel. Next, add the hotel rate per day, meals (be
sure to note if your hotel includes breakfast in its room rate), transportation costs, admission to museums and other attractions, and any other
entertainment expenses.

Table 5-1 offers some average costs for you to get started.

Table 5-1   What Things Cost in New Orleans

Expense	Cost
Taxi from the airport to the Central Business District or French Quarter	$24–$28; $12 per person for 3 or more passengers
Bus from airport to downtown	$1.50
St. Charles, Canal, or Riverfront streetcar ride for one (one-way)	$1.25
Riverfront streetcar ride for one (one-way)	$1.50
Bus ride for one (one-way)	$1.25
Taxi ride for one in the Quarter (add $1 for each extra passenger)	$5
Inexpensive ($) hotel room for two	under $100
Low to moderate ($$) hotel room for two	$100–$200
Moderate to high ($$$) hotel room for two	$201–$300
Expensive ($$$$) hotel room for two	more than $300
Moderately priced breakfast for two	$12–$16
Moderately priced lunch for two	$20–$30
Moderately priced dinner for two	$30–$50
Nonalcoholic drink	$1–$1.50
Bottle of beer	$1.50–$4
Cocktail	$3.50–$8
Cup of coffee	75¢–$1.50
Adult admission to New Orleans Museum of Art	$8
Theater ticket at Le Petit Theatre	$21–$26

The costs of some things, such as hotels, are relatively inflexible. Along with airfare or other transportation costs, lodging makes up the largest part of your expenditures. Other factors, such as transportation in the city, are relatively cheap. The incredible number of restaurants and nightlife choices in New Orleans vary as widely in price as they do in style, so it's up to you to go formal or casual and pay accordingly.

Of course, budgeting your vacation isn't so difficult when you're jotting down prices on a piece of paper in the comfort of your own home. Keeping track of your costs after you arrive, however, is another matter altogether. Remember that the key element in budget is "budge," so allow yourself some flexibility — start by tacking a good 10 percent or even 20 percent onto the final budget tally. Keep in mind that you can easily go from merely bending your budget to flat-out broke if you don't pay attention.

Transportation

Getting around the most popular parts of the city is a relative bargain. Many hotels and attractions lie within a few miles of one another in the French Quarter or Central Business District. If your destination is farther than you want to walk — or if you're visiting on a particularly hot day — a taxi ride is worth the cost. The average trip in or around the Quarter should be no more than $5.

For public transportation, hop on one of the city's buses or streetcars. Fares are $1.25 each time you get on (transfers cost an additional 25 cents), but a **VisiTour** pass, good for unlimited bus and streetcar rides, costs only $5 for one day and $12 for three days. Check with your hotel's concierge, or check with the **Regional Transit Authority** (☎ **504-248-3900;** www.norta.com) for information. Many hotels also offer free shuttles to and from the French Quarter or Central Business District. For more information on getting around the city, see Chapter 8.

Lodging

In this book, I share information about *rack rates* and how to save money in this area (details in Chapter 10), but hotels will still comprise a significant portion of your expenses. (*Rack rates* simply mean published rates and tend to be the highest rate paid.) You *can* find inexpensive rooms, though they're usually far from the center of town, or they don't offer much in the way of amenities. (Some guesthouses, for example, wanting to emulate that European feel, offer rooms that share a common bathroom for a cheaper rate, or a backpacker room that more closely resembles your closet at home.) If you want to stay relatively close to the French Quarter or the Central Business District, expect to spend a minimum of $80 to $100 a night.

Dining

Dining options in New Orleans range from dirt-cheap to astronomically high. Almost all options are tantalizing; you don't have to spend a lot of money for a great meal. If you want to save a buck or two, get coffee and beignets for breakfast at Café du Monde for about $2.50, a $5 po' boy for lunch at any one of a hundred places, and dinner for under $15 at a place such as Café Maspero in the Quarter.

However, if you feel like you can't come to New Orleans without having breakfast at Brennan's, dinner at Antoine's, or a special night out at one of the fancier restaurants listed in Chapter 11, make sure to put a little money aside and make reservations well in advance.

Sightseeing

Attractions are a somewhat more flexible expense. Of course, your budget for entrance fees and admissions depends on what you want to see. If you're traveling with your entire family, you can expect to shell out more for attractions than if you're backpacking with a buddy. Refer to the attraction listings in Chapter 12 and make a list of your "must-sees," and then figure out your costs from the ticket prices.

Shopping

The amount of money you need for shopping makes up another variable part of your budget. After all, you don't have to buy anything at all if that's your style, though self-restraint can be something of an alien concept in New Orleans. Even a scrupulous penny-counter can succumb to shopping fever when wandering the French Market or some of the souvenir shops in the French Quarter. As an international port city, New Orleans offers as many choices as you can imagine. If you're an antiques buff, you may want to leave your checks and credit cards at the hotel before going anywhere near Magazine or Royal streets.

If you're just looking for souvenirs to take home as proof of your trip, you can find whole colonies of shops selling postcards, posters, sunglasses, and T-shirts in the French Quarter. Being tourist shops, however, they aren't exactly cheap. If you want to save on souvenirs, ask someone to take your picture on Bourbon Street. Voilà! You now have an instant memento of your trip (assuming the person doesn't run away with your camera). See Chapter 13 for the lowdown on shopping in New Orleans.

Nightlife

Your entertainment dollars will likely stretch further in New Orleans than in a place such as New York, where a pair of tickets to the theater can require a second mortgage. Most of the nightlife in New Orleans is relatively inexpensive — but again, your personal preferences determine the final tally. You'll obviously spend more if you go to the opera than if you head to the Maple Leaf or the House of Blues for some local music. Turn to Chapter 17 for nightlife listings, and Chapter 15 for the performing arts scene.

Cutting Costs — If You Must

New Orleans really needs every tourist dollar, so if you can afford to splurge, go ahead; get or do what you want and feel good about it, too. But if you must stick to a budget, try these cost-saving tips:

✔ **Go off season.** If you can handle hot, humid weather, you can get some great deals from June through August — but remember that when I say hot, I mean blood-boiling, sweat-inducing hot. The first three weeks of December are also a good time for discounts.

✔ **Travel midweek.** If you can travel on a Tuesday, Wednesday, or Thursday, you may find cheaper flights to your destination. When you ask about airfares, see if you can get a cheaper rate by flying on a different day. For more tips on getting a good fare, see Chapter 5.

✔ **Try a package tour.** For many destinations, you can book airfare, hotel, ground transportation, and even some sightseeing just by making one call to a travel agent or packager for a price much less than if you put the trip together yourself. (See Chapter 5 for more on package tours.)

✔ **Reserve a room with a refrigerator and coffeemaker.** You don't have to slave over a hot stove to cut a few costs; several motels have minifridges and coffeemakers. Buying supplies for breakfast can save you money — and probably calories.

✔ **Always ask for discount rates.** Membership in AAA, frequent-flier plans, trade unions, AARP, or other groups may qualify you for savings on car rentals, plane tickets, hotel rooms, and even meals. Ask about everything; you may be pleasantly surprised.

✔ **Ask if your kids can stay in the room with you.** A room with two double beds usually doesn't cost any more than one with a queen-size bed. And many hotels don't charge you the additional person rate if the additional person is pint-size and related to you. Even if you have to pay $10 or $15 extra for a rollaway bed, you'll save hundreds by not taking two rooms.

✔ **Try expensive restaurants at lunch instead of dinner.** Lunch tabs are usually a fraction of what dinners cost at a top restaurant, and the menu often boasts many of the same specialties.

✔ **Get out of the Quarter.** Really. To many people, the French Quarter *is* New Orleans, and they want to stay where they think all the action happens. Although you'll certainly see plenty of action in the Quarter, New Orleans offers much more for you to see and experience. Plus, hotels outside the Quarter tend to charge less than those inside its borders. So if you don't mind a slightly longer trip to most attractions, book a room in Faubourg Marigny, Uptown, or along the Esplanade Ridge. Thanks to the new Canal streetcar, even Mid-City is convenient to downtown. (See Chapter 9 for detailed neighborhood descriptions and Chapter 10 for more on hotels.)

✔ **Take the streetcar.** What's more romantic than seeing New Orleans from the streetcar? Relax, and ride for only $1.25 (one-way). (See streetcar maps on p. 108 and 111 and see the St. Charles' "Streetcar Highlights" box on p. 256.)

Katrina's affect on the local economy

At $105 billion and counting, Hurricane Katrina is the costliest natural disaster in U.S. history. According to the Brookings Institute, the labor force in the Greater New Orleans area is 30 percent smaller one year post-Katrina and the unemployment rate of 7.2 percent, is higher than pre-Katrina. As tourism increases and people continue to return, the city will bounce back. For a list of charities accepting donations, see p. 38.

✔ **Walk a lot.** You can save money, get some exercise, and see the city the way it was meant to be seen — at a leisurely pace. Stay hydrated and invest in a good pair of walking shoes — the last thing you need on vacation is sore feet. (*Note:* Don't overdo the walking if you're in town during a really hot spell. And wear a hat — the sun is stronger than you may realize!)

✔ **Skip the souvenirs.** Your photographs and your memories could be your trip's best mementos. If you're concerned about money, avoid those Quarter tourist shops with their overpriced T-shirts, key chains, and other useless trinkets. After all, you don't really *need* those riverboat salt-and-pepper shakers, do you?

Handling Money

You're the best judge of how much cash you feel comfortable carrying or what alternative form of currency is your favorite. That's not going to change much on your vacation. True, you'll probably be moving around more and incurring more expenses than you generally do (unless you happen to eat out every meal when you're at home), and you may let your mind slip into vacation gear and not be as vigilant about your safety as when you're in work mode. But, those factors aside, the only type of payment that won't be quite as available to you away from home is your personal checkbook.

Using ATMs and carrying cash

The easiest and best way to get cash away from home is from an automated teller machine (ATM). The **Cirrus** (☎ **800-424-7787;** www.master card.com) and **PLUS** (☎ **800-843-7587;** www.visa.com) networks span the globe; look at the back of your bank card to see which network you're on, and then call or check online for ATM locations at your destination. Be sure you know your personal identification number (PIN) before you leave home, and be sure to find out your daily withdrawal limit before you depart. Also keep in mind that many banks impose a fee every time you use your card at a different bank's ATM, up to $1.50 for domestic transactions. On top of this, the bank from which you withdraw cash may charge its own fee. To compare banks' ATM fees within the United States, use www.bankrate.com.

Charging ahead with credit cards

Credit cards are a safe way to carry money: They also provide a convenient record of all your expenses. You can also withdraw cash advances from your credit cards at banks or ATMs, provided you know your PIN. If you've forgotten yours, or didn't even know you had one, call the number on the back of your credit card and ask the bank to send it to you. It usually takes five to seven business days, though some banks provide the number over the phone if you tell them your mother's maiden name or some other personal information.

Toting traveler's checks

These days, traveler's checks are less necessary because most cities have 24-hour ATMs that allow you to withdraw small amounts of cash as needed. However, keep in mind that you'll likely be charged an ATM withdrawal fee if the bank isn't your own. So if you're withdrawing money every day, you may be better off with traveler's checks — provided that you don't mind showing identification every time you want to cash one.

You can get traveler's checks at almost any bank. **American Express** offers denominations of $20, $50, $100, $500, and (for cardholders only) $1,000. You pay a service charge ranging from 1 to 4 percent. You can also get American Express traveler's checks over the phone by calling ☎ 800-221-7282; Amex gold and platinum cardholders who use this number are exempt from the 1 percent fee.

Visa offers traveler's checks at Citibank locations nationwide, as well as at several other banks. The service charge ranges between 1.5 and 2 percent; checks come in denominations of $20, $50, $100, $500, and $1,000. Call ☎ 800-732-1322 for information. AAA members can obtain Visa checks without a fee at most AAA offices or by calling ☎ 866-339-3378. **MasterCard** also offers traveler's checks. Call ☎ 800-223-9920 for a location near you.

 If you choose to carry traveler's checks, be sure to keep a record of their serial numbers separate from your checks in the event that they're stolen or lost. You'll get a refund faster if you know the numbers.

Dealing with a Lost or Stolen Wallet

Be sure to contact your credit-card companies the minute you discover your wallet has been lost or stolen and file a report at the nearest police precinct (in the French Quarter, go to the **New Orleans Police**

Department's 8th District at 334 Royal St.; ☎ **504-565-7530**). Your credit-card company or insurer may require a police report number or record of the loss. Most credit-card companies have an emergency toll-free number to call if your card is lost or stolen; they may be able to wire you a cash advance immediately or deliver an emergency credit card in a day or two. Call the following emergency numbers in the United States:

- ✔ **American Express** ☎ **800-221-7282** (for cardholders and traveler's check holders)
- ✔ **MasterCard** ☎ **800-307-7309** or 636-722-7111
- ✔ **Visa** ☎ **800-847-2911** or 410-581-9994

For other credit cards, call the toll-free number directory at ☎ **800-555-1212.**

Chapter 6

Getting to New Orleans

• •

In This Chapter

▶ Traveling to New Orleans by airplane, car, or other means
▶ Understanding how Katrina damage will affect your transport
▶ Considering the escorted or package tour options

• •

So you're ready to come to the Crescent City? Before you pack your bags and throw on those Mardi Gras beads, you have to decide how to get here. Many people rush through this part of the process and end up paying for it later. Even if you know you want to fly, considering your many travel options before you book a flight is worth your time. This chapter covers the pros and cons of using a travel agent and of booking an escorted or package tour. It also mentions some pointers to keep in mind if you choose a more independent route, be it by plane, car, or even train.

How Katrina Damage Will Affect Your Transport

Even months after the storm, transportation into and out of the city was still a mess. Some interstates and bridges leading into the city suffered damage requiring repair; the Twin Spans bridge, which crosses the east side of Lake Pontchartrain from New Orleans to Slidell, was utterly destroyed. The airport was not anywhere near full capacity and automobile traffic was just horrific. Everything is much closer to normal now and you should not notice any Katrina-related transport problems other than perhaps some increased auto traffic, especially during rush hour because so many people still work in the city but live elsewhere because their New Orleans home is gone. The Twin Spans bridge, now reopened, is busier than ever with traffic from Slidell and other cities on the Northshore.

Flying to New Orleans

All the major airlines fly to New Orleans's Louis Armstrong International Airport (airline code MSY, for those of you booking on the Web), among them **American Airlines** (☎ 800-433-7300; www.aa.com), **Continental**

(☎ **800-525-0280;** www.continental.com), **Delta** (☎ **800-221-1212;** www.delta.com), **Northwest** (☎ **800-225-2525;** www.nwa.com), **Southwest** (☎ **800-435-9792;** www.southwest.com), **United** (☎ **800-UNITED;** www.united.com) and **US Airways** (☎ **800-428-4322;** www.usairways.com). The airport is in Kenner, 15 miles west of the city.

Getting the best deal on your airfare

Competition among the major U.S. airlines is unlike that of any other industry. Every airline offers virtually the same product (basically, a coach seat is a coach seat is a . . .), yet prices can vary by hundreds of dollars.

Business travelers who need the flexibility to buy their tickets at the last minute and change their itineraries at a moment's notice — and who want to get home before the weekend — pay (or at least their companies pay) the premium rate, known as the *full fare.* But if you can book your ticket far in advance, stay over Saturday night, and are willing to travel midweek (Tues, Wed, or Thurs), you can qualify for the least expensive price — usually a fraction of the full fare. On most flights, even the shortest hops within the United States, the full fare is close to $1,000 or more, but a 7- or 14-day advance purchase ticket might cost less than half of that amount. Obviously, planning ahead pays.

The airlines also periodically hold sales, in which they lower the prices on their most popular routes. These fares have advance purchase requirements and date-of-travel restrictions, but you can't beat the prices. As you plan your vacation, keep your eyes open for these sales, which tend to take place in seasons of low travel volume — in New Orleans, that would be anytime in the summer and December.

Consolidators, also known as bucket shops, are great sources for international tickets, although they usually can't beat the Internet on fares within North America. Start by looking in Sunday newspaper travel sections; U.S. travelers should focus on the *New York Times, Los Angeles Times,* and *Miami Herald.*

Bucket-shop tickets are usually nonrefundable or rigged with stiff cancellation penalties, often as high as 50 to 75 percent of the ticket price, and some put you on charter airlines with questionable safety records.

Several reliable consolidators are worldwide and available on the Net. **STA Travel** (☎ **800-781-4040;** www.statravel.com), the world's leader in student travel, offers good fares for travelers of all ages. **FlyCheap** (☎ **800-FLY-CHEAP;** www.1800flycheap.com) is owned by package-holiday megalith MyTravel and has especially good access to fares for sunny destinations. **Air Tickets Direct** (☎ **800-778-3447;** www.airticketsdirect.com) is based in Montreal and leverages the currently weak Canadian dollar for low fares. Your best bet locally is **Uniglobe Americana Travel** (☎ **504-561-0588** or 504-561-8100).

Booking your flight online

The "big three" online travel agencies, **Expedia** (www.expedia.com), **Travelocity** (www.travelocity.com), and **Orbitz** (www.orbitz.com) sell most of the air tickets bought on the Internet. Each has different business deals with the airlines and may offer different fares on the same flights, so shop around. Expedia and Travelocity also can send you an **e-mail notification** when a cheap fare becomes available to your favorite destination. Of the smaller travel agency Web sites, **SideStep** (www.sidestep.com) receives good reviews from users. It's a browser add-on that purports to "search 140 sites at once," but in reality only beats competitors' fares as often as other sites do.

Great **last-minute deals** are available through free weekly e-mail services provided directly by the airlines. Most of these deals are announced on Tuesday or Wednesday and must be purchased online. Most are only valid for travel that weekend, but some (such as Southwest's) can be booked weeks or months in advance. Sign up for weekly e-mail alerts at airline Web sites or check megasites that compile comprehensive lists of last-minute specials, such as **Smarter Travel** (www.smartertravel.com). For last-minute trips, www.site59.com in the United States often has better deals than the major-label sites.

If you're willing to give up some control over your flight details, use an *opaque fare service* like **Priceline** (www.priceline.com) or **Hotwire** (www.hotwire.com). Both offer rock-bottom prices in exchange for travel on a "mystery airline" at a mysterious time of day, often with a mysterious change of planes en route. The mystery airlines are all major, well-known carriers — and the possibility of being sent from Philadelphia to Chicago via Tampa is remote. But your chances of getting a 6 a.m. or 11 p.m. flight are pretty high. Hotwire tells you flight prices before you buy; Priceline usually has better deals than Hotwire, but you have to play their "name our price" game. *Note:* In 2004, Priceline added nonopaque service to its roster. You now have the option to pick exact flights, times, and airlines from a list of offers — or opt to bid on opaque fares as before.

Great last-minute deals are also available directly from the airlines through a free e-mail service called *E-savers*. Each week, the airline sends you a list of discounted flights, usually leaving the upcoming Friday or Saturday and returning the following Monday or Tuesday. You can sign up for all the major airlines at one time by logging on to **Smarter Living** (www.smarterliving.com), or you can go to each individual airline's Web site. Airline sites also offer schedules, flight booking, and information on late-breaking bargains.

Driving to New Orleans

New Orleans is easily accessible by car. Interstate 10 runs directly through the city from east to west, and just north of the city is Interstate 12, which also travels from east to west. From I-12, you can connect with the Lake Pontchartrain Causeway and drive south to I-10 directly in the metro area or connect with either I-55 to the west of the city or I-59 to the east of the city. Both I-55 and I-59 flow from north to south and connect with I-10. You can also access the city by U.S. highways 11, 51, 61, and 90. For help planning your route into the city, see the "Greater New Orleans" map on the inside front cover of this book.

Before you pack the trunk, however, don't forget this bit of information: As far as sightseeing goes, New Orleans isn't an easy driving city. Getting around the city isn't impossible, but at many tourist destinations, such as restaurants, nightclubs, or antiques shops, you have to fend for yourself for on-street parking. In the French Quarter, on-street parking is as elusive as Shangri-La; even residents have perennial parking woes. In fact, finding free parking near most attractions is something of a crapshoot. Commercial lots are readily available, but they can be expensive, and their locations are sometimes inconvenient.

Again, I don't want to discourage you or scare you off, especially if you have no other option. But be warned: If you drive into New Orleans (especially if you're staying in the French Quarter), you're better served by taking public transportation around the Quarter and saving your car for excursions outside the district.

Arriving by Other Means

Would you prefer to pull in to New Orleans on a train, or perhaps ride in on a cruise? Here are a few options if you want to leave your car at home.

Riding the rails

An increasingly less popular, but scenic, option is to take a train. All trains arrive at New Orleans's **Union Passenger Terminal,** 1001 Loyola Ave. Call **Amtrak** (☎ **800-USA-RAIL** or 504-528-1610; www.amtrak.com) for specific information on train fares and schedules. Ask about senior-citizen discounts and other possible discounts when making a reservation.

Note: The terminal, located at the edge of the Central Business District, serves as both the train station and the Greyhound Bus Terminal.

Cruising into New Orleans

Taking a cruise ship into New Orleans is about as different a travel option as you can think of. The slow, luxurious nature of a sea cruise fits perfectly with the city's "big easy" reputation, and one of the city's most popular party tunes is the 1959 R&B hit "Sea Cruise," by local Frankie Ford.

As a major port, New Orleans is a stop for a number of cruise lines. If you miss a particular attraction during this trip, you can always catch it when your cruise ship stops here on your next major vacation. Or you can get really creative and schedule a Caribbean cruise right in the middle of your New Orleans vacation. **Carnival** (www.carnival.com), **Norwegian** (www.ncl.com), and **Crystal** (www.crystalluxurycruises.com) lines, for example, make stops in or have cruises disembarking from New Orleans. For a unique vessel, try Riverbarge Excursions (www.riverbarge.com).

You usually disembark at the **Julia Street Cruise Ship Terminals 1 and 2;** if you decide to take a cruise from New Orleans — for example, on Carnival's *Holiday* or *Conquest* — you board here, as well. The terminal was originally developed as part of the 1984 Louisiana World Exposition — only about five minutes on foot from the French Quarter. (For port information, call ☎ 504-522-2551.) Alternatively, many paddlewheel boats for upriver cruises and some southbound cruise ships depart from the **Robin Street Wharf.**

For more information on cruise ships as a vacation option, consider *Cruise Vacations For Dummies* by Fran Wenograd Golden (Wiley), a handy guide to navigating the world of cruise ships. For more information on cruises departing from New Orleans, check out **Cruise Deals for Less** (☎ 800-330-1001 or 504-885-7245; www.cruisedealsforless.com).

Joining an Escorted Tour

You may be one of the many people who love escorted tours. The tour company takes care of all the details, and tells you what to expect at each leg of your journey. You know your costs upfront and, in the case of the tame ones, you don't get many surprises. Escorted tours can take you to the maximum number of sights in the minimum amount of time with the least amount of hassle.

If you decide to go with an escorted tour, I strongly recommend purchasing travel insurance, especially if the tour operator asks to you pay upfront. But don't buy insurance from the tour operator! If the tour operator doesn't fulfill its obligation to provide you with the vacation you paid for, why would the tour operator fulfill its insurance obligations? Get travel insurance through an independent agency. (I tell you more about the ins and outs of travel insurance in Chapter 8.)

When choosing an escorted tour, along with finding out whether you have to put down a deposit and when final payment is due, ask a few simple questions before you buy:

✔ **What is the cancellation policy?** Can the tour operator cancel the trip if it doesn't get enough people? How late can you cancel if you're unable to go? Do you get a refund if you cancel? If the operator cancels?

✔ **How jam-packed is the schedule?** Does the tour schedule try to fit 25 hours into a 24-hour day, or does it give you ample time to relax by the pool or shop? If getting up at 7 a.m. every day and not returning to your hotel until 6 or 7 p.m. sounds like a grind, certain escorted tours may not be for you.

✔ **How large is the group?** The smaller the group, the less time you spend waiting for people to get on and off the bus. Tour operators may be evasive about this because they may not know the exact size of the group until everybody has made reservations, but they should be able to give you a rough estimate.

✔ **Is there a minimum group size?** Some tour operators have a minimum group size, and may cancel the tour if they don't book enough people. If a quota exists, find out what it is and how close they are to reaching it. Again, tour operators may be evasive in their answers, but the information may help you select a tour that's sure to happen.

✔ **What exactly is included?** Don't assume anything. You may have to pay to get yourself to and from the airport. A box lunch may be included in an excursion but drinks may be extra. Beer may be included but not wine. How much flexibility do you have? Can you opt out of certain activities, or does the bus leave once a day, with no exceptions? Are all your meals planned in advance? Can you choose your entree at dinner, or does everybody get the same chicken cutlet?

Depending on your recreational passions, I recommend one of the following tour companies:

✔ **Escape Holidays** (☎ **619-448-4489**; www.escapeholidays.com) creates custom tours for groups and independent "on your own" vacation packages, featuring the Essence Music Festival, Crescent City Haunts, and Holidays in New Orleans; call or e-mail for a price quote.

✔ **Menopausal Tours** (☎ **866-468-8646**; www.menopausaltours.com) caters specifically to women 40 and older. Ladies, get a group of girlfriends together for the "Jazz, Jambalaya & Beignets" tour, a little taste of everything New Orleans has to offer; prices start at $1,075 per person.

✔ **New Orleans Tours** (☎ **888-486-8687** or 504-592-0560; www.notours.com), offers traditional packages, like a Garden District Walking tour ($24 adults, $21 children ages 3–12), or the more adventurous seaplane tour, which flies over the French Quarter, Chalmette Battlefield, Lafitte, and more ($95 adults, $50 children ages 3–12).

Choosing a Package Tour

For many destinations, package tours can be a smart way to go. In several cases, a package tour that includes airfare, hotel, and transportation to and from the airport costs less than the hotel alone on a trip you book yourself. That's because packages are sold in bulk to tour operators, who resell them to the public. It's kind of like buying your vacation at a buy-in-bulk store — except the tour operator is the one who buys the 1,000-count box of garbage bags and resells them 10 at a time at a cost that undercuts the local supermarket.

Package tours can vary as much as those garbage bags, too. Some offer a better class of hotels than others, while some provide the same hotels for lower prices. Some book flights on scheduled airlines; others sell charters. In some packages, your choice of accommodations and travel days may be limited. Some let you choose between escorted vacations and independent vacations; others allow you to add on just a few excursions or escorted day-trips (also at discounted prices) without booking an entirely escorted tour.

To find package tours, check out the travel section of your local Sunday newspaper or the ads in the back of national travel magazines such as *Travel & Leisure, National Geographic Traveler,* and *Condé Nast Traveler.* **Liberty Travel** (call ☎ **888-271-1584** to find the store nearest you; www.libertytravel.com) is one of the biggest packagers in the Northeast and usually boasts a full-page ad in Sunday papers.

Another good source of package deals is the airlines themselves. Most major airlines offer air/land packages, including **American Airlines Vacations** (☎ 800-321-2121; www.aavacations.com), **Delta Vacations** (☎ 800-221-6666; www.deltavacations.com), **Continental Airlines Vacations** (☎ 800-301-3800; www.covacations.com), and **United Vacations** (☎ 888-854-3899; www.unitedvacations.com). Several big **online travel agencies** — Expedia, Travelocity, Orbitz, Site59, Frommer's (www.frommers.com), and www.lastminute.com — also do a brisk business in packages. If you're unsure about the pedigree of a smaller packager, check with the Better Business Bureau in the city where the company is based, or go online at www.bbb.org. If a packager won't tell you where it's based, don't fly with it.

New Orleans is a popular vacation destination, even post-Hurricane Katrina. You find no shortage of package tours — and no two are exactly alike (at least in terms of price). Some tours cater to people who want to be left to their own devices, while other tours target people who want a helping hand in searching out the local color. The following are just a few options:

  ✔ **Liberty Travel** (☎ **888-271-1584;** www.libertytravel.com) offers fairly bare-bones packages, which I liken to big-name hotel chains. Its packages are perfectly nice if you're just looking for a room, a cheap airline ticket, and maybe an attraction or two.

  ✔ If you want a package tour with a bit more character, consider **Destination Management, Inc. (DMI)** (☎ **800-471-8222** or 504-592-0500; www.dmineworleans.com). If Liberty Travel is like a generic, nationwide motor lodge, DMI is more like a small, independent hotel — not a mom-and-pop establishment, mind you, but a place that offers better atmosphere and service than the national chains. As a New Orleans–based company, DMI specializes in New Orleans vacation packages. DMI's packages center around different attractions and seasonal events, including Jazz Fest, Mardi Gras, the New Orleans Saints, Halloween — you name it, DMI has a package for it.

✔ **Festival Tours International** (☎ **310-454-4080;** www.gumbopages.com/festivaltours) offers a Jazz Fest tour. This tour is like the homey, bed-and-breakfast of New Orleans packages, with five-star service thrown in for good measure. The brainchild of Nancy Covey, this tour has atmosphere, character, culture, and slice-of-life authenticity. Unlike other packages for the New Orleans Jazz and Heritage Festival, the culture and heritage on this trip doesn't stop when you leave the event site. Covey also takes you on an insider's tour of Cajun Country, where you experience musicians currently making the scene.

Chapter 7

Catering to Special Travel Needs or Interests

In This Chapter

▶ Taking the kids along
▶ Going in your golden years
▶ Accommodating disabilities
▶ Finding gay-friendly activities

*I*f your idea of New Orleans comes courtesy of Hollywood, you may imagine a year-round bacchanal. Although you can find plenty of opportunities to party, the Big Easy offers much more. In fact, New Orleans is nothing if not a "one size fits all" vacation spot. Locals have always been gracious toward tourists; after Hurricane Katrina, you may find them to be even more accommodating because they have renewed pride in this unique city and are eager to share their passion for it.

Families

Although most people associate New Orleans with hard-core debauchery, the city is also a popular family destination. The farther away you get from Bourbon Street and the strip clubs in the French Quarter, the more family-friendly the city gets. But you don't have to leave the Quarter to find a wealth of kid-centric attractions and activities. New Orleans's unique history and its status as a nexus of different cultures provide for a number of fascinating landmarks, museums, and other sights of interest to children and adults.

 In Chapter 12 (and throughout the book), I highlight the attractions that your kids may like with the Kid Friendly icon. To get you started, the following is a list of places and activities guaranteed to keep kids entertained:

✔ Aquarium of the Americas (see p. 198)

✔ Audubon Zoo (see p. 201)

✔ City Park (see p. 203)

- ✔ Louisiana Children's Museum (see p. 206)

- ✔ Mimes, jugglers, musicians, and other street performers in the French Quarter, particularly at Jackson Square

- ✔ A ride across the river on the Canal Street Ferry (see box, p. 202)

You can also call **ACCENT on Children's Arrangements, Inc.** (☎ 504-524-1227; www.accentoca.com), a company that specializes in tours for children, especially for those whose parents are attending a convention.

Just because something touts itself as fun for kids doesn't necessarily make it fun for *you* and *your family*. Pointing your kids toward a museum that's "good for them" doesn't work and often results in eye rolling or the ubiquitous "Dad, you're a dork." I'm not ignorant of this reality, as many travel guides seem to be; in Chapter 12, I point out which attractions may be more age-appropriate for small fries than for jaded teens (and vice versa). I don't tell you not to bring your kids to a specific attraction. After all, you know your children better than I do, but I hope the guidance helps you plan a daily itinerary that the whole family can enjoy.

Celebrating Mardi Gras with the family

During **Mardi Gras** the French Quarter is no place to bring your kids. The farther into the Quarter you go, the raunchier the costumes become. You'd be amazed what people get away with. Also, many young women (and some not-so-young) are prone to lift up their shirts and bare their breasts at the slightest provocation. (Increasingly, men are flashing their private parts as well.) Although this practice originated as an incentive to get float riders to throw the best beads, it's evolved (or devolved) beyond that. In recent years, I've seen women consent to flash their breasts for camera-toting tourists in return for a free drink, a strand of beads, or even just an appreciative hoot.

If you'd like to shield your young ones from this bartering process, try the more family-friendly parade routes along **St. Charles Avenue** uptown. Or see the Mardi Gras listing on p. 206 for a selection of major **suburban parade routes** that are (for the most part) okay for the kids.

Planning with your kids

When on vacation, most kids hate nothing more than a daily itinerary, a history lesson, or anything else crammed down their throats. To help make your trip fun for you and your kids, let them participate in the planning process. Encourage them to read through this book and any tourist brochures you have. Allow them some input in organizing the sightseeing schedule. If they feel like the vacation belongs to them, too, they'll more likely have fun when they get there — and so will you.

Locating kid-friendly accommodations

Because New Orleans is a large tourist destination, you won't have any trouble finding a place to stay that accepts children. Of course, exceptions always exist. You won't likely find many cozy bed-and-breakfast establishments that accommodate children, for instance. But in major hotels, you'll have no problem.

Of course, after you find a hotel that accepts children, your work has just begun. Children are notoriously hard to please, and woe is the weary parent who doesn't take this into account when selecting a place to stay. Sure, most kids are just happy to be away from home and in close proximity to a rooftop swimming pool. But in case that isn't enough, many (if not most) hotels offer kid-friendly amenities, such as pay-per-view movies or in-house video/DVD rental, video games, and even goodies such as chocolate chip cookies upon check-in. Make sure to inquire about nearby restaurants with children's menus (that goes for the in-house restaurant as well).

Keeping the kids entertained

No matter how much planning you do, kids are still prone to fits of boredom and crankiness. Be sure to take along some toys or activities to help them through the rough patches. Depending on their age or tastes, pack coloring books, comics, books, or a portable radio or CD player to keep them occupied.

Be sure to keep your kids' endurance level in mind when planning your itinerary. Long walking tours can tire kids out faster than adults, and long waits can make them restless. This is where a portable radio or CD player can come in handy. Also, stagger events to keep them enjoyable for kids. A day of pounding the pavement may sap your child's enthusiasm for the next day's trip to that aquarium or zoo exhibit she's been dying to see. You also probably don't need me to tell you that a child's energy level fluctuates wildly, and your little munchkin could catch his second or third wind just as you're ready to collapse for the day. Try to keep an eye on such factors as sugar intake and other stimulants to avoid a serious case of child lag in the middle of a long afternoon.

Relying on babysitting services

If you want a night out on your own without the kids, some hotels provide babysitting services; check with your hotel's concierge or with the reservations clerk, or check the listings in Chapter 10. If your hotel doesn't provide such a service, you can contact an agency that watches your children while you wine and dine at Upperline. Employees of these agencies sit with your kids, take them on organized outings, or create a personalized itinerary:

> ✔ **ACCENT on Children's Arrangements, Inc.** (☎ 504-524-1227; www.accentoca.com); licensed, bonded, insured
>
> ✔ **Dependable Kid Care** (☎ 504-486-4001; www.dependablekidcare.com); licensed, bonded, insured

Seniors

Mention the fact that you're a senior citizen when you make your travel reservations. Although all the major U.S. airlines except America West have cancelled their senior discount and coupon book programs, many hotels still offer discounts for seniors. In most cities, people older than 60 qualify for reduced admission to theaters, museums, and other attractions, as well as discounted fares on public transportation.

Members of **AARP** (formerly known as the American Association of Retired Persons), 601 E St. NW, Washington, DC 20049 (☎ **888-687-2277** or 202-434-2277; www.aarp.org), get discounts on hotels, airfares, and car rentals. AARP offers members a wide range of benefits, including *AARP: The Magazine* and a monthly newsletter. Anyone older than 50 can join.

The **U.S. National Park Service** offers a **Golden Age Passport** that gives seniors 62 years or older lifetime entrance to all properties administered by the National Park Service — national parks, monuments, historic sites, recreation areas, and national wildlife refuges — for a one-time processing fee of $10, which must be purchased in person at any NPS facility that charges an entrance fee. (The Jean Lafitte National Historical Park and Preserve headquarters is located in the French Quarter; its satellite sites include the Chalmette Battlefield and National Cemetery 6 miles southeast of the city. See Chapter 12 for more details.) Besides free entry, a Golden Age Passport also offers a 50 percent discount on federal-use fees charged for such facilities as camping, swimming, parking, boat launching, and tours. For more information, go to www.nps.gov/fees_passes.htm or call ☎ **888-467-2757**.

Many reliable agencies and organizations target the 50-plus market. **Elderhostel** (☎ **877-426-8056**; www.elderhostel.org) arranges study programs for those aged 55 and older (and a spouse or companion of any age) around the world. Most courses last five to seven days in the United States, and many include airfare, accommodations in university dormitories or modest inns, meals, and tuition. One program, "L'Chaim Celebrate New Orleans' Cultural Heritage and Old World Charm," explores the local Jewish community and its contributions to the city since the 18th century.

Recommended publications offering travel resources and discounts for seniors include

- ✔ *The 50+ Traveler's Guidebook* by Anita Williams and Merrimac Dillon (St. Martin's Press)

- ✔ *101 Tips for Mature Travelers,* available from Grand Circle Travel (☎ **800-221-2610** or 617-350-7500; www.gct.com)

- ✔ *Travel 50 & Beyond,* a quarterly magazine (www.travel50and beyond.com)

- ✔ *Travel Unlimited: Uncommon Adventures for the Mature Traveler* by Alison Gardner (Avalon)

- ✔ *Unbelievably Good Deals and Great Adventures That You Absolutely Can't Get Unless You're Over 50* by Joann Rattner Heilman (McGraw-Hill)

Enjoying your stay in New Orleans depends in large part on how you plan for such variables as the distance between your hotel and the attractions you want to see as well as how you deal with the city's crazy weather. The following sections can help you make the best lodging and sightseeing decisions based on your own personal needs.

Lodging

Depending on your health, your hotel's location may be a more important consideration than it is for other travelers. If you plan to do a lot of sightseeing on foot, try to find a hotel that's central to a number of accessible attractions. If you plan to spend most of your time in the French Quarter, you're in good shape; almost everything in this relatively small but eventful area is within walking distance. If walking the Quarter's 13 blocks seems prohibitive for you or a companion, catching a cab is a wise, inexpensive alternative.

If you're outside the Quarter, make sure your hotel is convenient to public transportation and in a safe neighborhood. I recommend the **Pontchartrain Hotel** or the **St. Charles Guest House** (see p. 139) for safety and/or convenience to public transportation — both hotels are on St. Charles Avenue, where the streetcar travels. You can enjoy a brief, scenic walk from the streetcar stop to the St. Charles Guest House, located in the increasingly gentrified but still funky Lower Garden District.

No matter where you choose to stay, take a cab if you venture out at night; the extra couple of dollars is worth the security of being delivered right to your door.

Attractions

If you're staying in the French Quarter, you can find plenty of museums, historic landmarks, and other attractions close at hand, and a number of free sightseeing places (for example, **Jackson Square** or the **Moonwalk**) where you can watch the parade of life unfold before you. If you like to gamble, **Harrah's New Orleans Casino** is just across Canal Street from the **Aquarium of the Americas** and **Canal Place.** Check the listings in Chapter 12 for places of particular interest, as well as for information on senior discounts.

Weather

Whether you travel with a group or on your own, some of the best advice I can give you is to be mindful of the weather. In the summer, when tourism is generally down, you won't encounter as many crowds, which makes it a good time to visit. However, the heat and humidity can tire you out faster than normal, especially during the afternoons. If you're visiting in the summer, plan as many indoor activities as possible during the peak afternoon hours. When you do venture outside, carry some bottled water. (Check Chapter 4 for the lowdown on average temperatures during the year in New Orleans.)

If you get lost or separated from your group, have the number of a reliable cab company on hand. I recommend using **United Cab** (☎ **504-522-9771**), the largest and most reliable fleet in the city.

Travelers with Disabilities

Most disabilities shouldn't stop anybody from traveling. More options and resources are available than ever before.

The U.S. National Park Service offers a **Golden Access Passport** that gives free lifetime entrance to all properties administered by the National Park Service — national parks, monuments, historic sites, recreation areas, and national wildlife refuges — for persons who are visually impaired or permanently disabled, regardless of age. (The Jean Lafitte National Historical Park and Preserve headquarters is located in the French Quarter; its satellite sites include the Chalmette Battlefield and National Cemetery six miles southeast of the city. See Chapter 12 for more details.) You may pick up a Golden Access Passport at any NPS entrance fee area by showing proof of medically determined disability and eligibility for receiving benefits under federal law. Besides free entry, the Golden Access Passport also offers a 50 percent discount on federal-use fees charged for such facilities as camping, swimming, parking, boat launching, and tours. For more information, go to www.nps. gov/fees_passes.htm or call ☎ **888-467-2757.**

Many travel agencies offer customized tours and itineraries for travelers with disabilities. **Flying Wheels Travel** (☎ **507-451-5005;** www. flyingwheelstravel.com) offers escorted tours and cruises that emphasize sports and private tours in minivans with lifts. **Access-Able Travel Source** (☎ **303-232-2979;** www.access-able.com) offers extensive access information and advice for traveling around the world with disabilities. **Accessible Journeys** (☎ **800-846-4537** or 610-521-0339) offers trips for wheelchair travelers and their families and friends. **Wheelchair Getaways** (☎ **800-642-2042** or 504-738-2634; www. wheelchairgetaways.com) rents specially equipped vans with wheelchair lifts and other features for the disabled. The Louisiana office is located in Metairie, a suburb of New Orleans.

Avis Rent a Car has an "Avis Access" program that offers such services as a dedicated 24-hour toll-free number (☎ **888-879-4273**) for customers with special travel needs. Avis also offers helpful car features such as swivel seats, spinner knobs, and hand controls, and accessible bus service.

Organizations that offer assistance to disabled travelers include the **MossRehab** (www.mossresourcenet.org), which provides a library of accessible-travel resources online; **SATH (Society for Accessible Travel and Hospitality;** ☎ **212-447-7284;** www.sath.org; annual membership fees: $45 adults, $30 seniors and students), which offers a wealth of travel resources for all types of disabilities and informed recommendations on destinations, access guides, travel agents, tour operators, vehicle rentals, and companion services; and the **American Foundation for the Blind (AFB;** ☎ **800-232-5463;** www.afb.org), a referral resource for the blind or visually impaired that includes information on traveling with Seeing Eye dogs.

For more information specifically targeted to travelers with disabilities, the community Web site **iCan** (www.icanonline.net/channels/travel/index.cfm) has destination guides and several regular columns on accessible travel. Also check out the quarterly magazine **Emerging Horizons** ($14.95 per year, $19.95 outside the U.S.; www.emerginghorizons.com); **Twin Peaks Press** (☎ **360-694-2462**), offering travel-related books for travelers with special needs; and *Open World Magazine,* published by SATH (subscription: $13 per year, $21 outside the United States).

Anticipating building accessibility

Most of the historic sites and a few of the older hotels and restaurants in New Orleans may present problems for people with disabilities because they're exempt from the provisions of the Americans with Disabilities Act (ADA). I mention problematic places in the relevant chapters of this book, but call ahead and double-check.

All major hotels comply with the ADA, though some of the smaller hotels and most notably B&Bs either aren't in compliance or only partially so. Among hotels, the **Wyndham Canal Place** receives the biggest thumbs-up for accessibility, and the **Dauphine Orleans, Hotel Monteleone,** and **Royal Orleans** are also highly rated. Many major restaurants also comply, as I note in Chapter 11. If a place doesn't have a ramp, however, staffers are usually more than happy to help assist disabled patrons inside their establishments.

Planning for other New Orleans resources

A few resources within New Orleans can make your visit easier after you arrive in the Crescent City. Normally, the newer Canal Streetcar is wheelchair accessible, although that line's streetcars were flooded during Hurricane Katrina. So the historic St. Charles streetcars, which are not wheelchair accessible, are temporarily being used on Canal while repairs are made to the St. Charles Streetcar corridor. Please contact the **Regional Transit Authority** (☎ **504-248-3900;** www.norta.org) for updates on both streetcar lines and additional information. The RTA also has lift-equipped buses available for individuals as well as for groups. If you're hearing-impaired and have a telecommunications device for the deaf (TTY), the **Louisiana Relay Service** (☎ **800-947-5277**) offers a service that can connect you with non-TTY users. Travelers with disabilities can also receive assistance from **Resources for Independent Living** (☎ **504-522-1955**).

Gay and Lesbian Travelers

The **International Gay and Lesbian Travel Association** (IGLTA; ☎ **800-448-8550** or 954-776-2626; www.iglta.org) is the trade association for the gay and lesbian travel industry, and offers an online directory of gay- and lesbian-friendly travel businesses; go to its Web site and click on "Members."

Many agencies offer tours and travel itineraries specifically for gay and lesbian travelers. **Above and Beyond Tours** (☎ **800-397-2681;** www.abovebeyondtours.com) is the exclusive gay and lesbian tour operator for United Airlines. **Olivia Cruises & Resorts** (☎ **800-631-6277** or 510-655-0364; www.olivia.com) charters entire resorts and ships for exclusive lesbian vacations and offers smaller group experiences for both gay and lesbian travelers.

New Orleans is one of the most gay- and lesbian-friendly cities in the United States. You won't lack for bars, restaurants, hotels, or other businesses owned by or catering to gays and lesbians, especially in the French Quarter and neighboring Faubourg Marigny — the epicenter of the local gay scene.

New Orleans hosts a number of gay-themed or gay-friendly events year-round. **Southern Decadence** is a major festival for gay and lesbian tourists that takes place on Labor Day weekend. Halloween also has a sizable gay turnout, and, of course, the spectacle of **Mardi Gras** draws even bigger gay crowds (see Chapters 3 and 12). Despite the elitism of some krewes, Mardi Gras is generally an inclusive and unifying event, bringing together the city's disparate populations for one long party. The lower French Quarter even offers a gay-friendly celebration between St. Ann Street (the unofficial boundary that marks the gay section of the

Quarter) and Esplanade Avenue, where the Quarter ends. On Mardi Gras day, gays and lesbians converge around noon in front of the **Rawhide 2010 Bar** (see Chapter 17), at St. Ann and Burgundy streets, to see (and be seen in) outrageous costumes and to compete for the much sought-after Bourbon Street Award.

New Orleans's major gay publication is *Ambush* (☎ 800-876-1484 or 504-522-8047; www.ambushmag.com), providing excellent information on what's going on. You can find a copy in most gay-friendly establishments. In the relevant chapters of this book, I note gay-friendly choices for hotels, restaurants, and nightlife. Here are some additional suggestions:

✔ Best *hotel* choices for gay and lesbian travelers are the **Lafitte Guest House,** the **New Orleans Guest House,** and the **Ursuline Guest House,** all in the Quarter. If you're willing to travel a bit farther away, the **Macarty Park Guest House** in Bywater is about ten minutes by cab from the Esplanade boundary of the Quarter.

✔ Best *restaurant* picks are **Petunia's** and the **Quarter Scene** in the French Quarter and **Feelings Café** and **La Peniche** in the Marigny.

✔ Best gay *nightlife* choices are **The Bourbon Pub and Parade, Golden Lantern, Good Friends, Café Lafitte in Exile, MRB (Mississippi River Bottom), Oz,** and **Rawhide 2010,** all in the Quarter, and **The Phoenix** in the Marigny.

New Orleans has a network of services supporting the gay community. The following organizations can connect you with gay-friendly lodgings, help with travel arrangements, and offer food and entertainment recommendations.

✔ **Big Easy Lodging** (☎ 800-368-4876 or 504-433-2563; Fax: 504-391-1903; www.crescentcity.com/fql)

✔ **French Quarter Reservation Service** (☎ 800-523-9091 or 504-523-1246; www.neworleansreservations.com)

✔ **Gay New Orleans Online** (www.gayneworleans.com)

✔ **The Lesbian and Gay Community Center,** 2114 Decatur St. (☎ 504-945-1103; http://lgccno.net)

The following travel guides are available at most travel bookstores and gay and lesbian bookstores, such as New Orleans's own **Faubourg Marigny Bookstore** (600 Frenchmen St.; ☎ 504-943-9875), or you can order them from **Giovanni's Room** bookstore, 1145 Pine St., Philadelphia, PA 19107 (☎ 215-923-2960; www.giovannisroom.com; *Out and About* (☎ 800-929-2268 or 415-644-8044; www.outandabout.com), which offers guidebooks and a newsletter ($20/yr; 10 issues) packed with solid information on the global gay and lesbian scene; *Spartacus International Gay Guide* (Bruno Gmünder Verlag; www.spartacusworld.com/gayguide)

and *Odysseus,* both good, annual English-language guidebooks focused on gay men; the *Damron* guides (www.damron.com), with separate, annual books for gay men and lesbians; and *Gay Travel A to Z: The World of Gay & Lesbian Travel Options at Your Fingertips* by Marianne Ferrari (Ferrari International; Box 35575, Phoenix, AZ 85069), a very good gay and lesbian guidebook series.

Chapter 8

Taking Care of the Remaining Details

· ·

In This Chapter

▶ Renting a car or not
▶ Purchasing travel and medical insurance
▶ Staying healthy on your trip
▶ Connecting with your phone or computer
▶ Finding out the latest on airline security

· ·

*A*fter you book your hotel room and flight (or make other appropriate arrangements), you may assume that the rest of your trip is smooth sailing. But before you pat yourself on the back and skip ahead to the book's nightlife section (see Chapters 16 and 17), you still need to straighten out a few final details to avoid aggravation later.

Renting a Car — Don't!

Should you rent a car in New Orleans? The short answer is no — but a qualified no. If you plan to stay in the French Quarter, a car may be more of a headache than you really need on vacation. Many of the hotels, B&Bs, and guesthouses listed in this book have a limited number of parking spaces. If you stay in an area such as Faubourg Marigny, the Quarter is still just a short walk away.

Accommodations without adequate parking can point you to a nearby garage, but the garages aren't cheap. In some cases, you may have to park on the street, which can present a big problem in the Quarter, where parking spaces are a hot commodity. (Some people swear that they don't actually exist.)

For sightseeing in the Quarter, a car is more of a hindrance than an asset. All the streets are one-way, and on weekdays during daylight hours, Royal and Bourbon streets are closed to automobiles between the 300 and 700 blocks. In the Central Business District, congested traffic at peak hours and limited parking conspire to make a motorist's life difficult.

Also, New Orleans meter maids hand out more tickets than box-office attendants. Some signs noting restricted parking spaces are posted so far from the spaces themselves that you may miss them.

Of course, New Orleans offers much more than the very small French Quarter, especially where dining and nightlife are concerned. If you stay in one of the outlying areas, such as Uptown or the Garden District, you're more likely to find off-street parking.

 If you do rent (or bring) a car, steer clear of congested sightseeing areas such as the Quarter and the Central Business District and rely on public transportation instead.

Finding the car you need at the price you want

Car-rental rates vary even more than airline fares. The price depends on the size of the car, the length of time you keep it, where and when you pick it up and drop it off, where you take it, and a host of other factors. Asking a few key questions may save you hundreds of dollars:

- ✔ **Do you charge lower rates for the weekend compared to your weekday rates?** If you're keeping the car five or more days, a weekly rate may be cheaper than the daily rate. Ask if the rate is the same for pickup Friday morning as it is for Thursday night.

- ✔ **Do you assess a drop-off charge if I don't return the car to the same location?** Some do. Others, notably National, don't.

- ✔ **Is the rate cheaper if you pick up the car at a location in town rather than at the airport?** This may be cheaper — and more convenient — if you don't need a car for the trip to and from the airport.

- ✔ **Is age an issue?** Many car rental companies tack on a fee for drivers under 25, while some don't rent to them at all.

- ✔ **May I get the advertised price that I saw in the local newspaper?** If you did in fact see a rate, be sure to ask for it. Otherwise you may be charged the standard (higher) rate. Don't forget to mention membership in AAA, AARP, and trade unions. These memberships usually entitle you to discounts ranging from 5 percent to 30 percent.

   Check your frequent-flier accounts. Not only are your favorite (or at least most-used) airlines likely to have sent you discount coupons, but also most car rentals add at least 500 miles to your account.

You'll find desks for the following rental-car companies at the Louis Armstrong New Orleans International Airport:

- ✔ **Alamo** (☎ **800-GO-VALUE;** www.alamo.com)

- ✔ **Avis** (☎ **800-331-1212;** www.avis.com)

- ✔ **Budget** (☎ **800-527-0700;** www.budget.com)

 ✔ **Hertz** (☎ 800-654-3131; www.hertz.com)

 ✔ **National** (☎ 800-227-7368; www.nationalcar.com)

Additionally, **Enterprise Rent-A-Car** (☎ 800-736-8222; www.enterprise.com) maintains an office nearby on Airline Drive, and **Swifty Car Rental,** a local company (☎ 877-469-4007 or 504-733-2277; www.swiftycarrental.com), operates offices throughout the metropolitan area, including one near the airport.

Using the Internet to find deals

As with other aspects of planning your trip, using the Internet can make comparison-shopping for a car rental much easier. You can check rates at most of the major agencies' Web sites. Plus, all the major travel sites — **Travelocity** (www.travelocity.com), **Expedia** (www.expedia.com), **Orbitz** (www.orbitz.com), and **Smarter Travel** (www.smartertravel.com), for example — have search engines that can dig up discounted car-rental rates. Just enter the car size you want, the pickup and return dates, and location, and the server returns a price. You can even make the reservation through any of these sites.

Understanding the additional charges

In addition to the standard rental prices, other optional charges apply to most car rentals (and some not-so-optional charges, such as taxes). Many credit-card companies cover the *Collision Damage Waiver* (CDW), which requires you to pay for damage to the car in a collision. Check with your credit-card company before you go so you can avoid paying this hefty fee (as much as $20 a day).

The car-rental companies also offer additional *liability insurance* (if you harm others in an accident), *personal accident insurance* (if you harm yourself or your passengers), and *personal effects insurance* (if your luggage is stolen from your car). Your insurance policy on your car at home probably covers most of these unlikely occurrences. However, if your own insurance doesn't cover you for rentals or if you don't have auto insurance, definitely consider the additional coverage (ask your car-rental agent for more information). Unless you're toting around the Hope diamond, and you don't want to leave that in your car trunk anyway, you can probably skip the personal effects insurance, but driving around without liability or personal accident coverage is never a good idea. Even if you're a good driver, other people may not be, and liability claims can be complicated.

Some companies also offer *refueling packages,* in which you pay for your initial full tank of gas upfront and can return the car with an empty gas tank. The prices can be competitive with local gas prices, but you don't get credit for any gas remaining in the tank. If you reject this option, you pay only for the gas you use, but you have to return the car with a full tank or face charges of $3 to $4 a gallon for any shortfall. If you usually run late and a fueling stop might make you miss your plane, you're a perfect candidate for the fuel-purchase option.

Playing It Safe with Travel and Medical Insurance

Three kinds of travel insurance are available: trip-cancellation insurance, medical insurance, and lost luggage insurance. The cost of travel insurance varies widely, depending on the cost and length of your trip, your age and health, and the type of trip you're taking, but expect to pay between 5 percent and 8 percent of the vacation itself. Here is my advice on all three:

✔ **Trip-cancellation insurance** helps you get your money back if you have to back out of a trip, if you have to go home early, or if your travel supplier goes bankrupt. Allowed reasons for cancellation can range from sickness to natural disasters to the U.S. State Department declaring your destination unsafe for travel. (Insurers usually don't cover vague fears, though, as many travelers discovered who tried to cancel their trips in Oct 2001 because they were wary of flying.)

A good resource is **"Travel Guard Alerts,"** a list of companies considered high-risk by Travel Guard International (www.travel insured.com). Protect yourself further by paying for the insurance with a credit card. By law, consumers can get their money back on goods and services not received if they report the loss within 60 days after the charge is listed on their credit card statement.

Note: Many tour operators, particularly those offering trips to remote or high-risk areas, include insurance in the cost of the trip or can arrange insurance policies through a partnering provider, a convenient and often cost-effective way for the traveler to obtain insurance. Make sure the tour company is a reputable one. Some experts suggest you avoid buying insurance from the tour or cruise company you're traveling with. They say buying from a third-party insurer is better than putting all your money in one place.

✔ For domestic travel, buying **medical insurance** for your trip doesn't make sense for most travelers. Most existing health insurance policies cover you if you get sick away from home — but check before you go, particularly if you're insured by an HMO.

✔ **Lost luggage insurance** isn't necessary for most travelers. On domestic flights, checked baggage is covered up to $2,500 per ticketed passenger. On international flights (including U.S. portions of international trips), baggage coverage is limited to approximately $9.07 per pound, up to approximately $635 per checked bag. If you plan to check items more valuable than the standard liability, see if your homeowner's policy covers your valuables, get baggage insurance as part of your comprehensive travel-insurance package, or buy Travel Guard's "BagTrak" product. Don't buy insurance at the airport because it's usually overpriced. Be sure to take any valuables or irreplaceable items with you in your carry-on luggage because many valuables (including books, money, and electronics) aren't covered by airline policies.

If your luggage is lost, immediately file a lost-luggage claim at the airport, detailing the luggage contents. For most airlines, you must report delayed, damaged, or lost baggage within four hours of arrival. The airlines are required to deliver luggage, once found, directly to your house or destination free of charge.

For more information, contact one of the following recommended insurers:

- ✔ **Access America** (☎ **866-807-3982**; www.accessamerica.com)

- ✔ **Travel Guard International** (☎ **800-826-4919**; www.travelguard.com)

- ✔ **Travel Insured International** (☎ **800-243-3174**; www.travelinsured.com)

- ✔ **Travelex Insurance Services** (☎ **888-457-4602**; www.travelex-insurance.com)

Staying Healthy When You Travel

Getting sick will ruin your vacation, so I *strongly* advise against it (of course, last time I checked, the bugs weren't listening to me any more than they probably listen to you).

For domestic trips, most reliable healthcare plans provide coverage if you get sick away from home. For travel abroad, you may have to pay all medical costs upfront and be reimbursed later. For information on purchasing additional medical insurance for your trip, see the preceding section.

Talk to your doctor before leaving on a trip if you have a serious and/or chronic illness. For conditions such as epilepsy, diabetes, or heart problems, wear a **MedicAlert identification tag** (☎ **888-633-4298**; www.medicalert.org), which immediately alerts doctors to your condition and gives them access to your records through MedicAlert's 24-hour hotline. Contact the **International Association for Medical Assistance to Travelers (IAMAT;** ☎ **716-754-4883** or, in Canada, 416-652-0137; www.iamat.org) for tips on travel and health concerns in the countries you're visiting, and lists of local, English-speaking doctors. The United States **Centers for Disease Control and Prevention** (☎ **800-311-3435;** www.cdc.gov) provides up-to-date information on health hazards by region or country and offers tips on food safety.

Using a Cellphone across the United States

Just because your cellphone works at home doesn't mean it'll work else-where in the country (thanks to the fragmented cellphone system). It's a good bet that your phone will work in major cities. But take a look at your wireless company's coverage map on its Web site before heading out — T-Mobile, Sprint, and Nextel are particularly weak in rural areas. If you need to stay in touch at a destination where you know your phone won't work, **rent** a phone that does from **InTouch USA** (☎ **800-872-7626;** www.intouchglobal.com) or a rental-car location, but beware that you'll pay $1 a minute or more for airtime.

If you're not from the United States, you'll be appalled at the poor reach of the **GSM (Global System for Mobiles) wireless network,** which is used by much of the world. Your phone will probably work in most major U.S. cities, but it definitely won't work in many rural areas. (To see where GSM phones work in the United States, check out www.t-mobile.com/coverage/national_popup.asp.) And you may or may not be able to send text messages home. (International budget travelers like to send text messages home because it's much cheaper than making interna-tional calls.) Assume nothing — call your wireless provider and get the full scoop. In a worst-case scenario, you can always rent a phone; InTouch USA delivers to hotels.

Accessing the Internet Away from Home

Travelers have any number of ways to check their e-mail and access the Internet on the road. Of course, using your own laptop — or even a per-sonal digital assistant (PDA) or electronic organizer with a modem — gives you the most flexibility. But even if you don't have a computer, you can still access your e-mail and even your office computer from cybercafes.

New Orleans has plenty of cybercafes. Although no definitive directory for cybercafes is available — these are independent businesses, after all — but two places to start looking are at www.cybercaptive.com and www.cybercafe.com.

The **Cyber Bar and Café** at the **Contemporary Arts Center** (900 Camp St.; ☎ **504-523-1216**) in the Warehouse District is popular with the downtown crowd. In the French Quarter, storm the **Bastille Computer Café** (605–607 Toulouse St.; ☎ **504-581-1150**) or plug into **Royal Access** (621 Royal St.; ☎ **504-525-0401**).

Aside from formal cybercafes, most **youth hostels** nowadays have at least one computer through which you can access the Internet. And most **public libraries** offer Internet access free or for a small charge. Avoid **hotel business centers** unless you're willing to pay exorbitant rates.

Most major airports now have **Internet kiosks** scattered throughout their gates. These kiosks, which you also see in shopping malls, hotel lobbies, and tourist information offices, give you basic Web access for a per-minute fee that's usually higher than cybercafe prices. Only use Internet kiosks as a last resort because they're expensive.

To retrieve your e-mail, ask your **Internet Service Provider (ISP)** if it has a Web-based interface tied to your existing e-mail account. If your ISP doesn't have such an interface, you can use the free **mail2web** service (www.mail2web.com) to view and reply to your home e-mail. For more flexibility, you may want to open a free, Web-based e-mail account with **Yahoo! Mail** (http://mail.yahoo.com). (Microsoft's Hotmail is another popular option, but Hotmail has severe spam problems.) Your home ISP may be able to forward your e-mail to the Web-based account automatically.

If you need to access files on your office computer, look into a service called **GoToMyPC** (www.gotomypc.com). The service provides a Web-based interface for you to access and manipulate a distant PC from anywhere — even a cybercafe — provided your "target" PC is on and has an always-on connection to the Internet (such as with Road Runner cable). The service offers top-quality security, but if you're worried about hackers, use your own laptop rather than a cybercafe computer to access the GoToMyPC system.

If you're bringing your own computer, the buzzword in computer access to familiarize yourself with is **Wi-Fi** (wireless fidelity), and more and more hotels, cafes, and retailers are signing on as wireless "hotspots" from where you can get high-speed connection without cable wires, networking hardware, or a phone line. You can get Wi-Fi connection one of several ways. Many laptops have built-in Wi-Fi capability (an 802.11b wireless Ethernet connection). Mac owners have their own networking technology, Apple AirPort. If you have an older computer, you can plug in an 802.11b/**Wi-Fi card** (around $50) to your laptop.

You sign up for wireless access service much as you do cellphone service, through a plan offered by one of several commercial companies that have made wireless service available in airports, hotel lobbies, and coffee shops, primarily in the United States (followed by the United Kingdom and Japan). **T-Mobile Hotspot** (www.t-mobile.com/hotspot) serves up wireless connections at more than 1,000 Starbucks coffee shops nationwide. **Boingo** (www.boingo.com) and **Wayport** (www.wayport.com) have set up networks in airports and high-class hotel lobbies. iPass providers also give you access to a few hundred wireless hotel-lobby setups. Best of all, you don't need to be staying at the Four Seasons to use the hotel's network; just set yourself up on a nice couch in the lobby. The companies' pricing policies can be complex, with a variety of monthly, per-connection, and per-minute plans, but in general you pay around $30 a month for limited access — and as more and more companies jump on the wireless bandwagon, prices are likely to get even more competitive.

You can also find places that provide **free wireless networks** in cities around the world. To locate these free hotspots, go to www.personal telco.net/index.cgi/WirelessCommunities.

If Wi-Fi isn't available at your destination, most business-class hotels throughout the world offer dataports for laptop modems, and a few thousand hotels in the United States and Europe now offer free high-speed Internet access using an Ethernet network cable. You can bring your own cables, but most hotels rent them for around $10. Call your hotel in advance to see what your options are.

In addition, major ISPs have **local access numbers** around the world, allowing you to go online by simply placing a local call. Check your ISP's Web site or call its toll-free number and ask how you can use your current account away from home and how much it costs. If you're traveling outside the reach of your ISP, the **iPass** network has dial-up numbers in most of the world. You have to sign up with an iPass provider, who can then tell you how to set up your computer for your destination(s). For a list of iPass providers, go to www.ipass.com and click on "Individual Purchase." One solid provider is **i2roam** (www.i2roam.com; ☎ **866-811-6209** or 920-235-0475).

Wherever you go, bring a **connection kit** of the right power and phone adapters, a spare phone cord, and a spare Ethernet network cable — or find out whether your hotel supplies them to guests.

Keeping Up with Airline Security Measures

With the federalization of airport security, security procedures at U.S. airports are more stable and consistent than ever. Generally, you'll be fine if you arrive at the airport **one hour** before a domestic flight and **two hours** before an international flight. If you show up late, alert an airline employee and she'll probably whisk you to the front of the line.

Bring a **current, government-issued photo ID** such as a driver's license or passport. Keep your ID ready to show at check-in, the security checkpoint, and sometimes even the gate. (Children under 18 don't need government-issued photo IDs for domestic flights, but they do for international flights to most countries.)

In 2003, the Transportation Security Administration (TSA) phased out **gate check-in** at all U.S. airports. And **E-tickets** have made paper tickets nearly obsolete. Passengers with E-tickets can beat the ticket-counter lines by using airport **electronic kiosks** or even **online check-in** from your home computer. Online check-in involves logging on to your airline's Web site, accessing your reservation, and printing out your boarding pass — and the airline may even offer you bonus miles to do so! If you're using an airport kiosk, bring the credit card you used to book the ticket or your frequent-flier card. Print out your boarding pass from the kiosk and simply proceed to the security checkpoint with your pass and a photo ID. If you're checking bags or looking to snag an exit-row seat, you will be able to do so using most airline kiosks. Even the smaller airlines are employing the kiosk system, but always call your airline to make sure these alternatives are available. **Curbside check-in** is also a good way to avoid lines, although a few airlines still ban curbside check-in; call before you go.

Security checkpoint lines are getting shorter than they were during 2001 and 2002, but some doozies remain. If you have trouble standing for long periods of time, tell an airline employee; the airline can provide a wheelchair. Speed up security by **not wearing metal objects** such as big belt buckles. If you've got metallic body parts, a note from your doctor can prevent a long chat with the security screeners. Keep in mind that only **ticketed passengers** are allowed past security, except for folks escorting disabled passengers or children.

Federalization has stabilized **what you can carry on** and **what you can't.** Because of a terrorist plot thwarted in August 2006, all beverages, oils, gels, and creams have been banned, with just a few exceptions for liquid prescriptions and baby formulas. Log onto www.tsa.gov/travelers/ index.shtm for details. Bring food in your carryon rather than checking it because explosive-detection machines used on checked luggage have been known to mistake food (especially chocolate, for some reason) for bombs. Travelers in the United States are allowed one carry-on bag, plus a "personal item" such as a purse, briefcase, or laptop bag. Carryon hoarders can stuff all sorts of things into a laptop bag; as long as it has a laptop in it, it's still considered a personal item.

Airport screeners may decide that your checked luggage needs to be searched by hand. You can now purchase luggage locks that allow screeners to open and relock a checked bag if they need to hand-search your luggage. Look for Travel Sentry certified locks at luggage or travel shops and Brookstone stores (you can buy them online at www.brookstone. com). Luggage inspectors can open these TSA-approved locks with a special code or key. For more information on the locks, visit www.travel sentry.org. If you use something other than TSA-approved locks, your lock will be cut off your suitcase if a TSA agent needs to hand-search your luggage.

Part III

Settling into New Orleans

"I'll have the Cocoa Puffs Etouffée."

In this part . . .

You made it to New Orleans — or at least, you're finally ready to arrive. This part helps you get the lay of the land, with safety tips, public-transportation options and other convenient ways of getting around, and tips on where to find banks and ATMs (Chapter 9). You'll also get the scoop on booking a hotel room, with tips on rack rates and where to find good deals (Chapter 10).

We also get down to the meat and potatoes of your trip — yes, the food. A recent America Online and *Travel + Leisure* survey ranked New Orleans No. 1 in the United States for dining out, and you'll find out why (Chapter 11).

Chapter 9

Arriving and Getting Oriented

● ●

In This Chapter

▶ Finding your way from Point A (the airport) to Point B (your lodging)

▶ Figuring out the lay of the land

▶ Getting to know some of the neighborhoods

● ●

*N*ew Orleans can be a pretty confusing place, geographically speaking. Throw out your compass, because north, south, east, and west are meaningless in a city where the sun rises over the West Bank (which is, strictly speaking, to the east of the city). The Mississippi River replaces the magnetic poles as the focal point for getting your bearings here: Upriver is Uptown, downriver is downtown, and lakeside is toward Lake Pontchartrain.

The city began in the French Quarter, an area that covers 13 blocks between Canal Street and Esplanade Avenue, from the Mississippi River to North Rampart Street. The city's angular layout follows the bend in the river, making directions such as north, south, east, and west relatively useless. Consequently, you'll hear New Orleanians use the terms **riverside, lakeside, uptown,** and **downtown** in place of traditional directions. You'll have no problem if you remember that North Rampart Street is the "lakeside" boundary of the Quarter, Canal Street marks the beginning of "uptown," and the Quarter is "downtown." (These boundaries aren't immutable, however, and some locals may use different reference points. For example, people often refer to the Warehouse District, which is on the other side of Canal Street from the Quarter, as being downtown.)

Building numbers begin at 100 on either side of Canal Street. In the Quarter, however, the numbers start at the river with 400 because the river swallowed four blocks of numbered buildings before the levee was built. Street names change when they cross Canal Street — another reminder of Canal's traditional role as the border between the old, French New Orleans (the Quarter) and the new, American New Orleans. Bourbon Street, for example, becomes Carondelet as it stretches uptown.

This chapter reviews the best ways to enter the city, whether by land or by air. It also gives you the scoop on the different neighborhoods — including where to find them and what makes them unique.

Making Your Way to New Orleans

You know you want to visit New Orleans — but how do you want to get there? Choose the option that best fits your tastes, schedule, and budget.

Arriving by plane

If you fly into New Orleans, you arrive at Louis Armstrong International Airport, located a good 25-minute drive from the corporate limits of New Orleans in the suburb of Kenner. The airport's three-letter airport code, MSY, refers to the airport's former name, Moisant International — named for daredevil aviator John Blevins Moisant. (The SY refers to the fact that the airport sits on the site of a former stockyard.)

Moisant, as most locals still call it, isn't the flashiest, most ultramodern airport in the world. You've probably seen larger bus stations in New York, Chicago, or Atlanta, but Moisant's small size is a blessing in disguise. The whole place is compact; all concourses are attached to a single structure, and clear signage directs you to the baggage-claim area downstairs. Thus, getting around is more or less a snap. Additionally, you can find information booths throughout the airport and in the baggage-claim area. Also in the baggage-claim area is a branch of the **Traveler's Aid Society** (☎ 504-464-3522). Hours of service may vary because the aid desk is staffed by volunteers.

From the airport to the hotel by cab

The easiest way into town if you're traveling in a group of two or more people is to take a taxi. Cabs wait in line just outside the baggage-claim area, so you'll have no trouble finding one. Expect to pay around $28 for a taxi ride to the French Quarter or Central Business District for one or two people, or $12 each if your group includes more than two people. This price is more or less the same as the cost for a shuttle, and even cheaper if you're in a group of more than two or three. Taxis can hold a maximum of five passengers.

United Cab (☎ 504-522-9771) is the largest and arguably most reliable taxi company in the city. Their taxis are usually busy handling radio calls, however, so they don't wait in line with the other taxis at the airport. Two other reputable companies are **A Service** (☎ 504-834-1400) and **Metry Cab** (☎ 504-835-4242). You can also find plenty of mom-and-pop taxi operations hovering around the airport to catch your fare, most of which are reputable and won't rip you off. Still, exceptions always exist, so if you don't trust them, call one of the companies listed here.

Catching a cab safely

How can you tell if an airport taxi service is legitimate? For one thing, unless you're visiting during a heavy tourist season (Jazz Fest, Mardi Gras, or a big business convention) or you're sharing a cab with other travelers, avoid any driver who attempts to negotiate with you on the price. Negotiating is common during the previously mentioned events, but outside of those times I've heard of drivers quoting one price and then demanding another when they pull up to the hotel. Also, look at the car itself. If it looks professionally painted, you're probably safer than if you approach a car that looks as if someone hand-painted the information over the door. Don't enter a cab that doesn't have a phone number on the door, and don't get into a cab if something about the driver rubs you the wrong way; another cab will come along.

A trip into town usually takes about 25 to 30 minutes, though that number varies depending on where you're headed and what traffic is like on Interstate 10 (I-10), the city's main thoroughfare. Generally, tip between 10 and 15 percent.

From the airport to the hotel by shuttle bus

If you don't want to hail a cab, taking an airport shuttle bus is the next easiest option for getting into the city. Depending on your situation, taking a cab may be a more cost-effective and comfortable ride. You can find airport shuttle information desks in the airport, staffed 24 hours a day.

For $1.50, the **Downtown/Airport Express bus** takes you to the corner of Elk's Place and Tulane Avenue — a 30- to 40-minute ride. The bus leaves from the upper level near the down ramp about every 23 minutes from 5:30 a.m. to midnight (every 12–15 minutes during rush hours). The **Jefferson Transit Authority** (☎ **504-818-1077;** www.jefferson transit.org) can give you more information.

For $13, the **Airport Shuttle** takes you directly to your hotel from right outside the baggage area. Taking a taxi costs about the same, or less, and is more convenient, particularly if you have two or more passengers. The shuttle leaves every 10 to 15 minutes, but the ride can take up to an hour because you may have to go to several hotels before getting to your own. In comparison, a cab ride takes only about 25 to 30 minutes. Remember to reserve a spot on the shuttle if you intend to ride it back to the airport. To make your reservation, call ☎ **504-522-3500** or make arrangements through your hotel's concierge. The shuttle does offer wheelchair access.

From the airport to the hotel by "cool car" (rental car)

The New Orleans Police Department refers to a rental car as a "cool car" because undercover officers sometimes drive a rental car to make it seem as though they're tourists. You can find car-rental counters near the baggage-claim area of the airport. (See Chapter 8 for a list of car-rental companies that maintain offices in the airport.) To navigate your trip from the airport to your hotel, read the directions in the next section and check out the "Airport Driving Routes" map in this chapter.

Directions for driving from the airport

Follow one of the many signs at the airport to I-10 East. Take I-10 to the I-10/I-610 split, but *don't* take I-610, which branches off to your left. Continue following I-10, which branches right, until you reach the Superdome (you can't miss that). If you want to go to the French Quarter, follow I-10 to the left of the Superdome and take the Vieux Carré (French Quarter) exit. If you're trying to get to the Central Business District, stay to the right of the Superdome and exit at Loyola. If you want to reach the Garden District, stay to the right of the Superdome and take the St. Charles Avenue exit, which drops you squarely in the Lower Garden District, right on the cusp of Lee Circle and the Central Business District. Check with your hotel for exact directions.

Arriving by car

If you drive to New Orleans, you'll probably arrive by way of one of the major thoroughfares: highways 90 or 61 or Interstate 10. To see how your route flows into the Crescent City, see the "Airport Driving Routes" map in this chapter. Both highways 90 and 61 take you right into the city. If you're following I-10, refer to the previous section, "Directions for driving from the airport," for information on specific exits and road construction.

Arriving by train

If you're planning on chugging into New Orleans, your train arrives at the **Union Passenger Terminal** (☎ **504-528-1610;** www.amtrak.com) on Loyola Avenue in the Central Business District, just a few blocks from the French Quarter. Oddly enough, the station temporarily served as a post-Katrina jail. After you arrive at the station, taxis are available to take you into town. (If by some fluke they're not, call **United Cab** at ☎ **504-522-9771.**)

Figuring Out the Neighborhoods

Several towns and unincorporated areas extend along both the east and west banks of the Mississippi River to make up the New Orleans metropolitan area. This section gives a brief tour of some of the distinct local neighborhoods that make up the city (see the "New Orleans Neighborhoods," map below).

French Quarter (Vieux Carré)

Thankfully, the city's crown jewel remained high and dry after Hurricane Katrina. Founded in 1718, the Vieux Carré (or Old Square) comprised the original city of New Orleans and is now known as the French Quarter. The oldest neighborhood in New Orleans is bordered by North Rampart Street, Esplanade Avenue, Canal Street, and the Mississippi River. Many people enjoy the French Quarter for the European-style architecture surrounding Jackson Square (the old Ursuline Convent dates back to 1742), Bourbon Street, and the French Market. Despite its small size, it boasts more restaurants and bars per square inch than any other city (which is hyperbole, of course, but not by much). During Mardi Gras, the Quarter is Party Central. However, you won't find parades here (the narrow, one-way streets don't even allow buses, much less floats) but rather throngs of revelers, exhibitionists, and people-watchers. You can best enjoy the Quarter on foot, by carriage, or as part of an organized tour.

Central Business District

Canal Street, which did in fact look like a canal after Katrina, roughly bounds the district on the north, and the elevated Pontchartrain Expressway (I-90) bounds the district to the south, between Loyola Avenue and the Mississippi River. In the midst of the high-rise buildings, you can see bustling squares and parks, including the newly restored Piazza d'Italia, which was originally built in 1978 to recognize the contributions of the local Italian community. You can also find major attractions, such as the Superdome and World Trade Center, as well as a burgeoning Museum District, featuring the National D-Day Museum, Louisiana Children's Museum, Contemporary Arts Center, Ogden Museum of Southern Art, and the Confederate Museum. Luxury hotels and restaurants and the area's close proximity to the Quarter (without the attendant crowds) make it popular with tourists.

Warehouse District

You can find this area between Julia and St. Joseph's streets within the Central Business District, which also survived Katrina relatively unscathed. Once made up almost entirely of warehouses, adaptive reuse and revitalization has turned the neighborhood into an upscale residential neighborhood and Arts District, with most galleries located on what is known as Julia Row. The Convention Center, Riverwalk Shopping Center, music clubs, hotels, restaurants, and museums lure visitors.

Garden District

Due to its location not far from the river, the Garden District stayed dry after Katrina. Explore the Garden District — bordered by Jackson Avenue, St. Charles Avenue, Louisiana Avenue, and Magazine Street — via the St. Charles Streetcar and on foot. Originally part of the city of

New Orleans Neighborhoods

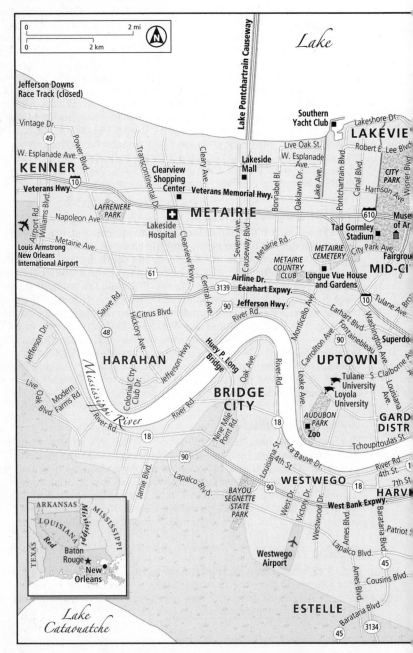

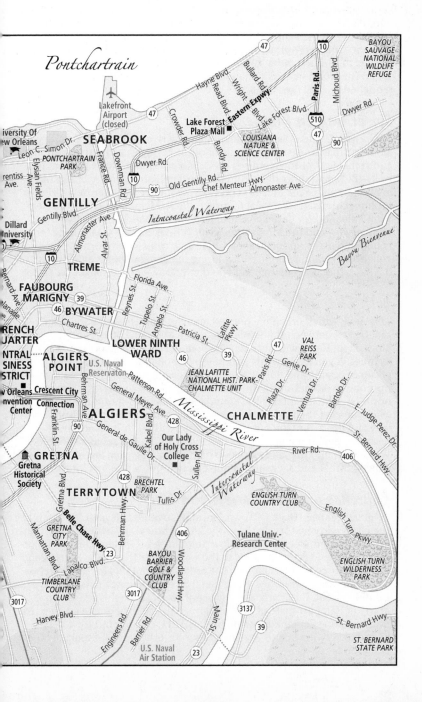

Pontchartrain

Lakefront Airport (closed)

47

Hayne Blvd.
Bullard Rd.
Wright Ave.
Read Blvd.
Crowder Rd.
Lake Forest Blvd.
Eastern Expwy.

47
10
Paris Rd.
Michoud Blvd.

BAYOU SAUVAGE NATIONAL WILDLIFE REFUGE

Dwyer Rd.

iversity Of w Orleans

Leon C. Simon Dr.
PONTCHARTRAIN PARK

SEABROOK

France Rd.
Downman Rd.

Dwyer Rd.

Lake Forest Plaza Mall

LOUISIANA NATURE & SCIENCE CENTER

510

47

90

Elysian Fields Ave.

rentiss Ave.

GENTILLY

Gentilly Blvd.

10
90

Old Gentilly Rd.
Chef Menteur Hwy.
Almonaster Ave.

Almonaster Ave.

Alvar St.

Dillard niversity

10

TREME

Florida Ave.

Intracoastal Waterway

Bayou Bienvenue

Bernard Hwy.
anade

FAUBOURG MARIGNY

39

BYWATER

46

Chartres St.

Reynes St.
Tupelo St.
Angela St.

Patricia St.

Lafitte Pkwy.

47

VAL REISS PARK

Genie Dr.

RENCH JARTER

LOWER NINTH WARD

46

39

Plaza Dr.

Ventura Dr.

Bartolo Dr.

NTRAL SINESS STRICT

ALGIERS POINT

U.S. Naval Reservaton

Patterson Rd.

JEAN LAFITTE NATIONAL HIST. PARK- CHALMETTE UNIT

E. Judge Perez Dr.

Orleans nvention Center

Crescent City Connection

General Meyer Ave.

Mississippi River

CHALMETTE

St. Bernard Hwy.

Behrman Ave.

ALGIERS

General de Gaulle Dr.

428

Kabel Blvd.

Our Lady of Holy Cross College

Sullen Pl.

River Rd.

406

90

Franklin St.

🏛 **GRETNA**
Gretna Historical Society

428

BRECHTEL PARK

Intercoastal Waterway

ENGLISH TURN COUNTRY CLUB

English Turn Pkwy.

Gretna Blvd.

TERRYTOWN

Tullis Dr.

Belle Chase Hwy.

GRETNA CITY PARK

23

Lapalco Blvd.

406

BAYOU BARRIER GOLF & COUNTRY CLUB

Woodland Hwy.

Tulane Univ.- Research Center

ENGLISH TURN WILDERNESS PARK

Manhattan Blvd.

TIMBERLANE COUNTRY CLUB

3017

3017

Harvey Blvd.

Engineers Rd.

Barrier Rd.

Main St.

3137

39

St. Bernard Hwy.

ST. BERNARD STATE PARK

U.S. Naval Air Station

23

Lafayette, it became a fashionable residential area after the United States purchased it and wealthy Americans took up residence there. Visitors come from all over the world to view the beautiful homes and gardens along St. Charles Avenue. Anne Rice's two former homes are located in this neighborhood, as is the beautifully restored cemetery Lafayette No. 1, and the world-famous restaurant **Commander's Palace,** restored and reopened in 2006 (see Chapter 11).

Lower Garden District

The Lower Garden District, which hugs the river and also stayed dry after Katrina, houses a number of modest cottages, attractive churches, and some elegant town houses on Coliseum Square. Developed in the early 1800s just downriver from the Garden District, many of its streets are named for Greek Muses — though most have peculiar New Orleans pronunciations. (Ask a local to direct you to Melpomene Street to hear what I mean.) St. Charles Avenue, Jackson Avenue, the Pontchartrain Expressway, and the Mississippi River border this area. Magazine Street is home to many antiques shops, sidewalk cafes, neighborhood bars, coffee shops, and boutiques. Exploring the area on foot is safe during the daytime, though I recommend you don't stray far from Magazine Street.

Irish Channel

This area, which originally housed many of New Orleans's Irish immigrants, lies between the Garden District's Magazine Street and the Mississippi River, with its sidewise boundaries at Jackson and Louisiana avenues. If you explore this part of the city on foot, only do so with a large group of people and during the day because it's not the safest neighborhood in town. During the 1800s, the area was a working-class neighborhood, which explains the abundance of double-shotgun cottages. (Shotguns get their name because a person can stand in the front doorway and fire a shotgun out the back door without hitting anything — and because they're reminiscent of looking down the barrel of a shotgun.) Walking around the antiques-shop district on Magazine Street and around Felicity Street and Jackson Avenue can give you a real feel for the area.

Churches and cemeteries: Mid-City

Originally called "Back O' Town," swamp covered this area for much of the city's early history. In the early 20th century, however, it was drained and developed. Because it is a low point in New Orleans, this neighborhood suffered severe flooding in the weeks after Hurricane Katrina and is in the process of rebuilding. The area, most notable for its churches and cemeteries, stretches along Canal Street between Esplanade Avenue, Perdido Street, City Park, and Derbigny Street (though some claim it starts at Rampart instead of Derbigny). You can experience some parts, notably along Esplanade itself and City Park, on foot; but for safety's sake, stick with a bus or organized tour for other areas, especially the cemeteries.

Uptown

Jackson Avenue, Claiborne Avenue, the Mississippi River, and Carrollton Avenue bound this district, the largest area in the city. You find Tulane and Loyola universities, breathtaking mansions, Audubon Park, Audubon Zoo, and churches and synagogues. Also in this area are the legendary music club **Tipitina's** (see Chapter 17) and several fine restaurants, such as **Pascal's Manale** (see Chapter 11). Magazine Street runs through the district and features antiques shops, boutiques, and art galleries. Normally, you could take the St. Charles Streetcar to explore, but the St. Charles streetcar remains closed as of this writing while undergoing hurricane-related repairs. Much of the area is perfect for walking or you can take the Magazine Street bus.

Faubourg Marigny

Faubourg Marigny lies downriver from, and immediately adjacent to, the French Quarter, bordered by Esplanade Avenue, St. Claude Avenue, Press Street, and the Mississippi River. This area stayed dry post-Katrina and was developed during the late 1700s as one of the earliest suburbs. Today it houses many Creole cottages and bed-and-breakfasts, as well as a range of residents — from bohemian to metrosexual. I hate to give the impression that the area is dangerous because overall it's very quaint and charming, but some areas can be dicey, so only explore the neighborhood on foot during daylight hours. Generally, Frenchmen Street, which is a hip entertainment area, is safe, as is most of the neighborhood close to the river. The farther toward Rampart and St. Claude you get, the riskier it becomes.

Bywater

Bywater, bounded by Press Street, St. Claude Avenue, Poland Avenue, and the Mississippi River, is just downriver from the French Quarter. Katrina was kind to it as this area did not flood. Some naysayers call this region "backwater" because at first glance it seems like a wasteland of light industry and run-down homes. In fact, Bywater is in the midst of a renaissance. Originally, artisans, free persons of color, and immigrants from Germany, Ireland, and Italy called this area home. Now artists, designers, and residents who simply can't afford the Quarter or Marigny live in its Creole cottages and Victorian shotguns. Within this mix are some funky neighborhood restaurants and bars.

Algiers Point

One of the city's original Creole suburbs, Algiers Point — which did not flood — is the only part of the city on the West Bank and it has changed little over the decades. Here you find some of the best-preserved small gingerbread and Creole cottages in New Orleans. The neighborhood has begun to attract a lot of attention as a historic landmark, and makes for a nice stroll during the day, though I'd stay in the car rather than walk on foot. (Like parts of Uptown, tranquil areas can give way to less-than-desirable areas at a moment's notice.) It's also becoming a popular neighborhood for locals. A former hole-in-the-wall club called the **Old Point Bar** (see Chapter 17) has established itself as a hip musical destination, adding to the neighborhood's cachet.

Finding Information After You Arrive

You can find a state-run **Tourist Information Center** (☎ 504-568-5661) in the French Quarter at 529 St. Ann St. in the historic Pontalba Buildings on the side of Jackson Square. Other information centers dot the city, many of them owned and operated by tour companies or other businesses. You can find tourist booths at these locations:

- ✔ **Canal and Convention Center Boulevard** (walk-up booth; ☎ 504-587-0739) at the beginning of the 300 block of Canal on the downtown side of the street

- ✔ Just outside the **World Trade Center** (walk-up booth; ☎ 504-587-0734) at 2 Canal St.

- ✔ Near the **Hard Rock Cafe** (walk-up booth; ☎ 504-587-0740) on the 400 block of North Peters Street

- ✔ **Julia and Convention Center Boulevard** (walk-up booth)

- ✔ **Poydras and Convention Center Boulevard** (walk-up booth)

- ✔ **New Orleans Metropolitan Convention & Visitors Bureau** (☎ 504-566-5011; www.nomcvb.com) at 2020 St. Charles Ave.

- ✔ **Vieux Carré Police Station** (small tourist information desk inside the station; ☎ 504-565-7530) at 334 Royal St.

Getting Around New Orleans

You'll probably spend most of your time in the French Quarter, which is only 6 blocks wide and 13 blocks long. Because the area is so small — and the narrow one-way streets, traffic congestion, strict traffic laws, and lack of on-street parking make driving a nightmare — I suggest you walk.

If you're cooped up in a car, you can't see the sights or hear the sounds of the French Quarter in the same way as on your own two feet. If you get tired, you can always hire a carriage and let the mule do the walking.

Use the daylight hours to explore; after dark, stick to well-lit areas with other people around. Watch out for pickpockets on Bourbon Street. Avoid contact with panhandlers, and be wary of people who approach you with a "hard-luck" story — their car broke down, they need money for gas, or their purse was stolen, for example — no matter how well dressed or sincere they seem. I'm not telling you to be rude, but use your judgment. Also avoid people (especially kids) who want to wager with you; a frequent ruse is "I bet I can tell you where you got your shoes." (You got 'em on your feet.) Or, "I bet I can spell your name." (Y-o-u-r-n-a-m-e.) As always, use common sense when exploring any area of the city.

New Orleans features a reliable and thorough public transportation system — streetcars and buses connect all neighborhoods that you may want to visit. Call the **Regional Transit Authority's Ride Line** at ☎ **504-248-3900** for maps, passes, and other information about streetcars or buses. Any of New Orleans's visitor information centers (including the main location at 529 St. Ann St. by Jackson Square) also have information on public transportation.

If you plan to use public transportation frequently during your stay, purchase a **VisiTour pass,** which entitles you to unlimited bus and streetcar rides. You can purchase one at most hotels and banks in the Quarter, Central Business District, and along Canal Street in one-day ($5) or three-day ($12) increments. Two booths also sell them: one outside the Aquarium of the Americas and the other on the 600 block of Decatur Street.

Hopping the St. Charles or Canal streetcars

Since 1835, the St. Charles line (see the "St. Charles Streetcar Route" map in this chapter) has serviced the Central Business District, Garden District, Lower Garden District, Uptown, and Carrollton neighborhoods. Unfortunately, for now, in order to view the scenic 7-mile ride (which begins at the corner of Carondelet and Canal streets and takes you from downtown to Uptown, or vice versa), you'll have to take the St. Charles bus. Most of the St. Charles Streetcar line continues to be closed for repairs due to Hurricane Katrina, but it should reopen in late 2007. However, the Central Business loop of the St. Charles streetcar line (from Carondelet and Canal Street to Lee Circle) should be up and running in early 2007. See www.norta.org for updates.

New Orleanians giddily anticipated the April 2004 return of the Canal Streetcar line (see the "Canal Streetcar Route" map in this chapter), 40 years after the last car ran and protesters threw tomatoes at the new buses. The 5½-mile ride heads up Canal, passing through the Central Business District and Mid-City, and ends at one of two destinations, either north on the Carrollton spur to the 1,500-acre urban oasis of City Park or farther west to the Cypress Grove and Greenwood cemeteries.

Riding either the Canal Streetcar or the St. Charles bus costs just $1.25 each way (exact change or a VisiTour pass is required). Chapter 12 has a list of sights to see while on the streetcar, which operates 24 hours a day. In order to maintain its distinction as a moving landmark by the National Register of Historic Places, the St. Charles Streetcar doesn't provide modern amenities such as air conditioning or handicap accessibility. However, the Canal Streetcar features air conditioning, wheelchair lifts, and a surprisingly quiet, high-tech braking system. The round-trip for either route takes 90 minutes to two hours.

Canal Streetcar Route

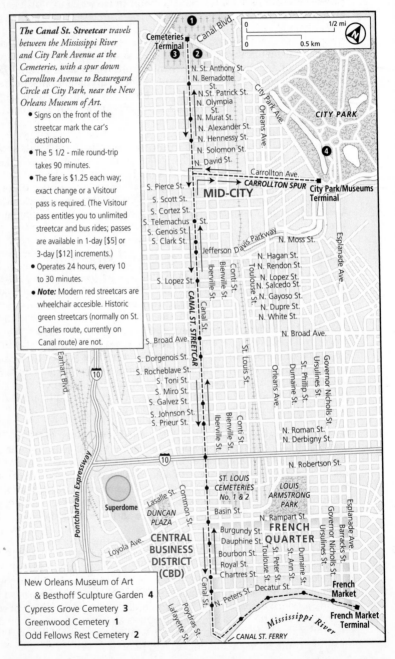

The Canal St. Streetcar travels between the Mississippi River and City Park Avenue at the Cemeteries, with a spur down Carrollton Avenue to Beauregard Circle at City Park, near the New Orleans Museum of Art.

- Signs on the front of the streetcar mark the car's destination.
- The 5 1/2 - mile round-trip takes 90 minutes.
- The fare is $1.25 each way; exact change or a Visitour pass is required. (The Visitour pass entitles you to unlimited streetcar and bus rides; passes are available in 1-day [$5] or 3-day [$12] increments.)
- Operates 24 hours, every 10 to 30 minutes.
- **Note:** Modern red streetcars are wheelchair accesible. Historic green streetcars (normally on St. Charles route, currently on Canal route) are not.

New Orleans Museum of Art
& Besthoff Sculpture Garden **4**
Cypress Grove Cemetery **3**
Greenwood Cemetery **1**
Odd Fellows Rest Cemetery **2**

0 — 1/2 mi
0 — 0.5 km

Canal Blvd.
Cemeteries Terminal
N. St. Anthony St.
N. Bernadotte St.
N. St. Patrick St.
N. Olympia St.
N. Murat St.
N. Alexander St.
N. Hennessy St.
N. Solomon St.
N. David St.
City Park Ave.
Orleans Ave.
CITY PARK

Carrollton Ave.
CARROLLTON SPUR City Park/Museums Terminal

S. Pierce St.
S. Scott St.
S. Cortez St.
S. Telemachus St.
S. Genois St.
S. Clark St.
MID-CITY
Jefferson Davis Parkway
N. Moss St.
Esplanade Ave.

S. Lopez St.
Bienville St.
Conti St.
Iberville St.
Toulouse St.
N. Hagan St.
N. Rendon St.
N. Lopez St.
N. Salcedo St.
N. Gayoso St.
N. Dupre St.
N. White St.
N. Broad Ave.

CANAL ST. STREETCAR
Canal St.

S. Broad Ave.
S. Dorgenois St.
S. Rocheblave St.
S. Toni St.
S. Miro St.
S. Galvez St.
S. Johnson St.
S. Prieur St.
St. Louis St.
Orleans Ave.
St. Phillip St.
Dumaine St.
Governor Nicholls St.
Ursulines St.
N. Roman St.
N. Derbigny St.

Iberville St.
Bienville St.
Conti St.

N. Robertson St.

Earhart Blvd.
10
Pontchartrain Expressway
10
Superdome
Lasalle St.
Common St.
DUNCAN PLAZA
CENTRAL BUSINESS DISTRICT (CBD)
Loyola Ave.
Poydras St.
Lafayette St.

ST. LOUIS CEMETERIES No. 1 & 2
Basin St.
Burgundy St.
Dauphine St.
Bourbon St.
Royal St.
Chartres St.
Canal St.
N. Peters St. Decatur St.
LOUIS ARMSTRONG PARK
N. Rampart St.
FRENCH QUARTER
St. Peter St.
St. Ann St.
Toulouse St.
Dumaine St.
Governor Nicholls St.
Ursulines St.
Esplanade Ave.
Barracks St.
French Market
French Market Terminal

Mississippi River
CANAL ST. FERRY

Generally, you don't have to wait too long for a streetcar — usually no more than half an hour. Downtown, you can board the St. Charles bus (or streetcar when it returns) at Canal and Carondelet (directly across Canal from Bourbon Street) and the Canal Streetcar at various stops along Canal Street on the eastern edge of the French Quarter. You can also board at a number of designated stops along St. Charles Avenue and Canal Street, respectively. Like taking a bus, you can get on and off the streetcar at will, but you have to pay each time you get back on.

The St. Charles line ends, rather inconveniently, at Palmer Park at Carrollton and Claiborne avenues where you can transfer to another bus for 25¢. Or, take the return trip and stop at one of the many restaurants and shops in the Riverbend (at the corner of St. Charles and Carrollton avenues).

Depending on which destination you choose, the Canal line ends at the cemeteries, which are safe to explore, or City Park. The latter features the New Orleans Museum of Art, the spectacular Besthoff Sculpture Garden, and the always-blooming New Orleans Botanical Garden, all of which have made an amazing recovery after flooding by Katrina. Families will want to head straight to **Children's Storyland,** an amusement park (rated one of the ten best in the country by *Child* magazine). As of this writing, the **Carousel Gardens,** which features a nostalgic, wooden-horse carousel ride, remain closed but people of all ages eagerly anticipate its reopening.

Because the streetcar is as much a mode of public transportation as a tourist attraction, it gets pretty crowded, especially at rush hour or when school lets out in the midafternoon. Also, the Canal Streetcar is packed during Jazz Fest because it's the cheapest and most convenient transportation to the Fair Grounds.

Riverfront seating: The Riverfront Streetcar

Established during the 1984 World's Fair, the Riverfront Streetcar line runs along the riverfront from the Convention Center to the far end of the French Quarter at Esplanade. The approximately 2-mile ride, which is a great way to see the river, costs $1.50 (exact change or a VisiTour pass is required). You can board, or get off, along that route at designated stops. The streetcar is wheelchair accessible.

By bus

Buses in New Orleans may generally be more convenient than streetcars, but they don't cover the same routes, and they're not anywhere *near* as picturesque. One or more bus lines connect most neighborhoods, and the fare is $1.25 (exact change or a VisiTour pass is required). Transfers cost 25¢, and buses are wheelchair accessible.

Because you're a visitor to New Orleans, you'll probably need to use only a few of the bus lines, such as **Tulane** (if you happen to stay on

Tulane Avenue) or **Magazine** (which runs through the Central Business District, Lower Garden District, and Uptown between the Garden District and the Irish Channel). Buses pick up passengers every other block or so along their routes at designated bus stops. Again, you can get more-specific information from the **Regional Transit Authority's Ride Line** at ☎ **504-248-3900** or by picking up one of the excellent city maps available at the **Visitor Information Center** at 529 St. Ann St.

By taxi

During the day, public transportation is perfectly safe, but I don't recommend taking it at night. You probably won't have any problems if you get on and off at well-lit major intersections, but I suggest a taxi if you're going somewhere not right on the line's route. A good neighborhood can take a turn for the worse in just a few short blocks.

Finding an available cab usually isn't too much trouble, with the exception of busy times such as rush hour or during bad weather. If a cab is empty, driving relatively slowly, and its "On Duty" sign isn't on (if it even has one), chances are it's looking for fares. But as in most major cities, the methods and habits of New Orleans cabbies can be inscrutable. A cab may be on its way to pick up a radio-call fare. Also, the cabbie may be on his lunch break, he may be scrutinizing potential fares for the most lucrative ride (to the airport), or he may just not like the way you look. If you're in a hurry, your best bet is always to call ahead for a cab.

The easiest places to find a taxi include the airport, the French Quarter, and the Central Business District. You can also spot cabs at stands near restaurants, at all the major hotels, and at some smaller hotels as well. If you can't find a cab on the street, call a taxi company. **United Cab** (☎ **504-522-9771**) is the largest and most reliable taxi company in the New Orleans area.

A ride for two people to most major tourist areas doesn't cost more than $10. All taxis cost $2.50 for the first ⅙ of a mile and 20¢ for each additional ⅙ of a mile (or $1.20 per mile). If you travel at a rate less than ⅙ of a mile per 40 seconds, the cabbie charges the additional 20¢ anyway. Add $1 for each additional person. The maximum number of passengers is five. You can also hire taxis for $30 an hour, though taxi companies impose a two-hour minimum and don't take you outside the New Orleans area.

During football and basketball games, Jazz Fest, and other special events, taxi drivers usually expect you to pay $3 per person or the meter rate, whichever is greater. Special events include regularly scheduled sporting events and/or concerts at the Superdome, Saenger Theater, Fair Grounds, and most other stadiums.

In the event that you leave a wallet, piece of luggage, or other important effect in a cab when you exit, call the cab company as soon as possible. Calmly tell the dispatcher your problem, and provide him or her with your route details ("I went from Audubon Park to Brennan's"). In case of

St. Charles Streetcar Route

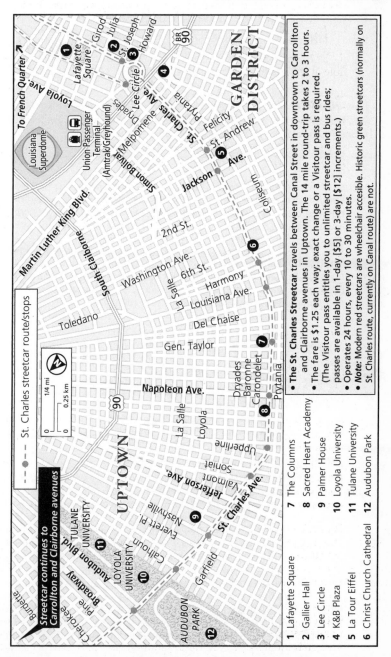

To French Quarter

Lafayette Square

BR 90

GARDEN DISTRICT

Loyola Ave.

Louisiana Superdome

Union Passenger Terminal (Amtrak/Greyhound)

Lee Circle

St. Charles Ave.

Melpomene
Dryades
Felicity

St. Andrew
Ave.

Simon Bolivar

Jackson

Martin Luther King Blvd.

South Claiborne

2nd St.

Coliseum

Washington Ave.
6th St.
La Salle
Harmony
Louisiana Ave.

Toledano

Del Chaise

Gen. Taylor

Dryades
Barone
Carondelet
Prytania

Napoleon Ave.

1/4 mi
0.25 km

La Salle
Loyola

UPTOWN

St. Charles Ave.

Upperline
Soniat
Valmont
Jefferson Ave.

Nashville

Everett Pl.

Calhoun

Broadway

TULANE UNIVERSITY

Audubon Blvd.

LOYOLA UNIVERSITY

Pine
Cherokee
Burdette

Garfield

AUDUBON PARK

- - - St. Charles streetcar route/stops

Streetcar continues to Carrollton and Clairborne avenues

• **The St. Charles Streetcar** travels between Canal Street in downtown to Carrollton and Clairborne avenues in Uptown. The 14 mile round-trip takes 2 to 3 hours.
• The fare is $1.25 each way; exact change or a Visitour pass is required. (The Visitour pass entitles you to unlimited streetcar and bus rides; passes are available in 1-day [$5] or 3-day [$12] increments.)
• Operates 24 hours, every 10 to 30 minutes.
• *Note:* Modern red streetcars are wheelchair accesible. Historic green streetcars (normally on St. Charles route, currently on Canal route) are not.

1 Lafayette Square
2 Gallier Hall
3 Lee Circle
4 K&B Plaza
5 La Tour Eiffel
6 Christ Church Cathedral

7 The Columns
8 Sacred Heart Academy
9 Palmer House
10 Loyola University
11 Tulane University
12 Audubon Park

Biking it

If you're feeling especially adventurous, rent a bike and take your own tour around New Orleans, using the information in this book as a guide. **Bicycle Michael's** (☎ **504-945-9505**; www.bicyclemichaels.com) and **French Quarter Bicycles** (☎ **504-529-3136**) are two good bets for rentals. Most cyclists in the city ride along the streets with the car traffic or along the popular bike trails in the greater New Orleans vicinity. For a comprehensive list of New Orleans bike shops and maps of bike trails, visit the **New Orleans Bicycle Club** Web site at www.neworleansbicycleclub.org.

situations such as this, noting your taxi driver's name (the license should be clearly posted) and the taxi's number (which should be painted on its trunk or on another visible space) is always a good idea.

By car

Though not impossible, driving in New Orleans *is* a big hassle. Parking is an issue (except in the French Quarter, where it's more of a myth). Navigation is confusing because street names change without warning and some streets have more twists and turns than an afternoon's worth of daytime soaps. As for other drivers . . . well, that's another story.

Avoiding the French Quarter

Before I go any further, however, absolutely the best, most essential tip I can give you about driving around New Orleans is to avoid driving in the French Quarter as much as possible. Why? Driving in the Quarter is a headache and a half. Unless you're paid to do it (that is, you're a cab driver), it's not worth the aggravation. The Quarter is small enough, with everything pretty close together, to navigate on foot.

Parking (or not parking) in the Quarter

Driving in the Quarter is a bad idea for a number of reasons, but the biggest is parking, which is practically nonexistent; even residents suffer constant parking woes. Parking spaces are scarce, and the ones that exist always seem to be occupied by people who got there before you — even if you get there at 4 a.m. Even if by fate you do find what seems to be an available spot, chances are it's illegal (of course, the sign pointing out this fact is probably obscured or on the other end of the street).

When choosing your hotel, find out whether your hotel has parking available. If you're staying in a French Quarter hotel that has parking, well, great, but limit your car usage to excursions outside the Quarter. Wait a minute, you're saying. What if I'm staying outside the Quarter, but I want to come in to visit? Good point. My advice is to take the Canal or

St. Charles streetcars if possible. Otherwise, park in one of the commercial parking lots on Decatur along the river and walk the rest of the way. You'll also see commercial lots inside the Quarter, notably for some of the bigger hotels, but they're often full, not to mention expensive. Aside from helping you avoid the hassle of finding a parking spot, parking in one of these lots is well worth the security of knowing you won't get towed — or vandalized.

Navigating the Quarter

The streets in the French Quarter are all one-way, which can make a simple right turn an elaborate affair. Additionally, certain tourist-heavy areas — notably Bourbon and Royal streets — are more congested than a Southern gourmand's arteries. Pedestrian traffic is thick, massive, and unrelenting, and no one shows much concern about stopping to let your car cross the street.

To further complicate matters, tourist traffic completely barricades the 300–700 blocks of Bourbon and Royal on weekdays during daylight hours, which turns the merely impractical into the impossible. Chartres Street is also closed on the blocks in front of the St. Louis Cathedral.

Additionally, the streets in the French Quarter are narrow, with no room to pass because on-street parking takes up almost half the available driving space. The lack of space is bad enough when you're stuck in a long line of traffic trying to navigate its way across Bourbon Street, but getting stuck behind a mule-drawn buggy is even worse.

Driving outside the Quarter

Outside the French Quarter, driving is a whole different story. In the Central Business District, getting around in your car is pretty much the same as in your main downtown area back home. Parking spots (at least free ones) can be hard to come by. Traffic can and will be heavy during morning and afternoon rush hour, and probably during lunch as well.

Enjoying a romantic carriage ride

You'll be hard pressed to resist the mule-drawn carriages at the Decatur Street end of Jackson Square (9 a.m.–midnight) if you have even one romantic bone in your body. You'll get a nonstop monologue on historic buildings, fascinating events of the past, and a legend or two. Most drivers charge around $8 for adults and $5 for children under 12. A private carriage tour, however, costs significantly more. Contact **Good Old Days Buggies** (☎ 504-523-0804) for a private tour, including hotel or restaurant pickup. See Chapter 12 for more information. (You can't ride this one, but the Roman Candy mule-drawn cart on St. Charles, about a half-mile downriver from Audubon Park, offers excellent taffy. My favorite flavor is chocolate.)

You can turn right on red throughout the city unless otherwise specified, but many streets are one-way, and many of those (most notably Tulane Avenue) don't allow left turns.

If you park on a parade route, block access to someone's driveway, or break other laws, your car may be towed away and impounded, and getting it back can cost you $100 or more. If you think your car has been towed, call the impounding lot (☎ 504-565-7235) or the Claiborne Auto Pound, 400 N. Claiborne Ave. (☎ 504-565-7450).

The driving situation is a little better uptown in the Garden District and other areas. You'll still encounter many one-way streets, however, and as always, free parking is hard to come by.

Avoiding local hazards: Potholes and drivers

Keep in mind that New Orleans's streets are famous for their potholes, some of which qualify as craters. Local drivers have developed a driving sixth sense; on certain streets, a sort of autopilot takes over that swerves your car this way or that to avoid wrecking your alignment on a nasty bump. Being new to the area, you haven't formed this psychic ability yet, and some potholes aren't so easy to see until after they've jolted you.

Last, but not least, are the New Orleans drivers themselves. Don't get me wrong — this is my home, and I love it — but the people here don't know how to drive. Many possess a dangerous mixture of arrogance and cluelessness on the road. Rubbernecking, idling in the passing lane, failure to yield or allow others to merge, and a complete lack of familiarity with turn signals are all trademark characteristics of local drivers. Consider yourself warned.

Chapter 10

Checking in at New Orleans's Best Hotels

● ●

In This Chapter

▶ Finding the hotel you want

▶ Locating the best price

▶ Turning up in New Orleans sans reservation

▶ Checking into the best hotels in the city

▶ Considering a few more hotel options

● ●

*M*ost visitors to New Orleans don't plan to spend much time in their hotel room, but there's something to be said for a good night's sleep. Or a sudden rain storm could encourage you to stick indoors for a little while, in which case, you want to be comfortable. Whether you decide to splurge on a luxurious suite at the Ritz-Carlton or take refuge in a Ramada, this chapter offers a variety of options — and aesthetics — in every price range. As a post-Katrina visitor, you might be pleasantly surprised to find some good deals and open rooms during the traditional tourism-heavy seasons of spring and fall.

Assessing Katrina's Effect on Area Hotels

For the most part, it was the bed-and-breakfast establishments, not the hotels, which fared worst, in terms of both damage and business, since tourism is still low in the area. I've seen "For Sale" signs on many properties, especially Mid-city, which is a shame; B&Bs such as House on Bayou Road and the Block-Keller House were the first accommodations to reopen after the storm, but they didn't get the support they needed.

Many downtown hotels were either damaged by looters or were roughed up by the crowds of locals seeking shelter from the storm. Many had roof damage and water damage as well; The Hotel Monaco had to close permanently, but other major hotels such as the Ritz-Carlton sustained damage but have already reopened. French quarter hotels held up better and had better security in place, so looting was less of an issue.

Getting to Know Your Options

When it comes to lodging, many travelers simply look for the cheapest accommodations they can find. Or they choose a hotel that's central to everything (usually right on Bourbon Street) but end up paying twice as much.

To make a hotel choice that best fits your needs, decide what's most important to you. Whatever your preferences, this chapter helps you weigh your options by outlining the advantages and disadvantages of staying in certain neighborhoods. It also gives you an idea of what you can expect to get, value-wise, for your dollar in New Orleans.

Since the 1960s the people of New Orleans have faithfully preserved the Quarter's architectural style. In fact, distinguishing between a new hotel that has been lovingly placed inside the shell of an older building and a hotel built from scratch isn't as easy as it sounds. Even motor hotels (which provide parking spots and have helped alleviate the ever-present problem of on-street parking) maintain a distinctly New Orleans look.

Of course, the city does have some high-rise chain hotels, but you only find them appropriately located in commercial sections, such as the Central Business District. Many of them have been customized to blend in with the scenery. Whatever your preference, New Orleans offers a variety of options.

Watch for the Kid Friendly icon, which points out hotels that are especially good for families.

Listings also note other special considerations, such as which hotels accommodate disabled travelers, which places are the most gay-friendly, which inspire romance, which are convenient to Mardi Gras parade routes, and so on.

Disabled travelers please take note: Hotels listed as wheelchair accessible may offer only a small number of these rooms, so ask about availability when you make your reservation. Also, "wheelchair accessible" doesn't necessarily mean that the hotel is up to the standards of the Americans with Disabilities Act (ADA) — the hotel may just be accessible from the street and have an elevator and wide doorways. I try to include any special information about steps, bathroom accessibility, or other access concerns.

You won't have any trouble finding atmosphere in this city — even in more modern neighborhoods. Despite the annual influx of hundreds of thousands of visitors, New Orleans has managed to keep historic districts such as the French Quarter free of skyscraper development. Because the city is below sea level, engineers found it to be quite a challenge to create stable, tall buildings. By the time they figured out how to do it, the French Quarter was a protected historic district that didn't allow new development disproportionate in size to its original buildings. In fact, the modest, four-story Pedesclaux-Lemonnier House at 640 Royal St. is still known as the "Skyscraper." It was built between 1795 and 1811 and is believed to be the first four-story building in New Orleans.

The chains: Tried and true

New Orleans has its share of national chain hotels, such as Holiday Inn, Hyatt, Marriott, Sheraton, Ramada, and Radisson. Although these hotels tend to have a homogeneous, seen-one-you've-seen-'em-all quality, the best ones adapt to the color and flavor of New Orleans, both outside and inside. (One good example is the **Holiday Inn-Chateau LeMoyne** in the French Quarter; see its listings later in this chapter.) These chain hotels usually attract business travelers with moderate expense accounts or families with children in tow. Many travelers prefer the consistency assured by a brand name. New Orleans features some fine chain hotels; this chapter lists the best ones.

Boutique hotels: Quiet luxury

Independent hotels — also called boutique hotels — are smaller in scope. They can be family-run, mom-and-pop operations (such as the **Hotel Villa Convento** in the French Quarter), or part of a small group of hotels owned by the same company but not part of a cookie-cutter chain. Boutique hotels may target a specific niche, such as older travelers or budget-minded business travelers. They're also usually cheaper than the bigger chains (though this rule isn't set in stone). Independent hotels are good spots to soak up local character, but they often have fewer amenities than chain hotels.

Motels and motor hotels: No frills

Motels are more or less like hotels, only stripped of the amenities. If you're willing to forego room service, a swimming pool, or atmosphere for a cheaper price, go with a motel. Of course, different types of motels exist — from the ubiquitous Motel 6 to seedy "no-tell motels" — but by and large, they're just places to sleep and shower. I don't recommend any lodging of this ilk in this book, concentrating instead on places with character and (usually) amenities; but you can find toll-free numbers for most of the major motel chains in any metropolitan phone book (and in the Appendix).

B&Bs and guesthouses: The personal touch

Sure, some of your nicer hotels offer fine service. However, *service* and *hospitality* aren't the same. For hospitality, head for a bed-and-breakfast. Breakfast — be it a full, belt-loosening extravaganza or (more likely) of the continental variety — is only part of the equation. After all, many hotels also offer a complimentary continental breakfast. So what sets a B&B apart? Basically, staying in a room in a B&B is a lot like being a guest in someone's home. In fact, most B&Bs *are* someone's home.

As with hotels, all B&Bs aren't created equal. Some are renovated houses fully dedicated to visitors, with a small living space for the caretaker's family tucked discreetly away, and a communal kitchen where visitors socialize over breakfast. Some are lavish manses, with antique furniture and floor-to-ceiling picture windows. Such picturesque spots may offer an impressive breakfast spread and perhaps a glass of wine in the afternoon as part of the service. Generally, the more you pay, the higher the level of service and hospitality.

Of course, what's in a name and what's offered can sometimes be vastly different. Many places that *call* themselves B&Bs are actually closer to what Europeans call a *home stay* — residences that rent out extra bedrooms, which may sound all well and good, but chances are they're neither licensed nor insured. You may not think the difference sounds like a big deal until you have an accident on the stairs, or you can't find a fire extinguisher or a safe exit during a fire. When inquiring about a B&B, find out whether it belongs to the **Louisiana Bed and Breakfast Association** (☎ 225-346-1857; www.louisianabandb.com). This association's members are licensed, insured, and regularly inspected for fire safety, sanitation, and up-to-date insurance, among other concerns. Be sure to contact the LBBA to verify membership.

I mention a few choice B&Bs in this chapter. If they interest you and you want more choices, calling a B&B reservation service is your best bet. The most reliable (and the most personable as well) is called, appropriately enough, **Bed and Breakfast, Inc. Reservation Service** (☎ 800-729-4640 or 504-488-4640; www.historiclodging.com). Other options are **Bed & Breakfast and Accommodations** (☎ 888-240-0070 or 504-838-0071; www.neworleansbandb.com), and **Garden District Bed & Breakfast** (☎ 504-895-4302; www.bedandbreakfast.com/new-orleans-louisiana.html).

Keep in mind that B&Bs are quite popular; regular visitors to Mardi Gras and Jazz Fest can reserve rooms up to a year in advance. So call early!

Similar to B&Bs are guesthouses, which are often closer in size and spirit to hotels, though the atmosphere is closer to a B&B. Like B&Bs, native New Orleanians (or in some cases, visitors who never left) often preside over them and imbue them with a special brand of hospitality. Like B&Bs, they're often furnished with antiques and are heavy on the quaint old-world charm or cozy, homelike atmosphere. Yet again, like B&Bs, guesthouses usually serve some sort of breakfast.

The difference between a B&B and a guesthouse comes down to size and, consequently, the level of service. In a B&B, you may be the only guest, or perhaps one out of six, and in intimate contact with its operators. A guesthouse, on the other hand, is often larger, and in all probability less intimate. Certainly, that may be exactly what you're looking for: more intimacy than a hotel, but without having to actually talk to anyone while you're still waking up at breakfast. (At other times, the differences between a place calling itself a guesthouse and a B&B are indistinguishable; the proprietors probably just thought that the words "guesthouse" sounded better.)

The upper-crust hotels: Top of the line

You know what I'm talking about here: the cream of the crop, the five-star, super-swanky affairs that play host to world leaders, top-level rock stars, and captains of industry. The rooms are spacious and gorgeous, the staff impeccably dressed and unfailingly solicitous, and the restaurants first-rate. Needless to say, the luxurious surroundings and pampering accommodations come with a hefty price tag.

Finding the Best Room Rate

The **rack rate** is the maximum rate a hotel charges for a room. It's the rate you get if you walk in off the street and ask for a room for the night. You sometimes see these rates printed on the fire/emergency exit diagrams posted on the back of your door.

Hotels are happy to charge you the rack rate, but you can almost always do better. Perhaps the best way to avoid paying the rack rate is surprisingly simple: Just ask for a cheaper or discounted rate. You may be pleasantly surprised.

In all but the smallest accommodations the rate you pay for a room depends on many factors — chief among them being how you make your reservation. A travel agent may be able to negotiate a better price with certain hotels than you can get. (That's because the hotel often gives the agent a discount in exchange for steering his or her business toward that hotel.) One of the benefits of a package tour is a discounted rate (see Chapter 5 for more details).

 Reserving a room through the hotel's toll-free number may also result in a lower rate than calling the hotel directly. On the other hand, the central reservations number may not know about discount rates at specific locations. For example, local franchises may offer a special group rate for a wedding or family reunion, but they may neglect to tell the central booking line. Your best bet is to call both the local number and the toll-free number and see which one gives you a better deal.

Room rates (even rack rates) change with the season, as occupancy rates rise and fall. But even within a given season, room prices are subject to change without notice, so the rates quoted in this book may be different from the actual rate you receive when you make your reservation. Be sure to mention membership in the American Automobile Association (AAA), AARP (formerly known as the American Association of Retired Persons), frequent-flier programs, and any other corporate rewards programs you can think of — or your Uncle Joe's Elks lodge in which you're an honorary inductee, for that matter — when you call to book. You never know when the affiliation may be worth a few dollars off your room rate.

The period between Thanksgiving and Christmas is another traditionally slow period. New Orleans can be quite pleasant at this time, especially if you're looking to avoid crowds. For more insight into seasonal and weather considerations, refer to Chapter 3.

Surfing the Web for hotel deals

You can generally shop online for hotels in one of two ways:

- ✔ By booking through the hotel's Web site
- ✔ By booking through an independent booking agency (or a fare-service agency like Priceline)

Internet hotel agencies have multiplied in mind-boggling numbers of late, competing for the business of millions of consumers surfing for accommodations around the world. This competitiveness can be a boon to consumers who have the patience and time to shop and compare the online sites for good deals — but shop they must, for prices can vary considerably from site to site. And keep in mind that hotels at the top of a site's listing may be there for no other reason than that they paid money to get the placement.

Of the "big three" sites, **Expedia** (www.expedia.com) offers a long list of special deals and "virtual tours" or photos of available rooms so you can see what you're paying for (a feature that helps counter the claims that the best rooms are often held back from bargain booking Web sites). **Travelocity** (www.travelocity.com) posts unvarnished customer reviews and ranks its properties according to the AAA rating system. Also reliable are **Hotels.com** and **Quikbook.com.** An excellent free program, **TravelAxe** (www.travelaxe.net), can help you search multiple hotel sites at once, even ones you may never have heard of — and conveniently lists the total price of the room, including the taxes and service charges. Another booking site, **Travelweb** (www.travelweb), is partly owned by the hotels it represents (including the Hilton, Hyatt, and Starwood chains) and is therefore plugged directly into the hotels' reservations systems — unlike independent online agencies, which have to fax or e-mail reservation requests to the hotel, a good portion of which get misplaced in the shuffle. More than once, travelers have arrived at the hotel, only to be told that they didn't have a reservation. To be fair, many of the major sites are undergoing improvements in service and ease of use, and Expedia will soon be able to plug directly into the reservations systems of many hotel chains — none of which can be bad news for consumers. In the meantime, **get a confirmation number** and **make a printout** of any online booking transaction.

In the opaque Web site category, **Priceline** (www.priceline.com) and **Hotwire** (www.hotwire.com) are even better for hotels than for airfares. With both sites, you're allowed to pick the neighborhood and quality level of your hotel before offering your money. Priceline's hotel product even covers Europe and Asia, though it's much better at getting five-star lodging for three-star prices than at finding anything at the bottom of the scale. On the down side, many hotels stick Priceline guests in their least desirable rooms. Be sure to go to the **BiddingforTravel** Web site (www.biddingfortravel.com) before bidding on a hotel room on Priceline; it features a fairly up-to-date list of hotels that Priceline uses in major cities. For both Priceline and Hotwire, you pay upfront, and the fee is nonrefundable. *Note:* Some hotels don't provide loyalty program credits or points or other frequent-stay amenities when you book a room through opaque online services.

Reserving the best room

After you make your reservation, asking one or two more pointed questions can go a long way toward making sure you get the best room. Always ask for a corner room. They're usually larger, quieter, and have more windows and light than standard rooms, and they don't always cost more. If the hotel is under renovation, request a room away from the construction. Inquire, too, about the location of the restaurants, bars, and discos in the hotel — all sources of annoying noise. If you aren't happy with your room when you arrive, talk to the front desk. If another room is available, the front desk staff should be happy to accommodate you, within reason.

Arriving without a Reservation

Assume that through circumstances beyond your control, you're suddenly plopped down in New Orleans without a hotel reservation. Don't panic. Unless Mardi Gras, Jazz Fest, or one of the other larger, room-hogging events is taking place, you'll likely find several hotels with available space. First, look through the listings in this chapter for hotels and call the ones that appeal to your preferences and budget. If that doesn't yield results, you have a few options:

✔ Call **Turbotrip.com** (☎ **800-473-STAY**), the **French Quarter Reservation Service** (☎ **800-523-9091** or 504-523-1246), or one of the B&B agencies listed elsewhere in this chapter.

✔ If you're stranded at one of the major French Quarter hotels and it's full, ask if the front desk staff can check around for you and see what other rooms are available. If the staff can't, check your luggage with the hotel in case someone cancels a reservation while you check around on your own.

Table 9-1		Key to Hotel Dollar Signs
Dollar Sign(s)	*Price Range*	*What to Expect*
$	Less than $100	These accommodations are relatively simple and inexpensive. Rooms likely are small, and televisions aren't necessarily provided. Parking isn't provided, but rather catch-as-you-can on the street.
$$	$101–$200	A bit classier, these midrange accommodations offer more room, more extras (such as irons, hair dryers, or a microwave), and a more convenient location than the preceding category.
$$$	$201–$300	Higher-class still, these accommodations begin to look plush. Think chocolates on your pillow, a classy restaurant, underground parking garages, maybe even expansive views of the water.
$$$$	$301 and up	These top-rated accommodations come with luxury amenities such as valet parking, on-premise spas, and in-room hot tubs and CD players — but you pay through the nose for 'em.

New Orleans's Best Hotels

Ashton's Bed & Breakfast
$$ Esplanade Ridge

Patrick and Karma Ashton's elegant 1861 Greek revival mansion is a standout on Esplanade Avenue, a natural ridge of land that saved it from severe flooding during Hurricane Katrina. However, the historic home did sustain some damage to one wall, which is in the process of being repaired. It's also given the Ashtons a long-sought opportunity to add some elegant architectural details and other updating. Be sure to admire the carefully restored original fixtures and woodwork, including a leaded-glass door and black onyx and marble fireplace mantels. If you like a European feel and claw-foot tubs, ask for the Pontalba or Napoleon room in the main house. If you prefer more modern amenities, request the Charpantier room in the former service quarters shaded by a 300-year-old live oak. The French Quarter is nine blocks away through some iffy areas, so come with a car or cab fare.

See map p. 128. 2023 Esplanade Ave., New Orleans, LA 70116. ☎ 800-725-4131 or 504-942-7048. Fax: 504-947-9382. www.ashtonsbb.com. *Parking: free. Rack rates: $105–$170 double (includes breakfast). AE, DC, DISC, MC, V. Call regarding wheelchair accessibility.*

B&W Courtyards Bed & Breakfast
$–$$ Faubourg Marigny

The coziness of this hospitable B&B may inspire you to forever forgo chain hotels. Current owners Rob Boyd and Kevin Wu went to ingenious lengths to convert three 19th-century buildings into appealingly quirky guest rooms. The four rooms and two suites are all completely different (you enter one of them through the bathroom). Though room size varies, the surroundings are uniformly beautiful with two small courtyards, a fountain, a Jacuzzi, and a sundeck. Breakfast is light but beautifully presented. They take good care of you here. Alas, such hospitality may come to an end as this property is on the market for $1,750,000 as of this writing. After Katrina, many business owners are facing difficult decisions or just wanting a change after such a life-changing event. Hopefully, B&W will be purchased by someone who maintains its well-earned rep.

See map p. 128. 2425 Chartres St., New Orleans, LA 70117. ☎ *800-585-5731 or 504-945-9418. Fax: 504-949-3483.* www.bandwcourtyards.com. *Parking: on-street available. Rack rates: $99–$250 double. AE, DISC, MC, V.*

Bienville House
$–$$$$ French Quarter

This moderately priced hotel, which you can't beat for location and price, was largely spared from Katrina's wrath with just a little wind and rain damage. The stately, old-world interior featuring hand-painted wall murals offers a respite from the near-constant bustle of Decatur Street. Rooms are small but comfortable and almost all of them have high ceilings. Some include wrought-iron balconies that overlook a relaxing flagstone courtyard, koi pond, and pool.

See map p. 124. 320 Decatur St. (4 blocks from Jackson Square), New Orleans, LA 70130. ☎ *800-535-7836 or 504-529-2345. Fax: 504-525-6079.* www.bienville house.com. *Valet parking: $20 cars; $25 sport utility vehicles. Rack rates: $89–$650 double (includes continental breakfast). AE, CB, DC, DISC, MC, V. Building and room entrances are wheelchair accessible; bathrooms aren't.*

Block-Keller House
$–$$ Mid-City

Innkeepers Bryan Block and Jeff Keller purchased and completely restored this classical-revival villa as a magnificent B&B just a couple years before Katrina hit. Six feet of standing water over the course of three weeks destroyed their once lovely basement guest rooms, however, the raised main house remained safe and dry. The elaborate parlor with its gorgeous stained-glass windows contrasts nicely with the simple Arts and Crafts dining room. Guests will enjoy exploring the luxurious accommodations of this historic beauty, not to mention the gentle companionship of resident Labradors Milo and Buster. The once lush gardens were ruined by the flood, but have been replanted. Thanks to the sub-tropical climate, they are quickly growing back. Flowers will replace the spot where the shady live oak once stood, another victim of the storm. As of this writing,

French Quarter Accommodations

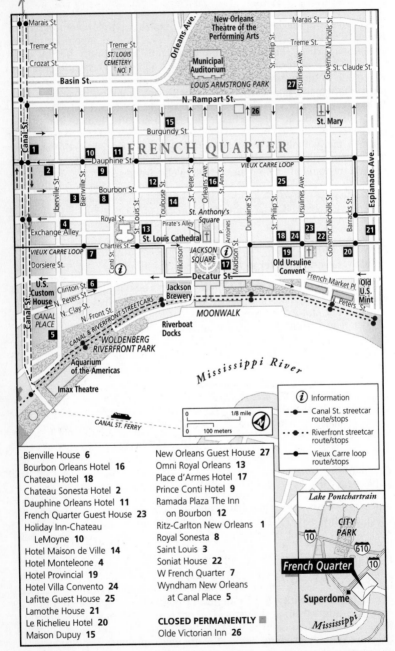

Bienville House **6**
Bourbon Orleans Hotel **16**
Chateau Hotel **18**
Chateau Sonesta Hotel **2**
Dauphine Orleans Hotel **11**
French Quarter Guest House **23**
Holiday Inn-Chateau
LeMoyne **10**
Hotel Maison de Ville **14**
Hotel Monteleone **4**
Hotel Provincial **19**
Hotel Villa Convento **24**
Lafitte Guest House **25**
Lamothe House **21**
Le Richelieu Hotel **20**
Maison Dupuy **15**

New Orleans Guest House **27**
Omni Royal Orleans **13**
Place d'Armes Hotel **17**
Prince Conti Hotel **9**
Ramada Plaza The Inn
on Bourbon **12**
Ritz-Carlton New Orleans **1**
Royal Sonesta **8**
Saint Louis **3**
Soniat House **22**
W French Quarter **7**
Wyndham New Orleans
at Canal Place **5**

CLOSED PERMANENTLY ▨
Olde Victorian Inn **26**

the Block-Keller House is listed for sale, so its future as a B&B is uncertain. For a mere $1,375,000, this grand home and business can be yours.

See map p. 128. 3620 Canal St. (on the new Canal Streetcar line), New Orleans, LA 70119. ☎ *877-588-3033 or 504-483-3033. Fax: 504-483-3032.* www.blockkeller house.com. *Parking: free. Rack rates: $90–$135 double (includes continental breakfast). AE, CB, DC, DISC, MC, V. Wheelchair accessible.*

Bourbon Orleans Hotel
$$–$$$ French Quarter

None of the rooms sustained damage from Katrina, which is quite fortunate considering the hotel spent more than $15 million on renovations preceding the storm. Determining this lavish hotel's best feature is impossible. Is it the central location at the corner of Bourbon and Orleans, the historical pedigree, or the extravagantly decorated public spaces? The extravagance, by the way, extends to the rooms — you find Golden Door Spa toiletries in your bathroom, and you can order room service through your television. The double rooms are comfortable and bigger than average. The bi-level suites feature living rooms with pullout sofa beds that are good for children, who will also appreciate the hotel's outdoor pool. Be sure to request a room closer to Royal Street and sidestep the clamor of Bourbon. The on-site restaurant offers good meals, and the elegant lobby features a nightly cocktail hour. In-room amenities include Wi-Fi, dataport and fax.

See map p. 124. 717 Orleans St. (directly behind St. Louis Cathedral), New Orleans, LA 70116. ☎ *504-523-2222. Fax: 504-525-8166.* www.bourbonorleans.com. *Valet parking: $30. Rack rates: $139–$329 double. Extra person: $30. AE, CB, DC, DISC, MC, V. Wheelchair accessible.*

Chateau Hotel
$–$$ French Quarter

One of the best buys in New Orleans, this hotel sits far enough off Bourbon Street to be quiet and intimate but is still within walking distance of virtually everything in the Quarter. Most of the rooms have antiques, giving the place a French provincial look. The rooms are a little on the dark side, but they're actually quite clean. The hotel includes a picturesque pool surrounded by a flagstone courtyard with chaise lounges. With your room fee you get a continental breakfast and newspaper. Seniors, be sure to ask about the 10 percent discount.

See map p. 124. 1001 Chartres St. (3 blocks from Jackson Square), New Orleans, LA 70116. ☎ *504-524-9636. Fax: 504-525-2989.* www.chateauhotel.com. *Parking: free. Rack rates: $89–$159 double. AE, CB, DC, MC, V. Wheelchair accessible but no bars in the bathrooms.*

Chateau Sonesta Hotel
$–$$$ French Quarter

Located in the former D. H. Holmes Department Store building — the 1913 facade has been retained — the Chateau Sonesta is one of the newest hotels in the Quarter. Flooding on Canal Street damaged its famous Clock Bar and required renovation of half of the hotel's rooms. Despite the older exterior, the rooms are large, if generic, and some feature balconies overlooking Bourbon Street. Among the noteworthy amenities are an outdoor pool, tropical courtyard and fountain, beauty salon, and health club. All rooms have minibars, and for those who can't escape their computers, the phones have dataports. Fans of the Pulitzer-Prize-winning novel, *A Confederacy of Dunces*, will be relieved to know that the statue of the book's unlikely hero, Ignatius Reilly, was safely stored during Katrina and is now back at the Canal Street entrance.

See map p. 124. 800 Iberville St. (at the corner of Dauphine St.), New Orleans, LA 70112. ☎ *800-SONESTA or 504-586-0800. Fax: 504-586-1987.* www.chateau sonesta.com. *Valet parking: $25. Rack rates: $99–$350 double. Extra person: $40. AE, CB, DC, DISC, MC, V. Wheelchair accessible.*

The Columns
$$–$$$ Uptown

The Columns is one of the few surviving examples of late-1880s Italianate homes designed by renowned local architect Thomas Sully (see two more Sully beauties at 4010 St. Charles Ave. and 1531 Carrollton Ave. from the streetcar). In 1915, a hurricane destroyed the original four-story tower but thankfully spared the rest. In 2005, Hurricane Katrina blew the roof off and caused considerable wind and water damage, though the gorgeous Victorian Lounge with its grand staircase and stained glass survived. This once magnificent home was in need of updating and maintenance prior to the storm, so this could be a blessing in disguise and renovations should be complete by the end of 2006. The room size reminds you that this hotel was a 19th-century home; some rooms are cozy in a way that suggests servants' quarters, while others are more expansive. I'm partial to the third-floor Pretty Baby Suite (named for the Brooke Shields movie filmed here), with its lovely Victorian decor. Its spacious, columned porch is a favorite meeting spot for locals, and hotel guests are encouraged to unwind on the huge second-floor balcony overlooking the avenue. Jazz bands sometimes serenade happy-hour patrons and always entertain the Sunday champagne brunch crowd.

See map p. 128. 3811 St. Charles Ave. (halfway between Louisiana and Napoleon avenues), New Orleans, LA 70115. ☎ *800-445-9308 or 504-899-9308. Fax: 504-899-8170.* www.thecolumns.com. *Parking: on-street available. Rack rates: $160–$230 double (includes southern breakfast). AE, MC, V.*

Dauphine Orleans Hotel
$$–$$$$ French Quarter

Katrina caused terrible roof damage to this luxurious establishment, though thankfully it's already been repaired and reopened. Here you'll find just the right blend of charming old-world history (ghosts have been sighted on the premises) and modern elegance, well removed from the madness of Bourbon Street. Lounge in one of the secluded courtyards or read for a spell in the guest library. Bird lovers also flocked to the hotel's buildings in the rear, which once served as the studio for John James Audubon. Among the eyebrow-raising amenities are a 24-hour fitness room, Nintendo for the kids, a Jacuzzi, an in-room safe for valuables, and complimentary French Quarter transportation. The staff can also hook you up with a babysitting service. Continental breakfast is served until 11 a.m., and complimentary tea is served every afternoon.

See map p. 124. 415 Dauphine St., New Orleans, LA 70116. ☎ *800-521-7111 or 504-586-1800. Fax: 504-586-1409.* www.dauphineorleans.com. *Valet parking: $18. Rack rates: $149–$269 double (include continental breakfast). Extra person: $20. Children under 17 free in parent's room. AE, CB, DC, DISC, MC, V. Wheelchair accessible.*

Doubletree Hotel New Orleans
$–$$$ Central Business District

Families will be happy to learn that this kid-friendly hotel has repaired its hurricane damage and reopened its doors. To their great credit, the staff took excellent care of guests stranded by the storm. Located at the foot of Canal Street, the Doubletree offers great views of the bustling Central Business District and the river. Sure, it's part of a chain, but the atmosphere is pleasant. Rooms are good-sized and comfortable; bathrooms are adequate. The hotel even features a rooftop pool that the kids can enjoy, as well as a fitness center. You also find a nice restaurant and a breakfast cafe on the first floor. The kicker for your small fry: Nintendo in every room and delicious chocolate-chip cookies when you check in. (They're so good, you may not want to share them with the kids.)

See map p. 128. 300 Canal St., New Orleans, LA 70130. ☎ *888-874-9074 or 504-581-1300. Fax: 504-212-3315.* http://doubletree.hilton.com. *Parking: valet, $22; self-parking next door at Harrah's Casino. Rack rates: $79–$229 double. Extra person: $20. AE, DC, DISC, MC, V. Wheelchair accessible.*

Fairmont Hotel
$–$$$ Central Business District

Hands down, this hotel is one of the city's most elegant and it promises to be even more so when it reopens on December 1, 2006, after extensive renovations and repairs. Given such amenities as a high-class restaurant,

New Orleans Accommodations

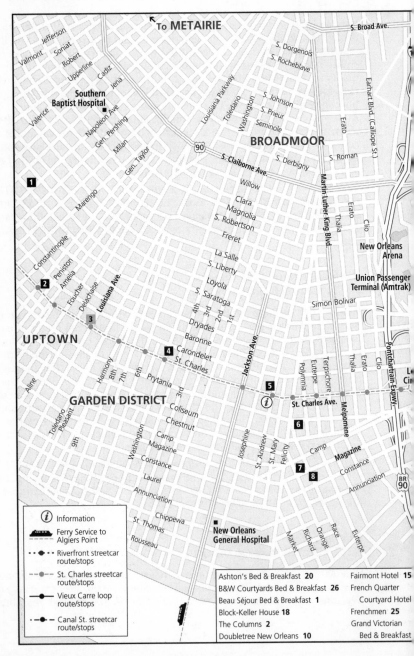

To METAIRIE

S. Broad Ave.

Jefferson
Valmont
Soniat
Robert
Upperline
Cadiz
Jena

S. Dorgenois
S. Rocheblave

Southern
Baptist Hospital

Napoleon Ave.
Gen. Pershing
Milan
Valence

Louisiana Parkway
Toledano
Washington
S. Johnson
S. Prieur
Seminole

Earhart Blvd. (Calliope St.)

Erato

Gen. Taylor

90

BROADMOOR

S. Claiborne Ave.
S. Derbigny
S. Roman

Marengo

Willow

1

Clara
Magnolia
S. Robertson
Freret
La Salle
S. Liberty
Loyola
S. Saratoga
4th 3rd 2nd 1st
Dryades
Baronne

Erato
Clio

New Orleans
Arena

Union Passenger
Terminal (Amtrak)

Martin Luther King Blvd.
Thalia

Simon Bolivar

Constantinople
Peniston
Amelia
Foucher
Delachaise

2

3

Louisiana Ave.

UPTOWN

Harmony
8th
7th
6th

Aline

Carondelet
St. Charles

4

Prytania
Pl.

GARDEN DISTRICT

Toledano
Pleasant
9th

Coliseum
Chestnut
Camp
Magazine
Constance
Laurel
Annunciation

Washington

Jackson Ave.

5

St. Charles Ave.

i

6

Josephine
St. Andrew
St. Mary
Felicity

Polymnia
Euterpe
Terpsichore
Melpomene

Thalia
Erato
Clio

Pontchartrain Expwy.

Le
Cir

7

8

Camp
Magazine
Constance
Annunciation

BR
90

Chippewa
St. Thomas
Rousseau

New Orleans
General Hospital

Market
Richard
Orange
Race

Euterpe

i Information

Ferry Service to
Algiers Point

• • ◆ • • Riverfront streetcar
route/stops

— ● — St. Charles streetcar
route/stops

—●— Vieux Carre loop
route/stops

— ● — Canal St. streetcar
route/stops

Ashton's Bed & Breakfast **20**		Fairmont Hotel **15**
B&W Courtyards Bed & Breakfast **26**		French Quarter
Beau Séjour Bed & Breakfast **1**		Courtyard Hotel
Block-Keller House **18**		Frenchmen **25**
The Columns **2**		Grand Victorian
Doubletree New Orleans **10**		Bed & Breakfast

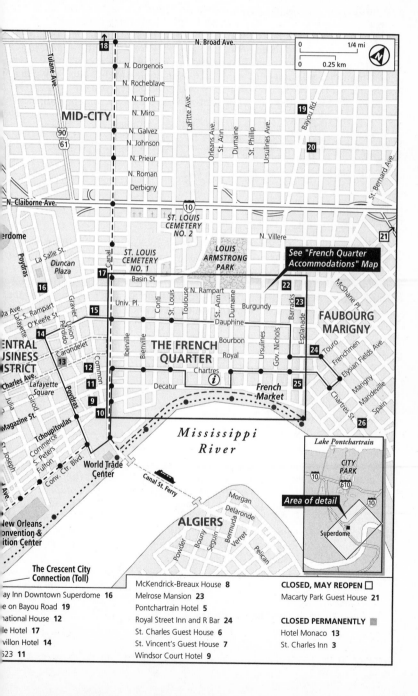

Tulane Ave.

N. Broad Ave.

0   1/4 mi
0   0.25 km

18

N. Dorgenois

N. Rocheblave

N. Tonti

MID-CITY

N. Miro

N. Galvez

N. Johnson

N. Prieur

N. Roman

Derbigny

90
61

LaFitte Ave.

Orleans Ave.

St. Ann

Dumaine

St. Phillip

Ursulines Ave.

Bayou Rd.

19

20

St. Bernard Ave.

N. Claiborne Ave.

10

ST. LOUIS
CEMETERY
NO. 2

N. Villere

21

erdome

Poydras

La Salle St.

*Duncan
Plaza*

16

ST. LOUIS
CEMETERY
NO. 1

Canal

17

Basin St.

**LOUIS
ARMSTRONG
PARK**

*See "French Quarter
Accommodations" Map*

McShane Pl.

Univ. Pl.

Conti

St. Louis

Toulouse

N. Rampart

St. Ann

Dumaine

Burgundy

Dauphine

22

Barracks

23

Esplanade

**FAUBOURG
MARIGNY**

Gravier

Union

Perdido

S. Rampart

O'Keefe St.

15

14

**CENTRAL
BUSINESS
DISTRICT**

Carondelet

13

12

Common

11

9

10

Iberville

Bienville

**THE FRENCH
QUARTER**

Bourbon

Royal

Chartres

Decatur

Ursulines

Gov. Nichols

Touro

24

Frenchmen

Elysian Fields Ave.

Marigny

Mandeville

Spain

*French
Market*

25

Chartres St.

26

Charles Ave.

*Lafayette
Square*

Julia

Girod

Poydras

Magazine St.

St. Joseph

Tchoupitoulas

Commerce

S. Peters

Fulton

Conv. Ctr. Blvd.

**World Trade
Center**

*Mississippi
River*

Lake Pontchartrain

Canal St. Ferry

Morgan

Delaronde

Bermuda

Verret

ALGIERS

Powder

Bouny

Seguin

Pelican

**CITY
PARK**

10

610

Area of detail

10

Superdome

**New Orleans
Convention &
Exhibition Center**

The Crescent City
Connection (Toll)

ay Inn Downtown Superdome **16**

e on Bayou Road **19**

national House **12**

le Hotel **17**

villon Hotel **14**

523 **11**

McKendrick-Breaux House **8**

Melrose Mansion **23**

Pontchartrain Hotel **5**

Royal Street Inn and R Bar **24**

St. Charles Guest House **6**

St. Vincent's Guest House **7**

Windsor Court Hotel **9**

CLOSED, MAY REOPEN ☐

Macarty Park Guest House **21**

CLOSED PERMANENTLY ▨

Hotel Monaco **13**

St. Charles Inn **3**

rooftop pool, workout area, and beauty shop, you may never want (or need) to leave. The hotel offers a lot of local lore: Huey Long used to hold court in the Sazerac bar on the first floor (see Chapter 16 for more information on this respected gathering place). President Bill Clinton often stayed here when in town. The rooms are as beautiful as you can expect for the price, and each one has its own fax machine for business travelers. A bonus for the tykes: Each room has Nintendo gear. If you visit during the winter, be sure to step inside the lobby to experience its one-of-a-kind holiday decorations.

See map p. 128. 123 Baronne St., New Orleans, LA 70112. ☎ 800-441-1414 or 504-529-7111. Fax: 504-529-4764. www.fairmont.com/neworleans. *Valet parking: $19. Rack rates: $99–$299 double. Children under 18 free in parents' room. AE, DC, DISC, MC, V. Wheelchair accessible.*

Frenchmen
$–$$$ Faubourg Marigny

High and dry, this friendly inn occupies two 1860s Creole townhouses and enjoys loyal repeat business from those who've fallen for its slightly funky charms. Rooms vary in size; some are downright tiny (if that's important, ask about size when making a reservation). Some rooms have private balconies; others are loft bedrooms with a sitting area. All are individually decorated and furnished with antiques. A tropical courtyard features a pool and hot tub.

See map p. 128. 417 Frenchmen St. (across the street from the Old U.S. Mint on Esplanade), New Orleans, LA 70116. ☎ 800-831-1781 or 504-948-2166. Fax: 504-948-2258. www.frenchmenhotel.com. *Free parking. Rack rates: $74–$299 double (includes breakfast). AE, DISC, MC, V.*

Grand Victorian Bed & Breakfast
$$–$$$$ Uptown

The name pretty much sums up this elegant B&B; the appointments here are grand, indeed, and remain intact post Katrina. Famed New Orleans architect Thomas Sully designed the house in 1893, and the proprietor Bonnie Rabe went to great lengths to restore the house to its original glory. The rooms vary in size but are uniformly elegant with handsome antique furniture; some bathrooms feature Jacuzzi tubs. A bountiful continental breakfast is offered either in the dining room or on the porte-cochere balcony. Business travelers can use available fax and copy machines, as well as dataports for computers.

See map p. 128. 2727 St. Charles Ave., New Orleans, LA 70130. ☎ 800-977-0008 or 504-895-1104. Fax: 504-896-8688. www.gvbb.com. *Parking: some on-street parking. Rack rates: $150–$350 double (includes breakfast; rates higher during special events). AE, DISC, MC, V. Wheelchair accessible.*

Holiday Inn-Chateau LeMoyne
$$–$$$ **French Quarter**

In contrast to its cousin in the Central Business District, this Holiday Inn sports an abundance of New Orleans–style character. Although the buildings are more than a century old (some of the rooms overlooking the courtyard are converted slave quarters), the historic ambience doesn't extend to the guest rooms, which are more or less standard for the chain, although comfortable. During its temporary Katrina-related closure, the hotel made some nice improvements, including new landscaping in the courtyard and around the pool, plus super service from staff who are happy to be back. It's just around the corner from Bourbon Street but nonetheless removed from the noise of the Quarter and convenient to Canal Street. The restaurant serves breakfast only, but you can order room service until 10 p.m. No video games in the rooms, but an outdoor heated pool and proximity to French Quarter attractions like the Aquarium of the Americas make this a good spot for the small fries.

See map p. 124. 301 Dauphine St. (just around the corner from the Deja Vu Bar & Grill), New Orleans, LA 70112. ☎ ***800-747-3279*** *or 504-581-1303. Fax: 504-523-5709.* www.sixcontinentshotels.com/holiday-inn. *Valet parking: $19. Rack rates: $159–$244 double. Extra person: $20. AE, CB, DC, DISC, MC, V. Wheelchair accessible.*

Holiday Inn-Downtown Superdome
$–$$ **Central Business District**

According to its Web site in August of 2006, "Guests will be required to sign a release form upon check-in due to post-hurricane conditions which are impacting the level of services and the length of occupancy we can provide at this time." That said, you might want to give the hotel a call to check on the status prior to making a reservation here. Accessibility is the key word when describing this hotel. Conveniently close to the Superdome and New Orleans Arena, it's a good bet for sports fans. It's also close to the city's business and financial centers and not too far from the French Quarter (though probably farther than you'd want to walk, especially at night). Each room has a balcony and a city view, but they're standard size for the chain and decorated in typical Holiday Inn style (not that there's anything wrong with that). The hotel also features a heated pool on the roof. In-room Nintendos and movies make this a good bet for kids.

See map p. 128. 330 Loyola Ave. (across from the Louisiana Supreme Court building), New Orleans, LA 70112. ☎ ***800-535-7830*** *or 504-581-1600. Fax: 504-522-0073.* www.holidayinndowntownsuperdome.com. *Parking: $11. Rack rates: $94–$209 double. Extra person: $20. Children 18 and under free in parent's room. AE, CB, DC, DISC, MC, V. Wheelchair accessible.*

Hotel Maison de Ville
$$–$$$ French Quarter

The Maison de Ville blends the charm and size of a B&B with the service and elegance of a five-star hotel, even post Katrina, when many hotels lost their staff and are having to make do with a smaller number. Perhaps that explains why Tennessee Williams was a frequent guest. Antiques are abundant, and a beautiful courtyard welcomes you with a fountain and banana trees. The rooms vary in size (some are downright tiny), so ask when you call, as price is no indication of what you get. In-room amenities include bathrobes, hair dryers, and other standard fare; two-bedroom cottages and suites have coffeemakers. Continental breakfast is served on a silver tray in your room, in the parlor, or on the patio. Complimentary sherry and port are served in the afternoon and evening. Unless you don't mind noisy streetscapes, ask for a room that doesn't overlook busy Bourbon. In fact, if peace and quiet is what you're after, I'd recommend the spacious Audubon Cottages, some of which have their own private courtyards.

See map p. 124. 727 Toulouse St. (½ block from Bourbon St.), New Orleans, LA 70130. ☎ *800-634-1600 or 504-561-5858. Fax: 504-528-9939.* www.maisondeville.com. *Valet parking: $18. Rack rates: $199–$249 double (includes continental breakfast and afternoon service of port and sherry). AE, DC, MC, V.*

Hotel Monteleone
$$–$$$ French Quarter

The largest and oldest hotel in the Quarter, the Hotel Monteleone is one of the best big hotels in New Orleans. Thankfully, Katrina completely spared it. The rooms come in a variety of styles, from smaller spaces to modern and comfortable family rooms to plush, antiques-filled suites. You can likely find a room here even when the rest of the city is booked. The hotel is famous for its extravagant lobby as well as for the revolving Carousel Bar, with its pleasing view of Royal Street. Laundry, a fitness center, Wi-Fi and a babysitting service top a list of amenities that also includes a heated rooftop pool and a hot tub. It's often voted the city's most romantic hotel and is one of only three hotels nationwide noted as a literary landmark by the Friends of the Library Association. Authors who have stayed here include William Faulkner, Richard Ford, Ernest Hemingway, Rebecca Wells, Eudora Welty, and Tennessee Williams

See map p. 124. 214 Royal St. (at the corner of Iberville), New Orleans, LA 70130. ☎ *800-535-9595 or 504-523-3341. Fax: 504-561-5803.* www.hotelmonteleone.com. *Valet parking: $27 cars, $32 SUVs. Rack rates: $199@nd$275 double. Extra person: $25. Children under 18 stay free in their parents' room. AE, CB, DC, DISC, MC, V.*

Hotel Provincial
$–$$$ French Quarter

Nestled in a series of 19th-century buildings, Hotel Provincial's atmosphere (including flickering gas lamps) makes it feel smaller and more intimate than it really is, more like a guesthouse than a hotel. Rooms have the high ceilings of an earlier age and are decorated with French and Creole antiques. The hotel is located in a quiet stretch of the French Quarter, so you can wind down in peace after a day of sightseeing. Local ghost hunters swear this place is haunted because it was used as a hospital during the Civil War. No damage occurred during Hurricane Katrina.

See map p. 124. 1024 Chartres St. (4 blocks from Jackson Square), New Orleans, LA 70116. ☎ *800-535-7922 or 504-581-4995. Fax: 504-581-1018.* www.hotel provincial.com. *Valet parking: $18. Rack rates: $79–$289 double. AE, CB, DC, DISC, MC, V. Wheelchair accessible.*

House on Bayou Road
$$–$$$$ Mid-City

Stepping into the luxurious quiet and elegance of this 18th-century home is like entering a time machine. The rooms and two cottages are individually decorated with antiques, though the small Creole cottage was damaged by a tree and is being repaired. The big barn was also destroyed by Katrina and the gardens suffered as well, though they have been replanted and will return as lush as ever. The staff serves a complimentary full plantation breakfast, and guests can help themselves to beverages in a minifridge throughout the day. Hostess Cynthia Reeves occasionally offers public cooking classes, for which guests receive a discount. Sadly, this historic treasure is for sale at the time of this writing, so its future as a B&B is uncertain.

See map p. 128. 2275 Bayou Rd. (1 mile from the Quarter along Esplanade; turn right at Bayou Road), New Orleans, LA 70119. ☎ *800-882-2968 or 504-945-0992. Fax: 504-945-0993.* www.houseonbayouroad.com. *Free off-street parking. Rack rates: $155–$320 double (includes breakfast). AE, MC, V.*

International House
$$–$$$$ Central Business District

Apparently, the youth and vigor of local developer Sean Cummings translates into sensual, state-of-the-art sanctuaries. The extraordinary International House — whose Beaux Arts building was constructed in 1906 to house the world's first trade center — now has a soul mate in Cummings' latest vision, Loft 523 (see "Runner-Up Hotels," later in this chapter). *Condé Nast Traveler-London* named International House one of the "Top 10 Boutique Hotels" in the United States, and I expect Loft 523 will soon follow suit. Suave locals savor drinks by candlelight in lovely *loa* (a voodoo word for deity or Holy Spirit). Guests can request any number of pampering packages, from the romantic "Southern Flower Bath" (massage for two is just the beginning) to "Voodoo Chic" (an authentic voodoo priestess transforms your room into a spiritual, personal altar). Busy moms and dads appreciate the "Kid Kit," a special welcome kit of New Orleans coloring books and crayons, a CD with lullabies, a cable movie schedule highlighting children's programming, daily delivery of the *Times-Picayune* turned to the kids' activities page, and surprise gift from local shopkeepers. Licensed, experienced nannies are available to watch little ones or take older kids on tours of local attractions. The hotel, along with Loft 523, are the only two in the city that are completely smoke free. There was no Katrina damage.

See map p. 128. 221 Camp St. (two blocks from the French Quarter), New Orleans, LA 70130. ☎ *800-633-5770 or 504-553-9550. Fax: 504-553-9560.* www.ihhotel.com. *Valet parking: $28. Rack rates: $149–$379 double. AE, DC, MC, V.*

Lafitte Guest House
$$–$$$ **French Quarter**

This eccentrically charming guesthouse is conveniently located on the quiet end of Bourbon Street, only a quick walk away from the action. Built in 1849, the three-story brick building features wrought-iron balconies on the second and third floors (the outside has been completely restored and looks great). There was substantial water damage post Katrina, so the guest house was closed for renovations and reopened in March 2006. The updating did not change the Victorian flair, though some are now more modern than others. Rooms vary in size; the penthouse suite (room 40) takes up the entire third floor and accommodates up to six people. Breakfast is brought to your room in the morning, and guests are invited to snack on wine and cheese for a "social" in the parlor in the afternoon. Dry cleaning and babysitting are also available. A sweet touch includes pralines on the pillows.

See map p. 124. 1003 Bourbon St. (at the corner of St. Philip), New Orleans, LA 70116. ☎ *800-331-7971 or 504-581-2678. Fax: 504-581-2677.* www.lafitteguesthouse. com. *Parking: $15. Rack rates: $159–$229 double (includes breakfast). Extra person: $25. AE, DC, DISC, MC, V.*

Lamothe House
$–$$$ **French Quarter**

If you don't like the shiny, homogenized feel of a chain hotel, the slightly faded, threadbare ambience of this place may be up your alley. Even the name suggests a Dickensian air of moth-eaten mustiness. A plain Creole-style facade belies the interior, which boasts a mossy, brick-lined court-yard with a fish-filled fountain and banana trees. You also find a swimming pool and hot-tub spa. The rooms, decorated with antiques, are well worn in a cozy way. Room sizes vary according to price, so ask when reserving. Minor renovations, such as swapping out old carpet, did not dampen its old-fashioned charm.

See map p. 124. 621 Esplanade Ave., New Orleans, LA 70116. ☎ *800-367-5858 or 504-947-1161. Fax: 504-943-6536.* www.lamothehouse.com. *Free parking. Rack rates: $74–$275 double (includes continental breakfast). AE, DISC, MC, V.*

Le Pavillon Hotel
$$ **Central Business District**

A unique blend of 17th-century grandeur and modern appointments makes this hotel truly elegant. The lobby is a dazzling array of chandeliers,

Oriental rugs, and detailed woodwork. A few of its windows were blown out by the storm but have since been replaced. Rooms of varying sizes feature original artwork and European and American antiques. Services include 24-hour room service, concierge, babysitting, laundry and dry cleaning, and a complimentary shoeshine. You can indulge yourself in complimentary hors d'oeuvres on weekday afternoons in the Gallery lounge or peanut-butter-and-jelly sandwiches served with chocolates and milk in the lobby each evening. Other amenities include a heated pool on the roof — whose damaged tiles were replaced — a fitness center, and a whirlpool spa.

See map p. 128. 833 Poydras St., New Orleans, LA 70112. ☎ ***800-535-9095** or 504-581-3111. Fax: 504-522-5543.* www.lepavillon.com. *Valet parking: $28. Rack rates: $149–$179 double. AE, CB, DC, DISC, MC, V. Wheelchair accessible.*

Le Richelieu Hotel
$–$$ French Quarter

Amazingly, the hotel reopened in April 2006 despite the water damage to 40 rooms when the roof sprung leaks during the storm. Located on the Esplanade edge of the Quarter, Le Richelieu offers convenience and tranquil old-world charm. Balconies overlooking the street or courtyard and pool accompany many rooms. You can order breakfast and lunch in the courtyard from the small in-house restaurant, or you can eat in the lounge adjacent to the pool. All rooms come with hair dryers, irons and ironing boards, and refrigerators. If you really want to go first class, ask for the VIP suite with its three bedrooms, kitchen, living area, dining area, and steam room. One of the nicest hotels in the Quarter in its price range, it's also the only hotel in the Quarter that offers free self-parking. Despite the surcharge, the hotel is very kid friendly with its away-from-Bourbon location and sunny pool. In fact, Sir Paul McCartney and his late wife, Linda, stayed here with their kids back in the day when he was working on a Wings album.

See map p. 124. 1234 Chartres St. (6 blocks from Jackson Square or 1 block from Esplanade), New Orleans, LA 70116. ☎ ***800-535-9653** or 504-529-2492. Fax: 504-524-8179.* www.lerichelieuhotel.com. *Free parking. Rack rates: $95–$180 double. Extra adult or child: $15. AE, CB, DC, DISC, MC, V.*

Maison Dupuy
$–$$$ French Quarter

Roof damage forced the Maison Dupuy to close temporarily, but it rebounded in April 2006. This picturesque hotel, made up of several town houses, has been the site of a cotton press (the first in the United States), a blacksmith shop, and a sheet-metal works. Today, it blends the clockwork efficiency of a large hotel with the attentive service of a B&B. You find desks and comfortable armchairs inside the large rooms, many of which have balconies that overlook the courtyard. On Sundays, the hotel restaurant serves a champagne and jazz brunch buffet. Dominique's is a nice place to wind down at the end of the day and enjoy award-winning cuisine. The hotel's amenities include a heated outdoor pool and Jacuzzi, an exercise room with treadmill and sauna, twice-daily maid service, and babysitting.

See map p. 124. 1001 Toulouse St. (2 blocks from Bourbon St.), New Orleans, LA 70112. ☎ *800-535-9177 or 504-586-8000. Fax: 504-525-5334.* www.maisondupuy.com. *Valet parking: $24 when available. Rack rates: $99–$269 double. AE, CB, DC, DISC, MC, V. Wheelchair accessible.*

McKendrick-Breaux House
$$ Lower Garden District

Closed a mere three weeks after Katrina, one of the city's best B&Bs played host to FEMA staff. It sits in the beautiful Garden District on a street known for its funky atmosphere and abundant dining and shopping options. The antiques-filled rooms are lovely and spacious (some bathrooms are just huge). Many rooms feature artwork by local artists for sale. The public areas are gorgeous and comfortable. Amenities include a hot tub, subtropical garden (fresh flowers may be waiting in your room), and a small pond whose resident turtle comes out for feedings. The owner provides perfect personal service while still giving guests plenty of privacy.

See map p. 128. 1474 Magazine St., New Orleans, LA 70130. ☎ *888-570-1700 or 504-586-1700. Fax: 504-522-7138.* www.mckendrick-breaux.com. *Free (but limited) parking. Rack rates: $135–$235 double (includes breakfast). AE, MC, V.*

Melrose Mansion
$$$ Faubourg Marigny

This restored mansion is intimate, romantic, and elegant — all adjectives that don't come cheap though lately, the service is not what it once was. Perhaps it's making do with a smaller staff post Katrina. The spacious accommodations have Victorian-era furnishings. Bed sizes, room sizes, and amenities vary; some have wet bars, Jacuzzi tubs, and separate seating rooms. A breakfast of muffins, fruit, and quiche is served in the parlor or in your room. The manse also offers a heated outdoor swimming pool and a menu of off-site services (Swedish massage, aromatherapy massage, manicures, and pedicures). This place is popular, so book as far in advance as possible, however, be aware that there is a strict cancellation policy.

See map p. 128. 937 Esplanade Ave. (at the corner of Burgundy), New Orleans, LA 70116. ☎ *800-650-3323 or 504-944-2255. Fax: 504-945-1794.* www.melrosegroup. com. *Valet parking: $23. Rack rates: $225–$250 double (includes champagne breakfast and cocktail hour). AE, DISC, MC, V.*

New Orleans Guest House
$–$$ French Quarter

This gay-friendly establishment, painted bright pink, sits just outside the Quarter, a stone's throw from Armstrong Park and Donna's (see Chapter 16). The 1848 Creole main house has spacious rooms, while the former slave quarters have accommodations that are even larger. Both buildings were completely renovated after roof damage thanks to Katrina. All rooms are tastefully decorated with different color schemes. The lush courtyard bravely withstood Katrina's winds and features a tropical garden with plenty of fresh greenery, a banana tree, and intricately carved old fountains (as well as beer and soda machines and a handy ice machine). Be sure to look for the resident kitty on the premises. Just as an FYI, the surrounding neighborhood is chancy at night the farther you get from Rampart, so take a cab rather than walk.

See map p. 124. 1118 Ursulines St. (1 block outside the Quarter just across Rampart St.), New Orleans, LA 70116. ☎ *800-562-1177 or 504-566-1177. Fax: 504-566-1179.* www.neworleans.com/nogh. *Free parking. Rack rates: $89–$119 double (includes continental breakfast). AE, MC, V.*

Omni Royal Orleans
$$–$$$$ **French Quarter**

This is one of the best chain hotels in the city because of its central location and excellent service. The hotel escaped any Katrina damage. Its richly decorated rooms aren't uniform in size, so communicate your needs when reserving. The one downside for families is that only a few rooms have two double beds, but the hotel can supply a rollaway bed. The rooftop swimming pool/observation deck appeals to kids, while parents appreciate the relatively cheap (and bonded) babysitting service. Amenities include terrycloth bathrobes (upon request), umbrellas, makeup mirrors, an extensively equipped fitness center, irons and ironing boards, and emergency mending and pressing services. The hotel's Rib Room is one of the city's premier restaurants (see Chapter 10).

See map p. 124. 621 St. Louis St., New Orleans, LA 70140. ☎ *800-THE-OMNI or 504-529-5333. Fax: 504-529-7089.* www.omniroyalorleans.com. *Valet parking: $28 plus tax. Rack rates: $169–$339 double. Children 18 and under free with parent. AE, CB, DC, DISC, MC, V. Wheelchair accessible.*

Pontchartrain Hotel
$–$$$$ **Garden District**

This cherished local landmark that dates back to the 1920s is normally an oasis of tranquility and beauty, but in the days following Katrina, what wasn't taken by looters were damaged by water from blown-out windows. Recent renovations have struck a nice balance between a worn, old-world feeling and a freshness of more modern hotels. Antique furnishings will no doubt be replaced. Rooms are comfortable and larger than most standard hotel rooms. Suites are named after the many celebrities of the '40s, '50s and '60s who stayed here, including Richard Burton, Carol Channing, Joan Fontaine and Mary Martin. The unique romantic ambience here is unmatched even in a city known for its atmosphere. Probably the biggest scandal was Rita Hayworth and Aly Kahn's secret trysts through neighboring suites. The hotel usually offers 24-hour room service and other amenities, however, room service, valet service and bell service are temporarily unavailable as the hotel continues to recuperate.

See map p. 128. 2031 St. Charles Ave., New Orleans, LA 70140. ☎ *800-777-6193 or 504-524-0581. Fax: 504-529-1165.* www.pontchartrainhotel.com. *Parking: $13. Rack rates: $95–$380 double. Extra person: $10; during special events $25. AE, CB, DC, DISC, MC, V. Wheelchair accessible.*

Prince Conti Hotel
$$ French Quarter

This small but friendly hotel boasts a congenial and helpful staff as well as a prime location just off Bourbon Street that isn't too noisy. The rooms are very comfortable, and many are furnished with antiques, but the bathrooms can be downright microscopic — toilets are practically on top of the sink. Travelers with kids should probably opt for the establishment's sister hotel, the Place d'Armes, which has a swimming pool and is farther removed from Bourbon Street. The Bombay Club, located on the first floor, is famous among locals for its genteel atmosphere and serves the best martinis in town (see Chapter 16). Fortunately, this hotel was basically untouched by Katrina.

See map p. 124. 830 Conti St. (at the corner of Dauphine St.), New Orleans, LA 70112. ☎ *800-366-2743 or 504-529-4172. Fax: 504-636-1046.* www.princecontihotel. com. *Valet parking: $20. Rack rates: $129–$199 double. AE, CB, DC, DISC, MC, V.*

Ramada Plaza The Inn on Bourbon Street
$$$ French Quarter

This nicely appointed hotel is located right on Bourbon Street and was spared by Katrina. As a result, its southern décor and amenities are sometimes lost on guests who just want to roll out of bed and into a bar or daiquiri shop. If you plan on sleeping while you're here (as opposed to just passing out), ask for an interior room, somewhat insulated from the street noise. But then you may not get a room with a balcony overlooking the action, which can be especially handy around Mardi Gras. (Decisions, decisions . . .) All rooms are standard in size, yet comfortable, and have king or double beds. Amenities include a fitness room, a business center, a jewelry shop, and a concierge who can put you in touch with babysitting services.

See map p. 124. 541 Bourbon St. (at the corner of Toulouse), New Orleans, LA 70130. ☎ *800-535-7891 or 504-524-7611. Fax: 504-568-9427.* www.innonbourbon.com. *Valet parking: $20. Rack rates: $219–$299 double. AE, CB, DC, DISC, MC, V. Wheelchair accessible.*

Ritz-Carlton New Orleans
$$–$$$$ French Quarter

Louisiana's only AAA Five Diamond luxury hotel stayed open in the weeks immediately following Katrina and as a result, has been closed for extensive renovations. The opening is anticipated for December 2006.

See map p. 124. 921 Canal St., New Orleans, LA 70112. ☎ ***800-241-3333*** *or 504-524-1331. Fax: 504-524-7233.* www.ritzcarlton.com/hotels/new_orleans.

Royal Sonesta
$$$–$$$$ French Quarter

The four-star Sonesta rightfully brags that it never closed during or after Katrina. It is always popular because it offers the best of both worlds: a Bourbon Street location and a gracious, classy hotel. Rooms are a bit more upscale than standard hotel rooms but otherwise pretty typical. Many feature balconies overlooking Bourbon Street, a side street, or a courtyard with a large pool. For a good night's sleep away from the noise of the street, request an inner room. The hotel features an exercise room, business center, excellent concierge service, and room service until 2 a.m. This hotel is the best place in the Quarter to catch a cab — they line up right at the corner.

See map p. 124. 300 Bourbon St. (3 blocks from Canal between Bienville and Conti), New Orleans, LA 70130. ☎ ***800-SONESTA*** *or 504-586-0300. Fax: 504-586-0335.* www.royalsonestano.com. *Parking: $23 cars, $25 SUVs. Rack rates: $249–$389 double. AE, CB, DC, DISC, MC, V. Wheelchair accessible.*

St. Charles Guest House
$ Lower Garden District

The guest house suffered Katrina damage, including fallen ceilings, broken siding and rampant looting. The owners cleaned up the mess and valiantly reopened in January 2006. Even with the renovations, character and economy are still the operative words here. The property consists of three separate, connected buildings, the oldest of which dates back about 100 years. Atmospheric touches balance out a general lack of modern conveniences; rooms don't include televisions or phones, though each building has its own pay phone (including one in a fascinating antique phone booth). Room sizes vary, with backpacker rooms available at the very low end, though these lack air conditioning and private baths. A continental breakfast is served in a cottagelike room that looks out on the courtyard and swimming pool.

See map p. 128. 1748 Prytania St., New Orleans, LA 70130. ☎ ***504-523-6556***. *Fax: 504-522-6340.* www.stcharlesguesthouse.com. *Parking: on-street available. Rack rates: $45–$95 double (includes continental breakfast). AE, MC, V.*

The Saint Louis
$$–$$$$ French Quarter

You find a splendid courtyard with a fountain at this small hotel right in the middle of the Quarter. Throughout the hotel, antique furniture, original oil paintings, and crystal chandeliers complement a Parisian-style decor. It was not affected by Katrina, however, it is undergoing a freshening up of the old-fashioned décor, with new carpeting, drapes and furniture. Rooms are standard but comfortable. Most face the courtyard and feature a balcony. The elegant, in-house Louis XVI restaurant serves fine French cuisine.

See map p. 124. 730 Bienville St. (½ block from Bourbon St.), New Orleans, LA 70130. ☎ *800-535-9111 or 504-581-7300. Fax: 504-679-5013.* www.stlouishotel.com. *Valet parking: $19. Rack rates: $145–$335 double. Children under 12 free in parent's room. AE, CB, DC, DISC, MC, V. Wheelchair accessible.*

Soniat House
$$$–$$$$ French Quarter

Located in a creative combination of three early 19th-century homes, Rodney and Frances Smith's tranquil hotel captures all the romance of the plantation era. It's no wonder *Travel + Leisure* once again pronounced Soniat House "one of the best hotels in the world." The rooms are comfortable, though bathrooms are small. Oriental rugs, fine French and English antiques, and beautiful paintings (some on loan from the New Orleans Museum of Art) furnish the rooms. More rooms (some have Jacuzzi bathtubs) are available in the annex of suites across the street. For an additional charge you can get a continental breakfast; the large, fluffy, baked-to-order biscuits and homemade strawberry preserves are worth the price alone. Thankfully, there was very little storm damage here.

See map p. 124. 1133 Chartres St. (across the street from the Old Ursuline Convent), New Orleans, LA 70116. ☎ *800-544-8808 or 504-522-0570. Fax: 504-522-7208.* www. soniathouse.com. *Valet parking: $25. Rack rates: $265–$325 double. Children under 13 not permitted. AE, MC, V.*

W French Quarter
$$$$ French Quarter

Katrina kept clear of this snazzy and upscale (in a nouveau-riche kind of way) W chain, which places as much emphasis on style as it does on service — both, just for the record, are quite good. Lounge in the comfort of your room's patio or balcony, or mingle with other beautiful people in the Living Room, the hotel's lounge. The "Whatever/Whenever" desk goes out of its way to accommodate, and ethernet connections, Internet-access televisions, dataports, and high-tech meeting rooms keep business travelers happy. Bacco, an acclaimed Italian/Creole restaurant, is on the premises (see Chapter 10). Pets are welcome guests for an additional $25 fee per night and a $100 non-refundable cleaning fee.

See map p. 124. 316 Chartres St., New Orleans, LA 70130. ☎ *800-448-4927 or 504-581-1200. Fax: 504-523-2910.* www.whotels.com/frenchquarter. *Valet parking: $30. Rack rates: $489–$514 double. Children under 16 free in parent's room. AE, CB, DC, DISC, MC, V. Wheelchair accessible.*

Windsor Court
$$–$$$$ Central Business District

Once voted by *Condé Nast Traveler* as the best hotel in North America, the Windsor is truly magnificent — from its Italian marble and antique furnishings to its impeccable service — and about as expensive as you'd expect. The hotel is 90 percent suites, though even the smaller guest rooms are spacious. All suites feature balconies or bay windows with views of the city or river. They also have fax machines, minibars, kitchenettes, living rooms, two dressing rooms, and marble bathrooms with plush robes, a hamper, high-end personal care items, and extra hair dryers. (Ask about amenities when you call because they aren't the same in each room.) The 24-hour suite service is much more luxurious than your average room service. Conference rooms are available for business travelers. The hotel also features a resort-size pool, a health club, laundry and dry cleaning, and in-room massage. If you can afford it, this hotel is the place to go for serious pampering. The hurricane caused minor damage that was quickly repaired.

See map p. 128. 300 Gravier St. (1 block from Canal St.), New Orleans, LA 70130. ☎ **888-596-0955** *or 504-523-6000. Fax: 504-596-4513.* www.windsorcourthotel. com. *Valet parking: $28. Rack rates: $195–$450 double; suites from $245. Children under 12 free in parent's room. AE, CB, DC, DISC, MC, V. Wheelchair accessible.*

Wyndham New Orleans at Canal Place
$$$$ French Quarter

High above the Quarter and the Mississippi River, the Wyndham was in no danger of flooding during Katrina. If you're a shopper, this large, luxurious hotel is the place for you. It's situated above the elegant Canal Place Shopping Center, which you can access directly by a glass elevator from the hotel's 11th floor lobby. The rooms have fine furnishings, including marble foyers and baths. The hotel boasts spectacular views of the Quarter and the Mississippi River, though none of the devastation wrought in other parts of the city. Business travelers are treated to amenities such as office supplies, a coffeemaker, and use of an in-room copier/printer/fax machine.

See map p. 124. 100 Iberville St. (1 block from the Aquarium), New Orleans, LA 70130. ☎ **800-996-3426** *or 504-566-7006. Fax: 504-553-5120.* www.wyndham.com/canal place. *Valet parking: $15. Rack rates: $159–$309 double. AE, CB, DC, DISC, MC, V. Wheelchair accessible.*

Runner-Up Hotels

If the suggestions in the previous section are all booked up, check out one of the options in this section. Some of these are just as charming and pleasant as the lodgings in the preceding listing, but they may be in a slightly out-of-the-way or dicey location (or I just ran out of space for them all). If you still can't find a room, see the "Finding the Best Room Rate" section earlier in this chapter for strategies on finding a last-minute bunk, listings of room-finding services specializing in hotels or B&Bs, and online-booking sources.

Beau Séjour Bed & Breakfast
$$–$$$ Uptown

See map p. 128. 1930 Napoleon Ave., New Orleans, LA, 70115. ☎ 888-897-9398 or 504-897-3746. Fax: 504-891-3340. www.beausejourbandb.com. *Parking: limited, on-street parking. Rack rates: $110–$175 double. AE, DISC, MC, V.*

French Quarter Courtyard Hotel
$$–$$$ Central Business District

See map p. 128. 1101 N. Rampart St. (a few blocks from the Quarter), New Orleans, LA 70116. Call ☎ 800-290-4233 or 504-522-7333. Fax: 504-522-3908. www.new orleans.com/fqch. *Valet parking: $15. Rack rates: $119–$289 double. Extra person: $15. Children 18 and under free with parent. AE, DC, DISC, MC, V. Wheelchair accessible.*

French Quarter Guest House
$$–$$$ French Quarter

See map p. 124. 623 Ursulines St., New Orleans, LA 70116. ☎ 800-887-2817 or 504-522-1793. Fax: 504-524-1902. Parking: $6 within walking distance. Rack rates: $79–$135 double (includes continental breakfast). Extra person: $10. AE, CB, DC, DISC, MC, V.

Hotel Villa Convento
$–$$ French Quarter

See map p. 124. 616 Ursulines St. (around the corner from the Old Ursuline Convent), New Orleans, LA 70116. ☎ 800-887-2817 or 504-522-1793. Fax: 504-524-1902. www.villaconvento.com. *Parking: $6 within walking distance. Rack rates: $89–$105 double (includes continental breakfast). Extra person: $10. AE, CB, DC, DISC, MC, V.*

LaSalle Hotel
$ Central Business District

See map p. 128. 1113 Canal St., New Orleans, LA 70112. ☎ 800-521-9450 or 504-523-5831. Fax: 504-525-2531. www.lhotellasalle.com. *Parking: $12. Rack rates: $85 double. Children under 12 free in parent's room. AE, DISC, MC, V.*

Loft 523
$$$–$$$$ Central Business District

See map p. 128. 523 Gravier St., New Orleans, LA 70112. ☎ 800-633-5770 or 504-200-6523. Fax: 504-200-6522. www.loft523.com. *Valet parking: $28. Rack rates: $259–$359 double; penthouse suites $859 and up. AE, DISC, MC, V.*

Macarty Park Guest House
$–$$ Bywater

It's unclear whether this beloved B&B will reopen. Note that it's located about ten minutes by cab from the Esplanade boundary of the Quarter.

See map p. 128. 3820 Burgundy St., New Orleans, LA 70117. ☎ *800-521-2790 or 504-943-4994. Fax: 504-943-4999.*

Olde Victorian Inn
French Quarter

This small but cozy B&B was a favorite, but new post-Katrina owners have yet to reopen it.

See map p. 124. 914 N. Rampart St., New Orleans, LA 70116 ☎ *800-725-2446 or 504-522-2446. Fax: 504-522-8646.*

Place d'Armes Hotel
$$–$$$$ French Quarter

See map p. 124. 625 St. Ann St. (just behind the Presbytere), New Orleans, LA 70118. ☎ *800-366-2743 or 504-524-4531. Fax: 504-571-2803.* www.placedarmes.com. *Parking: $20. Rack rates: $129–$199 double (includes continental breakfast). AE, CB, DC, DISC, MC, V. Wheelchair accessible.*

Royal Street Inn and R Bar
$–$$$ Faubourg Marigny

See map p. 128. 1431 Royal St., New Orleans, LA 70116. ☎ *800-449-5535 or 504-948-7499. Fax: 504-943-9880.* www.royalstreetinn.com. *Parking: free on-street parking with a visitor's permit (purchase at check-in). Rack rates: $100–$250 double (includes taxes and two drinks).*

St. Charles Inn
$ Garden District

Plans for the inn are unknown at press time.

See map p. 128. 3636 St. Charles Ave., New Orleans, LA 70115. ☎ *800-489-9908 or 504-899-8888. Fax: 504-899-8892.*

St. Vincent's Guest House
$ Lower Garden District

See map p. 128. 1507 Magazine St., New Orleans, LA 70130. ☎ *504-523-3411. Fax: 504-566-1518.* www.stvincentsguesthouse.com. *Parking: limited on-site parking. Rack rates: $59–$99 double (includes breakfast). Extra person: $10. AE, DC, DISC, MC, V. Wheelchair accessible.*

Index of Accommodations by Neighborhood

For neighborhood descriptions, see Chapter 8.

Bywater
Macarty Park Guest House ($–$$)

Central Business District
Doubletree Hotel New Orleans ($–$$$)
Fairmont Hotel ($–$$$)
French Quarter Courtyard
Hotel ($$–$$$)
Holiday Inn-Downtown Superdome
($–$$)
International House ($$–$$$$)
LaSalle Hotel ($)
Le Pavillon Hotel ($$)
Loft 523 ($$$–$$$$)
Windsor Court ($$–$$$$)

Faubourg Marigny
B&W Courtyards Bed &
Breakfast ($–$$)
Frenchmen ($–$$$)
Melrose Mansion ($$$)
Royal Street Inn and R Bar ($–$$$)

French Quarter
Bienville House ($–$$$$)
Bourbon Orleans Hotel ($$–$$$)
Chateau Hotel ($–$$)
Chateau Sonesta Hotel ($$–$$$)
Dauphine Orleans Hotel ($$–$$$$)
French Quarter Guest House ($$–$$$)
Holiday Inn-Chateau
LeMoyne ($$–$$$)
Hotel Maison de Ville ($$–$$$)
Hotel Monteleone ($$–$$$)
Hotel Provincial ($–$$)
Hotel Villa Convento ($–$$$)
Lafitte Guest House ($$–$$$)

Lamothe House ($–$$$)
Le Richelieu Hotel ($–$$)
Maison Dupuy ($–$$$)
New Orleans Guest House ($–$$)
Olde Victorian Inn ($$–$$$)
Omni Royal Orleans ($$–$$$$)
Place d'Armes Hotel ($$–$$$$)
Prince Conti Hotel ($$)
Ramada Plaza The Inn on Bourbon
Street ($$$)
Ritz-Carlton New Orleans ($$–$$$$)
Royal Sonesta ($$$–$$$$)
Saint Louis ($$–$$$$)
Soniat House ($$$–$$$$)
W French Quarter ($$$$)
Wyndham New Orleans at
Canal Place ($$$$)

Garden District
Pontchartrain Hotel ($–$$$$)
St. Charles Inn ($)

Lower Garden District
St. Charles Guest House ($)
St. Vincent's Guest House ($)

Mid-City
Ashton's Bed & Breakfast ($$)
Block-Keller House ($–$$)
House on Bayou Road ($$–$$$$)

Uptown
Beau Séjour Bed & Breakfast ($$–$$$)
The Columns ($$–$$$)
Grand Victorian Bed & Breakfast
($$–$$$$)

Index of Accommodations by Price

$

B&W Courtyards Bed & Breakfast (Faubourg Marigny)
Bienville House (French Quarter)
Block-Keller House (Mid-City)
Chateau Sonesta Hotel (French Quarter)
Chateau Hotel (French Quarter)
Doubletree Hotel New Orleans (Central Business District)
Fairmont Hotel (Central Business District)
Frenchmen (Faubourg Marigny)
Holiday Inn-Downtown Superdome (Central Business District)
Hotel Provincial (French Quarter)
Hotel Villa Convento (French Quarter)
Lamothe House (French Quarter)
LaSalle Hotel (Central Business District)
Le Richelieu Hotel (French Quarter)
Macarty Park Guest House (Bywater)
Maison Dupuy (French Quarter)
New Orleans Guest House (French Quarter)
Pontchartrain Hotel (Garden District)
Royal Street Inn and R Bar (Faubourg Marigny)
St. Charles Guest House (Lower Garden District)
St. Charles Inn (Garden District)
St. Vincent's Guest House (Lower Garden District)

$$

Ashton's Bed & Breakfast (Mid-City)
B&W Courtyards Bed & Breakfast (Faubourg Marigny)
Beau Séjour Bed & Breakfast (Uptown)
Bienville House (French Quarter)
Block-Keller House (Mid-City)
Bourbon Orleans Hotel (French Quarter)
Chateau Hotel (French Quarter)
Chateau Sonesta Hotel (French Quarter)
The Columns (Uptown)
Dauphine Orleans Hotel (French Quarter)
Doubletree Hotel New Orleans (Central Business District)
Fairmont Hotel (Central Business District)
Frenchmen (Faubourg Marigny)
French Quarter Courtyard Hotel (Central Business District)
French Quarter Guest House (French Quarter)
Grand Victorian Bed & Breakfast (Uptown)
Holiday Inn-Chateau LeMoyne (French Quarter)
Holiday Inn-Downtown Superdome (Central Business District)
Hotel Maison de Ville (French Quarter)
Hotel Monteleone (French Quarter)
Hotel Provincial (French Quarter)
Hotel Villa Convento (French Quarter)
House on Bayou Road (Mid-City)
International House (Central Business District)
Lafitte Guest House (French Quarter)
Lamothe House (French Quarter)
Le Pavillon Hotel (Central Business District)
Le Richelieu Hotel (French Quarter)
Macarty Park Guest House (Bywater)
Maison Dupuy (French Quarter)
New Orleans Guest House (French Quarter)
Olde Victorian Inn (French Quarter)
Omni Royal Orleans (French Quarter)
Place d'Armes Hotel (French Quarter)
Prince Conti Hotel (French Quarter)
Pontchartrain Hotel (Garden District)
Ritz-Carlton New Orleans (French Quarter)
Royal Street Inn and R Bar (Faubourg Marigny)
Saint Louis (French Quarter)
Windsor Court (Central Business District)

$$$

Beau Séjour Bed & Breakfast (Uptown)
Bienville House (French Quarter)
Bourbon Orleans Hotel (French Quarter)
Chateau Sonesta Hotel (French Quarter)
The Columns (Uptown)
Dauphine Orleans Hotel (French Quarter)
Doubletree Hotel New Orleans (Central Business District)
Fairmont Hotel (Central Business District)
French Quarter Courtyard Hotel (Central Business District)
French Quarter Guest House (French Quarter)
Frenchman (Faubourg Marigny)
Grand Victorian Bed & Breakfast (Uptown)
Holiday Inn-Chateau LeMoyne (French Quarter)
Hotel Maison de Ville (French Quarter)
Hotel Monteleone (French Quarter)
Hotel Provincial (French Quarter)
House on Bayou Road (Mid-City)
International House (Central Business District)
Lafitte Guest House (French Quarter)
Lamothe House (French Quarter)
Loft 523 (Central Business District)
Maison Dupuy (French Quarter)
Melrose Mansion (Faubourg Marigny)
Olde Victorian Inn (French Quarter)
Omni Royal Orleans (French Quarter)
Place d'Armes Hotel (French Quarter)
Pontchartrain Hotel (Garden District)
Ramada Plaza The Inn on Bourbon Street (French Quarter)
Ritz-Carlton New Orleans (French Quarter)
Royal Sonesta (French Quarter)
Royal Street Inn and R Bar (Faubourg Marigny)
Saint Louis (French Quarter)
Soniat House (French Quarter)
Windsor Court (Central Business District)

$$$$

Bienville House (French Quarter)
Dauphine Orleans Hotel (French Quarter)
Grand Victorian Bed & Breakfast (Uptown)
House on Bayou Road (Mid-City)
International House (Central Business District)
Loft 523 (Central Business District)
Omni Royal Orleans (French Quarter)
Place d'Armes Hotel (French Quarter)
Pontchartrain Hotel (Garden District)
Ritz-Carlton New Orleans (French Quarter)
Royal Sonesta (French Quarter)
Saint Louis (French Quarter)
Soniat House (French Quarter)
W French Quarter (French Quarter)
Windsor Court Hotel (Central Business District)
Wyndham New Orleans at Canal Place (French Quarter)

Chapter 11

Dining and Snacking in New Orleans

. . . .

In This Chapter

▶ Assessing restaurant activity post-Katrina

▶ Dishing up where the locals eat

▶ Navigating reservation and dress code policies

▶ Discovering the best restaurants in town

▶ Sampling the best places for snacks, sandwiches, and sweets

. . . .

*N*ew Orleans clings firmly to its reputation as a mecca for great food. The city's port-town status, unique ethnic mix, and proximity to Cajun Country all make it a combustible culinary-proving ground. Locals are happily spoiled by the rich tradition of good food, from crawfish étouffée to oyster po' boys to shrimp Creole. After living in exile in Illinois for a number of months after Katrina, I realized how spoiled I've been. Food elsewhere tastes so bland in comparison, and the only solution I've found so far is hot sauce. Almost everything you eat in New Orleans is fried or served in a rich, buttery sauce — or both. If this horrifies you, you've picked the wrong place to visit. Although the city offers some healthy alternatives, if you skip the decadent pleasures of a New Orleans meal, you're missing the point. Enjoy yourself here; eat responsibly when you get home.

Assessing Katrina's Effect on the Dining Scene

The dining scene did not change much from a tourist perspective because most of the restaurants you'll probably visit are on higher ground and did not flood. But from a local perspective, the difference is drastic. Steakhouses and soul food joints seemed to take a disproportionate beating. Some, like Commander's Palace, were closed for an extended period but then reopened (in their case, to great fanfare) whereas others, sadly, are permanently closed. Chateaubriand Steak House in Mid-City, Marisol in Faubourg Marigny, and Maximo's in the French Quarter all closed after their owners moved elsewhere. Katie's in Mid-City, where I used to go for shrimp or oyster po-boys, was flooded

Restaurants whose future remains uncertain

Bella Luna (914 N. Peters St., French Quarter; ☎ 504-529-1583; www.bellaluna restaurant.com). The City of New Orleans owns the building and no repairs to the roof have been made yet, so chef-proprietor Horst Pfiefer says he cannot reopen, though plans may change. For now he stays busy with his catering facility, The Foundry, in the Warehouse District.

Camellia Grill (626 S. Carrollton Ave., Carrollton/Uptown; ☎ 504-866-9573). The restaurant was closed before Katrina and is on the market. Let's hope the buyer returns this popular diner to its former glory and starts serving up its famous pecan waffles again soon.

Christian's (3835 Iberville St., Mid-City; ☎ 504-482-4924; www.christians restaurantneworleans.com). The Bergeron family is not sure whether they will reopen this restaurant, housed in a pink-pastel former church. If they do, the damage was so extensive that there may be some major changes.

Dooky Chase (2301 Orleans Ave., Treme; ☎ 504-821-2294; www.dookychase restaurant.com). Flood damage and looting has not kept owner/chef Leah Chase from promising that her famous Creole cooking and soul food will return. Menu highlights once included excellent gumbo, crispy fried chicken, and some of the city's best hot bread pudding — it's worth calling during your visit to see if it's reopened yet. Take a cab if you go, as the neighborhood's a bit dicey.

Dunbar's (4927 Freret St., Uptown; ☎ 504-899-0734). After flooding very badly, it's unclear whether his great soul food restaurant will return. Perhaps as the area around it recuperates, the owner will take steps to rebuild.

Gabrielle (3201 Esplanade Ave., Mid-City, ☎ 504-948-6233; www.gabrielle restaurant.com). This crowd-pleasing Parisian cafe, owned by Greg and Mary Sonnier, remained dry but a fallen tree punctured the roof and caused a lot of water damage anyway. They are not coming back to Mid-City but are contemplating a move to Uptown end of 2006.

Mandina's (3800 Canal St., Mid-City; ☎ 504-482-9179). As most locals know, the building housing Mandina's was not in great shape before the storm, but that was part of this beloved neighborhood restaurant's charm. Six feet of water didn't help the structure. However, the owners went against the odds and decided to renovate. They hope to reopen before the spring of 2007. See p. 182.

Ruth's Chris (711 N. Broad St., Mid-City; ☎ 504-486-0810; www.ruthschris.com). This is the original location for Ruth's Chris, but the company has long outgrown its family roots, so sentimentality no longer influences this restaurant's fate. I don't think it will reopen as the neighborhood was iffy before and now that it's damaged so badly, it will be a recovery zone for quite some time.

with 6 ft. of water; it was repaired but won't reopen. Michael's Mid-City Grill, which once offered great burgers and jukebox entertainment (and a daredevil $150 burger), will not return — a huge loss, in my opinion. Many restaurants in my neighborhood of Lakeview were destroyed, including Sid-Mar's, which had been built on land that was surrounded by water on three sides; I guess it was inevitable that it would be destroyed by a hurricane, but I had hoped that it would not be in my life-time. One of my saddest moments was trying to visit the restaurant and finding that all that remained of the place was the pilings (which the Army Corps of Engineers now owns as it seized the land near 17th Street Canal breach).

The list goes on and on. There are too many to name here, but you'll find that we've left all now-closed restaurants from our last edition on the maps (marked "closed permanently"), so you can get a glimpse of Katrina's effect. But again, remember it is neighborhoods outside of many of these maps that were hit the hardest.

And there are some whose fate could go either way. Owners of those establishments are faced with difficult questions: "Should I stay or go? If I rebuild, will the neighborhood return, too? Will visitors be willing to drive through areas in various stages of rebuilding to come to my restau-rant?" You'll find a box marked "Restaurants whose future remains uncertain" in this section. I've optimistically included as many restau-rants from the last edition as I could, and we've left them on the maps as well (marked "closed, may reopen"), in case they do reopen.

Those restaurants that are open still have their challenges, so please try to be understanding if they have limited menus, fewer waitstaff, and shorter hours of operation.

Getting the Dish on the Local Scene

National dining trends eventually show up in New Orleans, but hot chefs here mostly set their own trends, employing ingredients and methods from different cuisines and creating marvelous new combinations. In the aftermath of Katrina, I think New Orleans chefs take even more pride in how unique their menus are. More importantly, locals and tourists alike have an even better appreciation for it. As in Cajun and Creole cooking, fusion is a large part of what food in New Orleans is all about. Influences as varied as Spanish, Italian, West Indian, African, and Native American contribute to a wide range of choices — from eclectic gourmet dishes to down-home Southern cooking. (For additional information on local cui-sine, see Chapter 3.)

Thanks to the ubiquitous presence of celebrity chef and Food Network superstar Emeril Lagasse, Louisiana cooking has a higher profile than ever. His restaurants, **Emeril's, Nola,** and **Emeril's Delmonico,** draw large crowds looking for daring and creative Creole/New American cooking (and maybe a celebrity sighting or two). However, Lagasse is far from the only popular chef in New Orleans. Bayona's Susan Spicer, René Bistrot's René Bajeux, Restaurant August's John Besh, Upperline's Kenneth Smith, and Brigtsen's Frank Brigtsen are just a few of the names you're likely to hear bandied about by local foodies. One name I can almost guarantee you'll hear often in your gastronomic adventures is Brennan — with restaurants such as Bacco, Brennan's, Commander's Palace, Mr. B's Bistro, and Palace Café, this family is the dining scene's answer to the music scene's Neville and Marsalis dynasties.

The French Quarter

Although the Quarter is widely regarded as tourist headquarters, it has an almost unbelievable number of standout restaurants that locals regularly patronize. A list of the best is much too long to run here, but a partial sampling must include classy favorites such as **Arnaud's** and **Brennan's,** as well as wackier (and much cheaper) options such as **Café Maspero** and **Clover Grill.** Plenty of great spots exist in between those extremes, from the contemporary Italian fare at **Irene's Cuisine,** to the romantic ambience at **Bayona.**

Central Business and Warehouse Districts

Emeril's is one of the biggest names on the local scene — and with good reason. Locals also flock to **The New Orleans Grill** for one of the most elegant dining experiences in the city. On the other end of the scale, **Mother's** exemplary sandwiches are cheap (and a calorie-counter's nightmare), and **Taqueria Corona**'s mouth-watering combination platters (*uno y medio* with a shrimp *flauta* is my favorite) offer plenty of food for little money.

Carrollton, Garden District and Uptown

In the recent past, you could sum up your argument for the Garden District as a gourmet hot spot in just two words: **Commander's Palace.** After all, the James Beard Association voted it best restaurant in the United States a few years back — the food-industry equivalent of receiving an Oscar. Commander's reopened in October 2006 after a complete renovation. Also try **Restaurant August** and **René Bistrot.** Uptown, savvy gourmands flock to **Upperline** for chef Kenneth Smith and proprietor JoAnn Clevenger's creative Creole collaborations and **Brigtsen's** in the Riverbend. Farther out, but worth the trip, **Jacques-Imo's** has such an incredible vibe that locals endure as much as an hour-and-a-half wait — the highest praise imaginable in this town.

Mid-City

This neighborhood was absolutely devastated by flooding from Hurricane Katrina and parts of it remain in bad shape. As you can imagine, all of its restaurants suffered greatly as a result, but a surprising number are trying to make it, even without much of a resident population yet. The owner of the Creole **Dooky Chase** is committed to repairing and hopes to open in 2007. Before the storm, Mid-City's restaurant reputation was heating up thanks to the reinstated Canal Streetcar. On the Carrollton spur, you once found Gérard and Eveline Crozier's welcome return to fine dining with **Chateaubriand Steakhouse** and the newest location of popular Vietnamese chain **Pho Tau Bay,** but sadly, both are now closed for good. (The Pho Tau Bay on the West Bank did not flood and is still open.) At the intersection of Canal and Carrollton, **Juan's Flying Burrito** is back with its servers lip-synching speed metal and hip-hop. The owners of **Christian's,** which served French/Creole in a converted church, don't yet know if they will reopen. Everyone loved **Gabrielle** for its French cafe ambience and Creole/Cajun menu, however, hurricane damage forced the owners to consider relocating it Uptown. Serious steak lovers once herded into the original **Ruth's Chris Steak House** (where the popular chain originated), but it seems that the Broad Street location is doomed (see the box at the beginning of this chapter for an update). Personally, I could never decide which place I preferred for a po' boy — cheery, folksy **Katie's** or blue-collar, mom 'n' pop **Liuzza's,** home of the giant frozen beer mug. As long as they both come back, I promise to alternate visits to ensure they both get much-deserved support.

A word on tourist spots

Aside from the really obvious tourist draws, locals don't go out of their way to avoid too many restaurants. You *will,* however, find a disproportionate ratio of tourists to locals at such Cajun-leaning establishments as **K-Paul's, Michaul's,** and **Mulate's,** which isn't necessarily a reflection on the food itself. A large proportion of tourists usually just means that a restaurant is geared more toward visitor-friendly standby dishes, while locals familiar with the basics seek out more inventive fare. (In all fairness, **K-Paul's** is arguably an exception to this rule; its high tourist count has a lot to do with chef Paul Prudhomme's familiar name and French Quarter location.)

Making reservations

When a review recommends that you reserve a table at a restaurant, it generally means for dinner. You can usually get a table for two at lunch without having to wait too long (if at all). With a couple of exceptions (noted in the reviews), the same goes for breakfast.

Restaurants in New Orleans do a very brisk business except during the hot summer months. Consequently, make reservations before you even leave home if you want to dine at a certain restaurant at a particular time. You may need to reserve a table a month or more in advance, particularly during Mardi Gras and Jazz Fest, if you want to eat at one of the most famous restaurants. If you forgot to make reservations, arrive early — before noon (or even before 11:30 a.m.) for lunch and before 6:30 p.m. for dinner.

Dressing to dine

Legend has it that Antoine's restaurant once turned away Mick Jagger because he wasn't wearing a jacket. Whether that's true or not, top-of-the-line restaurants such as **Arnaud's** and **Commander's Palace** obviously require the full jacket-and-tie treatment. Other than that, though, New Orleans, being a tourist-dependent market, is pretty casual about dress codes. Most serious dining spots require the much less stringent "business casual" look (a nice shirt and a jacket or blazer; jeans are usually allowed, but only if they're in good condition — if you're uncertain, call the restaurant ahead of time). Even the best restaurants allow casual wear at lunch. And obviously, no one is going to kick you out of a corner po' boy shop for wearing shorts, flip-flops, and a Hawaiian print shirt. Check the individual restaurant listings that follow for special dress requirements.

Lighting up

When it comes to smoking in restaurants, New Orleans is slightly more lenient than the rest of the United States. Although many restaurants prohibit smoking or relegate it to certain sections (notably in the French Quarter, where space and atmosphere are at a premium), many others still tolerate it. If smoking is a priority for you, call ahead to find out the restaurant's policy.

Rewarding good service: Tips on gratuities

A general guideline for tipping is 15 to 20 percent, depending upon the level of service and quality of experience you receive. Because most restaurants are just getting by with a smaller staff, please be sure to generously tip those servers who make you happy. And if your service is somewhat slow, take a look around the dining room. Your server might be responsible for more tables than usual and doing the best he or she can. In fact, a few months after the storm, I went to dinner with some friends and clearly, the waitstaff was few and far between despite full tables and many more people waiting to be seated. So my friend's boyfriend helped bus tables! If he didn't already have a girlfriend, I guarantee you he would've gotten one soon enough before the night was over because he was a hero in the eyes of many. As more people return to the city and restaurants hire more staff, service will continue to improve.

Trying some of New Orleans's ethnic eats

As if the roulette wheel of local culinary combinations wasn't enough, New Orleans, like most mid-sized cities, also offers its fair share of ethnic fare. Although I don't go into great detail, check out a few of the best spots with this highly selective and subjective list.

Chinese: Five Happiness (3605 S. Carrollton Ave., Carrollton, ☎ 504-482-3935). Badly flooded by Katrina but now open.

Cuban: Liborio Cuban Restaurant (321 Magazine St., Lower Garden District, ☎ 504-581-9680). Reopened in October 2005 after cleaning up a huge mess from the defrosted refrigerators and freezer.

Japanese: Horinoya (920 Poydras St., Central Business District, ☎ 504-561-8914) and **Sekisui Samurai** (239 Decatur St., French Quarter, ☎ 504-525-9595), open for business.

Mediterranean: Moonlight Café (1921 Sophie Wright Place, Lower Garden District, ☎ 504-522-7313), badly looted after the storm, but owner Hassan Khaleghi is determined to return.

Mexican: Juan's Flying Burrito (2018 Magazine St., Lower Garden District, ☎ 504-569-0000; 4724 S. Carrollton Ave., Mid-City, ☎ 504-486-9950), both up and running despite flooding at Mid-City location, and **Taqueria Corona** (857 Fulton St., Warehouse District, ☎ 504-524-9805; 5932 Magazine St., Uptown, ☎ 504-897-3974), also up and running.

Middle Eastern: Lebanon's Cafe (1500 S. Carrollton Ave., Carrollton, ☎ 504-862-6200), and **Mona's** (3901 Banks St., Mid-City, ☎ 504-482-7743; 4126 Magazine St., Uptown, ☎ 504-894-9800; 3149 Calhoun St., Uptown, ☎ 504-861-2124), the Mid-City location went up in flames a couple years ago, possibly by an arsonist, but the restaurant prevailed. Then Katrina came and the building flooded with 5 feet of water, once again forcing the owners to decide whether they want to rebuild it yet again or focus on their other locations. They opted to save the Mid-City location and it is now open for business. Hurrah!

Thai: Basil Leaf (1438 S. Carrollton Ave., Carrollton, ☎ 504-862-9001), open for business.

Vietnamese: Lemon Grass Restaurant (217 Camp St., Central Business District, ☎ 504-523-1200) and **Pho Tau Bay** (216 N. Carrollton Ave., Mid-City, ☎ 504-485-SOUP; 1565 Tulane Ave., Central Business District, ☎ 504-524-4669), only the location on the West Bank is open as the two New Orleans locations flooded.

Trimming the Fat from Your Budget

I'm sure you won't be shocked to discover that many tourist places — especially in the French Quarter — charge inflated prices for "signature New Orleans dishes" simply because they can. Keep in mind that many

New Orleans specialties, such as jambalaya, étouffée, red beans and rice, muffulettas, and po' boy sandwiches were made with common ingredients out of economic necessity. Any place that charges you a ton of money for any of these is just ripping you off. You can find incredibly tasty versions of these staples very cheaply at any number of places, so go elsewhere.

Another way to save some dough without sacrificing the quality of your New Orleans dining experience is by visiting the city's fancier restaurants for lunch rather than dinner. Lunch menus almost always offer more-affordable versions of a particular institution's signature dishes. Eating lunch at the more expensive restaurants frees you up to frequent looser, less-expensive spots, such as Clover Grill or Franky and Johnny's for dinner.

Conversely, you may want to skip lunch altogether, fortifying yourself with a few snacks during your afternoon sightseeing. Of course, granola bars and the odd piece of fruit can only take you so far, in which case you can bend this idea slightly, maybe grabbing a Lucky Dog or a quick po' boy.

New Orleans's Best Restaurants

Grab your fork and get ready to loosen your belt a notch or two because this section explores New Orleans restaurants. I start with my picks of the best and/or most popular restaurants in the city, arranged alphabetically. The price range, neighborhood, and type of cuisine follow the restaurant name. After that, use the indexes to help you identify what best suits your tastes and needs.

The reviews also make note of which restaurants are wheelchair accessible. Call ahead to inquire, however, because some of these places may still be inconvenient — for instance, tables may be too close together.

One further note: Even if this whole book covered nothing but New Orleans restaurants, it still couldn't do justice to the many fine establishments in the city and its outskirts. These reviews are necessarily brief and to the point. Because space constraints prohibit me from highlighting every worthy establishment, this chapter is merely meant to provide a representative sampling, filled with no-brainers, conventional-wisdom choices, and my personal faves.

What the $ symbols mean

Dining in New Orleans ranges from low-key and friendly to white-gloved formal. To let you know what to expect price-wise, the restaurant listings in this chapter are accompanied by a dollar symbol ($), which gives you an idea of what a complete meal (including appetizer, entree, dessert, one drink, taxes, and tip) costs per person. Most listings contain more than one symbol — for example, $–$$ — to indicate the general price range you're likely to encounter at each restaurant. Aside from price ranges, the difference between one ranking and the next also reflects extras such as location, reputation, type of cuisine, atmosphere, interior, service, and view. Check out Table 11-1 for the lowdown on the dollar symbols.

Table 11-1	Key to Restaurant Dollar Signs
Dollar Sign(s)	*Price Range*
$	Less than $15
$$	$15–$30
$$$	$31–$45
$$$$	$46 or more

New Orleans's Top Restaurants from A to Z

Antoine's
$$–$$$$ **French Quarter   FRENCH/CREOLE**

Amazingly, Antoine's is still owned and operated by the family that founded it 160 years ago. The restaurant suffered wind and rain damage during Katrina; however, most of the building is now restored and ready to be of service. The biggest loss is the tragic passing of 71-year-old maitre'd Cliff Lachney, who tried to ride out hurricane Katrina at home with his handicapped son. Like so many others, they perished in flood waters. If you go to Antoine's, be sure to offer a toast in his memory, even if you never had the luck to meet him. The menu features old-world dishes such as *pompano* Pontchartrain (the grilled fillet is topped with tender crab-meat sautéed in butter) and *trout amandine.* The 15 dining rooms, some of which are still closed for repairs, run the gamut from plain to opulent, and some sort of caste system governs the seating process. (The front dining room is "reserved" for tourists, and locals are aghast to be mistakenly seated here.) Antoine's gets away with this by virtue of its place in New Orleans culinary history — it's the birthplace of Oysters Rockefeller. Save room for the enormous baked Alaska; after William Faulkner received the Nobel Prize for literature, he was served one inscribed "the Ignoble Prize."

See map p. 156. 713 St. Louis St. (a half block from Bourbon Street). ☎ *504-581-4422.* www.antoines.com. *Make reservations at least a week in advance for the weekend. Main courses: $22–$56 (most under $25). AE, DC, MC, V. Open: Mon and Thu–Sat 5:30–9:30 p.m.; Sun 11 a.m.–2 p.m. Jackets required for dinner. Wheelchair accessible.*

French Quarter Dining

Antoine's **11**
Arnaud's **17**
Bacco **13**
Bayona **16**
The Bistro at Maison de Ville **10**
Brennan's **15**
Café Maspero **7**
Court of Two Sisters **9**
Galatoire's **19**
Irene's Cuisine **4**
K-Paul's Louisiana Kitchen **14**
Mr. B's Bistro **20**
Olivier's **22**

Palace Café **21**
Peristyle **1**
Port of Call **2**
Ralph & Kacoo's **8**
Rib Room **12**
Tujague's **6**

CLOSED, MAY REOPEN ◇
Bella Luna **5**

CLOSED PERMANENTLY ◆
Maximo's **3**
Mike Anderson's Seafood **18**

Arnaud's
$$–$$$ French Quarter CREOLE

Founded in 1918, Arnaud's is a frequently overlooked classic New Orleans restaurant, which bodes well for locals. The restaurant sustained very minor storm damage. Unlike some other old-line haunts, the food's quality hasn't diminished with age, and neither has the decor, which features antique ceiling fans, flickering gas lamps, and dark wood paneling. The restaurant consists of 12 buildings connected by stairs and hallways — it sprawls leisurely over an entire city block. Start with the signature shrimp Arnaud marinated in tangy remoulade sauce, followed by Creole bouillabaisse or filet mignon (the latter rivals most local steakhouses). Only the most serious chocoholics can manage to devour every sinful spoonful of the Chocolate Devastation dessert. Before or after your meal, head upstairs to wander the spooky, dimly lit Mardi Gras Museum featuring costumes and other memorabilia owned by Arnaud's founder, Germaine Wells. For a less formal but no less pleasing experience, try Arnaud's neighboring brasserie, Remoulade.

See map p. 156. 813 Bienville (at the corner of Bourbon Street), an easy walk from anywhere in the French Quarter or Central Business District. ☎ *866-230-8895 or 504-523-5433.* www.arnauds.com. *Make reservations a week or more in advance for the weekend. Main courses: $19–$38. AE, DC, DISC, MC, V. Open: Daily 6–10 p.m., Sun jazz brunch 10 a.m.–2:30 p.m. Jackets required for dinner. Wheelchair accessible.*

Bacco
$–$$ French Quarter CREOLE/ITALIAN

Normally, I would be shocked to find plastic plates in a Brennan restaurant, but considering it was one of the brave few establishments to reopen a mere month after Katrina, they could've placed the food right in my hands and I wouldn't have cared. It was just such a joy to have good New Orleans food again, albeit a limited menu to start. With its Gothic arches and Venetian silk chandeliers, this sumptuously decorated testament to Brennan good taste combines the rich flair of Creole with the hearty comfort of Italian. Executive chef Chris Montero's signature dishes include housemade ravioli stuffed with Maine lobster and Gulf shrimp tossed in a champagne butter sauce garnished with caviar, and grilled tuna topped with seasonal seafood salsa. Like most Brennan restaurants, the desserts are always to die for, but I tend to play favorites. The fabulous tiramisu, topped with a light mascarpone cream, just melts in your mouth. Thank goodness President Bush spent an evening here during his first post-Katrina visit. It should help him remember why it's so important that New Orleans' culture — and cuisine — be saved.

See map p. 156. 310 Chartres St. (2 blocks from Bourbon Street, 2½ blocks from Canal Street, and 2½ blocks from Jackson Square). ☎ *504-522-2426.* www.bacco.com. *Make reservations a couple of days in advance for the weekend. Main courses: $15–$31. AE, DC, MC, V. Open: Daily 11:30 a.m.–2 p.m. and 6–10 p.m. Shorts and T-shirts are allowed. Wheelchair accessible.*

Bayona
$$–$$$ French Quarter   INTERNATIONAL

Bayona was chef-owner Susan Spicer's first foray into New Orleans dining and remains one of the city's most beloved institutions. It was such a relief to know that she returned to the post-Katrina kitchen. Housed in a 200-year-old Creole cottage, the mood is romantic and relaxed, yet invigorating. The only casualty of the storm was the wine cellar, which is tough, but it certainly could've been worse. Tasting the superb cream of garlic soup is worth forfeiting a kiss later, trust me (though I would encourage your dining partner to order the same). Any entree with lamb is heavenly, especially the peppered lamb loin with herbed goat cheese and Zinfandel sauce. Just when you think your taste buds are peaked, one bite of the toasted pecan roulade — with caramel mousse and praline syrup — and you'll reach new heights of ecstasy.

See map p. 156. 430 Dauphine St. (1 block from Bourbon Street). ☎ **504-525-4455.** www.bayona.com. *Reservations required for dinner, recommended for lunch. Main courses: $24–$28. AE, DC, DISC, MC, V. Open: Lunch Mon–Fri 11:30 a.m.–2 p.m.; dinner Mon–Thurs 6–9:30 p.m., Fri 6–10 p.m. and Sat 6–10:30 p.m. Dress is business casual. A low step and small restroom may pose problems for people with disabilities.*

The Bistro at Maison de Ville
$$–$$$ French Quarter   ECLECTIC/INTERNATIONAL

There was a little water damage here, but The Bistro was up and running again by Mardi Gras 2006. Stepping inside The Bistro is like entering a Parisian bistro, with its red leather banquettes, beveled-glass mirrors, natural wood flooring, and Impressionist-style paintings. One of the city's best-kept secrets, the Bistro is popular among locals for many reasons, from the intimate atmosphere to the inventive dishes and extensive wine list. The leap from "intimate" to "cramped" is short here, however, and the small size can also mean a good wait (especially when the theater crowd pours in). The menu changes every three months, but, depending on the season, you're likely to encounter and enjoy such options as confit of duck, house-smoked duck breast, grilled Italian sausage and cannelini bean cassoulet, or roasted pavé of salmon stuffed with crab, shrimp, and scallops and served with a grilled vegetable polenta cake.

See map p. 156. 733 Toulouse St. (in the Hotel Maison de Ville). ☎ **504-528-9206.** www.maisondeville.com. *Reservations recommended. Main courses: $29–$39. AE, DC, DISC, MC, V. Open: Daily 11 a.m.–2 p.m.; Thu–Sat 6–10 p.m. Dress is cocktail casual. Not accessible for wheelchairs.*

Brennan's
$$–$$$ French Quarter   BREAKFAST/CREOLE/FRENCH

One of New Orleans' most treasured restaurants was closed for eight months thanks to a mess caused by a defrosted freezer on the third floor. Of course, you've heard of Breakfast at Tiffany's. Well in New Orleans, the tradition is Breakfast at Brennan's. The morning repasts here have clogged generations of arteries with multicourse feasts featuring such sauce-laden options as Eggs Portuguese (poached and served in a puff pastry ladled with hollandaise), Eggs Benedict, Eggs Hussarde, and Trout Nancy (they're big on proper names here). Such extravagance isn't without its price; spending $50 on breakfast alone is easy (Shoney's all-you-can-eat, this ain't). In spite of the cost, Brennan's is always crowded at breakfast and lunch; expect a bit of a wait, even with a reservation. Dinners are generally calmer, especially if you can snag a table on the gas lamp–lined balcony.

See map p. 156. 417 Royal St. (1 block from Bourbon Street). ☎ **504-525-9711.** www. brennansneworleans.com. *Reservations recommended. Main courses: Breakfast: $15-$20; $35 for 3-course prix-fixe breakfast, dinner $29-$39. AE, DC, DISC, MC, V. Open: Daily 8 a.m.–2:30 p.m. and 6–10 p.m. Jacket recommended for men at dinner. Wheelchair accessible.*

Brigtsen's
$$ Carrollton/Uptown   CAJUN/CREOLE

I love that many of the city's finest restaurants are tucked into former homes. The atmosphere in this quaint Victorian cottage is both elegant and cozy, thanks to chef-owner Frank Brigtsen's expertise in the kitchen and his wife Marna's warm welcome at the door. Brigtsen's closed temporarily but returned to the scene before we became truly concerned about its future. The menu changes daily because Brigtsen prefers to use local ingredients whenever possible, but his reputation as one of the city's best chefs remains constant. Brigtsen knows his way around rabbit (a Creole mainstay), and the well-proportioned seafood platter allows you to sample flaky grilled fish, tender baked oyster, spicy deviled crab, and other creative incarnations. Dessert ranges from the familiar comforts of café au lait crème brûlée to the tangy surprise of homemade lemonade ice cream.

See map p. 164. 723 Dante St. (take the St. Charles Streetcar; get off at the corner of St. Charles and S. Carrollton avenues, and walk 3 blocks; take a taxi at night). ☎ **504-861-7610.** www.brigstens.com. *Reservations required. Main courses: $19-$28 (early bird specials available Tues–Thurs 5:30–6:30 p.m. — full meal for less than $20). AE, DC, MC, V. Open: Tues–Sat 5:30–10 p.m. Casual dress. Steps may prove a challenge for people with disabilities.*

Café Maspero
$ French Quarter   SANDWICHES/SEAFOOD

Nothing has changed for this local hangout since Katrina and we like it that way. This place is always packed, and for good reason (its Decatur Street location certainly doesn't hurt). Café Maspero serves seafood, grilled marinated chicken, and other familiar fare (though you won't find po' boys here), as well as kiddie-friendly items such as burgers and deli sandwiches — almost all served with fries, in impressively large portions, and at ridiculously low prices. That is, low in relation to the rest of the Quarter, anyway. The cafe also offers a huge selection of beers, wines, and

Mid-City Dining

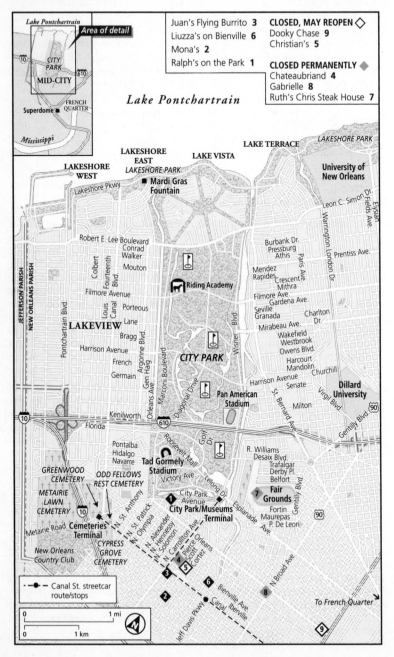

Juan's Flying Burrito **3**
Liuzza's on Bienville **6**
Mona's **2**
Ralph's on the Park **1**

CLOSED, MAY REOPEN ◇
Dooky Chase **9**
Christian's **5**

CLOSED PERMANENTLY ◆
Chateaubriand **4**
Gabrielle **8**
Ruth's Chris Steak House **7**

cocktails. (Don't confuse this restaurant with Maspero's Slave Exchange a few blocks away.)

See map p. 156. 601 Decatur St. (2 short blocks from Jackson Square and 3 blocks from Bourbon Street). ☎ *504-523-6250. Reservations aren't accepted, and the lines can be long at times, but they usually move fast. Main courses: $4.25–$9. No credit cards. Open: Sun–Thurs 11 a.m.–11 p.m. (until midnight Fri–Sat). No dress code. Wheelchair accessible, but the crowded tables and narrow doorways make maneuvering a challenge.*

Commander's Palace
Garden District   CREOLE

This New Orleans gem opened in October 2006 to great fanfare. Awarded the Lifetime Outstanding Restaurant Award from the James Beard Foundation, Commander's Palace always lived up to its reputation. Even in a city full of top-notch, elegant restaurants, Commander's Palace maintains a soft spot in locals' hearts with a winning combination of stellar service (you'll be pampered by several attendants throughout your meal), a grand setting (an 1880s Victorian House with a seemingly endless series of dining rooms and a gorgeous courtyard), and outstanding food. The sumptuous turtle soup with sherry is justly famous, and such bright spots as the boned Mississippi roasted quail (stuffed with an awesome Creole crawfish sausage) and the mixed grill (which features lamb and rabbit sausage) light up the menu. Lastly, when the staff suggests the bread pudding soufflé for dessert, you would be wise to do as they say.

See map p. 164. 1403 Washington Ave. (take the St. Charles Streetcar to Washington and walk 2 blocks along Washington Ave. toward the river; take a taxi at night). ☎ *504-899-8221.* www.commanderspalace.com. *Reservations required. Main courses: Full brunch $20–$32; main courses $29–$32; prix-fixe $29–$36. AE, DC, DISC, MC, V. Open: Mon–Fri 11:30 a.m.–2 p.m.; jazz brunch Sat 11: 30 a.m.–1 p.m., and Sun 10:30 a.m.–1:30 p.m.; daily 6–10 p.m. Men must wear a jacket and tie for dinner. Wheelchairs will need to navigate over one step. Complimentary valet parking.*

Court of Two Sisters
$$–$$$ French Quarter   CREOLE

The bottom line is that the atmosphere here — a historic building with a large, graceful courtyard (once again filled with flowers post-Katrina), soothing fountains, and a wishing well — is better than the food. A strolling jazz band serenades you during the daily jazz brunch, though most locals avoid it (the brunch, not the band) for fear of looking like tourists. The food is often impressive but rarely spectacular. The jazz brunch boasts more than 60 dishes, including meat, fowl, fish, vegetables, fresh fruits, homemade breads, and pastries. For dinner, stick to safe bets such as the chicken Michelle or shrimp remoulade (and keep in mind that the restaurant maintains a $15 minimum for dinner). Desserts are very good, though; splurge on the pecan pie or crêpes suzette. A children's menu offers shrimp or chicken fingers, with baked potato or fries, a fruit cup or ice cream, and milk. Kids 5 to 12 can also partake of the brunch buffet for $10.

See map p. 156. 613 Royal St. (1 block from Bourbon Street). ☎ *504-522-7261.* www.courtoftwosisters.com. *Reservations recommended. Main courses: $18–$30 (fixed-price meal available for $39); brunch $23. AE, CB, DC, DISC, MC, V. Open: Jazz brunch buffet daily 9 a.m.–3 p.m.; dinner 5:30–10 p.m. Shorts and T-shirts are allowed. Wheelchair accessible.*

Cuvée
$$ Central Business District   CREOLE/NEW AMERICAN

Because so many of New Orleans' culinary giants were closed for so long, Cuvée got a chance to really shine. Young executive chef Bob Iacovone experiments with seasonal ingredients and multicourse tasting menus. The cavernous exposed-brick dining room, lit by gaslight, sets a perfectly intimate mood for such contemporary French creations as seared sea scallop and vermouth-poached mussels with chorizo-stuffed pasta. I'm glad I saved room for the roasted banana tapioca pudding topped with brown sugar, rum ice cream and salted cashews. No doubt this establishment will continue to collect accolades and fans.

See map p. 164. 322 Magazine St. ☎ *504-587-9001.* www.restaurantcuvee.com. *Reservations recommended. Main courses: $18–$28. AE, DC, MC, V. Open: Mon–Sat 6–10 p.m. Wheelchair accessible.*

Dick & Jenny's
$–$$ Uptown   CREOLE/ECLECTIC

The decrepit bargeboard house on an industrial corridor doesn't look that appetizing, but inside you find a young Uptown crowd hungry for contemporary Creole dishes. The couple for whom the restaurant is named sold it to staff after Katrina, which made me a little wary. Thankfully, everything is as good if not better than it was before. You may want to fast earlier in the day to take advantage of the sumptuous starters like steamed artichoke with warm brie crab dip and an entree-cum-sampler Duck Quatro (duck prepared four ways: confit, foie gras, duck liver cognac flan, and seared breast with white beans). Desserts are deadly; linger over lemon mascarpone crêpes or delight in the crunch of the crispy chocolate fritter.

See map p. 164. 4501 Tchoupitoulas St. (5 miles from the Quarter — take a taxi). ☎ *504-894-9880. No reservations available. Main courses: $14–$23. AE, DISC, MC, V. Open: Tues–Thurs 5:30–10 p.m.; Fri–Sat 5:30–10:30 p.m. Steps and closely packed tables pose problems for people with wheelchairs.*

Elizabeth's
$–$$ Bywater   BREAKFAST/CREOLE

As home prices and rents rose in the French Quarter and Faubourg Marigny, artists and other creative types increasingly headed toward Bywater, which in turn re-energized the community and gave new life to the darling little shotguns, Creole cottages, and Italianate center halls.

Then Katrina came, and Elizabeth's changed hands, which I found rather worrisome. Thankfully, the only thing that really changed was the breakfast hours, which now start later. But who cares when you can eat praline bacon! Elizabeth's attracts locals from the farthest reaches of town because very few places offer breakfast period, much less the marvelous omelettes or waffles topped with cooked apples. If you're not an early bird, come for lunch or dinner instead. You can't go wrong with any seafood dish or sandwich. Daily specials like BBQ and meatloaf are winners, too. Service is refreshingly attentive.

See map p. 164. 601 Gallier St. (2 miles from the Quarter — take a taxi). ☎ *504-944-9272.* www.elizabeths-restaurant.com. *No reservations necessary. Main courses: $10–$25. MC, V. Open: Tues–Fri 10:30 a.m.–2:30 p.m.; Sat–Sun 9 a.m.–2:30 p.m.; Tues–Sat 5–10 p.m. A few small steps must be navigated for people with wheelchairs.*

Emeril's
$$–$$$ Warehouse District   CREOLE/NEW AMERICAN

Often the general public mistakes fame and money for super powers, so it came as no surprise that celebrity chef Emeril Lagasse was unfairly targeted as someone who didn't do much for the city in the weeks and months after Katrina. But guess what? The Bam Man is back with all three of his New Orleans restaurants up and running again, which employs locals and boosts tourism. I'd say that helps the city a lot! Lagasse's specialty is what he calls *"New* New Orleans Cuisine," using Creole tradition as a foundation while exploring bold new directions. The desserts outnumber the entrees here, and the menu changes often, but the rack of lamb and fresh duck are favorites, and the grilled, Creole-seasoned chicken is a crowd-pleaser as well. Don't miss the banana cream pie with banana crust and caramel drizzle sauce, which has reduced diners to moaning and pounding on the table to express their pleasure (I'm not kidding). Service can be a little snooty, but when the food is this good, it can be overlooked.

See map p. 164. 800 Tchoupitoulas (8 blocks from Canal — take a taxi). ☎ *504-528-9393.* www.emerils.com. *Reservations required. Main courses: $26–$39; a 7-course degustation menu (which changes nightly) is $65. AE, DC, DISC, MC, V. Open: Lunch Mon–Fri 11:30 a.m.–2 p.m.; daily 6–10 p.m. Casual dress. Wheelchair accessible.*

Galatoire's
$–$$ French Quarter   FRENCH

One of the classiest restaurants in New Orleans still guided by the same family who founded it in 1905, generations have stood in line here. Before the return of the second-floor dining area (closed since World War II), Galatoire's didn't accept reservations, and even made the Duke and Duchess of Windsor wait for a table — or so the legend goes. Before Katrina, locals liked to debate whether Galatoire's was still the best or merely coasting on its reputation? Those in the know (including those who

New Orleans Dining

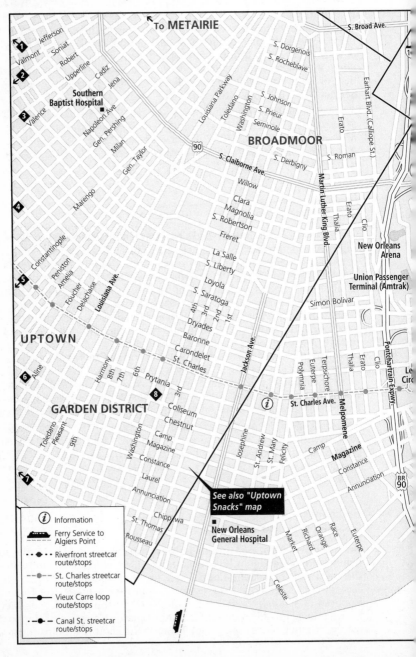

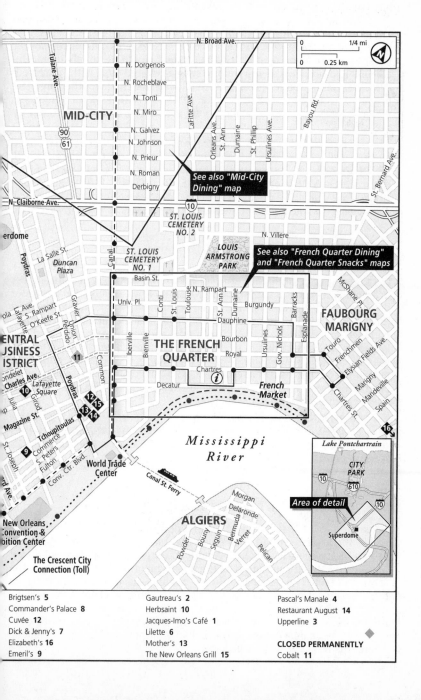

| 0 | | 1/4 mi |
| 0 | 0.25 km | |

MID-CITY

N. Dorgenois
N. Rocheblave
N. Tonti
N. Miro
N. Galvez
N. Johnson
N. Prieur
N. Roman
Derbigny

Tulane Ave.

N. Broad Ave.

Lafitte Ave.

Orleans Ave.
St. Ann
Dumaine
St. Phillip
Ursulines Ave.

Bayou Rd.

St. Bernard Ave.

See also "Mid-City Dining" map

N. Claiborne Ave.

erdome

ST. LOUIS CEMETERY NO. 2

LOUIS ARMSTRONG PARK

N. Villere

See also "French Quarter Dining" and "French Quarter Snacks" maps

FAUBOURG MARIGNY

La Salle St.
Duncan Plaza

ST. LOUIS CEMETERY NO. 1

Basin St.

Univ. Pl.

Canal

N. Rampart
Conti
St. Louis
Toulouse
St. Ann
Dumaine
Burgundy
Barracks
Esplanade

McShane Pl.

Dauphine

Touro
Frenchmen
Elysian Fields Ave.

THE FRENCH QUARTER

Iberville
Bienville
Bourbon
Royal
Ursulines
Gov. Nichols

ENTRAL
USINESS
ISTRICT

Gravier
O'Keefe St.
Union
Perdido
Common
Poydras

Chartres

Marigny
Mandeville
Spain

Decatur

French Market

Chartres St.

Charles Ave.
Lafayette Square

Magazine St.
Tchoupitoulas
Commerce
S. Peters
Fulton

World Trade Center

Mississippi River

Lake Pontchartrain

CITY PARK

Area of detail

Superdome

New Orleans Convention & bition Center

Canal St. Ferry

Morgan
Delaronde

ALGIERS

Powder
Bouny
Seguin
Bermuda
Verret
Pelican

The Crescent City Connection (Toll)

Brigtsen's **5**	Gautreau's **2**	Pascal's Manale **4**
Commander's Palace **8**	Herbsaint **10**	Restaurant August **14**
Cuvée **12**	Jacques-Imo's Café **1**	Upperline **3**
Dick & Jenny's **7**	Lilette **6**	
Elizabeth's **16**	Mother's **13**	**CLOSED PERMANENTLY**
Emeril's **9**	The New Orleans Grill **15**	Cobalt **11**

have made Sunday dinner here a tradition) say to order the trout amandine without sauce, or the red snapper or redfish topped with sautéed crabmeat meunière from the à la carte menu, and you'll be persuaded that this staunchly traditional spot is still a contender. This old-line restaurant is especially beloved post Katrina because it would be simply unimgainable if it had been lost. If you want to snag a coveted table in the mirrored, first-floor dining room — where heeled locals watch each other preen — prepare to join the long line outside. After you're in, look for Tennessee Williams's regular table — he always sat at the table in the front corner by the window.

See map p. 156. 209 Bourbon St. (located in the second block of Bourbon Street, an easy walk from anywhere in the Quarter or the Central Business District). ☎ *504-525-2021.* www.galatoires.com. *Reservations accepted for second-floor dining room only. Main courses: $14–$27. AE, DC, DISC, MC, V. Open: Sun Noon–10 p.m.; Tues–Sat 11:30 a.m.–10 p.m. Men must wear jackets for dinner and on Sun. The restaurant is wheelchair accessible, but the restrooms can be a problem.*

⅃ Gautreau's
$$–$$$ Uptown   CREOLE

I'm eagerly anticipating the return of this romantic Creole restaurant, set in an old converted neighborhood drugstore. It was remodeled after roof damage ruined the interior and some equipment, and it should be open for business by the time you read this. The upscale menu has typically included appetizers such as duck confit and eggplant crisps, and the grilled hanger steak (similar to flank) is a hit, though you may opt for the roasted chicken, served with wild mushrooms, garlic potatoes, and green beans. Try the triple-layer cheesecake (with chocolate, pecan, and almond layers) for dessert, or if it's available, the tarte tatin (apples and sun-dried cherries with a strawberry sorbet).

See map p. 164. 1728 Soniat St. (take the St. Charles Streetcar and walk 2½ blocks down Soniat away from the river; take a taxi at night). ☎ *504-899-7397. Reservations recommended. Main courses: $18–$34. DC, DISC, MC, V. Open: Mon–Sat 6–10 p.m. A few steps make the small restrooms inaccessible to wheelchairs.*

Herbsaint
$–$$ Central Business District   FRENCH/NEW AMERICAN

Acclaimed local chef Susan Spicer opened Herbsaint — named for the locally made pastis found in, among other places, the popular local cocktail, the Sazerac — as a French-American outpost. It instantly enhanced her already stellar reputation as the mastermind behind Bayona and the former Cobalt. The decor is suitably minimal, assuring no distractions from the adventurous cuisine. Offerings such as braised lamb shanks, duck confit, and fried frogs' legs dot a menu that veers between Gallic familiarity and New American experimentation. Satisfy your sweet tooth with coconut macadamia nut pie or the melt-in-your-mouth chocolate beignets. There was little storm damage here.

See map p. 164. 701 St. Charles Ave. ☎ *504-524-4114.* www.herbsaint.com. *Reservations recommended. Main courses: $14–$24. AE, DC, DISC, MC, V. Open: Lunch Mon–Fri 11:30 a.m.–2:30 p.m., Mon–Fri 11:30 a.m.–1:30 p.m.; Mon–Sat 5:30– 9:30 p.m. Dress is business casual. Wheelchair accessible.*

Irene's Cuisine
$–$$ French Quarter   FRENCH PROVENÇAL/ITALIAN

Closed briefly after Katrina, you can once again follow the scent of garlic — and locals — to this tiny restaurant located on the corner of a parking garage. Despite a brisk pace, the dark atmosphere (the waiters carry flashlights for a reason) can be really romantic. Start off with an appetizer of grilled shrimp served with just-so crunchy, panéed oysters. Follow that up with rack of lamb (served with a port wine sauce and herb garlic potatoes) or roasted chicken Rosmario, draped in a luxuriant rosemary gravy. If you're into the texture as well as the taste of the food, I recommend the bread pudding with roasted pecans for its alternating crunchy and creamy spoonfuls. Prepare to wait up to 90 minutes for a table; your patience will be amply rewarded.

See map p. 156. 539 St. Philip St. (3 short blocks from Jackson Square and 1 block from Decatur Street). ☎ *504-529-8811. Reservations not accepted (go early to avoid a wait) except for Christmas Eve, New Year's Eve, and Valentine's Day. Main courses: $14–$18. AE, MC, V. Open: Sun–Thurs 5:30–10:30 p.m. and Fri–Sat 5:30–11 p.m. Dress is casual to dressy. Wheelchair accessible.*

Jacques-Imo's Café
$–$$ Carrollton/Uptown   CREOLE/SOUL FOOD

Say it with me: *Jock*-a-moe's. People will gladly wait for more than an hour for some of the tastiest Southern soul food imaginable served in a cozy, low-lit dining room adorned by swamp murals. You can take the easy way out and order tender fried chicken or the stuffed pork chop, and no one would blame you. But the menu has a creative, experimental bent that's well worth pursuing compliments of owner Jack Leonardi (he's the guy in Bermuda shorts, even in winter) and chef Austin Leslie (you'll see him at work when you pass through the bustling kitchen to get to your table). A seafood-stocked Cajun bouillabaisse is an unexpected treat, as is the savory shrimp and alligator cheesecake appetizer in a rich, spicy cream. If you can find the room (and if you can, my hat's off to you), try the coffee bean crème brûlée dessert. Everything is still fine and funky here post-Katrina.

See map p. 164. 8324 Oak St. (2 blocks from Carrollton Avenue). ☎ *504-861-0886.* www.jacquesimoscafe.com. *Reservations accepted for parties of five or more. Main courses: $17–$25. AE, CB, DC, DISC, MC, V. Open: Mon–Thurs 5–10 p.m. and Fri–Sat 5–10:30 p.m. Casual attire. Wheelchair accessibility is a problem, though you can roll down a less-than-nice-looking alleyway to the back dining areas.*

K-Paul's Louisiana Kitchen
$$–$$$ French Quarter   CAJUN

The hoopla about Cajun cooking started back in the early '80s with living legend Paul Prudhomme and his renowned restaurant, which offers upscale (and high-priced) takes on traditional Cajun fare. Many of the red-hot chefs and restaurateurs in New Orleans today learned at the stove of Prudhomme. Clearly dedicated to New Orleans and its culinary tradition, Prudhomme founded "Chefs Cook for Katrina," a nonprofit organization that continues to make meals for tens of thousands of relief workers and clean-up crews. The menu, which changes daily and features a variety of extra-hot interpretations of the Cajun tradition, is known for its blackened redfish and Cajun martini. Also try anything with rabbit, the fiery gumbo, or the Cajun popcorn (fried crawfish tails). If it's available for dessert, order the sweet potato pecan pie with Chantilly cream. You won't find a children's menu per se, but several items are kid-compatible and nonspicy.

See map p. 156. 416 Chartres St. (between Conti and St. Louis streets). ☎ *504-524-7394.* www.kpauls.com. *Reservations suggested for upstairs dining room only; otherwise, you have to wait up to an hour. Main courses: Dinner $30–$40. AE, DC, DISC, MC, V. Open: Thu–Sat 11:30 a.m.–2:30 p.m.; Mon–Sat 5:30–10 p.m. Dress is business casual. Wheelchair accessible.*

Lilette
$$ Uptown   CREOLE/FRENCH

Typical of most Uptown restaurants, there was no flooding but *beaucoup* nasty refrigerators to throw away. Now Lilette is fresh and pretty once again. The namesake for chef-owner John Harris's quaint bistro was a French woman with whom he cooked during an extended stay in France. But Harris isn't content to stick to the classics; although he clearly respects tradition, he isn't afraid to experiment. A trademark dish is the spicy *boudin noir* (blood sausage) with cornichons and a house-made mustard sauce. Try the curious dessert goat cheese crème fraîche quenelles — little rounds of goat cheese crème fraîche with poached pears and topped with lavender honey. C'est magnifique!

See map p. 164. 3637 Magazine St. (4 miles from the Quarter — take a taxi). ☎ *504-895-1636.* www.liletterestaurant.com. *Reservations recommended. Main courses: $18–$30. AE, DISC, MC, V. Open: Tues–Sat 11:30 a.m.–2 p.m.; Tues–Thurs 6–10 p.m.; Fri–Sat 6–11 p.m. Steps and closely packed tables pose problems for people with wheelchairs.*

Liuzza's on Bienville
$ Mid-City   Italian/Sandwiches/Seafood

The flood waters flowed well above the bar of this rickety neighborhood joint, loved by locals since 1947. The owners initially didn't think they could reopen, but co-owner Michael Bordelon decided to get down to work. At one point, he had to board up the windows because concerned locals kept stopping by and interrupting his renovations. Just in time for

Jazz Fest 2006, Liuzza's opened with drinks only. Finally, in July 2006, their wonderful comfort food returned as well. While waiting for your main meal, crunch into their deep-fried onion rings and wash them down with beer (or root beer) in a frosted mug. Then look for the framed photo of the restaurant when it was under six feet of water and be glad that it's back. The children's menu offers chicken fingers, hamburgers, fried shrimp or oysters with a choice of potato salad, red beans, fries or cole slaw. I love any of their seafood po'boys and the Crawfish Telemachus — crawfish in a creamy sauce ladled over pasta — is super rich and delicious. Please remember, cash only!

See map p. 160. 3636 Bienville Ave. (2 miles from the Quarter — take a taxi or the Canal Streetcar). ☎ *504-482-9120.* www.liuzzas.com. *Main courses: $8–$15. Cash only (ATM conveniently located in the bar). Open: Tues–Sat 11 a.m.–9 p.m. Several steps and closely packed tables pose problems for people with wheelchairs.*

Mother's
$–$$ Central Business District   BREAKFAST/CREOLE/SANDWICHES/ SHORT ORDER

After being closed temporarily due to food spoilage and subsequent clean up, Mother's overstuffed, mountainous po' boys are back! The long lines and lack of atmosphere are minor qualms in the face of the Ferdi special — a giant roll stuffed with baked ham, roast beef, gravy, and other bits of beef debris that's just as delightfully, mouth-wateringly sloppy as it sounds. Mother's also offers "the world's best baked ham" as well as seafood platters, serviceable fried chicken, Creole offerings (gumbo, jambalaya), and of course, po' boys. Chicken strips are available for the kids, and most of the sandwiches and breakfast dishes are kid-friendly as well.

See map p. 164. 401 Poydras St. (easy walk from anywhere in the Quarter or Central Business District). ☎ *504-523-9656.* www.mothersrestaurant.net. *Reservations not accepted. Menu selections: $1.75–$20. AE, DISC, MC, V. Open: Mon–Sat 7:30 a.m.–8 p.m. No dress code. Wheelchair accessible.*

Mr. B's Bistro
French Quarter   CONTEMPORARY CREOLE

This once-bustling bistro is set to reopen by the time we go to print. Pre-Katrina, Mr. B's boasted white-glove-level service in a casual atmosphere, and regulars convened here daily for modern, spicy interpretations of Creole classics. Try the legendary crab cakes, the superb andouille sausage, and the hearty, country-style Gumbo Ya-Ya (the chicken and andouille sausage blend is my favorite; I recommend it gladly). The Cajun barbecued shrimp are large and plump, and served heads-on in a rich, thick, buttery sauce. If you come on a Sunday, show up early for the jazz brunch and bubbly.

See map p. 156. 201 Royal St. (1 block away from Bourbon or Canal street). ☎ *504-523-2078.* www.mrbsbistro.com. *Reservations are recommended. Main courses: $13–$19. Open: Daily 11 a.m.–10 p.m. AE, DC, DISC, MC, V. Casual attire. Wheelchair accessible.*

The New Orleans Grill
$$–$$$ Central Business District   INTERNATIONAL

Six months after Katrina, The New Orleans Grill returned to much fanfare. An exceptionally high level of service, food quality, and comfort makes The New Orleans Grill (on the second floor of the Windsor Court Hotel) an unforgettable dining experience — at a price you won't soon forget, either. The menu changes frequently and can include such fancy fare as moderately blackened filet of halibut, chilled oysters with frozen champagne ginger granita (champagne seasoned with ginger, which has been frozen into a sorbet), or a rich roasted goose. Eating here is an extravagant experience but not necessarily excessive.

See map p. 164. 300 Gravier St. (1 block from Canal). ☎ *504-522-1992.* www.windsorcourthotel.com. *Make reservations a week or two in advance. Main courses: $28–$39. AE, DC, DISC, MC, V. Open: Mon–Sat 7–10:30 a.m. and 11 a.m.– 2 p.m., Sun 7–9 a.m., Sun brunch 10:30 a.m.–2 p.m, Sun–Thu 6–10 p.m., and Fri– Sat 6–10:30 p.m. Jacket required and tie recommended at dinner. Wheelchair accessible.*

Olivier's
$–$$ French Quarter   CREOLE/FRENCH/SEAFOOD

Olivier's suffered minimal damage from Katrina and reopened quickly. Chef Armand Olivier hails from a family famous for its Creole cooking, and the menu is filled with dishes originated by ancestors going back to his great-great-grandmother. The Creole Rabbit is a version of a popular 19th-century Creole staple, braised and simmered in gravy to keep it moist and served with a rich oyster dressing. The beef Bourguignon is also good, with tenderloin tips simmered in a thick roux and served with pasta. I think the bread pudding dessert is moist, creamy and an absolutely perfect way to finish the meal. Service is highly professional and classy, and the decor is the same without being too fancy.

See map p. 156. 204 Decatur St. ☎ *504-525-7734.* www.olivierscreole.com. *Reservations are recommended. Main courses: $15–$20. Open: Thu–Tue 5–10 p.m. (closed Wed). AE, DC, DISC, MC, V. Casual attire. Wheelchair accessible.*

Palace Café
$$–$$$ French Quarter   CONTEMPORARY CREOLE

Immediately after Katrina, Canal Street as a whole didn't look too promising, but now that Palace Café has recuperated from flood damage, this historic avenue is on the rebound. Prepare to be pampered at Palace Cafe, another Brennan family creation whose motto seems to be service, service, and more service. At a recent visit, we had two waiters taking care of our every need, one of whom cracked us up with his witty one-liners. Their expertise was invaluable when trying to decide between the traditional dinner menu and seasonal specials, much less choose any one dish. I could eat the signature crabmeat cheesecake, with its crunchy pecan crust, as an appetizer, entree, and dessert — it is *that* good. If it's in season, you must succumb to the garlic-crusted softshell crab, which is flash fried and served on jalapeño corn pudding with fried plantains, green tomato crawfish relish, and avocado lime coulis. In perfect Brennan tradition, Palace Café offers a glorious dessert selection; the Ponchatoula strawberry shortcake topped with sweet double cream melts in your mouth. But if you've never had it, you absolutely must dip your spoon into their famous white-chocolate bread pudding — the best in town.

See map p. 156. 605 Canal St. (an easy walk from anywhere in the Quarter). ☎ *504-523-1661.* www.palacecafe.com. *Reservations recommended. Main courses: $19–$31. AE, DC, DISC, MC, V. Open: Mon–Fri 11:30 a.m.–2:30 p.m.; daily 5:30–11 p.m.; brunch Sat–Sun 10:30 a.m.–2:30 p.m. Dress is business casual. Wheelchair accessible. Complimentary validated parking at neighboring Marriott, Holiday Inn, and garage adjacent to Dickie Brennan's Steakhouse.*

Pascal's Manale
$–$$ Uptown   ITALIAN/SEAFOOD/STEAKHOUSE

Full of water then mold for weeks after Katrina, this Uptown favorite worked very hard to return to business as usual. It's known around town as Italian–New Orleans steakhouse, but that doesn't quite do justice to the slightly eccentric selection. Pascal's most popular item is its barbecued shrimp (a local favorite that originated here), which is actually marinated in an irresistible, spicy butter sauce, not barbecued. (These plump crustaceans are served with their heads on, so be forewarned if you don't like them that way.) Among other dishes, the combination pan roast features chopped oysters and crabmeat in a blend of shallots, parsley, and seasonings. Even with reservations, you may find a bit of a wait.

See map p. 164. 1838 Napoleon Ave. (take the St. Charles Streetcar to Napoleon and walk 3 blocks away from the river; take a taxi at night). ☎ *504-895-4877. Reservations recommended. Main courses: $11–$24. AE, CB, DC, DISC, MC, V. Open: Mon and Wed–Sat 5–9 p.m. or 10 p.m. depending on how busy it is (closed Sun Memorial Day weekend through Labor Day). Dress is business casual. Wheelchair accessible.*

Peristyle
$$ French Quarter   FRENCH/ITALIAN/NEW AMERICAN

When chef/owner Anne Kearney-Sand sold the restaurant to longtime friend Tom Wolfe of Wolfe's in neighboring suburb Metairie (since closed due to Katrina), locals were aghast and feared the worst. Kearney-Sand had owned the restaurant since 1995, and due to her talent and determination Peristyle flourished despite a devastating fire in 1999 that gutted the place. She excelled at anything, from appetizers to enticing entrees to surprise salads. New owner Wolfe did not have to deal with much Katrina damage; however, he is still trying to figure out what the new Peristyle will be. We continue to hope that he will persevere and make good on the old rep.

See map p. 156. 1041 Dumaine St. (3 blocks from Bourbon Street; take a taxi for safety). ☎ **504-593-9535.** *Reservations recommended. Main courses: $24–$28. AE, DC, MC, V. Open: Fri 11:30 a.m.–1:30 p.m., and Tues–Sat 6–9:30 p.m. Dress is business casual. The front step is a bit steep (about 6 inches), but once inside, navigating via wheelchair is easy.*

Port of Call
$–$$ French Quarter   HAMBURGERS/SANDWICHES

This character-filled, nautical-themed restaurant and bar is famous for its burgers, which locals generally agree are the best in town. They certainly are huge, weighing in at a half-pound without condiments or the accompanying baked potato (sorry, no fries). Steaks are another specialty, though I've found thickness and juiciness levels vary. The place really gets jumping late at night when the restaurant is dark and crowded, and attentive service is at a premium, but it's busy most all the time. For extra atmosphere, sit and eat at the bar. Take-out service is available.

See map p. 156. 838 Esplanade Ave. (take a taxi for safety). ☎ **504-523-0120.** www. portofcallneworleans.com. *Reservations are not accepted. Menu items: $6–$21. AE, MC, V. Open: Daily 7 a.m.–1 a.m. No dress code. Not accessible for wheelchairs.*

Ralph & Kacoo's
$–$$$ French Quarter   CREOLE/SEAFOOD

Despite ongoing repairs to storm damage, the New Orleans branch of this restaurant chain is usually crowded at all hours, though you seldom have to wait longer than 15 to 20 minutes. The time passes quickly if you spend it at the bar (a full-size replica of a fishing boat) downing drinks and raw oysters and people-watching. The onion rings alone are worth the wait, though the hush puppies and fried crawfish tails also prove popular. This restaurant is a solid, dependable (if not adventuresome) choice for seafood; the portions are large, the prices reasonable, and the fixings fresh. A kids' menu offers burgers and grilled cheese sandwiches and a shrimp boat.

See map p. 156. 519 Toulouse St. (2½ blocks from Bourbon Street and around the corner from Jackson Square). ☎ **504-522-5226.** www.ralphandkacoos.com. *Reservations recommended. Main courses: $14–$40. AE, DC, DISC, MC, V. Open: Mon–Thurs 4–10 p.m.; Fri 4–11 p.m.; Sat noon–11 p.m., Sun noon–9 p.m. Casual dress. Wheelchair accessible.*

Ralph's on the Park
$$ Mid-City   CREOLE/SEAFOOD

This latest Brennan establishment opened in the former Tavern on the Park building, but not before sprucing it up quite a bit. What a shame that the lovely results of all that time and money was under water for a few weeks thanks to Katrina. But in true dynasty fashion, Ralph's not only returned, but earned accolades as "Best Restaurant Post-Katrina," by readers of local *CityBusiness* magazine. I assumed the pre-Katrina view of City Park's magnificent live oaks was now spoiled, but miraculously, most live oaks fared pretty well and the Spanish moss is still there, draped over those enormous branches. While taking in the scenery, be sure to savor my favorite dish, the grilled lamb T-bone, which is served with housemade lamb crépinette, black lentils, roasted golden beets and finished with a natural lamb reduction and a red beet hummus. Please note that there is a vegetarian-only menu available and it's refreshingly untraditional.

See map p. 160. 900 City Park Ave. (3 blocks from the Canal Streetcar spur at the south entrance to City Park). ☎ *504-488-1000.* www.ralphsonthepark.com. *Reservations recommended. Main courses: $16–$29. AE, MC, V. Open: Tue–Sat 5:30–9:30 p.m. Dress is smart casual. Wheelchair accessible.*

Restaurant August
$$ Central Business District   CONTEMPORARY FRENCH

Born on the bayou, executive chef John Besh — recently nominated for a James Beard award — incorporates his southern Louisiana influences with those found in the South of France, culminating in exciting, experimental cuisine. He's also celebrated for pitching in to feed relief workers and clean-up crews in the weeks and months following Katrina. If available, you might want to try the playful "BLT," which is no diner staple but rather buster crabs, lettuce, and tomatoes on *pain perdu* (French toast). Other inspired entrees include Moroccan spice duck with sweet corn polenta, duck foie gras and dried fruit compote, and pan roast day boat grouper with lobster whipped potatoes and bouillabaisse jus. The dessert list is most intriguing; I went for the goat's milk cheesecake with bee pollen, honey ice cream, and Balsamic sauternes syrup and was very satisfied with my choice.

See map p. 164. 301 Tchoupitoulas St. (4 blocks from the Quarter; take a taxi at night). ☎ *504-299-9777.* www.rest-august.com. *Reservations recommended. Main courses: $20–$29. AE, DC, MC, V. Open: Fri 11 a.m.–2 p.m.; Tues–Sat 5:30–10 p.m. Dress is smart casual. Steps and closely packed tables make it problematic for people with wheelchairs.*

Rib Room
$$–$$$ French Quarter   SEAFOOD/STEAKHOUSE

The arched windows, high ceilings, and exposed brick remind me of a conservative British men's club, though acting genteel when tackling one of its filets, sirloins, or other meats isn't easy. The chef slow roasts the restaurant's specialty, prime rib, on a rotisserie over an open flame. Spit-roasted lamb, spit-roasted jumbo shrimp, and other satisfying dishes round out the menu. The Rib Room is a good alternative for those individuals tired of seafood or sauce-heavy Creole (though trading those rich creamy sauces for juicy, artery-hardening steak isn't much of a trade-off). There was no storm damage.

See map p. 156. 621 St. Louis St. (1 block from Bourbon Street in the Omni Royal Orleans Hotel). ☎ *504-529-7045.* www.omniroyalorleans.com. *Reservations recommended. Main courses: $24–$34. AE, DC, DISC, MC, V. Open: Daily 6:30–10:30 a.m., 11:30 a.m.–2:30 p.m., and 6–10 p.m. Dress is business casual. Wheelchair accessible.*

Tujague's
$$$ French Quarter   CREOLE

Opened in 1856, Tujague's (pronounced two-*jacks*) is one of the oldest restaurants in New Orleans and wasn't going to let a few roof leaks keep it from reopening in November 2005. It's a favorite institution among New Orleanians, but its simple, traditional charms aren't for everyone. The restaurant features no printed menu; instead, the waiters recite the limited but changing daily selections. Options frequently include the tender beef brisket with horseradish sauce (*very* spicy), shrimp remoulade (with a spicy mustard sauce), and a daily fish special. Ask for the Bonne Femme chicken, a baked garlic number from the original owner's recipe (the restaurant has it every night, but you have to request it). Finish with the classic bread pudding.

See map p. 156. 823 Decatur St. (1 short block from Jackson Square). ☎ *504-525-8676.* www.tujaguesrestaurant.com. *Reservations recommended. Main courses: 3-course lunch $15–$17; 6-course dinner $30–$36. AE, DC, DISC, MC, V. Open: Daily 11 a.m.–3 p.m. and 5–11 p.m. Casual attire. Wheelchair accessible.*

Upperline
$$ Uptown   ECLECTIC/CREOLE

Nestled in a largely residential section of Uptown that did not flood, JoAnn Clevenger's fabulous Upperline in a circa 1877 townhouse is every bit as inventive as bigger names such as Commander's Palace or Emeril's with far grander character. What other proprietor compiles lists of her favorite local music clubs, bookstores, artists, and (gasp!) favorite dishes at other restaurants, and shares them (by request) with patrons? No less extraordinary is how she and her head chef, Kenneth Smith, met; they're both vintage menu and out-of-print cookbook buffs and Smith asked a dealer in Michigan where he should find work. She suggested contacting Upperline, Clevenger hired him as an apprentice, and thus, culinary history was made. Speaking of which, Clevenger invented what is now a local staple, fried green tomatoes with shrimp remoulade — pay due homage and order it. I highly recommend the "Taste of New Orleans," a sampler of seven favorites served in three courses. ***Note:*** Don't come to Upperline if you're in a rush — you absolutely must make a night out of it. Savor the food and atmosphere, ask Clevenger questions (start with an inquiry about her enormous art collection displayed throughout the restaurant), and enjoy her only-in-New Orleans stories.

See map p. 164. 1413 Upperline St. (take the St. Charles Streetcar to the Upperline stop). ☎ *504-891-9822.* www.upperline.com. *Reservations required. Main*

_courses: $20–$27. AE, CB, DC, MC, V. Open: Wed–Sun 5:30–9:30 p.m. Casual attire.
Not accessible for wheelchairs._

Dining and Snacking on the Go

Snacking is a great American pastime, and New Orleans is nothing if not
a city of traditions. Plus, with the stress of post-Katrina life for many
locals, it should come as no surprise that New Orleans is stuffed to the
gills with snack food — from Lucky Dogs (hot dogs and sausage sold by
street vendors in giant hot dog-shaped carts) to the city's twin sandwich
staples, the po' boy and the muffuletta. This section suggests the best
places to go for these delights as well as bar food, late-night munchies,
beignets, and other sugary confections. It also cracks open the subject
of oysters and gives you my two cents on the longstanding debate as to
the best burger in town.

Savoring the muffuletta experience

What is a muffuletta, you ask? See Chapter 3 to find out more about this
savory sandwich. Here are a couple of places to try one:

- ✔ **Central Grocery** (923 Decatur St., French Quarter, ☎ 504-523-
  1620) makes the most likely winner in the great muffuletta debate.
  The place probably invented the muffuletta, so if you have just one,
  have it here. You can also buy many New Orleans spices and other
  deli items here as well. Many locals are stocking up because it was
  tough to do without when it was temporarily closed after Katrina.
  Tip: These things are so big you can easily split one.

- ✔ **Napoleon House** (500 Chartres St., French Quarter, ☎ 504-524-
  9752) is the sole seller of _hot_ muffulettas. Some locals find the very
  idea blasphemous, but others swear by it. This European-style cafe
  also serves other sandwiches, soups, jambalaya, and similar, moderately priced fare. Try the Pimm's Cup, a sweet-and-sour mix of
  lemonade, 7-Up, and Pimm's No. 1 — it's the bar's signature drink.
  The historic building — supposedly built for Napoleon (but
  unlikely) — fared well during Katrina, however, the shortened hours
  (only open until 6 p.m.) frustrate the usual late-night bar crowd.

Feasting on po' boys

You can put just about anything — ham, shrimp, oysters, roast beef —
between two slices of French bread and you've made yourself a po' boy.
See Chapter 3 to find out why these famously simple sandwiches are so
important to the local culture. Better yet, taste one by going to one (or
more!) of the following establishments:

- ✔ For the most popular po' boy spot in the Quarter, head to **Johnny's
  Po-boys** (511 St. Louis St., ☎ 504-524-8129). Family members are
  pitching in due to lack of staff, so please go support their efforts!

New Orleans Snacks

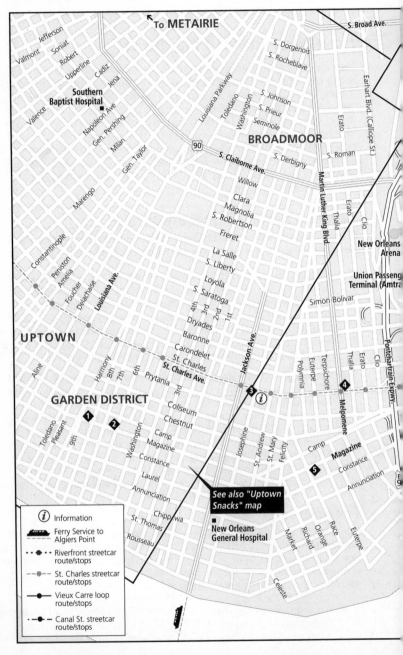

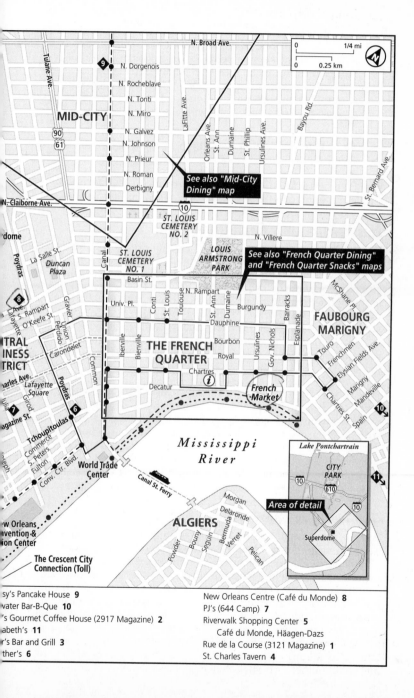

N. Broad Ave.

0   1/4 mi
0   0.25 km

9 N. Dorgenois
N. Rocheblave
N. Tonti
MID-CITY N. Miro
N. Galvez
(90) N. Johnson
(61) N. Prieur
N. Roman
Derbigny

Tulane Ave.

LaFitte Ave.

Orleans Ave.
St. Ann
Dumaine
St. Phillip
Ursulines Ave.

Bayou Rd.

St. Bernard Ave.

N. Claiborne Ave.

See also "Mid-City Dining" map

(10)
ST. LOUIS CEMETERY NO. 2

N. Villere

LOUIS ARMSTRONG PARK

See also "French Quarter Dining" and "French Quarter Snacks" maps

dome

La Salle St.
Duncan Plaza

Poydras

ST. LOUIS CEMETERY NO. 1

Basin St.

Canal

8
S. Rampart
O'Keefe St.
Graver
Union Perdido

Univ. Pl.

Conti
St. Louis
Toulouse
N. Rampart
St. Ann
Dumaine
Burgundy

Dauphine

St. Peter
Ursulines
Gov. Nichols
Barracks
Esplanade

McShane Pl.

FAUBOURG MARIGNY

CENTRAL BUSINESS DISTRICT

arles Ave.
Lafayette Square

Caronderlet

Iberville
Bienville

THE FRENCH QUARTER

Bourbon
Royal

Touro
Frenchmen

Elysian Fields Ave.

Magazine St.

Girod

7

6

Poydras

Common

Chartres
(i)

Decatur

French Market

Chartres St.

Marigny
Mandeville
Spain

10

Tchoupitoulas

Commerce
S. Peters
Fulton

Conv. Ctr. Blvd.

Mississippi River

Lake Pontchartrain

CITY PARK

(10)

(610)

11

seph

World Trade Center

Canal St. Ferry

Morgan
Delaronde

Area of detail

(10)

w Orleans
vention &
ion Center

ALGIERS

Powder
Bouny
Seguin
Bermuda
Verret
Pelican

Superdome

The Crescent City Connection (Toll)

sy's Pancake House **9**
vater Bar-B-Que **10**
's Gourmet Coffee House (2917 Magazine) **2**
abeth's **11**
r's Bar and Grill **3**
ther's **6**

New Orleans Centre (Café du Monde) **8**
PJ's (644 Camp) **7**
Riverwalk Shopping Center **5**
   Café du Monde, Häagen-Dazs
Rue de la Course (3121 Magazine) **1**
St. Charles Tavern **4**

- ✔ **Mother's** (401 Poydras St., ☎ 504-523-9656) serves a fine po' boy as does the **Napoleon House** (see the preceding section).

- ✔ In the Uptown area, **Domilise's** (5240 Annunciation St., ☎ **504-899-9126**) has been serving po' boys, as well as other hot dishes, for more than 75 years so they weren't about to let a little storm damage keep them closed for long. Try the "Peacemaker," a half-shrimp, half-oyster combination or a hot smoked sausage po' boy, dressed (see tip below), and with a bottle of Barq's.

- ✔ If you're tired of fried food, go for **Guy's** (5259 Magazine St., ☎ 504-891-5025) grilled shrimp po' boy (which requires an ice-cold root beer from the self-serve fridge).

When you order a po' boy, you'll be asked if you want it "dressed." Only say yes if you want lettuce, tomato, and mayonnaise on your sandwich.

Hankering for a hamburger

In New Orleans, sports, politics, and current events are popular topics. But those discussions are nothing compared to the amount of discourse spent on who makes the best burger in town. Many places make excellent burgers, but when you get right down it, this is a two-burger race between the **Port of Call** (838 Esplanade Ave., ☎ **504-523-0120**) and the **Clover Grill** (900 Bourbon St., ☎ **504-598-1010**). Both places make big burgers; the Port of Call's is a half-pound, while the Clover Grill's weighs in at a trim third of a pound. Both places keep their burgers juicy (the Clover cooks its burgers under a hubcap, believe it or not, to seal in the juices).

I used to heartily recommend **Michael's Mid-City Grill** (4139 Canal St.) if you had something special to celebrate, but severe flooding has put it out of business for good. For a mere $150, you'd get a burger topped with mushrooms, sour cream, and caviar — and a free bottle of Dom Perignon. The staff also took your photo to document the occasion, which was then tacked to the collage on the walls (you were far from the only person who bought the $150 burger!). I hate to think of all of those photos ruined by water and mold, all of those memories gone.

The world is your oyster

Katrina ruined many oyster beds by making brackish water a little too salty, so oysters were in short supply for awhile. Hopefully, the oyster population will return, given time. So if you get a chance to eat some, I say go for it and definitely savor the experience. I prefer my oysters fried and tucked inside a French bread, but some locals perfect the art of *oyster shooting* — slurping a raw oyster, often dressed with ketchup and horseradish, right out of its shell and letting it slide, virtually unchewed, right down the gullet. Oyster shooting may *sound* unappetizing, but try it once; it can sometimes be the right alternative to a heavy, sauce-laden meal. The following oyster bars also offer fried oysters, shrimp for peeling and dipping, and, when they're in season, plenty of boiled crawfish:

✔ **Acme Oyster House** (724 Iberville St., ☎ **504-522-5973**; 7306 Lakeshore Drive) spent $2 million on storm-related repairs, so you know they're *serious* about oysters. Get 'em raw, fried, or in over-stuffed po' boys. The Lakeshore location was devastated by flood-waters, and I doubt it will return.

✔ **Casamento's** (4330 Magazine St., ☎ **504-895-9761**) is mourning the untimely loss of 80-year-old Joe Casamento, whose father founded the restaurant. He lived above the restaurant, never took a vaca-tion, and it was believed that in nearly 40 years, he had never eaten anywhere else except the time he evacuated for a hurricane years ago and ate at a pancake house. He died the night he evacuated for Hurricane Katrina, possibly from heartbreak over the possible loss of his beloved restaurant and city. Please eat some oysters here in his honor. They are so incredibly good that Casamento's can afford to close for the summer (when oysters aren't at their peak) and locals are back in full force come fall. The homemade gumbo and oyster loaf are always worth the wait.

✔ **Felix's Restaurant and Oyster Bar** (739 Iberville St., ☎ **504-522-4440**) should be open by the time you read this. Feel free to eye the tempting Creole dishes, but keep in mind that they specialize in oysters and fried seafood.

Restaurant rescue for vegetarians

If you're a vegetarian traveler, your options in New Orleans are limited. If you can cook a food in animal fat, New Orleanians do. Ham and sausage even lurk in the red beans and rice. Nevertheless, a few places in town cater to the vegetarian market (though none of them are *exclusively* veg-etarian), and do a decent job of it, too.

✔ **Lebanon's Café** (1500 S. Carrollton Ave., Carrollton, ☎ **504-862-6200**) is extremely popular with the health- and money-conscious crowd, especially students and parents with little ones. When I need a veggie infusion, I order the sautéed vegetables topped with lightly browned goat cheese over basmati rice. The prices have increased since Katrina, but I think the food is well worth it.

✔ **Mona's** (3901 Banks St., Mid-City, ☎ **504-482-7743**; 4126 Magazine St., Uptown, ☎ **504-894-9800**; 3149 Calhoun St., Uptown, ☎ **504-861-2124**) is an unpretentious spot where people from all walks of life converge for Middle Eastern fare such as gyros, falafel, and the baba ganuj eggplant dip, with much to satisfy vegetarians with international palates. The Mid-City location flooded so be patient if there are still repairs going on during your visit.

✔ **Ralph's on the Park** (900 City Park Ave., Mid-City, ☎ **504-488-1000**) has fully recovered from flood damage and offers a special vegetar-ian menu if you ask for it.

French Quarter Snacks

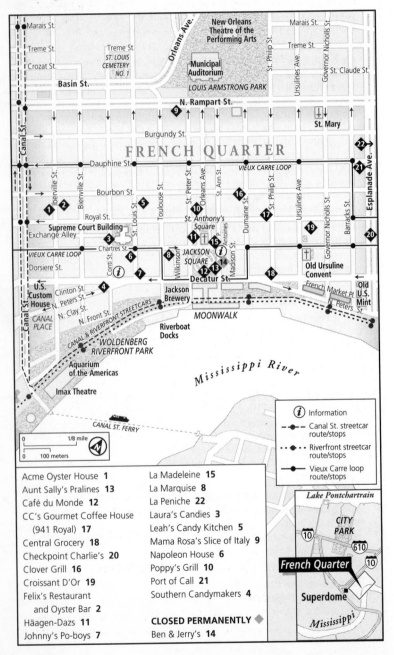

Acme Oyster House **1**

Aunt Sally's Pralines **13**

Café du Monde **12**

CC's Gourmet Coffee House
(941 Royal) **17**

Central Grocery **18**

Checkpoint Charlie's **20**

Clover Grill **16**

Croissant D'Or **19**

Felix's Restaurant
and Oyster Bar **2**

Häagen-Dazs **11**

Johnny's Po-boys **7**

La Madeleine **15**

La Marquise **8**

La Peniche **22**

Laura's Candies **3**

Leah's Candy Kitchen **5**

Mama Rosa's Slice of Italy **9**

Napoleon House **6**

Poppy's Grill **10**

Port of Call **21**

Southern Candymakers **4**

CLOSED PERMANENTLY ◆

Ben & Jerry's **14**

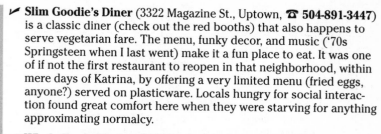

- ✔ **Slim Goodie's Diner** (3322 Magazine St., Uptown, ☎ **504-891-3447**) is a classic diner (check out the red booths) that also happens to serve vegetarian fare. The menu, funky decor, and music ('70s Springsteen when I last went) make it a fun place to eat. It was one of if not the first restaurant to reopen in that neighborhood, within mere days of Katrina, by offering a very limited menu (fried eggs, anyone?) served on plasticware. Locals hungry for social interaction found great comfort here when they were starving for anything approximating normalcy.

- ✔ **Whole Foods Market** (3135 Esplanade Ave., Mid-City; 5600 Magazine St., Uptown, ☎ **504-899-9119**), a local favorite for organic produce and vegetarian specialties, offers all items to go. In a prescient move, the quaint, smaller Mid-City location had closed prior to Katrina in favor of a sprawling big box location in the nearby suburb of Metairie.

Aside from these places, call ahead and ask if a particular restaurant that interests you features vegetarian entrees; a good number of them do. (Central Grocery, for example, offers a mean vegetable muffuletta.)

Lucky dogs: Street fare

A tradition in New Orleans since 1948, **Lucky Dog** carts became famous when spoofed in the Pulitzer Prize–winning book *A Confederacy of Dunces.* Missing in action for six months after Katrina, the carts that sell Lucky Dogs are once again on street corners throughout the French Quarter and Central Business District. (The carts spread out to other locations throughout the city during special events.) Spotting the carts is easy because they look like giant hot dogs.

Lucky Dogs are the perfect food for late-night revelers with a blood-alcohol volume of .05 percent or higher, and the carts are conveniently located throughout the Quarter to accommodate those who stumble out of nearby bars. A regular or foot-long hot dog or sausage dressed with the works (including chili) goes for less than $5.

A slice of pie

If you're in the mood for a familiar pepperoni pizza, or perhaps something a bit more gourmet, stop by one of these places:

- ✔ **Mama Rosa's Slice of Italy** (616 N. Rampart St., French Quarter, ☎ **504-523-5546**).

- ✔ **Reginelli's** (741 State St., Uptown, ☎ **504-899-1414**).

Neighborhood watch

For me, nothing quite tops people-watching at a diner or neighborhood joint, observing the ebb and flow of regular Janes and Joes in the tidal pool of the working world. The everyday give-and-take of greasy-spoon waitresses interacting with accountants, mechanics, and eccentrics is as fascinating to me as watching native tribal rituals is to an anthropologist. What follows, then, is a short and highly subjective list of neighborhood spots with just as much emphasis on character and atmosphere as on good food:

- ✔ **Betsy's Pancake House** (2542 Canal St., Mid-City, ☎ 504-822-0213) did indeed flood but this popular breakfast and lunch spot is open again and busy as ever. The waitresses will either annoy or amuse you; I find them to be fun.

- ✔ **Bywater Bar-B-Que** (3162 Dauphine St., Bywater, ☎ 504-944-4445) stayed high and dry and is the perfect place to harden your arteries with some prime barbecue. It also serves a decent burger and great pizza.

- ✔ **Franky and Johnny's** (321 Arabella St., Uptown, ☎ 504-899-9146) specializes in boiled seafood, but just about any of the sandwiches are rewarding. I love to play Ms. Pac-Man while waiting for my meal. They sustained little Katrina damage.

- ✔ **Liuzza's on Bienville** (3636 Bienville St., Mid-City, ☎ 504-482-9120) may be the mother of all neighborhood restaurants, especially after rising up again against all odds. Cool off with a giant frozen mug of beer and indulge in the popular "Frenchuletta," a muffuletta on French bread.

- ✔ **Mandina's** (3800 Canal St., Mid-City, ☎ 504-482-9179) suffered severe flooding but a sign claims, "We WILL return!" so here's hoping repairs and renovations continue to move along. This local legend aspires to some odd cross between stuffy upper-crust establishment and regular-Joe hangout. The sandwiches are good, but the real draws are daily specials such as red beans and rice or beef stew, as well as Italian and seafood dishes. Prepare for snobby waiters who can sniff out native New Orleanians from people who moved here from somewhere else; tourists don't stand a chance.

After-hours appetite

Clover Grill is one of the best places in town at which to eat in the predawn hours. Also in the French Quarter, **Poppy's Grill** and **Café du Monde** (800 Decatur St. at Jackson Square, ☎ 504-525-4544) are a couple of other reliable 24-hour snacking destinations. I'll never forget the first time I drove through the French Quarter after Katrina and found Café du Monde closed. It was just like a worst nightmare come true! Thank goodness they're back. But please don't feel like you must limit your options to them, nor to the French Quarter. You can find some late-night nourishment wherever you happen to be in New Orleans.

✔ **Clover Grill** (900 Bourbon St., French Quarter, ☎ **504-598-1010**) is a fun diner known for its juicy burgers (cooked under a hubcap to seal in the flavors), but it's now only open 24 hours on weekends. Bummer! Breakfast is served around the clock in a cheeky, whimsical atmosphere. This gay-friendly hangout also offers good shakes, malts, a painfully sweet icebox pie, and lots of coffee.

✔ **Igor's Bar and Grill** (2133 St. Charles Ave., Garden District, ☎ **504-522-2145**) offers 24-hour food, including the "world-famous" Igor burger, a good jukebox, and plenty of local atmosphere (and, again, self-serve laundry). It's also a good place to shoot pool.

✔ The down-home snacks and meals at **La Peniche** (1940 Dauphine St., Faubourg Marigny, ☎ **504-943-1460**) can really hit the spot. This gay-friendly spot has great half-pound hamburgers and homemade desserts; if the Oreo pie doesn't cause you to moan in ecstasy, call a mortician, because you must be dead. It used to be open 24 hours but now closes at 8 p.m.

✔ **Poppy's Grill** (717 St. Peter St., French Quarter, ☎ **504-524-3287**) is owned by the same folks who run Clover Grill, so the same lighthearted attitude prevails ("dancing in the aisles only"). It serves the same fabulous shakes, burgers, and other diner fare. That's not to say that Poppy's doesn't have its own unique qualities. Check out the scratch 'n' sniff menu or go for the blue plate special.

✔ **St. Charles Tavern** (1433 St. Charles Ave., Lower Garden District, ☎ **504-523-9823**) is also open 24 hours. The fare ranges from burgers to red beans and rice to Creole omelettes (stuffed with shrimp Creole). Don't be surprised if you find a short wait for a table even after 2 a.m.

Sipping a cup of joe

Since the 18th century, when European traders realized New Orleans was the logical importer of coffee from the Caribbean and South America, the Crescent City and coffee have remained inseparable. The devastation of Katrina demonstrated just how important New Orleans is as a port city to the rest of the nation. These are my favorite places to wake up in the morning:

✔ Open 24 hours, the original **Café du Monde** (800 Decatur St., French Quarter, ☎ **504-528-9933**) makes a legendary café au lait — strong New Orleans coffee flavored with chicory to make it less bitter and mixed with an equal portion of scalded milk. This prime place for people-watching has been around since 1862 and closed briefly after Katrina. (A handful of Café du Monde satellites are scattered around the city and suburbs.)

Uptown Snacks

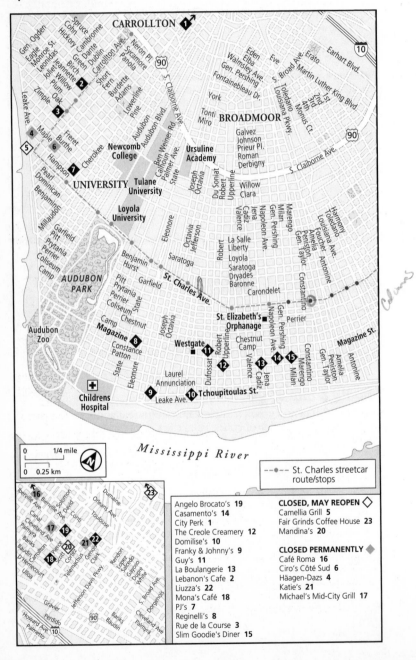

Angelo Brocato's **19**
Casamento's **14**
City Perk **1**
The Creole Creamery **12**
Domilise's **10**
Franky & Johnny's **9**
Guy's **11**
La Boulangerie **13**
Lebanon's Cafe **2**
Liuzza's **22**
Mona's Café **18**
PJ's **7**
Reginelli's **8**
Rue de la Course **3**
Slim Goodie's Diner **15**

CLOSED, MAY REOPEN ◇
Camellia Grill **5**
Fair Grinds Coffee House **23**
Mandina's **20**

CLOSED PERMANENTLY ◆
Café Roma **16**
Ciro's Côté Sud **6**
Häagen-Dazs **4**
Katie's **21**
Michael's Mid-City Grill **17**

---●--- St. Charles streetcar route/stops

Quick-stop java shops

The presence of two ubiquitous local coffee institutions in New Orleans is akin to that of Starbucks in the rest of the country (New Orleans has those too, by the way). **CC's Gourmet Coffee House** and **PJ's Coffee & Tea Co.** both have multiple locations throughout the metropolitan area. Of the two, I'm partial to homegrown PJ's with its funkier atmosphere.

Some of the more centrally located CC's locations include the following:

✓ 2917 Magazine St., Garden District (☎ 504-891-2115)

✓ 941 Royal St., French Quarter(☎ 504-581-6996)

Some of the more popular PJ's locations are the following:

✓ 7624 Maple St., Uptown (☎ 504-866-7031)

✓ 644 Camp St., Warehouse District (☎ 504-529-3658)

✓ **Café Fleur de Lis** (307 Chartres St., French Quarter, ☎ 504-529-9641) offers salads, light sandwiches and even a fruit bowl along with great coffee. It's probably the closest you'll find to a health store in New Orleans.

✓ **City Perk** (637 N. Carrollton Ave., Mid-City, ☎ 504-482-4847) was flooded badly and the owners have worked hard to repair and renovate it. It's an easy streetcar ride away thanks to the Canal line. This independent coffeehouse features friendly staff, consistently great drinks, vegan pastries, and yummy panini sandwiches. Grab a seat on the front patio or walk to nearby City Park (about six blocks) for an impromptu picnic. Dogs are welcome on the patio.

✓ **EnVie** (1241 Decatur St., French Quarter, ☎ 504-524-3689) was the first coffeehouse to reopen in the city post-Katrina. Its European style in both look and food (cheese boards!) complements the Crescent City. Breakfast is available until 2 p.m.

✓ **Fair Grinds Coffee House** (333 Ponce de Leon St., Mid-City, ☎ 504-948-3222) suffered severe flooding and is technically closed. But it now offers free coffee and Wi-Fi to area residents who rely on it as a meeting place as they work together to rebuild their community.

✓ **Rue de la Course** (1500 Magazine St., Lower Garden District; 3128 Magazine St., Uptown, ☎ 504-899-0242; 1140 S. Carrollton Ave., Carrollton, ☎ 504-861-4343) is modeled after 17th-century European coffeehouses, with cool, friendly college kids and locals hanging out and lingering over the morning paper. Chocolate lovers, order the iced cioccolato, which is an improvement on the standard iced mocha. A handful of these exist in the metropolitan area. I always thought that with its pressed-tin ceiling and odd mix of folks, the original location at 1500 Magazine was best, but that location has since been replaced by another coffee shop.

Beignets: Sweet treats

Beignets (pronounced ben-*yays*) are basically fried doughnuts generously covered with lots of powdered sugar. Novices may be tempted to shake off some of the sugar. Don't mess with it; the sugar tastes great, especially after the heat of the freshly baked beignet melts it. If anything, you end up adding *more* powdered sugar, courtesy of sugar shakers on the table. **Café du Monde** (800 Decatur St., ☎ 504-528-9933) is Beignet Central. They're a steal at three for about $1, and because the place is open 24 hours (every day but Christmas), you can satisfy your craving at any time. Other non-24-hour Café du Mondes are at the Riverwalk Shopping Center (1 Poydras St., ☎ 504-587-0841) and the New Orleans Centre shopping center (1400 Poydras St., ☎ 504-587-0842).

La patisserie

If you want to pretend that you're grabbing a snack back in French Colonial days, drop by one of these patisseries. Although they all offer seating, you may want to take your pastry to nearby Jackson Square to people-watch.

✔ **Croissant D'Or** (617 Ursulines St., ☎ 504-524-4663) is going strong and provides daily fresh-baked pastries for its sister location, La Marquise, as well, though this location has cheaper prices for the same delectable items. Ask the staff for the history behind the old "Ladies' Entrance" sign on the sidewalk. Opt for a seat beside the decrepit fountain in the outdoor courtyard and give the little sparrows a crumb or two.

✔ **La Boulangerie** (3143 Ponce de Leon St., ☎ 504-940-0577; 4526 Magazine St., ☎ 504-269-3777) offerings vary by location. The original spot on Magazine is a full bakery that is worth walking into for the smell alone. The Mid-City location is closed due to flooding and will be replaced by a wine store, Sip.

✔ **La Madeleine** (547 St. Ann St. ☎ 504-568-0073) was temporarily closed post-Katrina because of lack of staff, but should be open by the time you read this. Seek out its delectable French pastries and other light menu items. It also maintains locations in the Garden District and in the Riverbend.

✔ The lush courtyard at **La Marquise** (625 Chartres St., ☎ 504-524-0420) makes a great place to take a leisurely breakfast or an afternoon break. Croissant D'Or's sister shop offers all sorts of delicious pastries, soups, salads, and sandwiches. Serving hours are limited for now.

For your sweet tooth

The one word you need to know when discussing homegrown New Orleans–style sugary snacks is *pralines* (pronounced *praw*-leens, not *pray*-leens). Give these tasty confections (made with brown sugar and pecans) a try and you may become addicted. **Aunt Sally's Pralines** (810 Decatur St., ☎ 800-642-7257 or 504-944-6090) off-site warehouse and kitchen were flooded by Katrina, but the retail shop is up and running again. At **Southern Candymakers** (334 Decatur St., ☎ 800-344-9773 or 504-523-5544), you can watch the staff making the famous local candy. **Laura's Candies** (331 Chartres St., ☎ 800-992-9699 or 504-525-3880), open since 1913, offers pralines, fudge, and golf-ball-size truffles. **Evans Creole Candy Factory** (848 Decatur St., ☎ 504-522-7111), started in 1900, so you know they have perfected their praline recipe. Some people cast their vote for best praline to **Leah's Candy Kitchen** (714 St. Louis St., ☎ 504-523-5662), which is slowly getting back on its feet.

Screaming for ice cream

You can find ice-cream carts throughout the French Quarter, especially around Jackson Square. Or try **Häagen-Dazs Ice Cream Parlors** at 621 St. Peter St. (☎ 504-523-4001), the Riverwalk Shopping Center, and 1 Poydras St. (☎ 504-523-3566). Unfortunately, the Riverbend location (8108 Hampson St.) is permanently closed, as are both Ben & Jerry's on Jackson Square and in badly flooded City Park.

For a really special treat, head to **The Creole Creamery** (4924 Prytania St., ☎ 504-894-8680) for unusual gourmet flavors like bananas Foster and lemon garlic. Or take the Canal Streetcar to an old favorite, **Angelo Brocato's** (214 N. Carrollton Ave., ☎ 504-486-0078), which suffered great losses from flooding but worked hard to rebuild and is now open. Its creamy and rich gelato will make you an instant fan of Italian ice cream. If you're in the Lower Garden District, stop by **Sophie's Ice Cream Parlor** (1912 Magazine St., ☎ 504-561-0291), which specializes in seasonal homemade gelato and the "reverse" root beer float.

Technically, it's not ice cream, but if you're here during the summer, cool off with a New Orleans tradition: the sno ball. It's finely shaved ice dowsed in one or more flavored syrups. Locals also like to top their sno ball with condensed cream or whipped cream. You'll find sno ball stands throughout the city, but you absolutely must go to **Hansen's Sno Bliz** (4801 Tchoupitoulas St.; ☎ 504-891-9788). Founders Ernest and Mary Hansen started the business during the Depression and both died soon after Hurricane Katrina. Their granddaughter, Ashley Hansen, has taken over. **Plum Street Sno Balls** (1300 Plum St., ☎ 504-866-7996) has an amazing orchid-flavored sno ball that you just have to try to understand. (*Note:* Sno balls are seasonal, so only look for them Apr–Sept.)

Index of Establishments by Neighborhood

Carrollton/Garden District/Uptown

Basil Leaf (Thai, $–$$)
Brigtsen's (Cajun/Creole, $$)
Casamento's (Sandwiches/Seafood,
$–$$)
CC's Gourmet Coffee House
(Coffee/Sweets, $)
Commander's Palace (Creole, $$–$$$)
The Creole Creamery (Ice Cream, $)
Dick & Jenny's (Creole/Eclectic, $–$$)
Domilise's (Sandwiches/Seafood, $)
Five Happiness (Chinese, $–$$)
Franky & Johnny's
(Sandwiches/Seafood, $)
Gautreau's (Creole, $$–$$$)
Guy's (Sandwiches/Seafood, $)
Hansen's Sno Bliz (Sno Balls, $)
Igor's Bar & Grill (Sandwiches/
Seafood/Short Order, $)
Jacques-Imo's Café (Creole/Soul Food,
$–$$)
Juan's Flying Burrito (Mexican, $)
La Boulangerie (French/Sweets, $)
Lebanon's Café (Middle Eastern,
Sandwiches, $)
Liborio's Cuban Restaurant (Cuban, $)
Lilette (Creole/French, $$)
Mona's (Middle Eastern/
Sandwiches, $)
Pascal's Manale
(Italian/Seafood/Steakhouse, $–$$)
PJ's Coffee & Tea Co. (Coffee/
Sandwiches/Sweets, $)

Plum Street Sno Balls (Sno Balls, $)
Reginelli's (Pizza, Sandwiches, $)
Rue de la Course (Coffee/Sweets, $)
St. Charles Tavern (Sandwiches/
Seafood/Short Order, $)
Slim Goodie's Diner (Breakfast/
Sandwiches/Short Order/
Vegetarian, $)
Sophie's Ice Cream Parlor (Ice Cream/
Sweets, $)
Taqueria Corona (Mexican, $)
Upperline (Eclectic/Creole, $$)
Whole Foods (International/
Sandwiches/Vegetarian, $)

Mid-City

Angelo Brocato's (Sweets/
Ice Cream, $)
Betsy's Pancake House
(American/Breakfast/Sandwiches/
Short Order, $)
City Perk (Coffee/Sandwiches/
Sweets, $)
Fair Grinds Coffee House
(Coffee/Sweets, $)
Juan's Flying Burrito (Mexican, $)
Liuzza's on Bienville
(Italian/Sandwiches/Seafood, $)
Mona's (Middle Eastern/
Sandwiches, $)
Ralph's on the Park (Creole/
Seafood, $$)

Index of Establishments by Cuisine

American/New American

Betsy's Pancake House (Mid-City, $)
Bywater Bar-B-Que (Bywater, $)
Cuvée (Central Business District, $$)
Emeril's (Warehouse District, $$–$$$)
Herbsaint (Central Business District,
$–$$)
Peristyle (French Quarter, $$)

Breakfast

Betsy's Pancake House (Mid-City, $)
Brennan's (French Quarter, $$–$$$)

Clover Grill (French Quarter, $)
Elizabeth's (Bywater, $–$$)
Mother's (Central Business District,
$–$$)
The New Orleans Grill (Central
Business District, $$–$$$)
Poppy's Grill (French Quarter, $)
Slim Goodie's Diner (Uptown, $)

Cajun

Brigtsen's (Carrollton/Uptown, $$)
K-Paul's Louisiana Kitchen (French
Quarter, $$–$$$)

Chinese
Five Happiness (Uptown, $–$$)

Coffee
Café du Monde (French Quarter, $)
Café Fleur de Lis (French Quarter, $)
CC's Gourmet Coffee House (French Quarter/Garden District/Mid-City, $)
City Perk (Mid-City, $)
Croissant D'Or (French Quarter, $)
EnVie (French Quarter, $)
Fair Grinds Coffee House (Mid-City, $)
La Marquise (French Quarter, $)
PJ's Coffee & Tea Co. (Uptown/Warehouse District, $)
Rue de la Course (Carrollton/Uptown, $)

Contemporary Louisiana/French Provençal
Irene's Cuisine (French Quarter, $–$$)
Restaurant August (Central Business District, $$–$$$)

Creole
Antoine's (French Quarter, $$–$$$$)
Arnaud's (French Quarter, $$–$$$)
Bacco (French Quarter, $–$$)
Brennan's (French Quarter, $$–$$$)
Brigtsen's (Uptown/Carrolltown, $$)
Commander's Palace (Garden District, $$–$$$)
Court of Two Sisters (French Quarter, $$–$$$)
Cuvée (Central Business District, $$)
Dick & Jenny's (Uptown, $–$$)
Elizabeth's (Bywater, $–$$)
Emeril's (Warehouse District, $$–$$$)
Felix's Restaurant and Oyster Bar (French Quarter, $–$$)
Gautreau's (Uptown, $$–$$$)
Jacques-Imo's Café (Uptown, $–$$)
Lilette (Uptown, $$)
Mother's (Central Business District, $–$$)
Olivier's (French Quarter, $–$$)
Palace Café (French Quarter, $$–$$$)
Ralph & Kacoo's (French Quarter, $–$$$)
Ralph's on the Park (Mid-City, $$)
St. Charles Tavern (Garden District, $)
Tujaque's (French Quarter,$$$)
Upperline (Uptown, $$)

Cuban
Liborio's Cuban Restaurant (Garden District, $)

French
Antoine's (French Quarter, $$–$$$$)
Brennan's (French Quarter, $$–$$$)
Croissant D'Or (French Quarter, $)
Galatoire's (French Quarter, $–$$)
Herbsaint (Central Business District, $–$$)
La Boulangerie (Uptown, $)
Lilette (Uptown, $$)
Olivier's (French Quarter, $–$$)
Peristyle (French Quarter, $$)
Restaurant August (Central Business District,)

International/Eclectic
Bayona (French Quarter, $$–$$$)
The Bistro at Maison de Ville (French Quarter, $$–$$$)
Dick & Jenny's (Uptown, $–$$)
The New Orleans Grill (Central Business District, $$–$$$)
Upperline (Uptown, $$)
Whole Foods (Uptown, $)

Italian
Bacco (French Quarter, $–$$)
Irene's Cuisine (French Quarter, $–$$)
Liuzza's on Bienville (Mid-City, $)
Pascal's Manale (Uptown, $–$$)
Peristyle (French Quarter, $$)

Japanese
Horinoya (Central Business District, $–$$)
Sekisui Samurai (French Quarter, $–$$)

Mexican

Juan's Flying Burrito (Garden District/Mid-City, $)

Taqueria Corona (Uptown/Warehouse District, $)

Middle Eastern

Lebanon's Café (Carrollton/Uptown, $)

Mona's (Mid-City/Uptown, $)

Pizza

Mama Rosa's Slice of Italy (French Quarter, $)

Reginelli's (Sandwiches/Pizza, $)

Sandwiches/Hamburgers

Acme Oyster House (French Quarter, $–$$)

Betsy's Pancake House (Mid-City, $)

Bywater Bar-B-Que (Bywater, $)

Café Fleur de Lis (French Quarter, $)

Café Maspero (French Quarter, $)

Casamento's (Uptown, $–$$)

Central Grocery (French Quarter, $)

City Perk (Mid-City, $)

Clover Grill (French Quarter, $)

Domilise's (Uptown, $)

Elizabeth's (Bywater, $)

EnVie (French Quarter, $)

Franky & Johnny's (Uptown, $)

Guy's (Uptown, $)

Igor's Bar & Grill (Garden District, $)

Johnny's Po-boys (French Quarter, $–$$)

La Marquise (French Quarter, $)

La Peniche (Faubourg Marigny, $)

Lebanon's Café (Uptown, $)

Liuzza's on Bienville (Mid-City, $)

Lucky Dog (French Quarter, $)

Mama Rosa's Slice of Italy (French Quarter, $)

Mona's (Mid-City/Uptown, $)

Mother's (Central Business District, $–$$)

Napoleon House (French Quarter, $)

PJ's Coffee & Tea Co. (Uptown/Warehouse District, $)

Poppy's Grill (French Quarter, $)

Port of Call (French Quarter, $–$$)

Reginelli's (Sandwiches/Pizza, $)

Slim Goodie's Diner (Uptown, $)

St. Charles Tavern (Garden District, $)

Whole Foods (Uptown, $)

Seafood

Acme Oyster House (Sandwiches/Seafood, $–$$)

Café Maspero (French Quarter, $)

Casamento's (Uptown, $–$$)

Horinoya (Central Business District, $–$$)

Domilise's (Uptown, $)

Franky & Johnny's (Uptown, $)

Guy's (Uptown, $)

Igor's Bar & Grill (Garden District, $)

Johnny's Po-boys (French Quarter, $–$$)

Liuzza's on Bienville (Mid-City, $)

Mandina's (Mid-City, $–$$)

Olivier's (French Quarter, $–$$)

Pascal's Manale (Uptown, $–$$)

Ralph & Kacoo's (French Quarter, $–$$$)

Ralph's on the Park (Mid-City, $$)

Rib Room (French Quarter, $$–$$$)

Sekisui Samurai (French Quarter, $–$$)

St. Charles Tavern (Garden District, $)

Short Order

Betsy's Pancake House (Mid-City, $)

Clover Grill (French Quarter, $)

Igor's Bar & Grill (Garden District, $)

La Peniche (Faubourg Marigny, $)

Mother's (Central Business District, $–$$)

Poppy's Grill (French Quarter, $)

Slim Goodie's Diner (Uptown, $)

St. Charles Tavern (Garden District, $)

Soul Food

Jacques-Imo's Café (Uptown, $–$$)

Steakhouse

Pascal's Manale (Uptown, $–$$)

Rib Room (French Quarter, $$–$$$)

Sweets/Ice Cream/Sno Balls

Angelo Brocato's (Mid-City, $)
Aunt Sally's Pralines (French Quarter, $)
Café du Monde (French Quarter, $)
Café Fleur de Lis (French Quarter, $)
CC's Gourmet Coffee House (French Quarter/Garden District/Mid-City, $)
City Perk (Mid-City, $)
The Creole Creamery (Uptown, $)
Croissant D'Or (French Quarter, $)
EnVie (French Quarter, $)
Evans Creole Candy Factory (French Quarter, $)
Fair Grinds Coffee House (Mid-City, $)
Häagen-Dazs Ice Cream Parlor (French Quarter, $)
Hansen's Sno Bliz (Sno Balls, $)
La Boulangerie (Uptown, $)
La Madeleine (French Quarter, $)
La Marquise (French Quarter, $)
Laura's Candies (French Quarter, $)
Leah's Candy Kitchen (Sweets, $)

PJ's Coffee & Tea Co. (Uptown/Warehouse District, $)
Plum Street Sno Balls (Uptown, $)
Rue de la Course (Carrollton/Uptown, $)
Sophie's Ice Cream Parlor (Garden District, $)
Southern Candymakers (French Quarter, $)

Thai

Basil Leaf (Uptown, $–$$)

Vegetarian

Lebanon's Café (Uptown, $)
Mona's (Mid-City/Uptown, $)
Ralph's on the Park (Mid-City, $$)
Slim Goodie's Diner (Uptown, $)
Whole Foods (Uptown, $)

Vietnamese

Lemon Grass Restaurant (Central Business District, $–$$)

Index of Establishments by Price

Evans Creole Candy Factory (Sweets, French Quarter)
Fair Grinds Coffee House (Coffee/Sweets, Mid-City)
Five Happiness (Chinese, Uptown)
Franky & Johnny's (Sandwiches/Seafood, Uptown)
Galatoire's (French, French Quarter)
Guy's (Sandwiches/Seafood, Uptown)
Häagen-Dazs Ice Cream Parlor (Ice Cream, French Quarter)
Hansen's Sno Bliz (Sno Balls, Uptown)
Herbsaint (French/New American, Central Business District)
Horinoya (Japanese/Seafood, Central Business District)
Igor's Bar & Grill (Sandwiches/Seafood/Short Order, Garden District)
Irene's Cuisine (Italian/French Provençal, French Quarter)
Jacques-Imo's (Creole/Soul Food, Uptown)
Johnny's Po-boys (Sandwiches/Seafood, French Quarter)
Juan's Flying Burrito (Mexican, Mid-City/Garden District)
La Boulangerie (French/Sweets, Uptown)
La Marquise (Coffee/Sandwiches/Sweets, French Quarter)
La Peniche (Sandwiches/Hamburgers/Short Order, Faubourg Marigny)
Laura's Candies (Sweets, French Quarter)
Leah's Candy Kitchen (Sweets, French Quarter)
Lebanon's Café (Middle Eastern, Sandwiches, Mid-City)
Lemon Grass Restaurant (Vietnamese, Central Business District)
Liborio's Cuban Restaurant (Cuban, Garden District)
Liuzza's on Bienville (Italian/Sandwiches/Seafood, Mid-City)
Lucky Dog (Sandwiches, French Quarter)
Mama Rosa's Slice of Italy (Sandwiches/Pizza, French Quarter)
Mona's (Middle Eastern/Sandwiches, Mid-City/Uptown)

Mother's (Sandwiches/Creole/Short Order/Breakfast, Central Business District)
Napoleon House (Sandwiches, French Quarter)
Olivier's (Creole/French/Seafood, French Quarter)
Pascal's Manale (Italian/Seafood/Steakhouse, Uptown)
PJ's Coffee & Tea Co. (Coffee/Sandwiches, Uptown/Warehouse District)
Plum Street Sno Balls (Sno Balls, Uptown)
Poppy's Grill (Breakfast/Sandwiches/Hamburgers/Short Order, French Quarter)
Port of Call (Hamburgers, French Quarter)
Ralph & Kacoo's (Creole/Seafood, French Quarter)
Reginelli's (Pizza, Sandwiches, Uptown)
Rue de la Course (Coffee/Sweets, Carrollton/Garden District/Uptown)
St. Charles Tavern (Sandwiches/Seafood/Short Order, Garden District)
Sekisui Samurai (Japanese/Seafood, French Quarter)
Slim Goodie's Diner (Breakfast/Sandwiches/Short Order/Vegetarian, Uptown)
Sophie's Ice Cream Parlor (Ice Cream, Garden District)
Southern Candymakers (Sweets/Ice Cream, French Quarter)
Taqueria Corona (Mexican, Uptown/Warehouse District)
Upperline (Eclectic/Creole, Uptown)
Whole Foods (International/Sandwiches/Vegetarian, Uptown)

$$

Acme Oyster House (Sandwiches/Seafood, French Quarter)
Antoine's (Creole/French, French Quarter)
Arnaud's (Creole, French Quarter)
Bacco (Italian/Creole, French Quarter)
Basil Leaf (Thai, Uptown)

Bayona (International, French Quarter)

The Bistro at Maison de Ville (International/Eclectic, French Quarter)

Brennan's (French/Creole, French Quarter)

Brigtsen's (Cajun/Creole, Uptown/Carrollton)

Casamento's (Sandwiches/Seafood, Uptown)

Court of Two Sisters (Creole, French Quarter)

Cuvée (Creole/New American, Central Business District)

Commander's Palace (Creole, Garden District)

Dick & Jenny's (Creole/Eclectic, Uptown)

Elizabeth's (Breakfast/Creole, Bywater)

Emeril's (Creole/New American, Warehouse District)

Five Happiness (Chinese, Uptown)

Galatoire's (French, French Quarter)

Gautreau's (Creole, Uptown)

Herbsaint (French/New American, Central Business District)

Horinoya (Japanese/Seafood, Central Business District)

Irene's Cuisine (Italian/French Provençal, French Quarter)

Jacques-Imo's (Creole/Soul Food, Uptown)

Johnny's Po-boys (Sandwiches/Seafood, French Quarter)

K-Paul's Louisiana Kitchen (Cajun, French Quarter)

Lemon Grass Restaurant (Vietnamese, Central Business District)

Lilette (Creole/French, Uptown)

Mother's (Sandwiches/Creole/Short Order/Breakfast, Central Business District)

The New Orleans Grill (Central Business District)

Olivier's (Creole/French/Seafood, French Quarter)

Palace Café (Creole, French Quarter)

Pascal's Manale (Italian/Seafood/Steakhouse, Uptown)

Peristyle (French/Italian/New American, French Quarter)

Port of Call (Hamburgers, French Quarter)

Ralph & Kacoo's (Creole/Seafood, French Quarter)

Ralph's on the Park (Creole/Seafood)

Restaurant August (Contemporary French, Central Business District)

Rib Room (Steakhouse/Seafood, French Quarter)

Sekisui Samurai (Japanese/Seafood, French Quarter)

Upperline (Eclectic/Creole, Uptown)

$$$

Antoine's (Creole/French, French Quarter)

Arnaud's (Creole, French Quarter)

Bayona (International, French Quarter)

The Bistro at Maison de Ville (International/Eclectic, French Quarter)

Brennan's (French/Creole, French Quarter)

Commander's Palace (Creole, Garden District)

Court of Two Sisters (Creole, French Quarter)

Gautreau's (Creole, Uptown)

Emeril's (Creole/New American, Warehouse District)

K-Paul's Louisiana Kitchen (Cajun, French Quarter)

The New Orleans Grill (International, Central Business District)

Palace Café (Creole, French Quarter)

Ralph & Kacoo's (Creole/Seafood, French Quarter)

Rib Room (Steakhouse/Seafood, French Quarter)

Tujaque's (Creole, French Quarter)

$$$$

Antoine's (Creole/French, French Quarter)

Part IV
Exploring
New Orleans

"Honey, come on – that's part of the charm of New Orleans. Where else would they put a voodoo doll on your pillow instead of a mint at turndown?"

In this part . . .

You have at least one foolproof way to work off all the food you'll consume in New Orleans — sightseeing! Chapter 12 covers the absolute must-see attractions, followed by a comprehensive list of other worthwhile places and information on guided tours.

Chapter 13 familiarizes you with the city's diverse shopping areas, whether you want to browse the familiar brand-name department stores or comb through funky boutiques.

Chapter 14 suggests some great itineraries to help budget your time, and Chapter 15 throws in a couple of daytrips you may enjoy.

Chapter 12

Discovering New Orleans's Best Attractions

· ·

In This Chapter

▶ Reviewing the top attractions in town
▶ Assessing attractions post-Katrina
▶ Introducing additional sights by location and type
▶ Taking a guided tour
▶ Seeing the devastated areas

· ·

*T*hanks to great food and music, New Orleans has an embarrassment of cultural riches, even after Katrina. However, the thing about New Orleans that charms many people — and what we worry about losing as the city rebuilds — is its unique sense of character and identity. This chapter presents a selective, alphabetical list of the top places where you can soak up the best of the Crescent City, while also having a good time and maybe discovering something new along the way.

Assessing Katrina's Damage to City Attractions

Those attractions in severely flooded areas such as Mid-City and New Orleans East did not fare well for the most part and I strongly doubt they will return. For those in better shape, you might find that admission prices are lower but hours of operation are shorter due to a smaller pool of staff and/or anticipation of fewer visitors (for at least the first couple years after Katrina). Please keep in mind that prices will eventually increase, so now is the time when your tourist dollar will stretch a little further. A few places, such as the Audubon Zoo, slightly increased their admission prices, which is not much considering their losses that could've been passed on to you. Many businesses are making a concerted effort to keep prices reasonably low to encourage tourists to return, so again, this is to your advantage.

One of the most dramatic photos I saw in the weeks following Katrina was the image of a huge Six Flags roller coaster jutting out from what appeared to be a lake. This 140-acre theme park opened in 2000 as Jazzland Theme Park and was purchased by Six Flags soon thereafter. The amusement park was destroyed by storm surge and Category 3-plus winds. It is permanently closed.

New Orleans's Top Sights

No matter how you want to spend your time, New Orleans offers a multitude of choices. Read the following to get an idea.

Aquarium of the Americas
French Quarter

Before Katrina, this stylish, entertaining, and winningly educational aquarium — one of the top ten in the United States — featured breathtaking exhibits made you feel as if you were walking under water or exploring a tropical rain forest. In 2002, there was a public uproar when 10 aquarium visitors on a behind-the-scenes-tour fell into the 20-foot-deep, 400,000-gallon shark tank when the catwalk collapsed. Within 15 minutes, everyone was rescued and thankfully unharmed. The aquarium assured the public that safety was of the utmost concern and people continued coming to this popular destination. When Katrina came, all of the fish and animals survived the storm itself, however, as days passed without power and emergency generators began to give out, there was nothing the dedicated staff could do. They were then forced to evacuate for their own safety and upon their return four days later, most of the aquarium's 10,000 fish had died. Previous visitors will be happy to know that 250-pound sea turtle Midas, comic otter duo Buck and Emma, white alligator Spots and the African black-footed and Rockhopper penguins all survived. After eight months of renovations, the aquarium opened again, featuring many new fish and animals, some of which were donated by other institutions. The aquarium features an interactive, hands-on activity area for kids, along with popular exhibits of penguins (fed daily at 10:30 a.m. and 3 p.m.), sea horses, sharks and sting rays. Aquarium volunteers in blue or green shirts can answer your questions and steer you in the right direction if you're lost. Give yourself 1½ to 2 hours to see the aquarium.

See map p. 204. 1 Canal St. (at the Mississippi River). ☎ *800-774-7394 or 504-581-4629.* www.auduboninstitute.org. *Open: Tues–Sun 10 a.m.–5 p.m. Admission: $16 adults, $13 seniors, $9.50 children 2–12, children 2 and under get in free. Parking: 3-hour complimentary parking in the Hilton New Orleans Riverside parking lot with ticket stub. Wheelchair accessible.*

Armstrong Park
French Quarter

This historical spot, once the only place where slaves could congregate, used to be called Congo Square. (Congo Square still exists inside the park.)

New Orleans Attractions

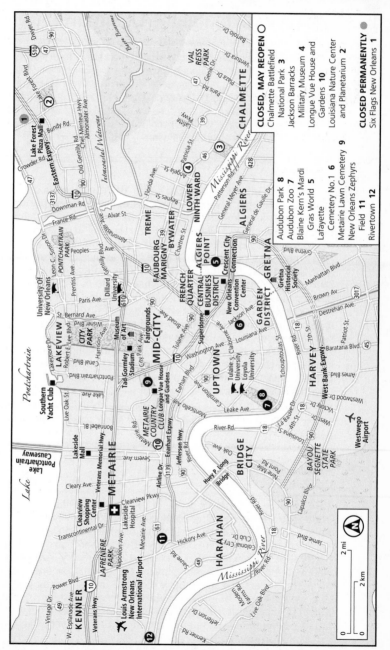

CLOSED, MAY REOPEN ○

Chalmette Battlefield
National Park **3**
Jackson Barracks
Military Museum **4**
Longue Vue House and
Gardens **10**
Louisiana Nature Center
and Planetarium **2**

CLOSED PERMANENTLY ●

Six Flags New Orleans **1**

Audubon Park **8**
Audubon Zoo **7**
Blaine Kern's Mardi
Gras World **5**
Lafayette
Cemetery No.1 **6**
Metairie Lawn Cemetery **9**
New Orleans Zephyrs
Field **11**
Rivertown **12**

A New Orleans IMAX experience

Next door to the Aquarium of the Americas is the IMAX Theatre (☎ **800-774-7394** or 504-581-4629), with large-screen 3-D documentaries (past shows have featured everything from dinosaurs to the Rolling Stones) that are sure to delight the kids. It sustained minor equipment damage and roof damage after Katrina but was able to reopen by May 2006. You can purchase tickets separately for $8 for adults and $5 for children 2–12 years old ($7 for seniors 65 and up), or save a couple of bucks with the aquarium/IMAX combination admission. Shows run hourly from 10 a.m.–6 p.m. (last show starts at 5 p.m.). Wheelchair accessible theater.

Transformed into a public park and dedicated to jazz legend Louis Armstrong, the park offers visitors stately sycamores, peaceful lagoons, and rolling grassy knolls. You can also find the Municipal Auditorium and the Mahalia Jackson Theater for the Performing Arts (see Chapter 16). As we go to print, Perseverance Hall, the Reimann House, and the Rabassa House are being restored and will be used as part of the much-anticipated New Orleans Jazz National Historical Park, which should open in spring 2007. During Mardi Gras, the all-canine Krewe of Barkus and its two- and four-legged fans gather here prior to the parade. Other park events can be more solemn; on the one-year anniversary of Hurricane Katrina, hundreds marched from the site of the Lower Ninth Ward levee break to the park in remembrance. The park entrance is just outside the Quarter in the Faubourg Tremé neighborhood at St. Ann and Rampart streets. The area is safe during the day, but I don't recommend venturing there at night unless you go as part of a large group or during an event. Give yourself 30 to 60 minutes to visit the park.

See map p. 204. On N. Rampart Street, between Toulouse and St. Phillip streets, facing the French Quarter. Open: seasonal hours. Admission: free. Wheelchair accessible.

Audubon Park
Uptown

This 340-acre public park is one of the most beautiful and tranquil spots in the city and named after John James Audubon, who briefly lived here. After Katrina, some of the young live oak trees and those weak from termite damage fell or had to be removed, but other than that, the park fared pretty well. It even survived serving as a temporary campground for the National Guard in the weeks following the storm. Now once again a refuge for nature lovers, it's also a busy social thoroughfare; bicyclists, joggers, dog walkers, and horseback riders (Cascade Stables closed prior to Katrina for a complete renovation which has now been put on hold indefinitely) come to enjoy the atmosphere and the scenery. Tucked into this sprawling expanse of land are tennis courts, riding and jogging paths, a public golf course, resident populations of squirrels and birds (keep an eye out for wood ducks, swans and egrets), and hundreds of gorgeous centuries-old live oaks. If you cross Magazine Street, you'll find Audubon Zoo (see details below) and beyond that, a park along the Mississippi River. Come here to have a picnic, exercise, or just relax by the fountain at the St. Charles Avenue entrance — but don't stay after dark. Allow 30 to 60 minutes for an appreciative stroll.

See map p. 199. 6500 St. Charles Ave. (across from Tulane and Loyola universities, nestled between St. Charles Avenue and Magazine Street). Take the St. Charles Streetcar (or bus) and get off in front of the park. ☎ *504-581-4629. Open: Daily 6 a.m.–10 p.m. Admission: free. Wheelchair accessible.*

Audubon Zoo
Uptown

Thanks to excellent hurricane preparation, all but three of the zoo's 1,800 animals, including some rare and endangered species, survived Katrina and live in this sprawling maze of lagoons, waterfalls, and vegetation. During the storm, staff members took refuge in the *art nouveau*-styled reptile building. Days later, their biggest challenges were food shortages and overheated pumps but they never gave up. At one point, relief workers were invited to visit for free, which was a very kind invitation on the part of the staff. Situated inside Audubon Park on the bank of the Mississippi River, the zoo features an array of exhibits, including a replica of a Louisiana swamp and the Dragon's Lair exhibit featuring spectacular 6- to 9-foot-long Komodo dragons, weighing on average 200 pounds, from Indonesia. The zoo boasts a white alligator, two white Bengal tigers named Rex and Zulu, and a host of other exotic animals. The Jaguar Jungle exhibit is a stunning acre-and-a-half replica of an ancient Mayan city filled with spider monkeys, macaws, iguanas, and other creatures; low-lying fog adds an air of mystery. Monkey Hill was artificially constructed by the Works Progress Administration in the 1930s, supposedly to demonstrate what a hill looked like to local kids since New Orleans is famously flat. The circa 1928 sea lion–pool, featuring neo-classical columns and allowing visitors to walk down one story and peer through windows at the sea lions swimming by, is still closed for renovations. Give yourself two to four hours to thoroughly enjoy the zoo.

See map p. 199. 6500 Magazine St. ☎ *800-774-7394 or 504-581-4629.* www.audubon institute.org. *Once it's running again, take the St. Charles Streetcar (or bus) and get off at the park entrance. A free shuttle through the park runs every 20 minutes. If you prefer, take the Magazine Street bus and get off at the zoo. Admission: $12 adults, $9 seniors (older than 65), and $7 children 2–12. Parking: free. Wheelchair accessible. Open: Tues–Fri 10 a.m.–4 p.m.; open till 5 p.m. weekends in the summer. Last ticket sold one hour before closing. Closed Mardi Gras day, the first Friday in May, Thanksgiving, and Christmas.*

Cruising from A(quarium) to Z(oo)

The popular ferry boat rides were discontinued after Katrina but should return in 2007. You can purchase a combination ticket for admission to both the Aquarium of the Americas and the Audubon Zoo, with a riverboat ride on the sternwheeler *John James Audubon* taking you between the two. Combination admissions for all three (cruise, aquarium, and zoo) will be available, with other combination admissions offered. Trips depart from the Riverwalk (in front of the aquarium) and from the zoo. (Call ☎ **800-774-7394** or 504-581-4629 for more information or to confirm schedule.)

Bourbon Street
French Quarter

As you walk along Bourbon Street, between the 100 and 1,000 blocks, you may feel like you've just crashed the world's largest ongoing, open-air fraternity party. This is New Orleans Party Central, for better or for worse, and at night it's definitely not a kids' attraction — unless you're a kid between the ages of 21 and 100. Bourbon Street is an odd mix of the authentic and the contrived, with its carnival-style barkers trying to lure you into strip clubs, its buggy drivers ferrying tourists, and its requisite street performers and scam artists competing for your attention (and your money). Most, if not all, bars on Bourbon Street (which is blocked off for pedestrians only) stay open until the wee, wee hours — some well into the morning. You can even take an alcoholic drink with you for a stroll — as long as you carry it in a plastic "go-cup." During the daylight hours, Bourbon Street becomes more relaxed and can almost look deserted. Only restaurants, T-shirt and souvenir shops, and a few bars stay open during the day. Depending on the ages of your children and your definition of family values, you may want your kids to see Bourbon Street only in daylight — or not at all. With the kids during the day, allow about an hour for a visit. If you're a bigger kid looking to cut loose at night, well, take your time.

Cabildo
French Quarter

The Cabildo, where the French government turned over the Louisiana Purchase to the United States in 1803, was built in 1795 as the Spanish seat of government. A fire in 1988 caused horrible damage to the historic building and it required five years of restoration to make it whole again. The Louisiana State Museum considers it "headquarters" for all of its French Quarter interests, and if you can't see every state museum, be sure to make time for at least this one. It sustained very minor damage to windows and shutters during Katrina. Worthwhile exhibits cover all aspects of life in early Louisiana, including antebellum music, mourning and burial customs, and the changing roles of women in the South. Each room seems more interesting than the one before. Allow at least an hour for your visit.

See map p. 204. 701 Chartres St. (at St. Ann Street on Jackson Square; 2 blocks from Bourbon Street). ☎ ***800-568-6968*** *or 504-568-6968.* http://lsm.crt.state.la.us/site/cabex.htm. *Admission: $5 adults, $4 students and seniors, free for children under 13. Wheelchair accessible, though the elevator is small. Open: Tues–Sun 9 a.m.–5 p.m.*

City Park
Mid-City

The Canal Streetcar takes you directly to City Park, which suffered greatly in the weeks after Katrina. At 1,500 acres, it's the fifth largest urban park in the United States and shelters the largest collection of mature live oaks in the world. Many of these beautiful trees — which have lived for hundreds of years — could not survive being under three- to eight-feet of brackish water for two weeks. Once the floodwaters receded, all of the grass, flowers, and bushes had died and brown muck covered everything. For years prior to Katrina, the trees and landscape did not receive the maintenance and care that it required due to lack of funds and staff because the park has never received money from the City of New Orleans or the state of Louisiana. However, the summer before Katrina, the park appeared to turn a corner with a master plan to increase revenue, revitalize underutilized sections of the park, and create more recreational opportunities, such as a skate park and dog agility center. Sadly, Katrina dashed that plan and the park was in worse shape than before. However, financial support from around the world has helped the cleanup and the flora and fauna are returning stronger than ever. Give yourself at least an hour to explore the park, two to three if you have children or want to linger at two or more of the spots listed here. (Much longer, of course, if you're going to play 18 holes of golf.) If you plan to visit the **New Orleans Museum of Art** (☎ **504-488-2631;** see listing later in this chapter), which is located on the park grounds, allow another hour to an hour and a half. For additional details on the following activities inside the park, go to the **City Park Web site** at www.neworleanscitypark.com.

The **Carousel Gardens** (☎ **504-482-4888**) in City Park house is currently closed. It boasts one of the country's few remaining carved wooden carousels, which survived Katrina but requires some repair. Two miniature trains take riders on a 2½-mile trip through the park. Also check out the small Ferris wheel and wading pool. The **Botanical Gardens** (☎ **504-483-9386**) was destroyed by floodwaters but amazing volunteers replanted everything, allowing it to reopen in March 2006. Though not as lush as before, I was pleasantly surprised to see how much growth there has been already. Explore 12 acres of gardens, fountains, ponds, and sculptures, plus a horticultural library and a gift shop. Open Tuesday through Saturday from 10 a.m. to 4:30 p.m., admission is free for the time being though donations of any amount are very welcome. Offering 26 larger-than-life storybook-themed play areas. **Storyland** (☎ **504-483-9381**) is great for children. Child

French Quarter Attractions

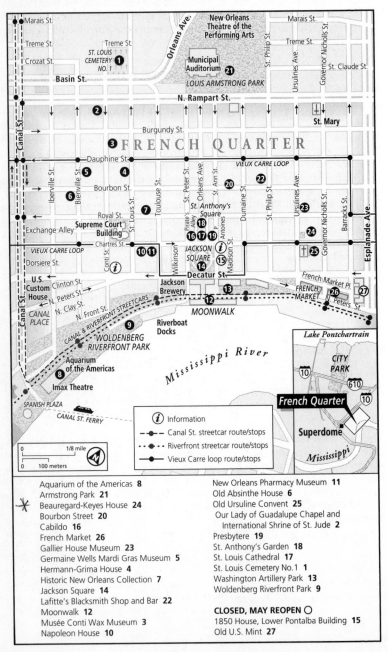

Aquarium of the Americas **8**
Armstrong Park **21**
Beauregard-Keyes House **24**
Bourbon Street **20**
Cabildo **16**
French Market **26**
Gallier House Museum **23**
Germaine Wells Mardi Gras Museum **5**
Hermann-Grima House **4**
Historic New Orleans Collection **7**
Jackson Square **14**
Lafitte's Blacksmith Shop and Bar **22**
Moonwalk **12**
Musée Conti Wax Museum **3**
Napoleon House **10**

New Orleans Pharmacy Museum **11**
Old Absinthe House **6**
Old Ursuline Convent **25**
Our Lady of Guadalupe Chapel and
   International Shrine of St. Jude **2**
Presbytere **19**
St. Anthony's Garden **18**
St. Louis Cathedral **17**
St. Louis Cemetery No.1 **1**
Washington Artillery Park **13**
Woldenberg Riverfront Park **9**

CLOSED, MAY REOPEN ○
1850 House, Lower Pontalba Building **15**
Old U.S. Mint **27**

magazine once rated it one of the 10 best in the country. Admission is $2, free for kids under 2. Other features of the park include the following:

- ✔ Four 18-hole public golf courses with lessons by PGA pros, electric carts, rentals, pro shop, and restaurant (☎ **504-483-9397**), are closed due to Katrina damage, however, the 100-tee driving range (☎ **504-483-9394**) is now open.

- ✔ Thirty-six tennis courts (☎ **504-483-9383**) are repaired and ready for play.

- ✔ Fishing (☎ **504-483-9371**) in the park's lagoons for bass, catfish, and perch. Permits are required and may be purchased on site — call or visit the city park Web site for details.

- ✔ Horseback rides, lessons, and pony rides (☎ **504-483-9398**).

See map p. 212. 1 Palm Drive. City Park is located all the way up Esplanade Avenue out of the French Quarter. ☎ ***504-482-4888.*** www.neworleanscitypark.com. *Take the Esplanade bus from the French Quarter and get off at the park. Open: sunrise til sunset. Parking: free. Wheelchair accessible.*

French Market
French Quarter

In the days after we evacuated and hearing news reports that the city was underwater, I was so worried that the French Quarter was completely destroyed, for without it, there simply is no New Orleans. The Quarter is its epicenter. This nexus of local trade, located on high ground right next to the river (from St. Phillip Street to the edge of the Quarter at Esplanade Avenue), did not flood and has been a fixture since the early 1700s. Its shops, flea market, and farmer's market are still neat places to shop for souvenirs, gifts, T-shirts, jewelry, arts and crafts, and fresh produce. Finish your shopping spree by indulging in some beignets at **Café du Monde,** located right along the market. Give yourself at least 30 to 60 minutes to wander the market.

See map p. 204. The French Market stretches along Decatur and N. Peters streets from St. Ann to Barracks. Admission: free. Wheelchair accessible. Open: most shops from 10 a.m.–6 p.m. daily. The Farmer's Market and Café du Monde are open 24 hours.

Jackson Square
French Quarter

President Bush stood here and publicly proclaimed that New Orleans would rebuild. Locals are determined to make good on his promise. Historically, Jackson Square served New Orleans as the place of execution, military parade ground, and town square. Today, the beautiful landscaping, trees, benches, and a tranquil fountain make this square one of the more popular public places in the city. Katrina did knock down two massive oak trees, which miraculously fell beside a marble statue of Jesus Christ — just snapping off the thumb and forefinger of an outstretched hand — located across from the 280-year-old St. Louis Cathedral. Along the ornate black-iron fence, artists set up shop on the sidewalk while mules stand along Decatur Street, patiently waiting to take tourists for a trip around the Quarter. Consult a tarot card reader or a psychic while watching clowns, street musicians, "living statues," and mimes vie for your tips. You can grab some ice cream, a soft drink, or another snack from a street vendor, or head for one of the restaurants located on each corner of the square. Allot 30 to 60 minutes to look around — considerably more if you decide to run away and join the street mimes.

See map p. 204. The square fronts the 700 block of Decatur Street and is bounded by Chartres, St. Ann, and St. Peter streets. www.jackson-square.com. *Admission: free. Open: seasonal hours, but usually from dawn to dusk.*

Louisiana Children's Museum
Warehouse District

This spacious, two-story interactive museum is really a playground in disguise. The hands-on exhibits open up the worlds of science and nature and role playing. Kids can be chefs, tugboat captains, or even TV anchors in a simulated television studio. Activities and exhibits include everything from a pint-sized grocery store to a "challenges" exhibit where they shoot hoops from a wheelchair and a math and physics lab. Allow 90 minutes to 2 hours. There was minimal storm damage.

See map p. 207. 420 Julia St. (4 blocks from the Convention Center). ☎ **504-523-1357.** www.lcm.org. *(Tues–Sat 9:30 a.m.–4:30 p.m; Sun noon–4:30 p.m; summer hours Mon 9:30 a.m.–4:30 p.m.). Admission: $7. Parking: Hourly lots nearby. Wheelchair accessible.*

Louisiana Nature Center and Planetarium
New Orleans East

The Nature Center was nestled in Joe Brown Park, an 85-acre stretch of Louisiana forest that was crushed by storm surge from the Gulf and Lake Pontchartrain. According to the Audubon Institute, which also manages the aquarium and zoo, the nature center will remain closed until further notice.

See map p. 199. Nature Center Drive in the Joe Brown Memorial Park.

Mardi Gras
Central Business District/French Quarter/Garden District/Mid-City/ Uptown

Although it's not confined to one physical location, Mardi Gras — the biggest free party thrown on the North American continent — is by far

Central Business District/Warehouse District Attractions

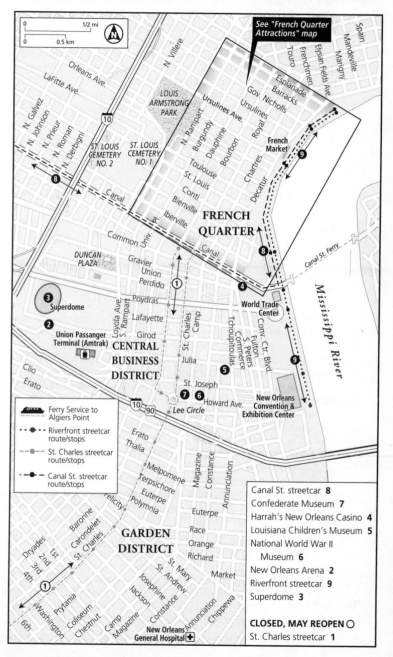

See "French Quarter Attractions" map

Canal St. streetcar **8**
Confederate Museum **7**
Harrah's New Orleans Casino **4**
Louisiana Children's Museum **5**
National World War II
   Museum **6**
New Orleans Arena **2**
Riverfront streetcar **9**
Superdome **3**

CLOSED, MAY REOPEN ○
St. Charles streetcar **1**

New Orleans's most popular attraction. You could write volumes about its rich and colorful history (and many people have; see Chapter 3). Revelers flock to the city from all over the United States — and the world — while some locals, who don't feel like fighting the crowds, hightail it out of town for the final few days. If you like crowds, you'll love joining the raucous street party in the French Quarter, especially on Bourbon Street between the 500 block and 1000 block. For these who prefer a little elbow room, I suggest you head as far Uptown as possible (think Napoleon Avenue). The 2006 Carnival season, while on a smaller scale than usual, gave locals a reason to smile and tourists extra incentive to visit and see the city at its spirited best.

For a family-friendly Mardi Gras experience, check out the parades in other parts of the city, most notably the parade route along **St. Charles Avenue** uptown. Also, the suburbs are increasingly becoming a haven for families. Although it's a bit of a drive, you can find a much more G-rated experience (okay, maybe PG-13) if you decamp along one of the major suburban parade routes. **Veterans Memorial Boulevard** in Metairie (on the East Bank of Jefferson Parish) or the **Westbank Expressway** (one of the main thoroughfares across the river, on the West Bank of Jefferson Parish) make

Mardi Gras Indians

Groups (or "tribes") of African American men who dress in elaborate Native American costumes are called "Mardi Gras Indians." Their elaborate, beaded suits (they prefer to say "suits," not "costumes") are their pride and joy, and they put serious work into them, usually taking a whole year to put one together. Feathers, sequins, headdresses — the costumes are spectacular. In the weeks after Katrina, as tribe members were allowed to return to their water-logged, moldy homes, some nailed their ruined costumes to the front of their houses, which was quite ghostly to behold. Some people say that the tradition originally developed as a way of showing thanks to Native Americans who helped escaped slaves. The Indian parades never follow an organized route, but roam at will. Fights used to break out when two different tribes met on the street, but today the tribes engage in an elaborate call-and-response ceremony instead. (Some Mardi Gras Indian tribes are also musical groups. The most popular these days is the Wild Magnolias, who have played and recorded albums with such luminaries as Dr. John, Bruce Hornsby, and Robbie Robertson.) Some Indians marched on Mardi Gras Day 2006 to show that their spirit could not be suppressed, while others sat it out, feeling that it was too soon to partake in traditional celebrations.

You can get a better understanding of these tribes at the **Backstreet Cultural Museum**, 1116 St. Claude Ave. (☎ **504-522-4806**; www.backstreetmuseum.org), located off the tourist path in a home in the Treme. See these fantastic, colorful suits up close in an intimate setting, where the affable owner Sylvester Francis also displays his collection of memorabilia from Jazz Funerals, Social Clubs, Second Lines, and more. The **Presbytere** (see p. 204) displays suits as well, but Backstreet is the real deal. Open Tuesday through Saturday from 10 a.m. to 5 p.m., and admission is $5.

Mardi Gras Parade Routes

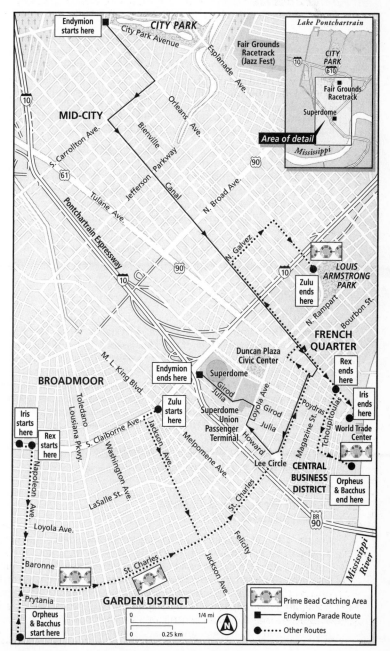

good spots. Compared to the bacchanalia on Bourbon Street, these sub-urban areas offer a whole other world. Sure, some drinking and partying goes on, but for the most part, they're good for a family outing.

If you drive a car to New Orleans, *never* park along a parade route for at least two hours before or after a parade. You'll see signs telling you the parade dates and times all over the place. If you choose to ignore these warnings, your car will be towed. The best bet for getting to Mardi Gras parades is to walk or take public transportation. Even for people who know how to get around, traffic is impossible, so if you must drive, give yourself plenty of time. Or call a cab; the number for **United Cab,** the city's largest and most well-known cab fleet, is ☎ 504-522-9771.

Your kids are sure to enjoy the Mardi Gras experience; costumes, crowds, and parades are quite a stimulant. Make sure your kids get plenty of sleep the night before so they don't tire out early. Mardi Gras certainly won't bore them, but it can make for a long day. Avoid spending the kids' college fund on overpriced Mardi Gras food by bringing snacks and drinks with you. Also, decide on a meeting place in advance in case someone gets lost or separated.

Citywide parades roll nearly every day in the two weeks prior to Mardi Gras day. Admission: free. Wheelchair accessible.

Moonwalk
French Quarter

Although the name conjures up that '80s dance move, the Moonwalk is a riverside path whose view of the Mississippi River and the Crescent City Connection (a twin-span bridge to Algiers Point, an established New Orleans neighborhood) makes for a romantic stroll. From the Moonwalk, you can watch river traffic coming into and going out of the second busiest port in the world. Named for Mayor Moon Landrieu, during whose admin-istration it was built, the Moonwalk is directly across the street from Jackson Square. Allow 10 to 15 minutes for general sightseeing, or more if you're looking for *amore*.

See map p. 204. Jackson Square. ☎ *504-587-0738. Admission: free. Wheelchair accessible. Open: 24 hours a day, but go before midnight for safety's sake.*

National World War II Museum
Central Business District

Contrary to initial reports, no looting took place here. This one-of-a-kind museum, formerly known as The National D-Day Museum, features quietly poignant and thought-provoking exhibits relating to D-Day, June 6, 1944, when the Allies stormed the beaches of Normandy and changed the course of World War II. The museum includes a 110-seat theater playing the Oscar-nominated documentary *D-Day Remembered.* The museum also features exhibits devoted to other beach landings and amphibious invasions during the war, often told through the personal stories and artifacts of the soldiers

Mardi huh? What the terms mean

Talking the talk and walking the walk are crucial if you plan to go to New Orleans during Mardi Gras. With these terms, you can talk the talk like a pro. Walking the walk, on the other hand, is entirely up to you.

- **Ball** or **Tableau Ball:** Krewes host these themed, masked balls. Themes change from year to year.

- **Boeuf Gras** (fattened calf): The calf represents ritual sacrifice, as well as the last meal eaten before Lent. It's also the symbol of Mardi Gras and the first float of the Rex parade.

- **Carnival:** A celebration beginning January 6 (the 12th night after Christmas) and ending Mardi Gras day.

- **Court:** A krewe's king, queen, and attendants.

- **Doubloon:** Krewes throw these metal coins during parades. They feature the logo of the krewe on one side and its theme for a particular year on the other.

- **Fat Tuesday:** Otherwise known as Mardi Gras, the last day before Ash Wednesday, which is the first day of Lent.

- **Favor:** Krewe members give these souvenirs, which feature the krewe's logo and date, to people who attend their ball.

- **Flambeaux:** Flaming torches carried by parade participants on foot; they aren't members of the krewe.

- **King Cake:** An oval, sugared pastry decorated with purple, gold, and green (Mardi Gras colors) that contains a small doll representing the baby Jesus.

- **Krewe:** The traditional word for a Carnival organization.

- **Lagniappe** (pronounced lan-*yap*): Loosely means "a little extra," and refers to any small gift or token — even a scrap of food or a free drink.

- **Mardi Gras:** French for "Fat Tuesday." Technically, if you say "Mardi Gras day," you're really saying "Fat Tuesday day."

- **Rex:** Latin for "king." The King of Carnival is Rex.

- **Second Line:** A group of people that follows a parade, dancing to the music. Also, a musical term that specifies a particular shuffling tempo popularized in much New Orleans music.

- **Throws:** Inexpensive trinkets thrown from floats to parade watchers, including doubloons, minifootballs, plastic swords, and spears and all sorts of knick-knacks. The most coveted throws are the gilded coconuts of the Zulu Social Aid and Pleasure Club.

Mid-City Attractions

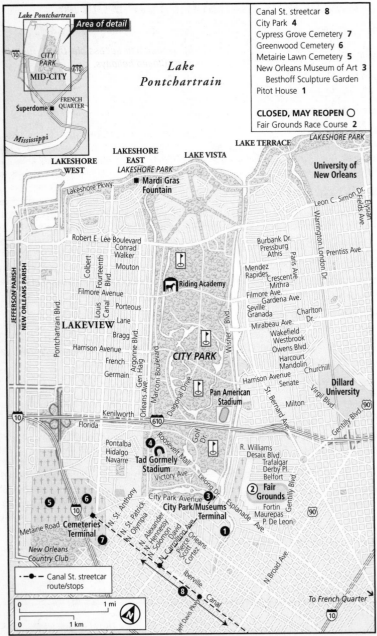

Canal St. streetcar **8**
City Park **4**
Cypress Grove Cemetery **7**
Greenwood Cemetery **6**
Metairie Lawn Cemetery **5**
New Orleans Museum of Art **3**
  Besthoff Sculpture Garden
Pitot House **1**

CLOSED, MAY REOPEN ○
Fair Grounds Race Course **2**

themselves. Allow one to two hours for the curious, at least half a day for serious history buffs.

See map p. 207. 945 Magazine St. (at Howard Avenue) ☎ **504-527-6012.** www.dday museum.org. *In the Warehouse District; enter on the Howard Avenue side. Admission: $14 adults, $8 seniors, $6 children under 18, children under 5 free. Parking: On-street and hourly lots available nearby. Wheelchair accessible. Open: Tues–Sat 9 a.m.–5 p.m. Open until 7 p.m. on Thursdays. Closed holidays.*

New Orleans Museum of Art
Mid-City

Take the Canal Streetcar to City Park, where a stately, oak-lined avenue leads you to New Orleans's premier fine arts museum, nicknamed "NOMA" by the locals. The museum was literally an island in flooded City Park, and a shelter for some staff who stayed and helped protect its valuable contents. You can find a magnificent 40,000-piece permanent collection of African American, Asian, European, and pre-Columbian works, including paintings, sculpture, and a decorative glass collection, plus ever-changing art exhibits from around the world. Past exhibits have featured works by Degas, Fabergé, and Monet, as well as Egyptian treasures and a commemoration of the Louisiana Purchase. The spectacular Besthoff Sculpture Garden has reopened and remains a study in contrasts with its natural backdrop of moss-draped oak trees and the clean lines of modern and contemporary sculpture. NOMA always has special exhibits and tours for kids. Allow two to three hours for your visit.

See map p. 212. 1 Collins Diboll Circle. ☎ **504-658-4100.** www.noma.org. *Admission: $8 adults, $7 seniors, $4 children 3–17; free to Louisiana residents; sculpture garden free (donations accepted), same hours as museum. Parking: free. Wheelchair accessible. Open: Tues–Sun 10 a.m.–4:30 p.m.*

Old U.S. Mint
French Quarter

Built in 1835, this huge Greek Revival building now belongs to the Louisiana State Museum, but it used to mint money for both the United States and the Confederacy. Pre-Katrina, it played host to a large exhibit showcasing New Orleans jazz. The museum features a comprehensive collection of pictures, musical instruments (including Louis Armstrong's first trumpet), and other artifacts that trace the development of jazz. Unfortunately, it sustained terrible damage from Katrina and is still closed for extensive renovations.

See map p. 204. 400 Esplanade Ave. ☎ **800-568-6968** *or 504-568-6968.* http://lsm.crt.state.la.us/mintex.htm.

Presbytere
French Quarter

This building was intended as a home for the Spanish clergy, but it took many years to finish and wound up being used as a courthouse instead.

Pre-Katrina, it was a branch of the Louisiana State Museum and home of a Mardi Gras exhibit, featuring colorful costumes and interactive displays on the festival's history. The building was damaged from Katrina then repaired and reopened in September 2006.

See map p. 204. 751 Chartres St. (at Jackson Square). ☎ *800-568-6968 or 504-568-6968.* http://lsm.crt.state.la.us. *Admission: $5 adults, $4 seniors and students, free for children under 12. Wheelchair accessible. Open: Tues–Sun 9 a.m.–5 p.m.*

St. Charles Streetcar and Canal Streetcar
Central Business District/Garden District/Uptown/Carrollton and Riverfront/Central Business District/Mid-City

The oldest continually operating streetcar system in the world, the St. Charles Streetcar began in 1835 as a mule-drawn railway and was electrified in 1893. In one of those quirky convergences of tradition and modernity that New Orleans is so famous for, the streetcar was both a national historic attraction *and* a functioning arm of the New Orleans public transit system. The Canal Streetcar began running again in April 2004 after 40 years of being out of service, proving that modern doesn't always mean better. The St. Charles line was closed due to storm damage and its green cars substituted for the Canal line since the new red cars in its Mid-City streetcar barn was destroyed by floodwaters. Hopefully, by the time you read this, the historic green cars will be rolling down St. Charles again and Canal will again have red, air-conditioned cars. Flip to Chapters 9 and 14 for information on the streetcar routes and attractions along the way. The St. Charles round-trip is about 14 miles and takes two to three hours; the Canal round-trip is nearly 11 miles and takes one to two hours.

☎ *504-248-3900.* www.norta.org. *Admission: $1.25 each way (exact change required); a VisiTour pass provides unlimited rides on streetcars or buses at a cost of $5 for 1 day or $12 for 3 days. Ask at your hotel or a tourist office for the nearest VisiTour pass vendor.*

St. Louis Cathedral
French Quarter

The oldest continuously operating cathedral in the United States, the St. Louis Cathedral dates from 1794, though the church was largely rebuilt in the 1850s. It has quite an interesting history and is the third building to stand on this spot. The first church was destroyed by a hurricane in 1722, and the second by the great fire of 1788. Supposedly the cathedral's bells were kept silent for religious reasons (it was Good Friday), so they didn't ring out to alarm folks of the fire, which went on to destroy more than 800 buildings. The first post-Katrina mass held in October 2005 was a very emotional event, allowing many locals to publicly mourn what was lost and pray for the strength to rebuild. The stained-glass windows and mural depicting the life of King Louis IX, the cathedral's patron saint, are especially beautiful. Located directly behind the cathedral, St. Anthony's

Garden is named for Pere Antoine, a popular rector who served New Orleans in the late 18th and early 19th centuries. Legend claims that many duels were fought here in the past. Now, however, the main attraction comes at night, when a huge shadow of Christ appears against the back of the church — thanks to a statue and a carefully placed spotlight. The garden isn't open for tours, but it is worth peeking into it from Royal Street, Pirates' Alley, or Pere Antoine's Alley.

See map p. 204. 615 Pere Antoine Alley (at Jackson Square). ☎ *504-525-9583.* www.stlouiscathedral.org. *Admission: Entry and tours are free, but donations are requested. Wheelchair accessible. Open: Tours are given Mon–Sat 9 a.m.– 5 p.m. and Sun 2–5 p.m.*

Finding More Cool Things to See and Do

Need to find an activity to keep the kids smiling and the teenager happy? Care to enlighten the historian inside you, or perhaps catch a game? The following suggestions should keep your diverse tastes and needs satisfied.

Especially for kids

Touring New Orleans with your small fry in tow will obviously be a drastically different experience from the one you'd have coming alone or with your significant other. But that doesn't mean you have to sacrifice for the sake of the kids. Finding attractions that appeal to all age groups is easier than you think. For example, a romantic riverboat ride (see "Dinner on the water: Riverboat cruises," later in this chapter for more information) also appeals to the young 'uns — just in a different way. Here are some kid-tested sights that you'll likely find interesting as well.

Blaine Kern's Mardi Gras World
Algiers

Algiers is a lesser known neighborhood of New Orleans that resides on the other side of the Mississippi River, known as the West Bank. Despite being sandwiched between the Gulf and the river, the West Bank did not flood at all during Katrina. If your visit doesn't coincide with Mardi Gras season, this place gives you a taste of what it's all about. You see people building and/or decorating a Mardi Gras float (this is where most of the floats in the city are made). You can watch a Mardi Gras film and even get your picture taken in a Mardi Gras costume. Furthermore, you get complimentary king cake and coffee. Budget around two hours to get here; take the tour and find your way back to the Quarter.

See map p. 199. 223 Newton St., Algiers Point. ☎ **800-362-8213** *or 504-361-7821.* www.mardigrasworld.com. *Take the Canal St. Ferry — free for pedestrians — and a van will meet you, take you to the site, and bring you back. (Van reservations only needed for parties of 15 or more.) Admission: $15 adults, $11 seniors (over 62), $7.25 children 3–12, free for children under 3. Parking: free. Wheelchair accessible. Open: Daily 9:30 a.m.–4:30 p.m. (closed some holidays)*

Chalmette Battlefield National Park
Chalmette

This park is the site of the historic Battle of New Orleans, where General Andrew Jackson and a ragtag band staged a desperate defense of the city against the British. This last major battle of the War of 1812 actually took place *after* the war was officially over — the participants just hadn't yet received word. Tragically, Chalmette was inundated with storm surge pushed up the Mississippi River Gulf Outlet, nicknamed "Mr. Go," an under-utilized channel dug up by the Army Corps of Engineers. Locals have demanded that the channel be forever closed to prevent this from happening again, but at press time, the battle raged on. Replica cannons, a reconstructed bunker, and the Chalmette Monument, which honors the battle's fallen soldiers, create a sense of history underscored by the collection of battlefield memorabilia housed in the visitor center. Also on the grounds is the Chalmette National Cemetery, which holds the bodies of 14,000 Union soldiers who died during the Civil War (as well as the bodies of American soldiers from every subsequent American war). Oddly enough, only one combatant from the Battle of New Orleans rests here. The battlefield grounds and public restrooms remain open to visitors, but the visitor center, Chalmette Monument, and the Malus-Beauregard House remain closed due to extensive damage.

See map p. 199. 8606 W. Saint Bernard Hwy., Chalmette. www.nps.gov/jela/chalmette-battlefield.htm. *Open: Mon–Thurs 7 a.m.–3 p.m.; Fri–Sat 9 a.m.–4:30 p.m.*

Musée Conti Wax Museum
French Quarter

After 40 years, this third-generation-owned and operated family business is still going strong and had no Katrina damage. The climate control here makes this a good place to escape from the heat. As you'd expect, you see the requisite Haunted Dungeon with its monsters and scenes from well-known horror tales. You also find a large section devoted to Louisiana legends such as Andrew Jackson, Marie Laveau, Napoleon Bonaparte, Huey Long, Pete Fountain, Louis Armstrong, and even a Mardi Gras Indian. Allow 30 to 60 minutes, unless you're procrastinating to beat the heat.

See map p. 204. 917 Conti St., near the corner of Burgundy. ☎ *800-233-5405 or 504-525-2605.* www.historyofneworleans.com. *Admission: $6.75 adults, $6.25 seniors (over 62), $5.75 children 4–17, free for children under 4. Parking: On-street and hourly lots within one block. Wheelchair accessible. Open: Mon–Sat 10 a.m.–5 p.m.*

Rivertown
Kenner

Offering a nice little tourist area along the banks of the Mississippi River, the city of Kenner sits about 10 miles northwest of the French Quarter.

Only a few areas flooded. A sort of town within a city, Rivertown is a great family spot for visitors, with a multitude of kid-friendly attractions. (*Note:* All the following Rivertown attractions share the same telephone number: ☎ **504-468-7231.**)

- ✔ Kids love the six working train layouts at the **Louisiana Toy Train Museum** at 519 Williams Blvd. It remains closed for renovations, so please call ahead.

- ✔ The planetarium and observatory at the **Freeport McMoRan Daily Living Science Center** (409 Williams Blvd.) is also worth a visit. Shows run at 2 p.m. Tuesday through Friday, with three shows on weekends. On Thursday through Saturday, 7:30 to 10:30 p.m., you can view the night sky.

- ✔ If your child likes magic, puppet shows, mimes, and stories, visit the **Children's Castle** at 503 Williams Blvd.

- ✔ Kids, as well as sports fans of all ages, get a kick out of seeing memorabilia and film clips of the New Orleans Saints NFL franchise at the **Saints Hall of Fame** at 415 Williams Blvd.

- ✔ You can see many animals, as well as a small aquarium, at the **Louisiana Wildlife Museum,** 303 Williams Blvd. The museum also features tales of everyday life from 1750 to 1850 told by people in period costume.

- ✔ Finally, the **Mardi Gras Museum of Jefferson Parish** (415 Williams Blvd.) caters to those people who didn't come during Mardi Gras, didn't visit Mardi Gras World, or just can't get enough Mardi Gras fun.

☎ *504-468-7231.* www.rivertownkenner.com. *All museums are within a 3-block area and an easy walk from each other. Admission: $3 for adults, $2.50 for seniors and children under 12; Planetarium and Megadome Cinema $6 for adults, $5 for seniors and kids; two-show combo tickets are $10 for adults, $8 for seniors and kids; three-show combo tickets are $15 for adults, $12 for seniors and kids. Parking: free. All museums are wheelchair accessible. Open: Tues–Sat 9 a.m.–5 p.m.*

Especially for teens

Most teenagers admit to a fondness for hanging out in that great social organism, the mall. If your teen fits in this category, the **Riverwalk, The Shops at Canal Place,** and **Jax Brewery** shopping centers (see Chapter 13) are good bets for shopping or just hangin' around.

If your kid likes vampires, that ultimate Goth magnet — the cemetery — is almost certainly to attract him or her. The cemeteries of New Orleans are attractions in their own right, filled with elegant statuary, crypts, and tombs, but youngsters find them especially appealing. (For information on guided cemetery tours, see "Spirited Fun: Cemetery tours, " at the end of this chapter.) This section lists some popular local haunts.

Lafayette Cemetery No. 1
Garden District

The cemetery remained intact post-Katrina. This place may not be as old as St. Louis Cemetery No. 1, but the Lafayette Cemetery No. 1 still features its share of large above-ground tombs. Anne Rice fans take note: This cemetery is also the family burial place of the fictional vampire Lestat. The cemetery has figured into many books and films, including the movie version of *Interview with the Vampire*. Touring the cemetery alone is unsafe. Only visit here on a guided tour (see the end of this chapter) or in a large group. Allow 30 to 60 minutes. Note that the famous **Commander's Palace** restaurant sits right across the street from the cemetery.

See map p. 199. 1400 block of Washington Avenue. Admission: free. Wheelchair accessible.

Metairie Lawn Cemetery
Metairie

The largest of all New Orleans cemeteries, Metairie is also the youngest (built after the Civil War). You find some of the most amazing tombs in the city here. Pick up a free cassette-tape tour (with player) at the office. Unlike most of the other cemeteries in New Orleans, you can tour the cemetery from your car or walk safely through it. Give yourself an hour.

See map p. 199. 5100 Pontchartrain Blvd. ☎ *504-486-6331. The Canal Streetcar takes you from the French Quarter to the cemeteries at the end of Canal Street. From there, the Metairie Cemetery is only a block or two (ask the driver), but you have to walk several more blocks from the street to the office. Admission: free. Wheelchair accessible.*

New Orleans Pharmacy Museum
French Quarter

Louis Dufilho, the first licensed pharmacist in the United States, opened an apothecary shop here in 1823. The Creole-style town home also served as his residence, and he supposedly grew herbs for his medicines in the courtyard. The museum opened in 1950, and it features lots of voodoo potions, giant syringes, bone saws, leeches, and other medical instruments, as well as a cosmetics counter (old-time pharmacists also manufactured makeup and perfumes). You'll quickly develop an appreciation for modern medicine. Allow 20 to 30 minutes.

See map p. 204. 514 Chartres St. (2 blocks from Bourbon Street). ☎ *504-565-8027.* www.pharmacymuseum.org. *Admission: $2 adults, $1 seniors and students, children under 12 free. Wheelchair accessible. Open: Tues–Sun 10 a.m.–5 p.m.*

St. Louis Cemetery No. 1
French Quarter

Founded in the late 1700s, this "city of the dead" is the oldest extant cemetery in the city and features large tombs, monuments, and smaller, unmarked niches that resemble baker's ovens. No Katrina damage occurred here. People still leave gifts at the tomb of legendary voodoo queen Marie Laveau to pay their respects and perhaps to ask for supernatural aid. Louis the vampire from Anne Rice's *Vampire Chronicles* has an empty tomb here, and the acid-dropping scene from *Easy Rider* was shot here. Only visit here in a large group or on an organized tour because the neighborhood is in a high-crime district. For this reason (and to avoid the errant ghoul or vampire), come only during daylight. Allow 30 to 60 minutes.

See map p. 204. 400 block of Basin Street (4 blocks from Bourbon Street). ☎ *504-482-5065. Admission: free, but organized tours aren't. Call Save Our Cemeteries at* ☎ *504-525-3377 for information on taking a tour. Wheelchair accessible for the most part, but some spots might pose problems.*

Especially for history buffs

Almost all the sights in this chapter have historic value, but here are a few that die-hard History Channel buffs don't want to miss.

1850 House, Lower Pontalba Building
French Quarter

Plans to reopen remain uncertain since this property is owned by the state, which experienced tough budget cuts since Katrina. The beautifully restored Pontalba Apartments (as they're locally known) were built in 1849, originally as individual town houses. The Baroness Pontalba built them in an effort to combat the deterioration of the older part of the city. The private courtyard, servants' quarters, and huge rooms with their high ceilings, marble fireplaces, and authentic period furniture allowed a fascinating look at the lifestyles of the rich and famous, 19th-century style. Allow 15 to 30 minutes.

See map p. 204. 523 St. Ann St. (on Jackson Square). ☎ *800-568-6968 or 504-568-6968.* http://lsm.crt.state.la.us/1850ex.htm.

Beauregard-Keyes House
French Quarter

This lovely house, built in 1826, is named for two of its most famous tenants: Confederate General Pierre Gustave Toutant Beauregard, who resided here after the Civil War, and author Frances Parkinson Keyes, who wrote many of her novels here, including the most famous, *Dinner at Antoine's.* Nothing is amiss post-Katrina. Take a gander at the twin staircases, the Doric columns, and the "raised cottage" architecture, and try to imagine what life was like when this place was a boardinghouse during the Civil War. The house itself isn't wheelchair accessible, but the beautiful garden adjoining the house is. Allot 45 to 75 minutes to peruse the house.

See map p. 204. 1113 Chartres St. (2 blocks from Bourbon Street). ☎ *504-523-7257. Admission: $5 adults, $4 seniors, students, and AAA members, $2 children ages 6–13, free for children under 6. Open: Mon–Sat 10 a.m.–3 p.m. Tours on the hour.*

Confederate Museum
Warehouse District

Billed as the oldest museum in Louisiana, this place has displayed Civil War artifacts since 1891 and was a trooper during Katrina. The memorabilia includes uniforms, photographs, guns, battle flags, swords, and personal belongings of Gen. Robert E. Lee, Gen. P. G. T. Beauregard, and Confederate president Jefferson Davis. The museum houses the second-largest collection of Confederate memorabilia in the United States. A visit to the museum takes about 30 to 60 minutes.

See map p. 207. 929 Camp St. ☎ *504-523-4522.* www.confederatemuseum.com. *If available, take the St. Charles Streetcar to Lee Circle and walk one block to Camp Street. Admission: $5 adults, $4 students and seniors, $2 children under 12. Parking: On-street and hourly lot nearby. Not accessible for wheelchairs. Open: Thurs–Sat 10 a.m.–4 p.m.*

Gallier House Museum
French Quarter

The museum was safe from the storm. Noted architect James Gallier once resided in this house, which people say served as the model for vampires Lestat and Louis's home in Anne Rice's *Vampire Chronicles.* The house was thoroughly modern back in 1857 — it has hot and cold running water and a bathroom. The guided tour gives you insight into mid-19th-century New Orleans life. Allow an hour to explore this modern miracle.

See map p. 204. 1132 Royal St. (1 block from Bourbon Street). ☎ *504-525-5661.* www. hgghh.org. *Admission: $6 adults, $5 seniors, students, AAA members and children 8–18, free for children under 8. Not accessible for wheelchairs. Open: Mon–Fri 10 a.m.–4 p.m.*

Germaine Wells Mardi Gras Museum
French Quarter

This museum, which houses the Mardi Gras gowns worn between 1910 and 1960 by former Arnaud's owner Germaine Wells, sits atop Arnaud's restaurant (see Chapter 11). Give yourself 15 to 20 minutes to peruse the costumes.

See map p. 204. 813 Bienville St. (½ block from Bourbon Street). ☎ *866-230-8892 or 504-523-5433.* www.arnauds.com/museum.html. *Admission: free. Not accessible for wheelchairs. Open during restaurant hours.*

Hermann-Grima House
French Quarter

Cooking demonstrations are held in the period kitchen of this 1832 house every Thursday from May through October. The house's interior depicts funeral customs of the time, except during December, when the house gets decorated for a "Creole style" Christmas. Tours cover both the house and the stable. Joint tours of this property and the Gallier House museum are available; call for details. Allow 30 to 60 minutes, or two hours or more for the combined tour.

See map p. 204. 820 St. Louis St. (½ block from Bourbon Street). ☎ **504-525-5661.** www.hgghh.org. *Admission: $6, $5 seniors, students, AAA members, and children 8 and older, free for children under 8. Wheelchair accessible, but call ahead so that workers can put out the portable ramp. Open: Mon–Fri 10 a.m.–4 p.m.*

Historic New Orleans Collection
French Quarter

If you want the lowdown on the evolution of New Orleans, visit this complex of buildings (one of which dates from 1792) where you can see art, maps, and original documents from Louisiana's past, all of which survived Katrina unscathed. The collection's research center provides a treasure trove of research materials. You find the research center in a beautifully restored courthouse and police station at 410 Charles St. The exhibits change periodically. Allow 30 to 60 minutes.

See map p. 204. 533 Royal St. (1 block from Bourbon Street). ☎ **504-523-4662.** www.hnoc.org. *Admission: free. Guided tours cost $4 and are given at 10 a.m., 11 a.m., 2 p.m., and 3 p.m. Wheelchair accessible. Open: Tues–Sat 10 a.m.–4:30 p.m.*

Jackson Barracks Military Museum
Holy Cross

Generals Robert E. Lee and Ulysses S. Grant served here prior to the Civil War; now it serves as headquarters for the Louisiana National Guard. The reason to visit is the military museum, where a chronological history traces the involvement of Louisiana soldiers in major wars and skirmishes from the American Revolution to today. You also see flags, guns, artillery pieces, uniforms, and other military hardware on display among the museum's artifacts. Allot 60 to 90 minutes to see the museum and to get there from the Quarter. *Note:* In 2004, Jackson Barracks was struck by lightning and the subsequent fire, although limited to the attic, forced the staff to move all historical artifacts to a safe location. Then in 2005, Hurricane Katrina happened. So please call ahead to ensure the museum has reopened.

See map p. 199. 6400 St. Claude Ave. ☎ **504-278-8242.** *Take the St. Claude bus and get off in front of the museum. Admission: free. Parking: free. Wheelchair accessible.*

Lafitte's Blacksmith Shop and Bar
French Quarter

Records verify this building's existence since 1772 though many insist that it's much older and is, in fact, the oldest building in the Mississippi Valley (try to overlook the hideous fake plaster job offered as a compromise when preservationists were concerned about the continued exposure of the historic bricks-between-post construction, pointing out that it was originally a stucco exterior, but the bar argued that its very identity was married to the exposed brick). Perhaps the forced *faux* renovation helped it withstand Katrina as it weathered the storm just fine. According to legend, the pirate Jean Lafitte and his brother Pierre used it as a front for their illegal activities, posing as blacksmiths while selling ill-gotten pirate booty (and, some say, slaves). Since 1944, it's been a bar, and was the preferred haunt of Tennessee Williams. Kids can't go inside, but you can get an excellent view of the dark interior through the open doorway. Only budget a couple of minutes here, unless you plan to have a drink or two.

See map p. 204. 941 Bourbon St. ☎ *504-522-9377. Admission: no cover charge. Part of it is not accessible to wheelchairs. Open: daily 11 a.m.–close (no set closing time).*

Napoleon House
French Quarter

People claim that Mayor Nicholas Girod's home was offered to the exiled Napoleon Bonaparte as a refuge, but Napoleon died before the scheme got off the ground. Some doubt this tale's veracity, claiming that the building was built after Napoleon's death. Whatever the truth, the building's been trading on this near brush with glory ever since, and it's become a favorite spot of bohemian locals in recent decades. Today, the Napolean House bar and cafe provides patrons with a dark and quiet atmosphere, though the hours have been significantly shortened. Unless you want to grab a drink or a bite to eat, only allow yourself a few minutes here. Kids are also welcome.

See map p. 204. 500 Chartres St. (at the corner of Chartres and St. Louis streets, 2 blocks from Bourbon Street and Jackson Square). ☎ *504-524-9752. Admission: no cover. Wheelchair accessible. Open: Fri–Wed 11:30 a.m.–6 p.m.*

Old Absinthe House
French Quarter

According to legend, Andrew Jackson and the Lafitte brothers (pirates Jean and Pierre) met in this 1806 building to plan the Battle of New Orleans. During Prohibition, it was a speakeasy. The drink for which the bar is named is illegal these days, so the bar serves anisette instead — which tastes like absinthe but, thankfully, doesn't cause brain damage. Stop here for a few minutes to look around, or longer if you're going to drink. Because it's a bar, kids aren't allowed inside. No Katrina damage of note.

See map p. 204. 240 Bourbon St. ☎ *504-523-3181.* www.oldabsinthehouse.com. *Admission: no cover. Wheelchair accessible. Open: Daily from 9 a.m. till whenever they decide to close.*

Old Ursuline Convent
French Quarter

Some people say this structure is the oldest building in New Orleans and the entire Mississippi Valley, as well as the only surviving building from the French colonial period in what is now the United States. Erected between 1745 and 1752, it was once run by the Sisters of Ursula, who had the first girls-only school in the United States. In 1831, the state assembly met here. Today, it houses a Catholic archive with documents that go back to 1718. Everything is in order post-Katrina. Give yourself 60 to 75 minutes to see it all.

See map p. 204. 1100 Chartres St. (2 blocks from Bourbon Street). ☎ 504-529-3040. Admission: $5 adults, $4 seniors, $3 students, children under 8 free. Not accessible for wheelchairs. Open: tours run Tues–Fri 10 a.m.–3 p.m. on the hour (closed for lunch at noon); Sat–Sun 11:15 a.m., 1 p.m., and 2 p.m.

Our Lady of Guadalupe Chapel and International Shrine of St. Jude
French Quarter

Erected in 1826 across the street from St. Louis Cemetery No. 1, Our Lady served as a convenient place to hold funerals for victims of yellow fever and other diseases. Our Lady serves as a shrine to both St. Jude (saint of impossible causes) and a guy called St. Expedite. Legend claims that this saint's statue showed up at the church in a crate, marked only with the word "expedite" stamped on the outside. The name stuck, and today people know him as the saint to whom you pray when you want things in a hurry (I'm not making this up). No doubt many New Orleanians are calling on him for a quick rebuilding of their homes, businesses and the city in general. Allow 15 minutes.

See map p. 204. 411 N. Rampart St. (3 blocks from Bourbon St.). ☎ 504-525-1551. www.saintjudeshrine.com. *Admission: free. Wheelchair accessible. Open: Daily 7 a.m.–7 p.m.*

Pitot House
Mid-City

Located on a ridge of land between Esplanade Avenue and Bayou St. John, the Pitot House survived Katrina, thankfully. James Pitot, the first mayor of incorporated New Orleans, moved this beautiful house in 1810, which was originally built on a different spot in the late 1700s. This excellent example of an 18th-century, West Indies–style plantation home features wide galleries and large columns. It is owned by the Louisiana Landmark Society, which uses the home as its headquarters. Seeing the house takes one to two hours plus transportation time.

See map p. 212. 1440 Moss St. (near City Park). ☎ 504-482-0312. Admission: $5 adults, $4 seniors and students, $2 children under 12. Parking: free. The first floor is wheelchair accessible, but the second floor isn't. Open: Wed–Sat 10 a.m.–3 p.m.

Enjoying the outdoors: Parks and gardens
New Orleans boasts a number of areas of interest to fans of the outdoors. Whether you're looking for spacious parks or impressive gardens, check out these choice selections.

Longue Vue House and Gardens
New Orleans

Natural and formal gardens, gorgeous fountains, and tranquil ponds form the backdrop for this beautiful Greek Revival mansion, which sits at the end of an oak-lined drive just minutes from downtown New Orleans. Inside, savor the beautiful antiques, rice-paper wall coverings, Oriental carpets, and other lovely touches. Families enjoy the Discovery Garden, a half-acre, interactive garden for children of all ages. A visit here takes one to two hours plus transportation time. During Katrina, roof leaks caused damage to some of its collections, while flooding destroyed some gardens that took years to design and grow. However, the site reopened in April 2006 and continues to refurbish and replant.

See map p. 199. 7 Bamboo Rd. ☎ *504-488-5488.* www.longuevue.com. *Garden and shop open: Mon–Sat 10 a.m.–5 p.m.; Sun 1 p.m.–5 p.m. House tours Wed–Sat 10 a.m.–5 p.m.; Sun 1 p.m.–5 p.m.; Mon and Tues by special appointment.*

Washington Artillery Park
French Quarter

This spot and Jackson Square have long been two of the most popular places for tourists and young people. Street performers often run through their routines for tips in front of the steps leading to the top of the levee (which double as seats for a small amphitheater). This place had fallen into disrepair for awhile, but the Audubon Institute prettied it up a few years ago by relandscaping the area, reopening the public restrooms, and providing a tourist information center.

Just west of the French Market, along the riverfront. ☎ *504-587-0738. Admission: free. Wheelchair accessible. Open: 9 a.m. to dusk.*

Woldenberg Riverfront Park
French Quarter

This park, which features almost 20 acres of green grass, open space, and hundreds of trees and shrubs, makes for a nice break along the Mississippi River. This area has historically been the city's promenade; nowadays it stretches from the Moonwalk to the Aquarium of the Americas and features works by popular local artists. At night, or even during the day, take a romantic stroll and watch the many ships sail by.

Riverfront behind the 500 block of Decatur Street. ☎ *504-587-0738. Admission: free. Wheelchair accessible. Open: dawn to 10 p.m.*

If you're the sporting (or betting) type

Granted, the Crescent City isn't a sports mecca on the order of, say, Chicago or New York, but it does offer some areas of interest for gamers and fans of major- and minor-league franchises, including the NFL's New Orleans Saints, of course, the city's long-suffering football team, as well as the family favorite New Orleans Zephyrs minor-league baseball club.

In 2002, New Orleans officially became the NBA home of the former Charlotte Hornets, salving the deep wound left in the local hoops consciousness when the New Orleans Jazz packed up for Utah back in 1979. After the hurricane, both the Saints and the Hornets were welcomed by other clubs around the country while they waited for their hometown arenas to be repaired.

Fair Grounds Race Course
Mid-City

One of the oldest racetracks in the country, this course has hosted Pat Garrett, Frank James (brother of Jesse and a betting commissioner), and Generals Ulysses S. Grant and George Custer, among others. The racing season runs from Thanksgiving Day to late March, though flooding from Katrina prevented it from opening in time for the 2005–2006 season; it is expected to reopen in time for the 2006–2007 season. The New Orleans Jazz and Heritage Festival (also known as Jazz Fest) is held here every year during the last weekend of April and the first weekend of May and attracted 350,000 to the first festival held after Katrina.

See map p. 212. 1751 Gentilly Blvd., Mid-City (approximately ten minutes by car from the Central Business District and the French Quarter). ☎ **504-944-5515.** www.fgno.com.

Harrah's New Orleans Casino
Central Business District

Because gambling is a hot-button issue around here, I'm neither advocating nor condemning it as an attraction, family or otherwise. Nevertheless, this place is *huge,* both in terms of its size and its impact (for good or ill) on the local community. You may want to take a look at it for those reasons alone.

See map p. 207. 512 S. Peters St. ☎ **800-VIP-JAZZ** or 504-533-6000. www.harrahs.com/our_casinos/nor. *Parking: Valet and garage parking are available; call the information number for prices and other details. The casino is wheelchair accessible. Open: 24 hours.*

New Orleans Arena
Central Business District

This arena shares many facilities with its neighbor and older sibling, the Superdome, including parking spaces, power, water, and staff. Smaller than the Superdome but larger than other area venues, it hosts sporting events (including some Tulane University basketball home games), concerts, and other touring events. The arena is also home to the New Orleans Hornets NBA team, which relocated from Charlotte at the end of the 2001–02 basketball season.

See map p. 207. 1501 Girod St. (next to the Superdome, even though the street names are different). ☎ **504-587-3663.** www.neworleansarena.com. *Wheelchair accessible.*

Mississippi gaming: Riverboat casinos

Harrah's isn't the only craps game in town. You may also want to look into a couple of riverboat casinos in the area:

✔ **The Boomtown Belle Casino** resides in Harvey (4132 Peters Rd., located about 15 miles due south of the French Quarter; ☎ **504-366-7711**; www.boomtownneworleans.com). The taxi ride costs about $24.

✔ In Kenner, you find the **Treasure Chest Casino** (5050 Williams Blvd., 15 miles northwest of the French Quarter; ☎ **504-443-8000**; www.treasurechestcasino.com). Many locals give this casino the highest marks of the casinos mentioned here. A taxi runs about $24.

New Orleans Zephyrs Field
East Jefferson

Although New Orleans doesn't host a major league baseball team, it does have the Zephyrs — the AAA farm team of the Houston Astros. Since their arrival in New Orleans in the 1990s, the Zephyrs have become a popular team among jaded local sports fans.

See map p. 199. 6000 Airline Dr., East Jefferson. ☎ *504-734-5155. See* www.zephyrsbaseball.com *for game times and admission. Located approximately 9 miles from the French Quarter, on the way to the airport. Take the Airline bus and get off by the stadium.*

Superdome
Central Business District

The Superdome served as a last-resort hurricane shelter, and as you most likely saw on the news, the city was not prepared to care for the nearly 20,000 people who sought shelter here during the storm. Health conditions quickly moved from bad to worse; it is reported that at least 3 elderly people died here during the storm. (Initial reports of rape and rampant violence were later discredited.) After a $186-million restoration, the Superdome reopened on September 25, 2006, when the Saints beat the Falcons to much fanfare. One of the largest buildings in the world in terms of diameter (680 feet), the Superdome provides a climate-controlled environment for 76,000 New Orleans Saints fans or more than 100,000 concertgoers. The Superdome also hosts trade shows and conventions.

See map p. 207. 1500 Poydras. ☎ *504-587-3663;* www.superdome.com. *Take the Poydras bus and get off in front of the Superdome.*

Seeing New Orleans by Guided Tour

To tour or not to tour? That is the question. The answer depends on
your idea of a vacation. If you prefer to be independent and take a spon-
taneous approach, you'll probably be happier doing your own thing.
If you enjoy socializing and knowing what to expect, a tour could be
exactly what you want. You can get an entertaining overview of the city
(or of a specific part of it, such as the French Quarter or the Garden
District) by taking a guided tour. Depending on the tour operator you
choose, you'll definitely see some good sights, (hopefully) be entertained by your guide, and discover a thing or two.

Bear in mind, that as often as not your tour will offer more entertainment value than historical significance. I mention some exceptions in
this chapter, but most tours here are Show Biz, baby. They all mean well,
and most of them even have their facts right, but you'll also get plenty of
drama, intrigue, history, and innuendo — New Orleans's rich history
more than holds its own with daytime soaps.

Nevertheless, tours are still a lot of fun and a nice way to meet other
people. They can also provide the perfect compromise for those days
when you're trying to balance your aching feet against the urge to get
out and see some sights. General orientation tours and specialty tours
make up the two main types of guided tours. You find information on
both types in this section.

Time versus info: General orientation tours

If you only have limited time but still want to experience as much as possible, consider a general orientation tour. Riding around the city on a
half-hour carriage tour, you get a condensed New Orleans history lesson,

---

Help! I've been de-toured

If you're interested in taking a tour, keep your eyes open. Some hotel concierges have
been known to take kickbacks from certain tour operators to steer business exclusively to them. Obviously, not every concierge is on the take, but your best bet would
be to book any tours directly through the operator; no reputable operator will force
you to go through a third party.

If you can't find sufficient tour information at your hotel, call or visit the **State Office of
Tourism** (529 St. Ann St., right on Jackson Square; ☎ **504-568-5661**). Aside from offering a multitude of booklets, brochures, and other such material, the staff also has
someone from the New Orleans Convention and Visitor's Bureau on hand to give you
the straight dope on tours and attractions, and to steer you toward a reputable tour
that's right for your budget, needs, or time frame. For more information on tourist
offices, see Chapter 9.

find out about the local architecture, locate the good clubs, and see the attractions. However, general information is all that you'll get. Walking tours and bus tours may take a little longer, but with a thorough guide, you can walk away feeling like you're in the know.

Cooling off with a bus tour

If you can't take the heat, a bus tour — where you can see the sights without leaving the air conditioning — is just your cup of iced tea. Aside from seeing the whole city, you can also take a tour that goes outside of town to plantations or swamps. Licensed guides narrate these tours, and buses come variously equipped with TVs, VCRs, and DVDs, stereo sound, bathrooms, cellphones, and equipment for travelers with disabilities. (If a particular amenity is important to you, make sure to ask for the appropriate bus ahead of time.)

One of the oldest and most reliable tour companies, **New Orleans Tours** (☎ 504-592-0560) offers city and neighborhood tours by bus, as well as riverboat cruises, swamp tours, plantation tours, walking tours, nightlife tours, jazz tours, and combination tours. For more options, check out these other tour companies as well:

- ✔ **Dixieland Tours** (☎ 800-489-8747)

- ✔ **Gray Line** (☎ 800-535-7786 or 504-569-1401) — offering special — and somewhat controversial — "Devastation Tours" (see Chapter 2 for more information)

- ✔ **Hotard Coaches** (☎ 504-944-0253)

Strolling the Quarter

Because the French Quarter is the oldest and arguably most interesting part of New Orleans, most tourists focus on this area. No large buses are allowed in the Quarter (though you will see smaller buses and vans), so walking is your best option for getting around.

Strolling around the French Quarter on your own is the best way to see the area. Traveling on your own gives you the freedom to linger in a pastry shop or park, stop to watch street entertainers, poke your head in all the cute stores you find, admire the local architecture, or follow your nose into off-the-beaten-path nooks and crannies. Chapter 14 lists several itineraries for walking tours that you can take on your own. If you still feel like you want to bring someone along to tell you what you're seeing, contact **Friends of the Cabildo** (☎ 504-523-3939), a non-profit group that gives two-hour walking tours of the French Quarter. Cost is $12 for adults, $10 for seniors and students, and free for kids 12 and under. See our interview with tour guide Rebecca Sell on p. 17.

Because the French Quarter is part of the Jean Lafitte National Park, you can also get a free tour from the **National Park Service**. The service offers only one tour each day at 9:30 a.m., and each person must pick up his or her own ticket. The tickets are given out starting at 9 a.m. on a

French Quarter?

"People are surprised to learn that the French Quarter is actually not French. It would be more accurate to call it the Spanish/American/Caribbean Quarter. There were two devastating fires in the late 1700's that destroyed all of the French buildings except for the Ursuline Convent (that building dates back from 1752; it's the oldest in the Mississippi River Valley). The Spanish enacted building codes to prevent such a disaster from ever occurring again, and many of the builders were refugees from the slave revolts in San Domingue (Haiti). People always get a chuckle to then learn that our very first Spanish governor in the city was a fellow by the name of Don Alejandro O'Reilly. It sounds strange, but it's true: the fellow we now consider the father of Spanish Louisiana was actually an Irish soldier of fortune."

—*Rebecca Sell gives walking tours of the French Quarter through Friends of the Cabildo (☎ 504-523-3939). See our interview with her on p. 17.*

first-come, first-served basis. For more information, stop by the **Visitor's Information Center** at 419 Decatur St. or call ☎ **504-589-2133.**

University of New Orleans professor emeritus W. Kenneth Holditch (who really knows his stuff) leads the **Heritage Literary Tours** (732 Frenchmen St., ☎ **504-949-9805**). He gives a general tour centered on the literary legacy of the French Quarter (which has played host to a considerable number of famous and colorful writers over the years) as well as a more specialized tour about Tennessee Williams. If you arrange it in advance, he can (probably) design a tour for you around a specific author. He's a character in his own right, and his tours are fun, informative, and loaded with anecdotes. Tours are $20 for adults and $10 for students; call ahead if you have something specific in mind.

Riding in style: Carriage tours

Like bus tours, a carriage tour may or may not be up your alley. Riding through the French Quarter in a mule-drawn carriage certainly gives you a more intimate experience than riding around in a bus with 50 or 60 other name-tag-wearing passengers. It can also be quite romantic with the hypnotic clip-clop of the mules' hooves. A good carriage driver can show you the highlights of the Quarter in just 30 minutes; spend an hour touring, and you'll feel like a native.

Carriage rides stay in the Quarter, and no one guarantees the veracity of the information you receive. Some drivers are licensed tour guides, though most aren't. Nevertheless, each one has his or her area of expertise. Some have eaten their way through the city, some are historians, and others pride themselves on knowing the location of every bar. One driver may regale you with ghost stories, another may tell you jokes, and a third may not say much. Talk to the driver for a minute and try to gauge his or her personality before hopping in.

Most of the carriages in the Quarter line up along Decatur Street at Jackson Square and at carriage stands at the corners of Royal and St. Louis, Bourbon and Conti, or Bourbon and Toulouse. Also keep your eyes open for carriages cruising throughout the Quarter or parked on a corner waiting for a fare.

You see two types of carriages: the large hard-topped, bus-like models that you share with anybody else that comes along, and the smaller convertible models that you hire individually for your party. Generally, carriages have abandoned the per-person rates, charging $50 for a half-hour ride and $105 for an hour (the latter price includes picking you up from your hotel).

If your tour lasts less than 30 minutes, your driver is giving you a "zip tour." If this is the case, confront the driver and find out if the tour can be extended. If the driver doesn't comply, complain to the driver's boss. If the driver refuses to give you the boss's name, write down the driver's name (if you know it), the company name, and the carriage number (on its side or back), and call the city's **Taxicab Bureau** (☎ **504-565-6272**) to complain.

If you want a carriage to pick you up, call one of the following licensed carriage companies:

- ✔ **Good Old Days Buggies** (☎ **504-523-0804**)
- ✔ **Mid-City Carriages** (☎ **504-581-4415**) — They're not currently operating (call for updates), but their story is worth noting: After Katrina, dedicated employees rescued the mules and horses from the flooded stable and brought them to a parking lot where they waited for help to arrive. Six days later, they led the animals to the interstate, loaded them into trailers and drove them to safety in Baton Rouge, where they still remain.
- ✔ **Old Quarter Tours** (☎ **504-944-0446**)
- ✔ **Royal Carriages** (☎ **504-943-8820**)

Filling a niche: Specialty tours

Specialty tours are good bets if you're deeply interested in a particular subject. Although anyone can parrot the touristy info you'll get on a basic orientation tour, you'll more likely sound like an expert to family and friends back home if you take a specialty tour.

Gay New Orleans

The Bienville Foundation's **Gay Heritage Tour** (☎ **504-945-6789**) is a 2½-hour tour that shows you the city from a gay-friendly perspective. You explore the Quarter and hear about such figures as Tennessee Williams, Clay Shaw, and Ellen DeGeneres. Robert Batson, the knowledgeable and personable tour guide, also explains the importance of various gay landmarks. The $20 tour leaves from **Alternatives** (a gay-targeted gift shop at

909 Bourbon St.); days and times vary seasonally (the tour doesn't run during Aug or Dec), so be sure to call for information.

Discovering New Orleans's African American heritage

If you want to delve into New Orleans's history of Africans and African Americans, contact **African American Heritage Tours** (☎ 504-288-3478). Tours include trips to plantations, Xavier University (the first Black Catholic university in the United States), and a narrative on historic sites such as Liberty Bank, which was founded by African Americans.

Hepcats unite: Jazz tours

 Photographer for the *Times-Picayune* and well-known local jazz historian John McCusker leads **John McCusker's Cradle of Jazz Tour** (☎ 504-282-3583). He takes visitors on a bargain-priced ($25), 2½-hour van tour every Saturday morning that traces the history of New Orleans jazz. He points out the spots where jazz was born, where it matured, and where performers such as Louis Armstrong were born or played their music. You must make reservations in advance.

Spirited Fun: Cemetery, vampire, and ghost tours

 Many cemeteries simply aren't safe unless you're with an organized group. I strongly advise against wandering through any cemetery (especially St. Louis No. 2) alone or without an official tour.

The members of **Save Our Cemeteries** (☎ 504-525-3377), a nonprofit organization, do more to restore and maintain New Orleans's cemeteries than anyone else. Their tours are a good crash course for newcomers to the subject.

Fred Hatfield (☎ 504-891-4862), a semi-retired native New Orleanian, has spent his whole life in the neighborhood of **Lafayette Cemetery No. 1.** Consequently, he's done extensive research on the people buried there, as any good neighbor would do. His combination walking tours of the Garden District and Lafayette No. 1 take about two hours and cost $14 per person; he also gives individual tours of the cemetery for $9. All tours require a minimum of four people. He's usually home, so give him a call.

Many visitors have raved about the wealth and quality of information they receive from **Historic New Orleans Walking Tours** (☎ 504-947-2120; www.tourneworleans.com). Here you can find a number of French Quarter tours, including tours for history and "mystique," as well as the following cemetery tours:

   ✔ The **Cemetery/Voodoo Tour** takes you to the tomb of Marie Laveau and to an actual voodoo temple. You get the straight facts about voodoo's West African religious roots and its modern-day practitioners. In short, it's long on the authentic and short on the wink-wink-nudge-nudge sensationalism you may get elsewhere. You also see other famous burial sites and hear the stories of some legendary locals.

✔ The **Garden District/Cemetery Tour** tours this historic neighborhood pointing out rocker Trent Reznor's former castle, Indianapolis Colts quarterback Peyton Manning's boyhood home, and Anne Rice's former manse.

✔ **Haunted History Tours** (☎ 504-861-2727; www.hauntedhistory tours.com) offers vampire and cemetery tours. You can also opt for the Haunted History Tour itself, which details various ghost stories and legends in the Quarter. The tour is entertaining, but don't put too much stock in the "facts."

✔ **Magic Walking Tours** (☎ 504-588-9693) even lets you go on a vampire hunt. If you're really lucky, your guide may even let you carry the wooden stake and mallet.

✔ **Weekend Jazz Walk** (☎ 504-947-2120) explores jazz landmarks such as Storyville, Congo Square, J&M Studio and more.

No petting the gators: Swamp tours

Swamp tours can be a great deal of fun. You see some incredible scenery and wildlife, you're out on the water, and you get a feel for what it's like to live out on the bayous. Your guide may call alligators up to the boat for a little snack of chicken, but be careful to keep your hands inside the boat because gators can't always tell the difference.

You can find plenty of swampland worth exploring within the metro area, but the really isolated swamp areas lie three hours outside the city.

✔ **Cypress Swamp Tours** (☎ 504-581-4501) tour the Bayou Segnette area (near Westwego, on the West Bank across the Crescent City Connection) for $22 per adult and $12 for children under 12.

✔ **Dr. Paul Wagner,** a well-known swamp ecologist and a national conservationist, gives excellent tours of the Honey Island Swamp area. His **Honey Island Swamp Tours** (☎ 504-242-5877 or 985-641-1769) cost $20 per person.

✔ **Gator Swamp Tours** (☎ 800-875-4287 or 504-484-6100) also have good tours of the Honey Island Swamp, approximately 40 minutes east of New Orleans; they charge $20 per adult and $10 for children under 12.

✔ **Jean Lafitte Swamp Tours** (☎ 800-445-4109 or 504-587-1719) tour the Bayou aux Carpes, a patch of private land flush with all sorts of wildlife near the intercoastal canal, just 20 minutes from the Crescent City Connection; cost is $24 for adults and $13 for children under 12.

Ask when calling about the length of each tour whether the tours are private or public, and how many people are allowed on one tour. You don't want one that's too crowded.

Other tour companies operate in the Atchafalaya Basin, a vast swamp about 2½ hours west of New Orleans, between Baton Rouge and Lafayette. These include **McGee's Landing** (☎ **800-445-6681** or 318-228-2384) and bilingual (English/French) tours with **Angelle's Atchafalaya Basin Swamp Tours** (☎ **337-228-8567**). The basin is pretty big, so the good tours take more time; you may want to budget your afternoon around it.

Shopping for old stuff: Antique tours

Macon Riddle's Antique Tours (☎ **504-899-3027;** www.neworleans antiquing.com) provides an enthusiastic and educational way to see New Orleans's antique districts, which are all the more prized after Katrina. Macon Riddle picks you up at your hotel, takes you on a customized antique shopping tour, and even makes lunch reservations for you. She even takes care of shipping your antique finds home.

Dinner on the water: Riverboat cruises

Riverboat cruises are extremely popular in New Orleans, as you may expect. Gambling cruises, however, are a thing of the past (riverboat casinos rarely leave the dock, because most gamblers want to be able to come and go at will). You can still find harbor cruises, dinner and dancing cruises, river cruises, and combination cruises where you also visit the Audubon Zoo or Chalmette Battlefield. The riverboats come in several different forms: steam- or diesel-powered, with their paddle wheels on the side or on the stern, and so forth. Companies and boats offering riverboat tours include the following:

- ✔ **Creole Queen Paddle Wheel Tours** (☎ **800-445-4109** or 504-524-0814)

- ✔ **John James Audubon** (☎ **800-233-BOAT** or 504-586-8777)

- ✔ **New Orleans Steamboat Co.** (☎ 800-233-BOAT or 504-586-8777)

Chapter 13

Shopping the Local Stores

*V*acation shopping is an odd thing. You'd think that spending yet *more* money is the last thing a vacationer would want to do. But for whatever reason, whether trying to find that perfect memento of their trip or suddenly deciding to redecorate their home with antiques, vacationers shop here — a *lot*.

This chapter explores shopping in New Orleans from a couple different angles. It runs through the big-name stores, neighborhood markets, and the major shopping areas, some of which feature antiques shops and art galleries.

Assessing Katrina's Damage to the City's Shops

One thing you may have learned from all of the post-Katrina coverage of New Orleans is its importance to the rest of the nation as an international port, which gives it a huge advantage over other American cities for the shopping vacationer. Normally, if you can name it, you can probably find it in New Orleans, though post-Katrina problems with distribution and mail service caused stock woes for many shopkeepers. By the time you arrive, this should be much improved.

Shop hours will vary considerably as businesses juggle the need to be open with the lack of employees or other resources. Also, many are struggling just to stay open, and may be forced to close their doors before your arrival. So if you have a particular store in mind, call ahead. Please do your best to support these shops; your purchases will help boost the city's economy.

Surveying the Scene

Your shopping options in New Orleans aren't limited to things such as home furnishings, pottery, and designer clothing — also on hand is quite a bit of local artwork and imported fine jewelry. Don't neglect the locally crafted jewelry, however. Some local designers, such as Mignon Faget, work with such innovation and creativity that their shops seem more like art galleries.

If you're shopping for antiques or contemporary art, you can find plenty on Royal and Magazine streets, which are both really bustling after the storm. Royal Street boasts the finest, most expensive goods; Magazine Street promises more bargain-basement finds. Also in that area, and on Julia Street, are the city's art galleries. (I cover these areas individually later in this chapter.)

A word on sales tax: Weigh your options carefully if buying a large, expensive item. Because sales tax in New Orleans is 9 percent, you may save money by having the item shipped to you at home. Of course you pay for shipping and handling instead of the sales tax, but the difference may be in your favor.

A program called **Louisiana Tax-Free Shopping** benefits shoppers who hail from other countries. If you aren't from the United States, look for store windows with this program's logo; these merchants give you a tax-refund voucher that you can cash in, either at the airport or by mail. To take advantage of this program, you need a valid foreign passport and round-trip airline ticket. Call ☎ 504-568-5323 for details.

Checking Out the Big Names

Because corporate America has made inroads here during the last half-century, local homegrown institutions have found it difficult to compete with the deep pockets of the big-name corporations. As a result, New Orleans is now almost exclusively the province of the big-name corporate chains. Here's a list of the big players that have since reopened:

- ✔ **Brooks Brothers:** The Shops at Canal Place, 300 block of Canal Street (☎ 504-522-4200; www.brooksbrothers.com); open Monday to Saturday from 10 a.m. to 7 p.m., and Sunday from noon to 6 p.m.

- ✔ **Gucci:** The Shops at Canal Place, 300 block of Canal Street (☎ 504-524-5544; www.gucci.com); open Monday to Saturday from 10 a.m. to 7 p.m., and Sunday from noon to 6 p.m.

- ✔ **Lord & Taylor:** New Orleans Centre, 1400 Poydras St. (☎ 504-581-5673; www.lordandtaylor.com); open Monday to Saturday from 10 a.m. to 8 p.m., and Sunday from noon to 6 p.m.

New Orleans Shopping

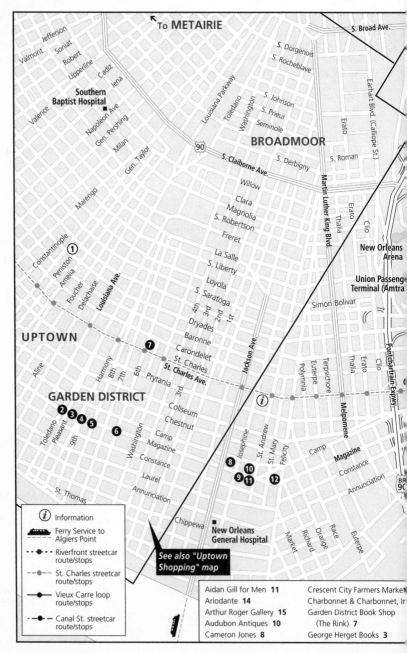

To METAIRIE

S. Broad Ave.

Jefferson
Valmont
Soniat
Robert
Upperline
Cadiz
Jena

S. Dorgenois
S. Rocheblave

Earhart Blvd. (Calliope St.)

Southern
Baptist Hospital

Louisiana Parkway
Toledano
Washington
S. Johnson
S. Prieur
Seminole

Erato

Napoleon Ave.
Gen. Pershing
Milan
Gen. Taylor

Valence

BROADMOOR

Martin Luther King Blvd.

Erato
Thalia
Clio

90

S. Claiborne Ave.
S. Derbigny
S. Roman

New Orleans
Arena

Marengo

Willow

Clara
Magnolia
S. Robertson
Freret

Union Passenge
Terminal (Amtra

Constantinople
Peniston
Amelia
Foucher
Delachaise

1

La Salle
S. Liberty
Loyola
S. Saratoga
4th 3rd 2nd 1st
Dryades
Baronne
Carondelet
St. Charles
St. Charles Ave.

Simon Bolivar

Louisiana Ave.

UPTOWN

7

Aline

Harmony
8th 7th 6th
Prytania 3rd

Jackson Ave.

Terpsichore
Polymnia
Euterpe

Thalia
Erato
Clio

Pontchartrain Expwy.

GARDEN DISTRICT

2 3 4 5

6

Coliseum
Chestnut
Camp
Magazine
Constance
Laurel
Annunciation

i

Josephine
St. Andrew
St. Mary
Felicity

Camp

Melpomene

Magazine

Constance

Annunciation

BR
90

Toledano
Pleasant
9th

Washington

8

9 11
10

12

Chippewa

New Orleans
General Hospital

Race
Orange
Richard
Market

Euterpe

St. Thomas

i Information

Ferry Service to
Algiers Point

•••• Riverfront streetcar
route/stops

--- St. Charles streetcar
route/stops

— Vieux Carre loop
route/stops

•-•- Canal St. streetcar
route/stops

See also "Uptown
Shopping" map

Aidan Gill for Men 11
Ariodante 14
Arthur Roger Gallery 15
Audubon Antiques 10
Cameron Jones 8

Crescent City Farmers Market
Charbonnet & Charbonnet, Ir
Garden District Book Shop
(The Rink) 7
George Herget Books 3

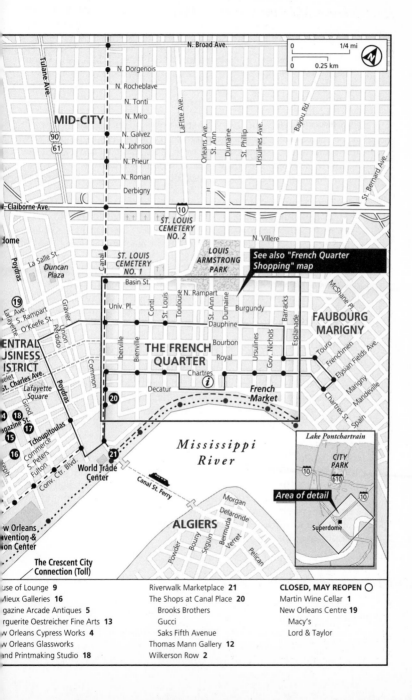

N. Broad Ave.

N. Dorgenois
N. Rocheblave
N. Tonti
N. Miro
N. Galvez
N. Johnson
N. Prieur
N. Roman
Derbigny

Tulane Ave.

MID-CITY

90
61

LaFitte Ave.
Orleans Ave.
St. Ann
Dumaine
St. Phillip
Ursulines Ave.

Bayou Rd.

St. Bernard Ave.

. Claiborne Ave.

10

**ST. LOUIS
CEMETERY
NO. 2**

N. Villere

**LOUIS
ARMSTRONG
PARK**

*See also "French Quarter
Shopping" map*

McShane Pl.

**FAUBOURG
MARIGNY**

dome

La Salle St.
Duncan
Plaza

Canal

**ST. LOUIS
CEMETERY
NO. 1**

Basin St.

Poydras

19

Ave.
S. Rampart
O'Keefe St.
Lafayette

Gravier

Union

Perdido

Univ. Pl.

Conti
St. Louis
Toulouse

N. Rampart

St. Ann
Dumaine

Burgundy

Dauphine

Barracks

Esplanade

Touro
Frenchmen
Elysian Fields Ave.

**ENTRAL
USINESS
ISTRICT**

St. Charles Ave.

Lafayette
Square

Poydras

Girod

Common

Iberville
Bienville

**THE FRENCH
QUARTER**

Bourbon
Royal

Chartres

Decatur

Ursulines

Gov. Nichols

ⓘ

**French
Market**

Chartres St.

Marigny
Mandeville
Spain

4 18
St.
Magazine
17
15
16
Commerce
S. Peters

Tchoupitoulas

Fulton

Conv. Ctr. Blvd.

21

**World Trade
Center**

*Mississippi
River*

Canal St. Ferry

Morgan
Delaronde

ALGIERS

Powder
Bouny
Seguin
Bermuda
Verret
Pelican

Lake Pontchartrain

**CITY
PARK**

10
610

Area of detail

Superdome

10

w Orleans
vention &
ion Center

**The Crescent City
Connection (Toll)**

0   1/4 mi
0   0.25 km

---

use of Lounge **9**
Vieux Galleries **16**
gazine Arcade Antiques **5**
rguerite Oestreicher Fine Arts **13**
w Orleans Cypress Works **4**
w Orleans Glassworks
and Printmaking Studio **18**

Riverwalk Marketplace **21**
The Shops at Canal Place **20**
  Brooks Brothers
  Gucci
  Saks Fifth Avenue
Thomas Mann Gallery **12**
Wilkerson Row **2**

CLOSED, MAY REOPEN ◯
Martin Wine Cellar **1**
New Orleans Centre **19**
  Macy's
  Lord & Taylor

- **Macy's:** New Orleans Centre, 1400 Poydras St. (☎ 800-456-2297 or 504-592-5985; www.macys.com); open Monday to Saturday from 10 a.m. to 9:30 p.m., and Sunday from 11 a.m. to 7 p.m.

- **Saks Fifth Avenue:** The Shops at Canal Place, 300 block of Canal Street (☎ 504-524-2200; www.saksfifthavenue.com); open Monday to Saturday from 10 a.m. to 7 p.m., and Sunday from noon to 6 p.m.

These big-name stores, of course, need a place to house their wares, and New Orleans offers plenty of alternatives for shoppers hoping to meet all their shopping needs under one roof. In addition to the Canal Place Shopping Center (see the "Canal Street" section, later in this chapter), the following shopping areas are good choices for a little mall-browsing:

- **Jackson Brewery:** Just across from Jackson Square (600 Decatur St.; ☎ 504-566-7245; www.jacksonbrewery.com), the old **Jax Brewery** is now a complex of shops, cafes, restaurants, and entertainment spots. Look for gourmet and Cajun and Creole foodstuffs, fashions, toys, hats, crafts, pipes, posters, and souvenirs. You also find a huge **Virgin Megastore** (☎ 504-671-8988) and for pet lovers, **Woof & Whiskers** (☎ 504-568-0065). The Brewery hours are Sunday to Thursday from 10 a.m. to 9 p.m., and Friday to Saturday from 10 a.m. to 10 p.m. Note that many shops in the Brewery close at 5:30 or 6 p.m.

- **New Orleans Centre:** This place (1400 Poydras St.; ☎ 504-568-0000; www.neworleanscentre.com) offers upscale department stores, such as **Lord & Taylor** and **Macy's,** plus three levels of specialty shops, restaurants, and a huge food court. Add on the fancy office tower and you get plenty of foot traffic in this spacious environment. Hours are Monday to Saturday from 10 a.m. to 8 p.m., and Sunday from noon to 6 p.m.

- **Riverwalk Marketplace:** Actually a covered mall running along the river from Poydras Street to the Convention Center (1 Poydras St.; ☎ 504-522-1555; www.riverwalkmarketplace.com), this is a popular venue that's also quite atmospheric. Take a break from shopping and just watch the river roll by or the occasional free entertainment. Among the more than 100 specialty shops are such big hitters as **Eddie Bauer, The Sharper Image,** and **Banana Republic**, plus several eateries.

Going to Market

New Orleans's long-time street market is the **French Market** (☎ 504-522-2621), a complex of shops that begins on Decatur Street across from Jackson Square that sits on high ground and never flooded. In the market, you can find candy, cookware, fashions, crafts, toys, New Orleans memorabilia, candles — all manner of goodies, though you really have to look for the true gems. Also in the complex are **Café du Monde** (☎ 504-581-2914) and the **Farmer's Market** and **Flea Market** (☎ 504-596-3420), which are located in the 1200 block of North Peters. Hours are from 10 a.m. to 6 p.m. (Café du Monde is open 24 hours.)

The original **Crescent City Farmers Market** (700 Magazine St.; ☎ 504-861-5898; www.crescentcityfarmersmarket.org) is held every Saturday from 8 a.m. to noon in a parking lot at the corner of Magazine and Girod streets in the Warehouse District. Japanese journalist Ryoko Sato, who has studied American farmers markets for years, generously donated $7,000 to the department of Loyola University that runs the Crescent City Farmers Market. It offers fresh local produce, flowers, cooking demonstrations, and more. Plenty of free, off-street parking is available because it's a Saturday and the meter maids aren't out and about. Depending on where you're staying, you may be able to walk here. Come early for the best selection, or wait for the cooking demonstration at 10 a.m.

Discovering the Best Shopping Neighborhoods

The trick to shopping in New Orleans is knowing where to go. The major shopping areas you want to visit are the French Quarter, the Central Business District, the Warehouse District, and along Magazine Street, both in the Garden District and the Uptown area. Thankfully, all of these neighborhoods were spared from major flooding — some had no water at all — which gives you an idea of just how large New Orleans was because 80 percent of the city was underwater at one point. The best strategy for shopping in these neighborhoods is to just wander around and see which shops catch your eye. Here is a rundown of the city's best shopping areas and the scoop on what you can find inside.

French Quarter

This section breaks down some of the Quarter's more prominent shopping streets — Bourbon, Decatur, and Royal. But first, I take a quick look at some of the noteworthy shops found elsewhere in the Quarter.

- ✔ **Animal Art** (617 Chartres St.; ☎ 504-529-4407) is for animal lovers because it features fine furniture, paintings, ceramics, and more, all depicting its namesake.

- ✔ **Chi-Wa-Wa Ga-Ga** (37 French Market Place; ☎ 504-581-4242) is the small store for small dogs, offering off-the-rack clothes, costumes, and accessories for your (or your friend's) well-dressed pooch.

- ✔ **Faulkner House Books** (624 Pirates Alley; ☎ 504-524-2940) is a national literary landmark as it was once the home of Nobel Prize–winner William Faulkner, who wrote his early works *Mosquitoes* and *Soldiers' Pay* here. The one room (and hallway) of this private home may be small in comparison to chain bookstores, but it boasts possibly the finest selection per square foot of any bookstore on the planet. The stock tends to be highly collectible and literary, including a large collection of first-edition Faulkners and rare and first-edition classics by other authors. Roof leaks did cause some damage to the owners' living quarters above the shop, but everything has since been repaired.

✔ **Kaboom** (901 Barracks St.; ☎ **504-529-5780**) is a used-book store that primarily stocks fiction, but with a little digging, you can turn up some real gems.

✔ **Latin's Hand** (1025 N. Peters St.; ☎ **504-529-5254**) features hammocks, dresses, jackets, sandals, and leather goods, all imported from places such as Brazil, El Salvador, Guatemala, Bolivia, and Mexico.

✔ **Tower Records** (408 N. Peters St.; ☎ **504-529-4411**) is part of the well-known national chain, but this location distinguishes itself with an extensive collection of local and regional music.

Bourbon Street

If you're looking for silly slogan T-shirts or the usual trinkets and souvenirs, check out Bourbon Street. Of course, most of the stuff is of the "My Grandma Went to Bourbon Street and All I Got Was This Stupid T-Shirt" variety, and if you're seen buying that kind of stuff, forget about trying to blend in: You've just slapped the scarlet "T" (for tourist) on your shirt, and it ain't coming off. (On the plus side, it's one of the few places in the world you can window-shop while carrying a large plastic cup full of booze.)

If you're looking for something a little different, **Marie Laveau's House of Voodoo** (739 Bourbon St., ☎ **504-581-3751**), a popular attraction in the French Quarter, is a good place to find a voodoo doll (though hopefully you don't need one). The resident psychic and palm reader can give you a reading as well.

Canal Street

Longtime fans of and visitors to New Orleans may remember when Canal Street was *the* place to shop. With the return of the Canal Streetcar, look for increased commercial ventures, shops, and restaurants along the route. For now, **The Shops at Canal Place,** located at the foot of Canal Street (365 Canal St.; ☎ **504-522-9200** or 504-581-5400), represents the extent of the Canal Street shopping experience — but it's a plush one, with polished marble floors, a landscaped atrium, fountains, and pools. A small fire after Katrina — which was highly suspicious because there was no electricity or gas at the time — postponed its reopening, but renovations were completed fairly quickly. This mall features more than 50 shops. It's open Monday to Wednesday from 10 a.m. to 6 p.m., Thursday from 10 a.m. to 8 p.m., Friday and Saturday from 10 a.m. to 7 p.m., and Sunday from noon to 6 p.m.

French Quarter Shopping

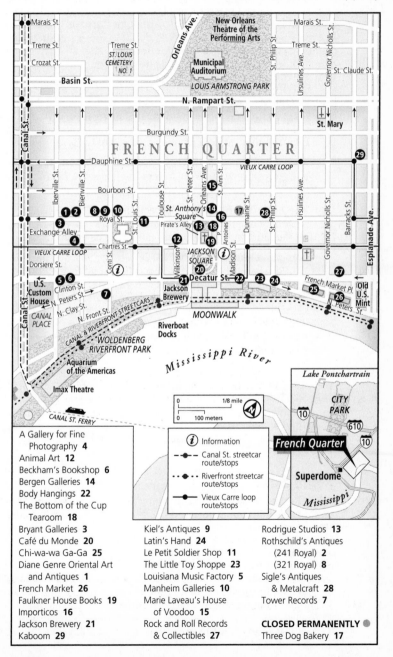

A Gallery for Fine
  Photography **4**
Animal Art **12**
Beckham's Bookshop **6**
Bergen Galleries **14**
Body Hangings **22**
The Bottom of the Cup
  Tearoom **18**
Bryant Galleries **3**
Café du Monde **20**
Chi-wa-wa Ga-Ga **25**
Diane Genre Oriental Art
  and Antiques **1**
French Market **26**
Faulkner House Books **19**
Importicos **16**
Jackson Brewery **21**
Kaboom **29**

Kiel's Antiques **9**
Latin's Hand **24**
Le Petit Soldier Shop **11**
The Little Toy Shoppe **23**
Louisiana Music Factory **5**
Manheim Galleries **10**
Marie Laveau's House
  of Voodoo **15**
Rock and Roll Records
  & Collectibles **27**

Rodrigue Studios **13**
Rothschild's Antiques
  (241 Royal) **2**
  (321 Royal) **8**
Sigle's Antiques
  & Metalcraft **28**
Tower Records **7**

CLOSED PERMANENTLY ●
Three Dog Bakery **17**

Decatur Street

One of the French Quarter's main drags, Decatur Street runs along the river and gets a lot of foot traffic. Although the main attraction is the **Jax Brewery** (which I mention more in depth in the "Checking Out the Big Names" section, earlier in this chapter), you also find a number of worthwhile shops for serious collectors and enthusiasts. Among the best are the following:

- ✔ **Beckham's Bookshop** (228 Decatur St.; ☎ **504-522-9875**) is a real treasure trove for book and music lovers alike, with two levels of old editions, rare secondhand books, and thousands of classical LPs. You may get lost wandering the musty, Byzantine aisles.

- ✔ **Body Hangings** (835 Decatur St.; ☎ **800-574-1823** or 504-524-9856), in case you're wondering, refers to cloaks, which are this store's specialty. A selection of capes and scarves is also available.

- ✔ **The Little Toy Shoppe** (900 Decatur St.; ☎ **504-522-6588**) presents strikingly beautiful dolls as well as wooden toys from Germany, stuffed animals, tea sets, and miniature cars and trucks.

- ✔ **Louisiana Music Factory** (210 Decatur St.; ☎ **504-586-1094;** www. louisianamusicfactory.com) offers a large selection of regional music, including Cajun, zydeco, R&B, jazz, blues, and gospel. The Factory also sells reference books, posters, and T-shirts, and occasionally provides live in-store performances and beer bashes. More than just a record store, it's an integral part of the city's music community and local musicians need your support more than ever. If you can't make it to the clubs to hear them live, then please pick up a CD or two here.

- ✔ **Rock and Roll Records & Collectibles** (1214 Decatur St.; ☎ **504-561-5683**), despite its name, has a lot more than just rock-and-roll on sale. The owners claim to have the biggest and best collection of vinyl anywhere, and that includes 45s and 78s. Indeed, the collection even takes up floor space. There's no telling what you can find here.

Royal Street

Along Royal Street you can find many fine-art galleries and shops selling antiques, jewelry, perfume, and candy as well as shops for coin and stamp collectors.

First, check out these general-interest sites:

- ✔ **The Bottom of the Cup Tearoom** (732 Royal St.; ☎ **504-523-1204**) is supposedly the oldest tearoom in the United States. You can have someone read your tarot cards or tea leaves or build your astrological chart; you can also get a reading from "pure clairvoyant psychics." I can't vouch for their accuracy, but they're sure a lot cheaper than those 1-900 psychic lines. The store offers books, jewelry, crystal balls, tarot cards, crystals, and healing wands.

✔ **Importicos** (736 Royal St.; ☎ **504-523-3100**) features an international selection of hand-crafted silver jewelry; pottery; textiles; leather, wood, stone, and metal items; and teak, mahogany, and wrought-iron furniture.

✔ **Le Petit Soldier Shop** (528 Royal St.; ☎ **504-523-7741**), as its name implies, sells miniature soldiers made by local artists. Armies represent a span from ancient Greece up to Desert Storm, and you can find quite a few miniatures that resemble major figures in military history, such as Eisenhower, Grant, Lee, Hitler, and Napoleon. Also available is a good-size collection of medals and decorations.

For antiques, check out these places:

✔ **Diane Genre Oriental Art and Antiques** (431 Royal St.; ☎ **504-595-8945**) is a nice change of pace if you've looked at too many European antiques. It offers East Asian porcelains, 18th-century Japanese woodblock prints, and Chinese and Japanese textiles, scrolls, screens, engravings, and lacquers.

✔ **Kiel's Antiques** (325 Royal St.; ☎ **504-522-4552**) was established in 1899 and is still a family business. It houses a considerable collection of 18th- and 19th-century French and English furniture, chandeliers, jewelry, and other items.

✔ **Manheim Galleries** (403@nd409 Royal St.; ☎ **504-568-1901**) showcases a huge collection of Continental, English, and Oriental furnishings, along with porcelain, jade, silver, and fine paintings.

✔ **Rothschild's Antiques** (241 and 321 Royal St.; ☎ **504-523-5816** or 504-523-2281) isn't only an antiques store but also a full-service jeweler. Look for antique and custom-made jewelry among the more standard offerings of antique silver, marble mantels, porcelain, and English and French furnishings.

✔ **Sigle's Antiques & Metalcraft** (935 Royal St.; ☎ **504-522-7647**) is the place if you're a big fan of the lacy ironwork that distinguishes French Quarter balconies. Sigle's offers some of its antique ironwork already converted into more-packable household items such as planters.

If you're in the mood for fine art, visit these galleries:

✔ **A Gallery for Fine Photography** (241 Chartres St.; ☎ **504-568-1313**; www.agallery.com) offers rare photographs and books from the 19th and 20th centuries, with an emphasis on New Orleans and Southern history and contemporary culture. The owner calls it "the only museum in the world that's for sale"; I agree.

✔ **Bergen Galleries** (730 Royal St.; ☎ **800-621-6179** or 504-523-7882; www.bergenputmangallery.com) boasts the South's largest selection of posters and prints. It also specializes in New Orleans, Louisiana Cajun, and African-American fine art. The service here is extremely personable.

✔ **Bryant Galleries** (316 Royal St.; ☎ **800-844-1994** or 504-525-5584; www.bryantgalleries.com) represents a number of American and European artists. Look for glasswork, graphic art, and bronzes depicting jazz themes. The staff is quite friendly here.

✔ **Rodrigue Studios** (721 Royal St.; ☎ **504-581-4244**) features the famous Blue Dog by Cajun artist George Rodrigue, who began painting blue portraits of his late dog for a children's book in 1984. Now his work has achieved international renown, hanging in galleries in Munich and Yokohama. Take a trip here to see this canine pop icon in home territory. Rodrigue created special prints featuring the Blue Dog to raise funds for charities helping New Orleans come back. So far, he has raised nearly $500,000. Go to www.bluedog relief.com to see the unique prints and order online if you can't make it to the gallery.

Warehouse District

Julia Street, from Camp Street down to the river and along some of its side streets, is your best bet for contemporary art galleries in New Orleans (an area known as the Arts District). Of course, some of the works are a bit pricey, but collectors can get some good deals and casual viewers can take in lots of fine art. While on Julia Street be sure to check out these places:

✔ **Ariodante Contemporary Craft Gallery** (535 Julia St.; ☎ **504-524-3233**) features hand-crafted furniture, glass, ceramics, jewelry, and decorative accessories.

✔ **Arthur Roger Gallery** (432 Julia St.; ☎ **504-522-1999**) has played a large role in nurturing the local art community and developing ties to the New York art scene. This beautiful gallery represents a number of prominent artists such as John Waters and local artist Robert Gordy. Roger says his gallery spaces were spared during Katrina, but several artists' studios were flooded. "But I can tell you that every artist who was displaced has emphatically stated to me that they are coming back to New Orleans," Roger says. "Every artist who is already in New Orleans is staying here. Our singular community of artists will remain intact and their spirit is still vital." The gallery's Project Space is in the Arts District at 730 Tchoupitoulas St.

✔ **LeMieux Galleries** (332 Julia St.; ☎ **504-522-5988**) showcases the work of local and regional craftspeople as well as contemporary artists from Louisiana and the Gulf Coast.

✔ **Marguerite Oestreicher Fine Arts** (726 Julia St.; ☎ **504-581-9253**) has consistently been a showcase for emerging artists, with a focus on contemporary painting, sculpture, and photography.

Magazine Street, Garden District, and Uptown

Running from Canal Street to Audubon Park, Magazine Street offers 6 miles of almost 150 shops: some in 19th-century brick storefronts, others in quaint, cottage-like buildings. Overall, it's a very unique, funky stretch; the 5400 and 5500 blocks (between Jefferson Avenue and Joseph Street) are my favorite stretch. Because it's a less ritzy area of the city, you can usually find some bargains here. Look for antiques, art galleries, boutiques, crafts, fashion, and custom-designed furniture. Looting was a huge problem in the weeks after Katrina, forcing some businesses to remain closed for a much longer period of time or causing the owners to wonder if they wanted to return at all.

I'm not pointing a finger at any of the antiques dealers or shops here, but in general, it helps to be discerning when looking at antiques. You never know; someone may have passed off an everyday household item as a priceless family heirloom. As the song says, you better shop around. Some places ask entirely too much money for their wares when a little digging can find you something very similar at a much more reasonable price.

Following are some noteworthy shops on Magazine Street, from art galleries to antiques stores and more, which were doing fine as of press time:

✔ **Aidan Gill for Men** (2026 Magazine St.; ☎ **504-587-9090**) carries everything to maintain a man's good looks, from handmade shaving gear to luxurious creams and soaps as well as timeless fashion accessories. Owner Aidan Gill and his staff also provide hairstyling and old-fashioned hot-towel shaves.

✔ **Audubon Antiques** (2025 Magazine St.; ☎ **504-581-5704**) stocks everything from curios to authentic antique treasures spread out over two floors.

✔ **Beaucoup Books** (3951 Magazine St.; ☎ **504-895-2663**) is another popular independent bookseller with a strong emphasis on local and regional reference books plus a children's room. After more than 20 years in the same location, the rent was raised and the store moved further down Magazine. It's better than ever. Ask owner Mary Price Dunbar for her picks.

✔ **Cameron Jones** (2127 Magazine St.; ☎ **504-524-3119**) is a surprise respite from heavy old antiques, with its eclectic, contemporary collection of home accent pieces, furniture, custom-designed rugs, original art works, unusual lighting fixtures, and soothing wall fountains.

✔ **Charbonnet & Charbonnet, Inc.** (2728 Magazine St.; ☎ **504-891-9948**) is the place to go for country pine; theyhave beautiful English and Irish pieces on display, and custom furnishings are also built on site.

✔ **Garden District Book Shop** (2727 Prytania St.; ☎ **504-895-2266**) is a popular independent bookstore beloved by local fans. Anne Rice has used it as a starting point for a number of her book-signing tours; the store usually keeps a number of signed Rice books on hand. However, you can find much more.

✔ **George Herget Books** (3109 Magazine St.; ☎ **504-891-5595**) has more than 20,000 rare and used books on any subject you can think of.

✔ **House of Lounge** (2044 Magazine St.; ☎ **504-671-8300**) offers a sexy, sophisticated collection of designer lingerie and loungewear for women and smoking jackets and more for men. Erin Brockovich couldn't resist spending hundreds of dollars when she stopped by.

✔ **Magazine Arcade Antiques** (3017 Magazine St.; ☎ **504-895-5451**) carries an excellent selection of 18th- and 19th-century furnishings as well as music boxes, dollhouse miniatures, porcelain, antique toys, and a host of other treasures. Budget a fair amount of time for this place.

✔ **Magic Box** (5508 Magazine St.; ☎ **504-899-0117**) is a treasure trove of toys for kids of all ages.

✔ **Maple Street Book Shop** (7523 Maple St.; ☎ **504-866-4916**) is quintessentially New Orleans, from its curled and yellowed photo murals to its shotgun home. Founded by her mother more than 40 years ago, daughter Rhoda Faust carries on Maple Street's promise to "Fight the Stupids!" The Walker Percy and Ellen Gilchrist collections are literary eye candy.

✔ **Martin Wine Cellar** (3500 Magazine St.; ☎ **504-899-7411**) carries an expansive selection of wines, spirits, and champagnes for unexpectedly reasonable prices. Also on hand are preserves, coffees, teas, crackers, biscotti, cookies, and cheeses. There is no deli but it does offer gourmet take-out. Note that the original store at 3827 Baronne Street was damaged in flooding, and it's not clear if they'll eventually return or stay on Magazine Street.

✔ **Mignon Faget** (3801 Magazine St.; ☎ **504-891-2005**) features fine jewelry designed by local artist Mignon Faget, whose muses are nature and Louisiana motifs. (I adore the sterling-silver Creole Cottage Key Ring and the unique Red Bean Tie Tack.) Her gallery also offers home accessories, signature fragrances, stationery, baby clothing, and more.

✔ **Mimi** (5500 Magazine St.; ☎ **504-269-6464**) is an upscale women's boutique (in a marvelously restored Arts and Crafts brick building) featuring clothing and accessories designed by Donna Karan, Michael Kors, and other fashion trendsetters.

Uptown Shopping

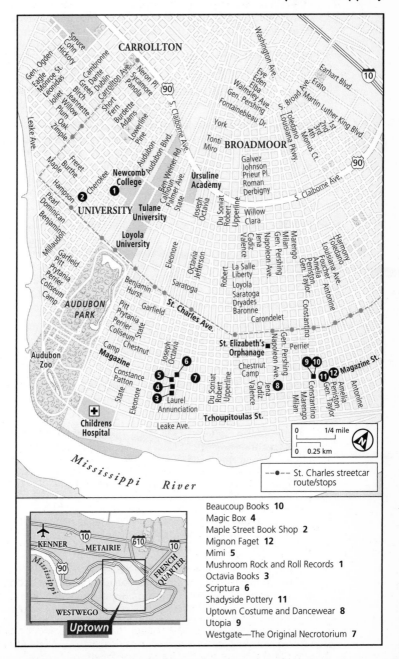

Beaucoup Books **10**
Magic Box **4**
Maple Street Book Shop **2**
Mignon Faget **12**
Mimi **5**
Mushroom Rock and Roll Records **1**
Octavia Books **3**
Scriptura **6**
Shadyside Pottery **11**
Uptown Costume and Dancewear **8**
Utopia **9**
Westgate—The Original Necrotorium **7**

✔ **Mushroom Rock and Roll Records** (1037 Broadway St.; ☎ 504-866-6065), located on Fraternity Row in the university area in the heart of Uptown, is a hip little place that is good for alternative music. As if that weren't enough, frugal students enjoy the comprehensive collection of used CDs (though they're not arranged in any particular order, so happy digging) and a large selection of T-shirts and other paraphernalia.

✔ **New Orleans Cypress Works** (3105 Magazine St.; ☎ 504-891-0001) designs custom furniture using antique cypress and heart of pine.

✔ **New Orleans Glassworks and Printmaking Studio** (727 Magazine St.; ☎ 504-529-7277) displays blown-glass sculptures, lampworking, bronze pours, printmaking, and bookbinding. The heart of the activity here is a state-of-the-art, 800-pound furnace. Visitors can commission glass, hand-bound books, or prints, as well as watch daily demonstrations of glassblowing, glass painting, metal sculpture, and other arts.

✔ **Octavia Books** (513 Octavia St.; ☎ 504-899-READ). Husband-and-wife proprietors Tom Lowenburg and Judith Lafitte handpick books of regional and national interest stocked in a spacious, modern setting complete with outdoor patio and waterfall. Their renovation of a 100-year-old former grocery earned them Best of New Orleans Architecture honors from *New Orleans Magazine* and a Golden Hammer award from the City of New Orleans.

✔ **Scriptura** (5423 Magazine St.; ☎ 504-897-5555) carries a unique assortment of paper products from around the world, including fine stationery, leather journals, and greeting cards plus writing instruments and custom wax seals.

✔ At **Shadyside Pottery** (3823 Magazine St.; ☎ 504-897-1710) you can witness the creation of *raku,* a particular type of pottery that has a cracked look.

✔ **Thomas Mann Gallery** (1804 Magazine St.; ☎ 504-581-2113) features "techno-romantic" jewelry designer Thomas Mann, who claims a lot of the credit for bringing contemporary jewelry and sculpture to New Orleans. This store/gallery seeks to "redefine contemporary living" via its eclectic collection of jewelry, lighting, and home furnishings.

✔ **Uptown Costume & Dancewear** (4326 Magazine St.; ☎ 504-895-7969) is the place to go for spooky monster masks, hats, wigs, makeup, and all kinds of mischievous mask wear.

✔ **Utopia** (3953 Magazine St.; ☎ 504-899-8488) also lost its lease (prior to the storm) and now shares a cozy double with former neighbor Beaucou Books. It has a unique collection of contemporary clothing, jewelry, accessories, and gifts as well as playful, fun furniture designed by David Marsh.

✓ **Westgate — The Original Necrotorium** (5219 Magazine St.; ☎ 504-
899-3077; www.westgatenecromantic.com) celebrates the inner
Goth, a one-stop shop for death-related items including "necroman-
tic" art and jewelry (featuring plenty of skeletons and other death
images). The book section offers related titles. Although some
people may find the artwork disturbing, open-minded visitors with
a healthy dose of curiosity will appreciate its unique offerings.

✓ **Wilkerson Row** (3137 Magazine St.; ☎ 504-899-3311) is an award-
winning furniture shop whose custom designs are influenced by
19th-century New Orleans architecture.

Chapter 14

Following an Itinerary: Four Great Options

Although I give a lot of lip service to exploring New Orleans on your own, the truth is, you do need some structure. However, that doesn't preclude fun. This chapter presents suggestions on what to do if your time is limited or if you're bringing your family.

New Orleans in One Day

If you're only in New Orleans for one day, spend the whole day in the French Quarter (see Chapters 3, 9, and 14). As much as I stress throughout this book that New Orleans is more than this historic district, I'd never advise you not to take in the Quarter's sights. It *is* the single most popular attraction in the city for good reason, with a lot of culture, history, and lore in its small (6 blocks wide by 13 blocks long) confines.

To get into the spirit of the city, take your time getting started in the morning with a visit to **Café du Monde** (see Chapter 11) for **beignets** (fried doughnuts covered in powdered sugar) washed down with a **café au lait.** After lingering for a bit at Café du Monde, begin the day's touring with a 30- to 60-minute stop at historic **Jackson Square** (see Chapter 12). While in the neighborhood, check out the **Cabildo** and the **Presbytere** (see Chapter 12), allowing roughly an hour for each. Then wander over to the **St. Louis Cathedral,** on the north side of the square at 721 Chartres (see Chapter 12), for a short 15-minute go-through. Afterward, pop in at **Faulkner House Books** (see Chapter 13) for a little bit of literary history and maybe to buy a rare first-edition hardback or two. You may also want to gander at the beautifully restored **Beauregard-Keyes House** (see Chapter 12) at 1113 Chartres St.; allow about 45 minutes to one hour.

New Orleans in One Day

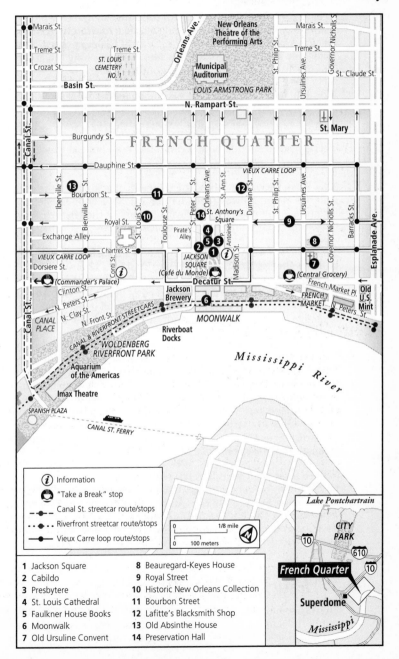

Marais St.
Treme St.
Crozat St.
Basin St.
ST. LOUIS CEMETERY NO. 1
Treme St.
Orleans Ave.
New Orleans Theatre of the Performing Arts
Municipal Auditorium
LOUIS ARMSTRONG PARK
St. Philip St.
Marais St.
Treme St.
Ursulines Ave.
Governor Nicholls S
St. Claude St.

N. Rampart St.

Canal St.
Burgundy St.
FRENCH QUARTER
St. Mary

Dauphine St.
VIEUX CARRE LOOP

Iberville St.
13 Bourbon St.
Bienville St.
Royal St.
Exchange Alley
Chartres St.
VIEUX CARRE LOOP
Dorsiere St.
St. Louis St.
10
Toulouse St.
St. Peter St.
11
Orleans Ave.
St. Ann St.
14 St. Anthony's Square
Pirate's Alley
4
5 **3**
2 **1**
JACKSON SQUARE
(Café du Monde)
Antoines
Madison St.
Dumaine St.
12
St. Philip St.
Ursulines Ave.
9
8
(Central Grocery)
7
Governor Nicholls St.
Barracks St.
Esplanade Ave.

(Commander's Palace)
Clinton St.
N. Peters St.
N. Clay St.
CANAL PLACE
CANAL & RIVERFRONT STREETCARS
N. Front St.
Jackson Brewery
6
Decatur St.
MOONWALK
French Market Pl.
FRENCH MARKET
N. Peters St.
Old U.S. Mint

WOLDENBERG RIVERFRONT PARK
Riverboat Docks
Mississippi River
Aquarium of the Americas
Imax Theatre
SPANISH PLAZA
CANAL ST. FERRY

(i) Information
"Take a Break" stop
Canal St. streetcar route/stops
Riverfront streetcar route/stops
Vieux Carre loop route/stops

0   1/8 mile
0   100 meters

Lake Pontchartrain
CITY PARK
10
610
French Quarter
10
Superdome
Mississippi

1 Jackson Square
2 Cabildo
3 Presbytere
4 St. Louis Cathedral
5 Faulkner House Books
6 Moonwalk
7 Old Ursuline Convent
8 Beauregard-Keyes House
9 Royal Street
10 Historic New Orleans Collection
11 Bourbon Street
12 Lafitte's Blacksmith Shop
13 Old Absinthe House
14 Preservation Hall

Right about now, you may realize that all you had for breakfast was the rough equivalent of three very sugary donuts. My suggestion is to forego an actual sit-down restaurant and roll some sightseeing into your lunch. Stroll down to Decatur Street and sample a **muffuletta** (one of New Orleans's premier sandwiches) at **Central Grocery** (see Chapter 11). Take your sandwich across the street, wander along the **Moonwalk** (see Chapter 12), and eat by the banks of the Mississippi.

After lunch, a little walking helps the digestive process. Wind your way up Ursulines to the **Old Ursuline Convent** and tour the oldest surviving building in the Mississippi Valley (see Chapter 12). Allow about an hour before wandering over to the **Beauregard-Keyes House** across the street; plan to spend about 45 minutes to an hour at this literary land-mark (see Chapter 12).

Next, walk westward down **Royal Street,** checking out the shops and galleries along the way (see Chapter 13). Save enough energy for the insightful exhibits on New Orleans history at the **Historic New Orleans Collection** (see Chapter 12) for a nice overview.

Steel yourself for a predinner stroll down **Bourbon Street.** Stop in at **Lafitte's Blacksmith Shop and Bar** (Chapters 12 and 17) for a drink, and darned if you won't absorb some more history in the process. To con-tinue the historical theme, you can hang out at the **Old Absinthe House** (Chapters 12 and 17), sipping an anisette, and imagine what it must have been like back in the days of Andrew Jackson and Jean Lafitte.

For dinner, only one place is worth considering if you only have one day in town. If its has reopened, please make a reservation at **Commander's Palace** (see Chapter 11), widely considered one of the best restaurants in the United States. Visiting celebrities regularly stop to relax in the lux-urious dining rooms (all decorated in New Orleans flair). The restaurant is a bit pricey, but the pampering, food, and luxurious surroundings are well worth the cost. If it still remains closed at the time of your visit, **Upperline** (see Chapter 11) offers fine Creole food, an eclectic art collec-tion and the most congenial hostess-proprietor in the city.

Make a pit stop at your hotel to recharge your batteries because you haven't had the complete New Orleans experience until you've heard some music. Start out in the Quarter, first heading to **Preservation Hall** (see Chapter 16), if it has finally reopened, for authentic, traditional jazz. Then head back to **Bourbon Street,** which by now should be in full swing.

New Orleans in Three Days

For **day one** of this itinerary, see the preceding section to get the most out of the famous French Quarter. Start **day two** by adhering to my New Orleans Golden Rule: Get out of the Quarter!

If you're staying in the French Quarter, have breakfast at the breezy and friendly **Clover Grill** (see Chapter 11). From there, head down to Decatur Street for a glimpse of the Mississippi River and to look for souvenirs at **Jax Brewery** (see Chapter 13). Allow about an hour to an hour and a half. Next, cross Canal Street and head into the **Warehouse District** (see Chapter 9), specifically toward **Julia Street,** a bustling corridor of art galleries (see Chapter 13). If you prefer to eat a late breakfast, stop in at **Mother's** (see Chapter 11) for your fill of good diner food.

From there make your way by streetcar, auto, or other propulsive means (*not* by foot) to the **Garden District** (see Chapter 9). You can take a walking tour (see Chapter 12) or stroll around on your own to admire the stately elegance of the gorgeous manses, especially those along St. Charles Avenue and Prytania Street. Closer to the river, along **Magazine Street,** the elegance gives way to a loose and funky vibe. Here you find smaller shotguns and cottages (see Chapter 3), and more art galleries and antiques shops (see Chapter 13). Allow at least two hours to explore the district.

For lunch, Uptown offers several great options. I recommend **Franky & Johnny's** (just off Magazine at Arabella Street; see Chapter 11) for filling sandwiches and New Orleans staples. Afterward, take a cab to **City Park** (see Chapter 12) and spend a little time enjoying its tranquil charms. While you're there, you simply must wander the halls of the **New Orleans Museum of Art** and reflect on its marvelous **Besthoff Sculpture Garden** (see Chapter 12). Allow two to three hours for the park, museum, and garden.

If you're feeling hungry, cross the bridge at Bayou St. John to Esplanade Avenue and grab a snack and caffeine at **Fair Grinds Coffee House** (see Chapter 11). Take a cab from the park along grand old Esplanade Avenue and gaze at the funky neighborhood that's home to the Fair Grounds Race Course. Esplanade takes you right up to the border of the French Quarter.

After a little downtime at your hotel — or additional French Quarter touring for the truly hearty — treat yourself to a quintessential (and fairly cheap) French Quarter dining experience slurping down raw oysters at **Acme Oyster House** (see Chapter 11). If seafood isn't your thing, head to the Quarter's edge and grab a burger at **Port of Call** (see Chapter 11). Either way, you dine relatively cheaply and rub elbows with some down-to-earth locals.

Now, get ready for some music. Digest and unwind with a drink at a local watering hole. I recommend **Molly's at the Market** (see Chapter 17), a homey hangout that won me over with its charming atmosphere and friendliness. Next, hop across Esplanade to **Frenchmen Street** (see Chapter 17) for a whirlwind tour of jazz, funk, and world music. You can easily spend an evening at just one of these clubs, but I recommend that

New Orleans in Three Days

To METAIRIE

Jefferson
Valmont
Soniat
Robert
Upperline
Cadiz
Jena

Southern
Baptist Hospital
Valence
Napoleon Ave.
Gen. Pershing
Milan
Gen. Taylor

S. Dorgenois
S. Rocheblave
S. Broad Ave.
Earhart Blvd. (Calliope St.)

Louisiana Parkway
Toledano
Washington
Seminole
S. Johnson
S. Prieur

BROADMOOR

90

S. Claiborne Ave.
S. Derbigny
S. Roman

Willow
Clara
Magnolia
S. Robertson
Freret

Erato
Thalia
Clio

Martin Luther King Blvd.

Marengo

La Salle
S. Liberty
Loyola
S. Saratoga
4th
3rd
2nd
1st
Dryades
Baronne
Carondelet
St. Charles

**New Orleans
Arena**

**Union Passenger
Terminal (Amtrak)**

Simon Bolivar

Constantinople
Peniston
Amelia
Foucher
Delachaise
Louisiana Ave.

14

UPTOWN

Aline
Harmony
8th
7th
6th
Prytania
3rd

Coliseum

GARDEN DISTRICT

Toledano
Pleasant
9th

Washington
Camp
Magazine
Constance
Laurel

Chestnut

Annunciation

Chippewa
St. Thomas
Rousseau

3

Jackson Ave.

Josephine
St. Andrew
St. Mary
Felicity

Polymnia
Euterpe
Terpsichore
Melpomene

St. Charles Ave.

Polymnia
Euterpe
Terpsichore
Thalia
Erato
Clio

Le
Cir

Pontchartrain Expwy.

4

Camp
Magazine
Constance
Annunciation

Race
Orange
Richard
Market
Celeste

**New Orleans
General Hospital**

BR
90

13

Lake Pontchartrain

**CITY
PARK**

10
610
10

Area of detail

Superdome

(i) Information

"Take a Break" stop

Ferry Service to
Algiers Point

- • - Riverfront streetcar
route/stops

— • — St. Charles streetcar
route/stops

—●— Vieux Carre loop
route/stops

— ● — Canal St. streetcar
route/stops

1

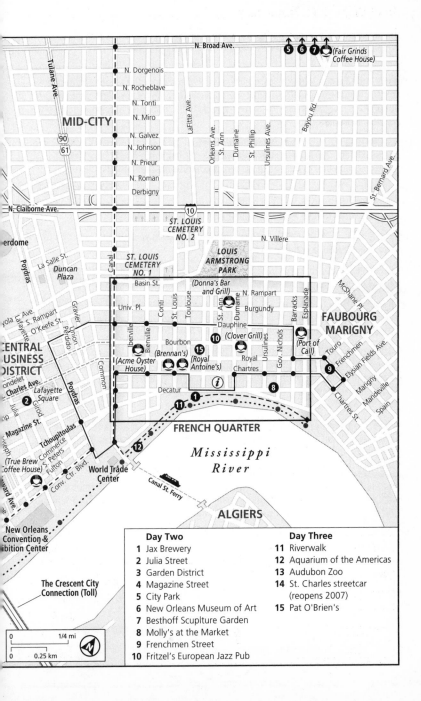

MID-CITY

CENTRAL BUSINESS DISTRICT

FAUBOURG MARIGNY

FRENCH QUARTER

LOUIS ARMSTRONG PARK

ST. LOUIS CEMETERY NO. 2

ST. LOUIS CEMETERY NO. 1

Duncan Plaza

Lafayette Square

Mississippi River

ALGIERS

World Trade Center

New Orleans Convention & Exhibition Center

The Crescent City Connection (Toll)

Canal St. Ferry

(Fair Grinds Coffee House)

(Donna's Bar and Grill)

(Clover Grill)

(Brennan's)

(Acme Oyster House)

(Royal Antoine's)

(Port of Call)

(True Brew Coffee House)

Day Two	Day Three
1 Jax Brewery	11 Riverwalk
2 Julia Street	12 Aquarium of the Americas
3 Garden District	13 Audubon Zoo
4 Magazine Street	14 St. Charles streetcar
5 City Park	(reopens 2007)
6 New Orleans Museum of Art	15 Pat O'Brien's
7 Besthoff Scuplture Garden	
8 Molly's at the Market	
9 Frenchmen Street	
10 Fritzel's European Jazz Pub	

0   1/4 mi

0   0.25 km

Streetcar highlights

Taking the St. Charles Streetcar (or bus in case you visit while it's closed, through late 2007)? Watch for these sights along the way. (For a map of the streetcar route, see Chapter 9.) When traveling from the French Quarter through the Garden District toward Audubon Park, note that odd-numbered addresses are on the right, even-numbered addresses on the left.

✔ After passing Julia and St. Joseph streets, you go around Lee Circle. That's General Robert E. Lee atop the massive column. Note that he's facing north so that his back won't be to the Yankees. The statue was erected in 1884.

✔ At 2040 St. Charles is La Tour Eiffel. If it looks like the Eiffel Tower in Paris, that's because it actually *was* a part of the tower, built in Paris as an upper-level restaurant and then moved to New Orleans and reassembled in 1936.

✔ The Columns Hotel (1883), located at 3811 St. Charles, was the location of a Storyville bordello in the movie *Pretty Baby*.

✔ Does the Palmer House at 5705 St. Charles look familiar? If you've seen *Gone With the Wind,* it should, It's a replica of Tara.

✔ Audubon Park (extending all the way from St. Charles to the Mississippi River) was the site of the 1884 World's Industrial and Cotton Centennial Exposition. The renowned Audubon Zoo is on the far side of the park.

✔ After passing Tulane University and the old St. Mary's Dominican College (now Loyola's Broadway campus), you enter what used to be the town of Carrollton, named for General William Carroll, a commander at the Battle of New Orleans. Carrollton was founded in 1833 and incorporated in 1845. New Orleans annexed the city in 1874.

✔ After the streetcar turns right onto Carondelet, look ahead and a little to the left. The tall building with the cupola at 325 Carondelet is the Hibernia Bank Building (1921), the tallest building in the city until 1962. The cupola is lit at night in colors that change with the seasons.

Taking the Canal Streetcar? (For a map of the streetcar route, see Chapter 9.) New Orleans's former main street was undergoing a well-received revival but severe flooding did a lot of damage to this up-and-coming corridor. Keep an eye out for:

✔ Block-Keller House (3620 Canal St.), a magnificently restored classical-revival villa now serving as a B&B. Hosts Bryan Block and Jeff Keller repaired flood damage, but currently have it on the market, so let's hope that the buyer continues their success.

✔ City Park, the New Orleans Museum of Art, and the Besthoff Sculpture Garden at the end of the Carrollton spur.

✔ The former upscale brothel at 4332 Canal St. infamously busted by the FBI.

✔ The Cypress Grove and Greenwood cemeteries at the end of the line (no pun intended).

you stroll from place to place. After a couple hours, head over to **Fritzel's European Jazz Pub** (Chapter 16) to catch a late-night jam session before collapsing into bed.

After using day two to sample the city's charms beyond the French Quarter (though you've really only scratched the surface), treat **day three** as a reward, indulging in some of the more touristy but no less entertaining sights, including the hedonistic pleasures of a breakfast at **Brennan's** (see Chapter 11). Allow about an hour to savor the experience. From there, head over to **Riverwalk Marketplace** (Chapter 13) to finish up any last-minute shopping, followed by a tour of the amazing **Aquarium of the Americas** (Chapter 12). Allow one to two hours to take it all in (closer to two to include a film at the **IMAX Theater**).

Next, if the streetcar is running, take it to the world-renowned **Audubon Zoo** (see Chapter 14). If your plentiful Brennan's breakfast has begun to wear off, grab lunch (or at least a snack) at the zoo or across Magazine Street at the Audubon Golf Clubhouse. Allow about two hours. Next, travel back to the French Quarter by riverboat or — assuming it's literally back on track — by the **St. Charles Streetcar** (see Chapter 14), which provides a scenic glimpse of the city's grandest boulevard. (See the sidebar "Streetcar highlights" in this chapter for a list of sights to see along the way.)

Return to your hotel to rest up for another signature New Orleans dining experience — dinner at **Antoine's** (see Chapter 11). After dinner, take a leisurely last stroll through the Quarter, making sure to stop at **Pat O'Brien's** (see Chapter 17), where the expansive courtyard, complete with flaming fountain, is touristy but cool in a kitschy way. Then wind your way to the Rampart Street border of the Quarter, where you can finish the night with some eclectic New Orleans music — and more than a little atmosphere — at **Donna's Bar and Grill** (Chapter 15).

New Orleans in Five Days

If you're in town for more than three days, see the preceding section to get the most out of your first three days. For **day four** of this itinerary get out of the city completely. I recommend you choose from one of the day-trip suggestions in Chapter 15.

If you like regional music, start driving to Lafayette and make a day of touring **Atchafalaya Basin,** shopping at **Acadian Village,** and a night of Cajun dining and dancing at **Randol's Restaurant and Cajun Dance Hall.** If you're too tired to drive back to the city, check in at the 1820s **Bois des Chenes Inn,** a former cattle and sugar cane plantation, for a good night's sleep.

If you like the outdoors, head south to Lafitte. Spend the morning at **Barataria Preserve** followed by lunch at **Restaurant des Familles** in nearby Crown Point or an English tea at **Victoria Inn & Gardens.** Then spend the afternoon communing with alligators on a swamp tour, courtesy of **L'il Cajun Swamp Tours,** before dining at **Voleo's.** Again, if you're too tired to return to the city, stay overnight at Victoria Inn & Gardens. If you like to fish, you're welcome to fish off the pier or ask hosts Roy and Dale Ross if they can set up a fishing charter for you with **Captain Phil Robichaux.** Prepare to get up super early the next day to catch some reds (tasty red fish) and maybe a crab or two.

For **day five,** you have your pick of lovely plantation homes along River Road. My personal favorites are **Laura,** for including the slave community in its tours and maintaining the slave cabins (instead of having destroyed them as some plantations did) and its resurrection after a devastating fire in 2004; **Oak Alley,** for its beautiful oak-lined avenue and fantasy of Southern plantation living; and the 54,000-square-foot **Nottoway,** known locally as the White Castle for its formidable presence. Along the way you can feast on fresh seafood at **B & C Seafood Market & Cajun Deli** (about a mile from Laura). For details on the establishments I recommend visiting on days four and five, see Chapter 15.

New Orleans for Families with Kids

If you have young ones, you might want to steer clear of devastated areas. Whereas teenagers might be fascinated by seeing history in the making as flooded areas rebuild. Happily, more than enough diversions are available that appeal to grown-ups and little ones alike.

On **day one,** start with a breakfast at **Café du Monde** (see Chapter 11) followed by a brief walk through the French Quarter, taking in **Jackson Square** (see Chapter 12) and maybe a historic home or two. But spend the majority of the morning enjoying the many delights of the **Aquarium of the Americas** (see Chapter 12), allowing one to two hours before a brief lunch either on-site or at one of many nearby restaurants. After lunch, if it's running, take the St. Charles Streetcar (or bus) to the **Audubon Zoo** (see Chapter 12), where you can while away the afternoon (allow at least two hours) ooh-ing and aah-ing the wildlife on display. Again, if it's running, take the St. Charles Streetcar (or bus; see Chapter 9) to wind your way back toward downtown, disembarking near Lee Circle, the Quarter a short hop away by cab. Grab a bite at **Café Maspero** (see Chapter 11) and retire to your hotel to rest up for the next day. If you or the kids get restless, a **carriage ride** (see Chapter 9) is a pleasant way to enjoy the sights of the French Quarter.

On **day two,** after breakfast at **Mother's** or **Clover Grill,** a cheerful gay-friendly establishment (see Chapter 12), take the Canal Street Ferry (it's free, and departs from the foot of Canal Street every quarter hour; a pedestrian-only commuter boat also runs at 15-minute intervals) to **Blaine Kern's Mardi Gras World** (see Chapter 12), where you'll spend the morning (about two hours round-trip) looking at floats-in-progress and finding out some interesting tidbits about Carnival. Afterward, the ferry takes you back to the Quarter (it costs a dollar this way), where you can do a bit more walking around, taking in the **Moonwalk** and the Mississippi and perhaps even the open-air **French Market** (see Chapter 12). Take your time, but budget about 20 minutes to have a quintessential New Orleans lunch courtesy of **Central Grocery** (see Chapter 11) before taking the Canal Streetcar to **City Park** (see Chapter 12). Here you can enjoy the **New Orleans Museum of Art,** the **Besthoff Sculpture Garden,** and if it has reopened, the park's **Carousel Gardens** (see Chapter 12), allowing about two and a half to four hours, depending on your stamina, before hopping a cab back to your hotel and dinner at **Remoulade** (309 Bourbon St., ☎ **504-523-0377**), a kid- and budget-friendly cousin to the legendary **Arnaud's** (see Chapter 11). Squeeze in a bit more strolling in the evening, but be sure to rest up for the following day.

Day three starts with a leisurely jazz brunch at **Court of Two Sisters** (see Chapter 11) before stopping by the **Presbytere** (see Chapter 12), if it's open again, for an entertaining look at Mardi Gras memorabilia. Then take a short hop to the Warehouse District for the fun, interactive exhibits at the **Louisiana Children's Museum** (see Chapter 12). Allow about an hour at each museum.

Follow it up with some shopping and a quick lunch at **Jax Brewery** (see Chapter 13) or the **Riverwalk Marketplace** (see Chapter 13) if you went to the Children's Museum. In the past, I recommended a fun-filled afternoon at **Six Flags New Orleans** (see Chapter 12) or a jaunt out to the **Louisiana Nature Center and Planetarium** (see Chapter 12), but both of these locations were devastated by storm surge. Six Flags is permanently closed but I am optimistic about the fate of the nature center.

After days of super rich local food, go easy on dinner and walk off some of those calories, enjoying one last look at the French Quarter by night, perhaps enjoying a final, lingering gaze out over the Mississippi by **Washington Artillery Park** (see Chapter 12). Then take time for souvenir packing and sleep before heading back home.

New Orleans for Families with Kids

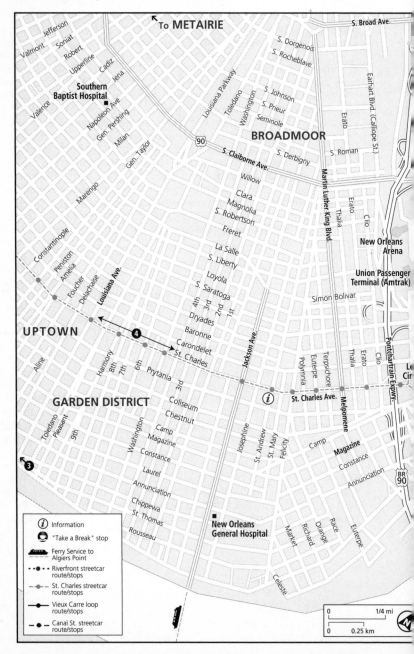

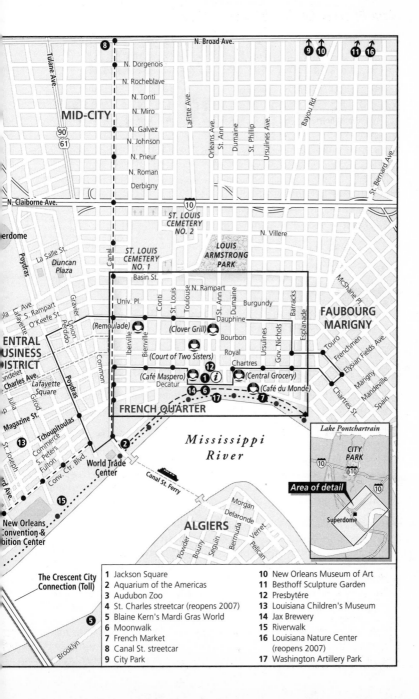

The Crescent City Connection (Toll)

1 Jackson Square
2 Aquarium of the Americas
3 Audubon Zoo
4 St. Charles streetcar (reopens 2007)
5 Blaine Kern's Mardi Gras World
6 Moonwalk
7 French Market
8 Canal St. streetcar
9 City Park

10 New Orleans Museum of Art
11 Besthoff Sculpture Garden
12 Presbytére
13 Louisiana Children's Museum
14 Jax Brewery
15 Riverwalk
16 Louisiana Nature Center (reopens 2007)
17 Washington Artillery Park

Chapter 15

Going Beyond New Orleans: Three Daytrips

In This Chapter

▶ Spending a day in Cajun Country
▶ Taking a sightseeing tour of remarkable plantation homes
▶ Getting back to nature — without driving all day to do it

*Y*ou could probably spend your next three or four vacations in the Crescent City and still not get to everything on your list. But sometimes you just need to get away from urban life. So gas up the car, get out your maps, and hit the road.

Daytrip No. 1: Discovering Cajun Country

This daytrip takes you to Lafayette, the heart of Cajun Country, where you discover this unique region's food, culture, and music.

The **Lafayette Parish Convention and Visitors Commission** (P.O. Box 52066, Lafayette, LA 70505, ☎ **800-346-1958** in the United States, 800-543-5340 in Canada, or 337-232-3737; fax: 337-232-0161; www.lafayette travel.com) can give you the scoop on all Lafayette has to offer. If you plan to come out this way, call for a brochure. They may even persuade you to extend your stay.

Creoles, *zydeco* (popular music of southern Louisiana combining tunes of French origin with elements of Caribbean music and the blues and that features guitar, washboard, and accordion) musicians, and non-Cajun residents don't much care for the "Cajun Country" label. Also, many citizens of Acadian descent aren't too wild about it either, especially in large urban centers such as Lafayette. Although the people here are proud of their heritage, some of them bristle at the rather touristy simplification of the term. If you drive through Lafayette, you can find that it's a city like any other. You don't have to abandon your car and paddle through dense swamp to get to a hotel or restaurant, nor do you encounter fiddle-playing *Deliverance* extras on every street corner and front porch.

Where in the world is Cajun Country?

Cajuns are the descendants of Acadians, settlers who were forced out of their established colony in Nova Scotia in the mid–18th century. Arriving in the French colony of Louisiana, they found themselves in relative isolation, farming in the low-lying wetlands and developing their own distinct culture. To experience some true Cajun culture, you need to drive two to three hours from New Orleans to Lafayette. There, you can find the food, music, and lifestyle that developed as the Acadians mingled with their neighbors and became an integral part of Louisiana life and lore.

Getting to Lafayette

Lafayette (167 miles — give or take a few — west of New Orleans) is a straight shot from New Orleans on Interstate 10. Drive in mid- to late morning so that you don't get caught in rush-hour traffic in Baton Rouge or Lafayette — or New Orleans, for that matter. After Katrina, traffic in the Greater New Orleans area has increased dreadfully as people who scattered outside New Orleans are now coming back full- or part-time. Try to be patient and listen to www.wwoz.org if the pace slows down.

Taking a tour of Cajun Country

The New Orleans area offers some authentic swamp tours, but the Atchafalaya Basin holds the distinction of being the third-largest swamp in the United States. A boat tour is a great way to experience this mystical region. **Angelle's Atchafalaya Basin Swamp Tours** (see map p. 264; Whiskey River Landing, P.O. Box 111, Cecilia, LA 70521; ☎ **337-228-8567,** www.angelleswhiskeyriver.com) operates tours in glass-bottomed boats or smaller, open boats. To get to the swamp from I-10, take Exit 115 to Henderson, go through Henderson to the levee, and turn right. The landing is the fourth exit on the left. Fares are $12 for adults, $10 for seniors (55 and up), and $6 for children. Departures are at 10 a.m., 1 p.m., and 3 p.m. daily (weather permitting).

Seeing the sights of Cajun Country

The sights in this daytrip wet your feet in the bayous of the Cajun experience. What's a bayou, exactly? Coming from the Choctaw word meaning "small stream," a *bayou* is a sluggish offshoot of a lake or river that flows through swampland — and an integral part of swampland culture.

Acadian Village

Acadian Village is a reconstructed (actually, reassembled) Cajun bayou community in which houses have been transported from their original location to this site beside a sleepy bayou. If you're the exploring type, take the footpath and venture along the bayou's banks. Peek inside the

Daytrip No. 1: Discovering Cajun Country

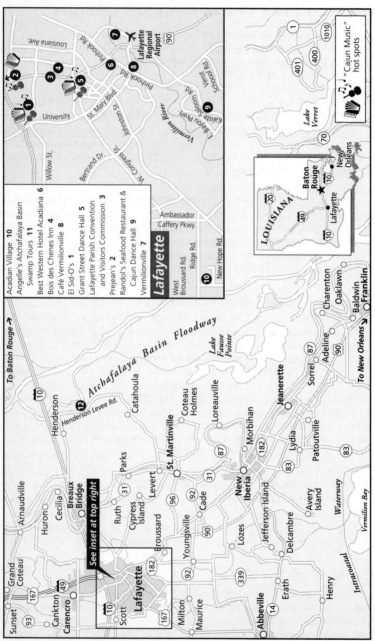

Acadian Village **10**
Angelle's Atchafalaya Basin Swamp Tours **11**
Best Western Hotel Acadiana **6**
Bois des Chenes Inn **4**
Café Vermilionville **8**
El Sid-O's **1**
Grant Street Dance Hall **5**
Lafayette Parish Convention and Visitors Commission **3**
Prejean's **2**
Randol's Seafood Restaurant & Cajun Dance Hall **9**
Vermilionville **7**

houses to glimpse the Cajun furniture. The gift shop sells Cajun handicrafts and books. Allow one to two hours.

See map p. 264. 200 Greenleaf Dr., Lafayette, LA 70506. ☎ ***800-962-9133*** *or 337-981-2364. Fax: 337-988-4554.* www.acadianvillage.org. *Take I-10 from Lafayette to Exit 97. Go south on Highway 93 to Ridge Road and then take a right on Ridge Road followed by a left on West Broussard. Admission: $7 adults, $6 seniors, $4 children 6–14; free for children under 6. Open: daily 10 a.m.–5 p.m.*

Vermilionville

Vermilionville is a small village on Bayou Vermilion that attempts to recreate Cajun life as it existed in the 18th and 19th centuries. Costumed staff members demonstrate crafts from the period. Shows feature Cajun music and dancing, and the restaurant serves authentic Cajun fare. Although it's a bit contrived, Vermilionville is fun and informative nonetheless. Allow one to two hours.

See map p. 264. 300 Fisher Rd., Lafayette, LA 70508. ☎ ***866-99-BAYOU*** *or 337-233-4077. Fax: 337-233-1694.* www.vermilionville.org. *Take I-10 from Lafayette to Exit 103A. Get on the Evangeline Thruway going south until you get to Surrey Street and then follow the signs. Closed most major holidays. Admission: $8 adults, $6.50 seniors, $5 students; free for children under 6. Open: Tues–Sun 10 a.m.–4 p.m.*

Where to stay in Cajun Country

If you want to enjoy the area's nightlife (see the "Passing a good time: Cajun Country nightlife" sidebar in this chapter), plan to spend the night in Lafayette rather than make the two-hour drive back to New Orleans.

Best Western Hotel Acadiana
$$–$$$$

The Hotel Acadiana offers great value for your vacation dollar, providing all the conveniences you'd expect in a large chain hotel, including a complimentary airport shuttle. The hotel's restaurant, Bayou Bistro, serves great Cajun food, and the hotel itself is located close to local sights.

See map p. 264. 1801 W. Pinhook Rd., Lafayette, LA 70508. ☎ ***800-874-4664*** *in Louisiana, 800-826-8386 in the United States and Canada, or 337-233-8120. Fax: 337-234-9667.* www.bestwestern.com/hotelacadiana. *Parking: free. Rates: $79–$210 double. AE, DC, DISC, MC, V.*

Bois des Chenes Inn
$$–$$$

Once the center of a 3,000-acre cattle and sugar cane plantation, this plantation home is now a small but lovely bed-and-breakfast. With only five accommodations — two suites in the main plantation home and three rooms in the carriage house — each room has been lovingly restored and furnished with Louisiana French antiques. Room rates include not only a Louisiana-style breakfast but a bottle of wine and a tour of the house as well. Also available are nature and bird-watching trips into Atchafalaya Swamp, as well as guided fishing and hunting trips. These adventures are conducted by the inn's owner, a retired geologist.

See map p. 264. 338 N. Sterling St., Lafayette, LA 70501. ☎ *337-233-7816.* www. members.aol.com/boisdchene/bois.htm. *Parking: free. Rates: $100–$150 double. Rates include breakfast. Extra person $30. AE, MC, V.*

Where to dine in Cajun Country

Although all these restaurants have their merits — and very strong ones at that — if you have time for only one, I recommend Prejean's.

Café Vermilionville
$$–$$$

Want atmosphere? Café Vermilionville is located in a meticulously restored Acadian cypress house dating back to 1799. With plenty of fresh seafood on the menu, specialties include Creole bronze shrimp and the unique Louisiana Crawfish Madness, which is crawfish tails prepared according to the chef's mood: au gratin, étouffée, fried, or in crawfish beignets (oh yes, crawfish beignets).

See map p. 264. 1304 W. Pinhook Rd., Lafayette, LA 70508. ☎ *337-237-0100.* www. cafev.com. *Reservations and appropriate attire recommended. Main courses: $17–$26. AE, DC, DISC, MC, V. Open: Mon–Fri 11 a.m.–2 p.m. and Mon–Sat 5:30–10 p.m.*

Prejean's
$–$$

While in the heart of Cajun Country, treat yourself to a night at Prejean's, *the* spot for nouvelle Cajun cooking. Although it gives the appearance of being simply another family restaurant, the bill of fare reveals this place to be one of the finest restaurants in Acadiana, with some of the best ingredients and recipes you'll find in Cajun cuisine. Highlights include crawfish enchiladas, crawfish étouffée, grilled or fried oysters, gumbo, shrimp, and alligator. Kids can dine on burgers or chicken fingers. Live Cajun music plays nightly at 7 p.m.

See map p. 264. 3480 I-49 North, Lafayette, LA 70507 (next to the Evangeline Downs Racetrack). ☎ *337-896-3247.* www.prejeans.com. *Reservations strongly recommended. Main courses: $15–$26; children's menu $3.50–$8.95. AE, DC, DISC, MC, V. Open: Sun–Thurs 7 a.m.–10 p.m. and Fri–Sat 7 a.m.–11 p.m.*

Randol's Restaurant and Cajun Dance Hall
$–$$

For the full Cajun experience, go to Randol's and enjoy live Cajun music with your cuisine. Randol's serves up seafood fresh from the bayou, prepared any way you want it: fried, steamed, blackened, or grilled. The house specialty seafood platter guarantees to fill you up. It includes a cup of

---

Passing a good time: Cajun Country nightlife

While in Lafayette, check out some of the local nightlife. A visit to **El Sid-O's** (see map p. 264; 1523 Martin Luther King Dr. in Lafayette), a hot spot for zydeco music, is an essential stop. The place is run by Sid Williams, whose brother Nathan is an acclaimed zydeco musician and leader of the popular group Nathan and the Zydeco Cha-Chas. The decor may not be very fancy, but that just adds to its appeal. A lot of zydeco history has gone down between these walls. Call ☎ 337-235-0647 to find out who's playing.

Grant Street Dance Hall (see map p. 264; 113 W. Grant St. in Lafayette) is the place where out-of-town rock bands are most apt to play when they pass through town (unless they're stadium-sized acts filling the nearby Cajundome). Local bands also call this place home, from alternative-rock outfits to Cajun and brass bands. Call ☎ 337-237-8513 or visit www.grantstreetdancehall.com for information.

---

seafood gumbo, fried shrimp, fried oysters, fried catfish, stuffed crab, crawfish étouffée, deviled crab, and coleslaw. With live music every night at 7 p.m., you can take in a few dances before, during, and after your meal.

See map p. 264. 2320 Kaliste Saloom Rd., Lafayette, LA 70508. ☎ *800-962-2586 or 337-981-7080. Fax: 318-981-7083.* www.randols.com. *Reservations for 20 or more only. Main courses: $7.95–$18. MC, V. Open: Sun–Thurs 5 p.m.–10 p.m. and Fri–Sat 5 p.m.–11 p.m.*

Daytrip No. 2: Plantations along the Great River Road

Once the focal point of a self-sustaining community, plantation homes flourished in Louisiana from the 1820s to the beginning of the Civil War. Although dozens of grand, beautiful homes once dotted the landscape (particularly around the Mississippi River because the homes were generally built near riverfronts), today the number has dwindled to a relative few. All were spared Katrina's wrath, however, with less than half the usual visitors, they are still struggling and need your support. This trip meanders along the river between New Orleans and Baton Rouge, stopping at a number of stately plantation homes along the way.

Getting to the plantations

This trip follows Interstate 10 west of New Orleans. Each plantation listing includes driving times and directions. The plantations are listed in the order in which they appear on the "Daytrip No. 2: Plantations along the Great River Road" map, running north from New Orleans along the Mississippi River. Keep in mind that the river winds a bit, so some distances may be deceiving.

Taking a plantation tour

All plantations listed in this section offer guided tours. Most present engaging historical details about the homes and their owners; I especially recommend you visit Laura and Destrehan Manor. Except where otherwise noted, tours generally last between 30 to 45 minutes. Some plantations schedule tours continuously (that is, a tour begins whenever a group arrives asking for one) or every 15 minutes or so. The Oak Alley and Houmas House tours begin on the half-hour. See the individual listings for admission prices.

Seeing the sights

Houses are spread apart and individual visits can take some time — seeing all the homes in a single day is unlikely. My advice is to pace yourself and find out how far you get by midday (or even midmorning). With a home or two under your belt, go through the list and concentrate on the ones that appeal to you the most. If you only have time for two or three, you can check out Laura, Oak Alley, and Madewood in one day at a comfortable pace. Allow one to one and a half hours for each visit, two and a half hours if you're a serious enthusiast.

With the exception of Destrehan Manor, with an elevator to the second floor, these plantation homes are rough going for those traveling in wheelchairs.

Destrehan Manor

The oldest plantation open to the public in the Lower Mississippi Valley, and the site of some of the largest live oaks in the country, Destrehan Manor was built in 1787 by a free person of color and restored using some of the earliest methods of construction. (In a nice touch, one room has been deliberately spared the renovation process, allowing a glimpse of the true ravages of age.) A cameo in the film *Interview with a Vampire,* along with its proximity to New Orleans, has made this a popular attraction. Guided tours start every 20 minutes.

See map p. 269. 13034 River Rd., Destrehan, LA 70047. ☎ *985-764-9315. Fax 985-725-1929.* www.destrehanplantation.org. *Located approximately 25 miles from New Orleans. Take I-10 West to Exit 220 (I-310 South), stay on I-310 for about 6 miles, exit onto River Road, and turn left at the light. Admission: $10 adults, $5 teenagers, $3 children 6–12; free for children under 6. Open: daily 9 a.m.–4 p.m.*

Houmas House Plantation & Gardens

The grand live oaks, magnolias, and formal gardens alone are worth the trip. The structure is actually two houses joined together; the original was built in 1790, and in 1840 a larger, Greek Revival–style house was built next to it (some time in the intervening years, a roof was built over both, joining them together). This bit of architectural jury-rigging adds to the intrigue.

Daytrip No. 2: Plantations along the Great River Road

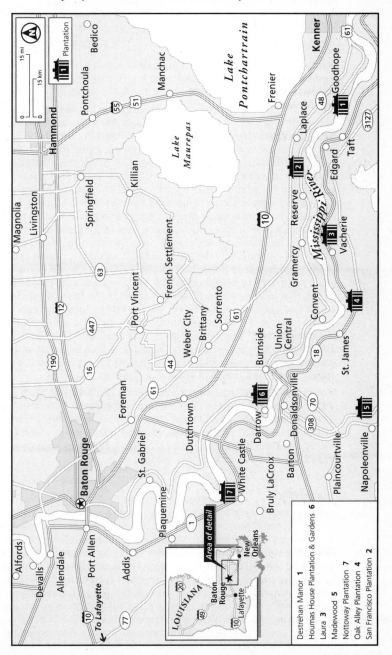

Destrehan Manor **1**
Houmas House Plantation & Gardens **6**
Laura **3**
Madewood **5**
Nottoway Plantation **7**
Oak Alley Plantation **4**
San Francisco Plantation **2**

See map p. 269. 40136 Highway 942 Burnside, LA 70725 (58 miles from New Orleans). ☎ **888-323-8314** or 225-473-7841. Fax: 225-474-0480. www.houmashouse.com. Take I-10 from New Orleans or Baton Rouge, exit onto Highway 44 to Burnside, turn right on Highway 942. Admission: $10 adults, $6 children 13–17, $3 children 6–12; free for children under 6. Open: daily Feb–Oct 10 a.m.–5 p.m. and Nov–Jan 10 a.m.–4 p.m. Closed holidays.

Laura: A Creole Plantation

This is the belle of the ball, the one plantation home you should definitely see and I nearly cried when I heard about the devastating fire in 2004 that nearly burned it to the ground. It says something about the strength and determination of the owners that Laura was open for tour the very next day. Now they are restoring the original layout of the plantation, which is being documented by the History Channel. You'll find a refreshing, educational atmosphere rather than the touristy patronization you might get from other homes. General manager Normal Marmillion and his outstanding staff share what daily life on a sugar plantation was like for both the masters and the slaves (a disappointingly rare insight on most plantation tours) in the 18th and 19th centuries. This cultural history of Louisiana Creoles is astoundingly detailed thanks to former occupant Laura Locoul's diary. The house is a brightly painted, classic Creole home — perhaps plain compared to neighboring Oak Alley — sheltering more than 375 original artifacts spanning a 200-year period in the lives of one family. Basic tours last about an hour. If you want a longer tour, you can schedule in advance a special 90-minute tour; topics include "Women on the Creole Plantation" and "Plantation Slaves, Artisans, and Folklore." The famous Br'er Rabbit stories were first collected here by a folklorist in the 1870s. Be sure to walk the grounds afterward to view the slave cabins, overseer cottages, barns, and the 1829 Maison de Reprise.

See map p. 269. 2247 Highway 18, Vacherie, LA 70090. ☎ **888-799-7690** or 225-265-7690. www.lauraplantation.com. Located about 60 miles from New Orleans. Take I-10 West about 28 miles from New Orleans to Exit 194 (Gramercy). Cross the bridge and turn left onto Highway 18 (River Road); travel about 4 more miles. Admission: $10 adults, $5 students and children 6–17; free for children under 6. Open: daily 9:30 a.m.–5 p.m. Closed major holidays.

Madewood

Another must-see stop on this route, Madewood is an imposing two-story Greek Revival mansion with a bit of history behind it (surprise, surprise!). The owner commissioned it solely for the purpose of outdoing his brother, who had a grand house of his own. The construction took eight years, including four just to cut the lumber and make the bricks. In a cruel twist of fate, the owner died of yellow fever just before the house's completion. Current owner Keith Marshall's parents bought and saved it from disrepair in 1964, and photos of the laborious restoration process are a revelation. Marshall and his wife, Millie Ball (travel editor for *The Times-Picayune*), are gracious hosts who tell delightful stories. You can stay overnight, either in the main house for $225, or in a more secluded raised cottage. (A bronze plaque notes that Brad Pitt slept here while filming *Interview with the Vampire*.)

See map p. 269. 4250 Highway 308, Napoleonville, LA 70390. ☎ *800-375-7151 or 985-369-7151. Fax: 985-369-9848.* www.madewood.com. *Located approximately 72 miles from New Orleans. Take I-10 West from New Orleans to Exit 182 (Donaldsonville). Cross the Sunshine Bridge onto Highway 70; follow it to Spur 70. Follow signs that say "Bayou Plantations," turn left onto Highway 308, and then travel south about 6 miles. Admission: $8 adults, $4 children and students. Open: daily 10 a.m.–4 p.m. Closed holidays.*

Nottoway Plantation

The last stop on this tour is a comparative stone's throw (about 25 miles) from Baton Rouge. The house has a formidable presence, with 22 enormous columns and its original slate roof. Sixty-four rooms cover more than 54,000 square feet, including a grand ballroom, beautiful archways, and original crystal chandeliers. It was saved from Civil War destruction by a Northern gunboat officer who had once been a guest here. You can have lunch or dinner in the restaurant, and stay overnight in one of the restored bedrooms for between $125 and $250 a night. The rate includes a full plantation breakfast, a wake-up tray of muffins, juice, and coffee, and a house tour.

See map p. 269. 30970 Mississippi River Rd. (P.O. Box 160), White Castle, LA 70788. ☎ *866-LASOUTH or 225-545-2730. Fax: 225-545-8632.* www.nottoway.com. *Located 69 miles from New Orleans. From New Orleans, follow I-10 West to the Highway 22 exit, and then turn left on Highway 70 across Sunshine Bridge; exit onto Highway 1 and drive 14 miles north through Donaldsonville. From Baton Rouge, take I-10 West to the Plaquemine exit and then Highway 1 south for 18 miles. Admission: $10 adults, $4 children 5 to 12; free for children under 5. Open: daily 9 a.m.–5 p.m. Last tour begins at 4:30 p.m. Closed Dec 25.*

Oak Alley Plantation

Originally named Bon Sejour, the most popular plantation home in Louisiana gets its current name from a quarter-mile alleyway of live oaks. Along with Laura and Madewood, this is the best bet for those wishing to abridge this trip into a "best of" tour, offering exactly what the word "plantation" conjures up. A nonprofit foundation runs the place, and authentically costumed guides lead tours. The mansion has been lovingly restored, though its furnishings range from antiques to modern. You can stay the night (it also serves as a bed-and-breakfast), with rates from $105 to $135. On-site is a restaurant open for breakfast and lunch.

See map p. 269. 3645 Highway 18, Vacherie, LA 70090. ☎ *800-44-ALLEY or 225-265-2151. Fax: 225-265-7035.* www.oakalleyplantation.com. *Located 60 miles from New Orleans. Take I-10 West to Exit 194 (Gramercy). Turn left on Highway 641 (South), and follow the highway, which turns into Highway 3213. Continue over the Veteran's Memorial Bridge. Turn left onto Highway 18 and drive 7½ miles to the plantation. Admission: $10 adults, $5 students, $3 children 6–12; free for children under 6. No credit cards accepted. Open: daily Mar–Oct 9 a.m.–5:30 p.m. and Nov–Feb 9 a.m.– 5 p.m. Closed in the a.m. on New Year's Day (call for details), Thanksgiving, Christmas.*

San Francisco Plantation

This fanciful home's broad galleries resemble a ship's double decks, and atop two sets of stairs is a broad main portal much like a steamboat's grand salon. English and French 18th-century furniture and paintings are featured as part of the restoration. The contrast between the plantation and its neighbor, a huge oil refinery practically in its backyard, is a bit jarring but oddly enough adds some poignant perspective on how much the times have changed.

See map p. 269. 2646 Highway 44 (P.O. 950), Garyville, LA 70051. ☎ 888-322-1756 or 985-535-2341. Fax: 985-535-5450. www.sanfranciscoplantation.org. *Located approximately 35 miles from New Orleans. Take I-10 West to U.S. 51 (23 miles). Turn south and continue for 3 miles to Highway 44 and then go west for 5 miles. Admission: $10 adults, $5 students 13–18, $3 children 6–12; free for children under 6. Open: daily 9:30 a.m.–5 p.m. Closed major holidays and Mardi Gras.*

Where to stay and dine

For accommodations at a plantation, see the preceding listings for Oak Alley Plantation, Madewood, and Nottoway Plantation.

For dining, see the preceding listings for Oak Alley Plantation (lunch) and Nottoway Plantation (lunch and dinner). Two noteworthy eateries near Houmas House are **The Cabin** (see map p. 269; 5405 Hwy. 44 at the intersection of Highway 22, in Burnside, approximately 3 miles from Houmas House; ☎ 225-473-3007; www.thecabinrestaurant.com) and **Hymel's** (see map p. 269; 8740 Hwy. 44 in Convent, approximately 8 miles south of Burnside; ☎ 225-562-7031). Near Laura and Oak Alley, I like the family operation **B & C Seafood Market & Cajun Deli** (see map p. 269; 2155 Hwy. 18 in Vacherie, about 1 mile from Laura; ☎ 225-265-8356).

Daytrip No. 3: New Orleans Nature Getaway

This trip takes you a world away from the other experiences in this book and gets you back to New Orleans in time for an evening out. Grab breakfast at one of your favorite local morning spots before driving across the Mississippi River on the Crescent City Connection to the West Bank. Spend the morning at **Barataria Preserve** followed by lunch at **Restaurant des Familles** in nearby Crown Point or an English tea at **Victoria Inn & Gardens** in Lafitte. Then spend the afternoon communing with alligators on a swamp tour before dining at **Voleo's.** This area fared well during hurricane Katrina, however, it was completely flooded by storm surge from hurricane Rita a few weeks later. At a recent visit, I was so relieved to see that everything was dry and coming back. The locals are nothing if not determined to preserve their unique way of life and share it with you.

Getting back to nature

In New Orleans, get on Interstate 10 East heading toward the Mississippi River and the West Bank. (Yes, it's the West Bank, though it's directly *east* of New Orleans. Go figure.) Cross the Crescent City Connection; after you're over it becomes the West Bank Expressway, an elevated thoroughfare that connects a good deal of the West Bank. Go to Exit 4B, Barataria Boulevard, and get off, turning left at the second stoplight onto Barataria Boulevard. Then drive about 9 miles to Barataria Preserve.

Taking a swamp tour

Lil' Cajun Swamp and Shrimping Tours (see map p. 274; Hwy. 301, just outside Jean Lafitte National Park, next to Frank's Boat Launch; ☎ 800-725-3213 or 504-689-3213; www.lilcajunswamptours.com) are led by Captain Cyrus Blanchard, one character of a tour guide who isn't afraid to give his opinion on anything. (Be sure to ask about his pet alligator, Julie.) His tour includes Bayou Barataria and is roughly two hours long. Admission is $17 adults, $15 seniors, $13 children 4 to 12, and free for children under 4. Tour times are 10 a.m. and 2 p.m. The boat is wheelchair accessible, but the bathrooms aren't.

Seeing the sights

The **Barataria Preserve** is a branch of the **Jean Lafitte National Historical Park and Preserve,** which encompasses several locations around the state. The preserve sprawls over approximately 20,000 acres of hardwood forest, cypress swampland, and freshwater marshlands, with 8 miles of hiking trails (including 2½ miles of boardwalk) and waterways, preserving a representative sample of the environment of the delta, including bayous, swamps, marshes, and natural levee forests.

The wildlife preserve was once home to prehistoric human settlements (archaeologists have unearthed village sites along the bayous dating back some 2,000 years). The trails and waterways make it a natural spot for hiking and exploration, and for getting some perspective on the peoples who settled this area, which was a delta formed by the Mississippi River some 2,500 years ago. You can easily lose yourself here, either taking a "natural history walk," striking out on your own along the pathways, or exploring the 9 miles of canoe trails (closed to motorized boats and accessible by three canoe launch docks; see canoe rental information later in this section), as well as 20 miles of waterways accessible to all types of craft. Picnic tables are scattered throughout, and fishing (with a valid Louisiana fishing license) and hunting and trapping (by permit only) are allowed; the marshes are dotted with recreational hunting and fishing camps. Hunting permits and fishing licenses can be purchased online at www.wlf.state.la.us or at a nearby marina — the closest is 2 miles away at Cochiara's Marina, 4477 Jean Lafitte Blvd. in Lafitte, ☎ 504-689-3701. *Note:* Bring mosquito repellent!

Head to the **Visitor Center** (see map p. 274; 6488 Barataria Blvd. in Marrero; ☎ 504-589-2330; www.nps.gov/jela/Barataria Preserve. htm) for maps, exhibits, and films. Trails in the preserve are open daily

Daytrip No. 3: New Orleans Nature Getaway

To Airport

Huey P. Long Bridge

48

90

541

BRIDGE CITY

St. Charles Ave.

Napoleon Ave.

90

Louisiana Ave.

B.R. 90

ALGIERS

Franklin St.

Audubon Park & Zoo

Mississippi River

Crescent City Connection Bridge

90

18

WESTWEGO

Westbank Expressway

18

MARRERO

18

HARVEY

4th St.

GRETNA

To Houma & Luling

Lapaico Blvd.

B.R. 90

45

Barataria Blvd.

Peters Rd.

Lapaico Blvd.

23

BAYOU SEGNETTE STATE PARK

Bayou Segnette

3134

45

Bayou des

Intracoastal Waterway

Lake Cataouatche

Bayou Bardeaux

Bayou Couba

Couba Island

Lake Salvador

❶

JEAN LAFITTE NATIONAL HISTORICAL PARK

Familles

❷

❹

❸ ❺

303

Bayou Barn **4**

Captain Phil Robichaux **9**

Jean Lafitte Information Center **6**

Jean Lafitte Inn **3**

Jean Lafitte National Historical Park **1**

Jean Lafitte National Historical Park Visitor Center **2**

Lil' Cajun Swamp and Shrimping Tours **7**

Restaurant des Familles **5**

Victoria Inn & Gardens **8**

Voleo's **10**

301

45

❻

Intracoastal Waterway Hi-Rise Bridge

❼

Bayou Villars

Kerner Bridge

■ Town of Jean Lafitte

Intracoastal Waterway

Bayou Barataria

Goose Bayou Bridge

Bayou Villars

Bayou Perot

3257

Town of Lafitte

■

❽

❿ ❾

Bayou Rigolettes

Canoeing

Fishing

Hiking

Shrimping

from 7 a.m. to 7 p.m. (during daylight savings hours) and 7 a.m. to 5 p.m. (standard time), and the visitor center is open daily from 9 a.m. to 5 p.m. (closed on Christmas Day). No admission fee is required, though donations are welcome. The visitor center, restrooms, and the Bayou Coquille Trail are all wheelchair accessible.

Canoe rentals are available at **Bayou Barn** (see map p. 274; 7145 Barataria Blvd. in Crown Point; ☎ 504-689-2663), next door to Restaurant des Familles (mentioned in the following paragraph) and **Jean Lafitte Inn** (see map p. 274; ☎ 504-689-3271), located next to the park just off Barataria Boulevard (before you get to the Lafitte/LaRose Highway, which you cross on your way to Restaurant des Familles). The last time I canoed the bayou, I accidentally bopped an alligator on its head with my paddle (they sleep just below the surface). The adventure continued when a heavy thunderstorm (complete with lightning bolts) hit just after the halfway point. Scary stuff, but it was still a refreshing change of pace from the city. Rentals must be returned by dark at either location.

Where to dine

For lunch, select from seafood, Cajun, or Creole dishes (I can't resist the spicy shrimp balls) while overlooking a picturesque bayou at **Restaurant des Familles** (see map p. 274; 7163 Barataria Blvd. in Crown Point; ☎ 504-689-7834). The restaurant is open Tuesday through Saturday for lunch and dinner (as well as Sun for brunch).

Alternatively, treat yourself to a feast for all the senses with an afternoon tea and garden tour at **Victoria Inn & Gardens** (see map p. 274; 4707 Jean Lafitte Blvd. in Lafitte; ☎ 800-689-4797 or 504-689-4757; www. victoriainn.com). The inn flooded badly from Rita's storm surge, ruining the garden-level rooms which are now being restored. All of the lovely gardens had to be replanted, so it's a little sparse. But thanks to the sub-tropical climate, it will become lush again in no time. The unique pool in the center of a "reverse-P" pier over the lake is fine, however, the pier was twisted by the storm, giving it a funhouse mirror look. You can still walk on it and take a dip in the pool. The teas — specially blended for the inn — are served in delicate, antique china cups with a mouth-watering assortment of tea breads, scones, finger sandwiches, and sweets. I recommend you sit on the gallery overlooking the Shakespeare Herb Garden, which is filling in nicely and is also where my husband and I got married eight years ago. Tea is served daily from 2 p.m. to 3:30 p.m. Reservations are required; $18 per person (garden tours are free). Dinner is available Wednesday through Sunday from 6–9:30 p.m. at **The Restaurant at Victoria Inn,** featuring Creole cuisine by candlelight. For me, it's always a toss-up between the pan-seared redfish and filet mignon topped with crawfish. Be sure to save room for dessert!

You may like what you see during the tour — that lakeside pool is as refreshing as it looks — and decide to stay. Hosts Roy and Dale Ross see to your every need, whether its reserving a saltwater fishing excursion with **Captain Phil Robichaux** (☎ 504-689-2006) or giving you frank recommendations on local attractions. Single rooms cost $98, doubles and queens $115, luxury suites with Jacuzzi from $145. Well-behaved dogs are welcome; call ahead for details.

For dinner, go to **Voleo's** (see map p. 274; 5134 Nunez St. in Lafitte; ☎ 504-689-2482), where former Paul Prudhomme apprentice David Volion presides over award-winning Cajun, Creole, and German dishes at cheap bayou prices. It took on three feet of water during Rita and reopened in October. This is one of my favorite places to eat in all of Greater New Orleans. Try the sinfully rich seafood gumbo or signature flounder Lafitte and you'll taste why.

Part V
Living It Up After Dark: New Orleans Nightlife

The 5th Wave   By Rich Tennant

JAZZ GROUPS TO AVOID   RICHTENNANT

The Modern Saw Quartet

Jazz fusion group: Return to Whatever

The Balloon Jazz Orchestra

In this part . . .

New Orleans after dark is nothing like New Orleans during the day. The experience is completely different — with its own landmarks, history, and etiquette. Chapter 16 delves into the local theater and performing arts scenes, while Chapter 17 focuses on the city's best clubs and bars, whether you want the quickie tourist experience or something more authentic. Chapter 17 also ferrets out the best spots for real-deal Cajun and zydeco music.

Chapter 16

Applauding the Cultural Scene

● ●

In This Chapter

▶ Assessing post-Katrina damage to the cultural life

▶ Finding out what's playing and where to get tickets

▶ Getting the lowdown on the New Orleans theater scene

▶ Making the New Orleans opera, ballet, and orchestra scenes

● ●

*T*he performing arts likely aren't the first thing you think of when coming to New Orleans. After all, in terms of size, scale, and importance, the scene here is a far cry from, say, New York City's. No one comes to New Orleans on vacation with the express purpose of seeing the ballet or some edgy, off-Broadway fare. What New Orleans *is* known for is its food, music, and rich history (in no particular order). But you can make a strong argument in favor of its performing arts taking a respectable fourth place.

Assessing Katrina's Effect on the City's Cultural Life

Historically, New Orleans has enjoyed status as a small but thriving center for the performing arts; at one time, it boasted what was the continent's first opera house. The city hasn't seen the likes of that heady heyday in decades, but the theater and performing arts thrive in a city as creative and multicultural as this one. Needless to say, with fewer visitors and locals strapped for cash, the city's theaters and other performing arts venues and organizations — and the actors and musicians who play there — are not doing as well as they should. So please, take in a show and help them get back in the spotlight.

Finding Out What's Playing and Getting Tickets

The *Times-Picayune* (in its weekly **Lagniappe** entertainment section) and *Gambit Weekly* are good places to look for listings, reviews, and previews of major arts events. If you're looking for information before you arrive, try their Web sites: www.nola.com and www.bestofneworleans.com, respectively. Another good source is the local CitySearch site (http://neworleans.citysearch.com).

New Orleans doesn't have a local ticket broker such as New York's TKTS. Tickets to most local productions are easily available through the venue's box office, and most of the larger spaces (such as the Saenger, the Orpheum, and the Contemporary Arts Center) take credit cards; they also usually offer tickets via **Ticketmaster** (☎ 504-522-5555). Smaller theaters accept cash only (though Southern Rep and NORD accept local checks) at the door the night of the show. For a popular event, such as an opera production or a Broadway touring company, reserve in advance, or ask your hotel concierge (assuming your hotel has one) to find out about acquiring tickets for you.

Raising the Curtain on the Performing Arts

Do you have a free evening and want to take in a show, catch the symphony, or enjoy an opera? If so, the following section can give you all the details.

Theater

New Orleans actually boasts a good theater scene, a tight community that makes up in passion, creativity, and quality what it lacks in size. Though no heir apparent to Tennessee Williams is waiting in the wings to usher the city into a glorious new age, theater in New Orleans is much more than touring companies of national productions and amateur dinner theater (though you find plenty of both). New Orleans boasts a handful of inventive local companies staging intriguing original works or creative reinterpretations of classics (and usually drawing pretty good crowds). Of course, tried-and-true standby fare such as *The Fantasticks* is always being produced somewhere, by someone, at any time.

So what's hot right now? As you would expect, national tours of big-name productions are always popular. Whenever you come, the Saenger Theatre on Canal Street will most likely offer that season's hot ticket, whether it be *Proof* or *The Producers*. Local classics, such as anything written by Williams, are a good bet.

Without further ado, the following lists the more prominent theater spaces in the city:

✔ One of the city's major hubs for the arts, **Contemporary Arts Center** (900 Camp St. in the Warehouse District; ☎ **504-528-3800;** www. cacno.org) reopened in January 2006 and features exhibits of contemporary art (of course). It also hosts some small productions in its intimate performance spaces, most recently related to Katrina. You find experimental works by local playwrights as well as the occasional comedy and musical (concerts, dance productions, and film screenings also take place here). The rooms are small enough that no seat is really bad. Food and drink are also on the premises via the Cyber Bar & Cafe. The CAC itself has no dress code, though the promoters/producers of specific shows or events may impose one.

✔ **le chat noir** (715 St. Charles Ave. in the Central Business District; ☎ **504-581-5812;** www.cabaretlechatnoir.com) is one of the hippest, hottest spots in the city. The intimate (135-seat) space lends itself to give-and-take exchanges between audience and performers. Typical fare may include a one-woman (or -man) show of the life and songs of French chanteuse Edith Piaf, a performance art piece with audience participation, or a set by a singer or local jazz band. Stick around after the show; the piano bar on Saturday nights has been compared favorably to the edgy, unpredictable vibe of Parisian cabaret. Attire is semiformal. Come a little early to socialize and sip a Black Cat at Bar Noir, open Tuesday through Saturday from 7 p.m., (about one hour before showtime).

✔ The show must go on! **Le Petit Theatre du Vieux Carre** (616 St. Peter St. in the French Quarter; ☎ **504-522-2081**) fared well during Katrina and is home to one of the oldest nonprofessional theater troupes in the United States and will proudly present its 90th season in 2006-2007. The main performance stage, open from September to June, generally presents well-chosen plays and musicals. A smaller performance space sports edgier, experimental fare from local writers. Supposedly, a ghost named Caroline haunts the attic; she is believed to be an actress who, in 1927 while cavorting with the director, fell off the third-story balcony overlooking the flagstone courtyard and died. Theatre employees claim that if they can't find something, they simply ask Caroline and 15 minutes later, the item mysteriously appears.

✔ **NORD Theater** (705 Lafayette St. in Gallier Hall, one block from Poydras Street in the Central Business District; ☎ **504-565-7860**), a long-running arm of the New Orleans Recreation Department, is primarily a vehicle for local children, though the productions and target audience aren't limited to children. It did fine during Katrina, staying high and dry. The summer production is usually kid-oriented, while the fall one is a better bet for adults. The theater stages four productions a year, mostly musicals — Broadway, off-Broadway, or original. This comfortable, intimate theater (seating capacity is 120) has plenty of legroom, and no dress code.

✔ The venerable **Saenger Theatre** (143 N. Rampart St; ☎ **504-525-1052;** www.saengertheatre.com) opened in 1927, and is listed on the National Register of Historic Places. Due to significant damage from Katrina — including loss of the historic organ console to flood and major roof damage — the theater postponed its 2006-2007 season. Upon its return, join locals in the audience for touring theater productions (some are Best Musical Tony Award winners) and popular performances by everyone from David Bowie to Neil Young and comedians like *The Daily Show*'s Lewis Black.

✔ **Southern Rep Theatre** (The Shops at Canal Place; ☎ 504-522-6545; www.southernrep.com) stayed high and dry during Katrina. The popular theater focuses on Southern playwrights and actors, and benefits from a convenient location on the lip of the Quarter at Canal Street; plenty of validated parking is in the shopping center's spacious, multilevel garage. The pace slows down in summer, but it does have children's programs. Performance space is intimate, but comfortable, as befits its high-rise digs; the atmosphere (and dress code) is casual.

✔ **Zeitgeist Multi-Disciplinary Arts Center** (1724 Oretha Castle Haley Blvd.; ☎ 504-525-2767; www.zeitgeistinc.net), which complements the Contemporary Arts Center, celebrates its 20th anniversary in November 2006. The bill of fare is left of center all the way, from performance art to edgy original plays and independent films — everything from Andy Warhol to Leni Riefenstahl to original works on growing up gay in New Orleans.

In keeping with its casual vibe, New Orleans is pretty lax about dress codes. Exceptions exist, of course, but generally you can get by with a basic business-casual look. At le chat noir, which aspires to a hip atmosphere where dressing up is half the fun, a semiformal approach is required. But after that, it's fair game.

Symphony

Most people, including the locals, often overlook the **Louisiana Philharmonic Orchestra** (☎ 504-523-6530; www.lpomusic.com) in favor of the city's hopping bar and club scene. It's a shame because the LPO is a delightful way to spend an evening. Music lovers around the world offered donations and support to help this vital cultural organization stay intact and new music director Carlos Miguel Prieto infuses the symphony with new blood. The season runs from September through May.

Opera

The **New Orleans Opera Association** (☎ 800-881-4459 or 504-529-2278; www.neworleansopera.org) has been around since 1943, providing local opera buffs with a steady diet of classic performances each season. The company is talented and professional; this isn't the local amateur hour. Often, the association features a star performer from, say, the Metropolitan Opera Company, with local talents in supporting roles. The fare runs from familiar classics to new, edgy works.

Dining before (and after) the show

You'll have no trouble making an evening of dining and theater in New Orleans. If you're lucky, you can find a restaurant that matches the mood and feel of the play, musical, or piece you're going to see. A playbill for a touring show at the Saenger Theatre, for example, will likely include ads placed by the **Palace Café** (see Chapter 11) and **Dominique's** (in the **Maison Dupuy** hotel, 1001 Toulouse St.; ☎ 504-522-8800). If you want to mingle, head to the **Sazerac** bar in the Fairmont Hotel (see Chapter 17) to see and be seen by some of the city's elite. These establishments are a fine start (or finish) to an evening at the elegant Saenger.

On your way to or from Southern Rep, a host of French Quarter choices are nearby, although I prefer the bistro elegance of **Mr. B's Bistro** (see Chapter 11), which should be open by the end of 2006. If you're looking for something more casual, try an over-stuffed oyster po' boy at **Acme Oyster House** (see Chapter 11). For a performance at Le Petit, the nearby **The Bistro at Maison de Ville** is a favorite of theater patrons and performers; the elegant **Court of Two Sisters** is also a good spot (see Chapter 11 for both). To satisfy your post-theater munchies, head down St. Peter to Dumaine and plop yourself down at the **Clover Grill**, the "happiest grill on earth" (see Chapter 11).

In the Central Business District, the family-friendly **Bon Ton Café** (401 Magazine St.; ☎ 504-524-3386) is the perfect complement to an evening at NORD Theater. Nothing nearby mirrors the unique Parisian cabaret experience at le chat noir, though **Mother's** provides some amusing contrast (see Chapter 11). Closer in spirit, the **Veranda** (inside the **Hotel Inter-Continental,** 444 St. Charles Ave.; ☎ 504-585-4383) — whose extraordinary glass-enclosed courtyard was destroyed by Katrina but is now completely restored — and **Palace Café** (see Chapter 11) are a straight shot down St. Charles Avenue.

Dance

The **Delta Festival Ballet** is comprised primarily of area talent that performs a seasonal schedule, including a popular annual production of *The Nutcracker* at Christmastime. Call ☎ 504-836-7166 for performance calendar, ticket prices, and other information. The **New Orleans Ballet Association,** despite its name, isn't a local company. Instead, it presents a schedule of touring shows. The season generally runs from September to June. Tickets are available through Ticketmaster (☎ 504-522-5555) or through the Association box office (☎ 504-522-0996).

Chapter 17

Hitting the Clubs and Bars

• •

In This Chapter

▶ Assessing post-Katrina nightlife

▶ Checking out French Quarter nightlife

▶ Finding the best bars and clubs elsewhere in the city

▶ Discovering a spot to suit your style, from hip hangouts to piano bars

• •

*T*hings have always been more laidback here, especially after dark, when the city marches to the beat of a decidedly different drummer than during the weekday 9-to-5 grind. And I don't just mean the slinky, greasy rhythms of funk and R&B or the stately clip of vintage jazz. I'm talking about mood. The city grows livelier; for proof, you need walk no farther than the nearest bar.

What makes for a cool bar? Smart alecks might say any bar that didn't flood. But really, it depends on who you ask. Some people want a nice, dark watering hole, while others want a high-energy dance workout and the chance to discreetly bump into an anonymous member of their preferred sex. This chapter explores all the nooks and crannies of New Orleans's bar scene. It stops in at some rowdy saloons, upscale bars, dance clubs, and your regular hole-in-the-wall dives.

 Keep in mind that the selections throughout this chapter aren't all-inclusive. Because New Orleans boasts more bars and music clubs per capita than almost any other city in the United States, you'll doubtless find a host of other happening places on your own. For comprehensive club and bar listings, go online prior to your arrival or pick up a free copy of *Gambit Weekly* (see Chapter 4 or go to www.bestofneworleans.com) or *Offbeat* magazine (see Appendix or go to www.offbeat.com) at your hotel or nearby coffeehouse or retail store. Every Friday, the *Times-Picayune* publishes *Lagniappe*, it's pull-out entertainment section (see Chapter 4).

 If you're here for **Mardi Gras** (see Chapters 7 and 12 for more information), you may notice that after the last float rolls by, the party simply relocates to another spot, such as a bar. Club owners usually book exciting, party-friendly acts, even on Sunday and Monday nights when many spots would otherwise be dark. If you base your dream image of New

Orleans on the constant street-party scenes you've seen in the movies, Mardi Gras is your time.

Assessing Katrina's Effect on the City's Nightlife

Sadly, many musicians lived in Treme and the Lower Ninth Ward, which were badly flooded by storm surge and broken levees. In addition to losing their homes, they also lost their livelihood. One of my neighbors in Lakeview is Benny Grunch, who leads the city's most popular "Yat" band, Benny Grunch & the Bunch (www.bennygrunch.com). (He came to a party at my house celebrating my first *New Orleans For Dummies* book, and people talked about it for weeks afterwards — a real live celebrity showed up at Julia's house!) Benny has famously stayed in the city, but he lost his guitars, keyboard, master tapes, and CD inventory in the storm and has had to rebound. Many other bands had to decide whether to stay in the city, as many bars and clubs were closed for a few weeks after the storm at best (and some are still shuttered). Bands that lost members are now collaborating, and musicians often play with several groups.

A few examples: Named after one of the liveliest clubs in the early days of jazz (and for a tune made famous by legendary cornet player Buddy Bolden), the **Funky Butt** (714 N. Rampart St.) closed for good, much to everyone's dismay. **O'Flaherty's Irish Channel Pub** (514 Toulouse St.; ☎ 504-529-1317) was a popular pub, but severe damage to the structure forced the owner to close for good and flee to Texas. The **Saturn Bar** (3067 St. Claude Ave. in Bywater; ☎ 504-949-7532) offered renegade ambience and cheap drinks, with veteran barflies and slumming celebrities drinking side by side. It was severely damaged by Katrina and then owner O'Neil Broyard passed away, but his family say they are determined to come back.

Despite the generous financial support of music lovers around the world, there is still concern that many musicians — including some whose musical families have been around for generations — won't come back. Without its native musical sons and daughters, New Orleans would not be New Orleans. So please, support our unique, homegrown music by going to live shows, buying CDs and telling your friends about this city's unique soundtrack.

Playing by the Rules

Some people may be disappointed to discover that the legal drinking age in Louisiana is 21 — for years, it was 18. If you're of drinking age, however, you'll be delighted to know that you can legally walk along any public street with a drink in your hand (though the drink must be in a plastic cup, called a *go-* or *geaux-cup*). Drinking alcohol in a vehicle is illegal, even if you're just a passenger. So if you feel the need to imbibe while getting somewhere, stick to the sidewalks.

Unless otherwise noted, most places listed in this chapter don't usually charge a cover (though all bets are off during Mardi Gras or Jazz Fest). For locations of nightlife spots inside and outside the French Quarter, refer to the maps later in this chapter.

Entering the Neon Party Zone: French Quarter Nightlife

Tourist nightlife centers around the French Quarter, as you may have guessed. Keep in mind, however, that the key word here is "tourist." Tons of clubs are concentrated here, many solely to cater to the constant influx of visitors (with *some* notable exceptions to this rule). Some are cheap, some are tacky; many are both. Of course, you can find some genuinely good haunts here as well. Where the French Quarter is concerned, the epicenter of nightlife is Bourbon Street.

Drinking in Bourbon Street

Having just cautioned you against relying too much on the Quarter bar scene, I don't want to discourage you from stepping onto world-famous Bourbon Street altogether. (My husband still shakes his head at my insistence that his visiting parents walk at least one block of Bourbon, but I felt it was important that when they returned to their Midwest hometown, they could tell everyone that they had in fact experienced it. That's one of the first questions your family, friends, and coworkers will ask: Did you go to Bourbon Street? Imagine their reaction if you said no! They may make you go back.) But if you stroll down Bourbon and assume that you've experienced all that New Orleans nightlife has to offer, well, you know what they say about people who assume . . . .

Sure, Bourbon Street is a tourist attraction, first and foremost. Like Beale Street in Memphis, it became an attraction because of something genuine and authentic, but almost all vestiges of that elusive something have been replaced by glitter, glitz, and spectacle. Still, seedy as it can be, Bourbon Street can also be a fun barrage of sights, sounds, and smells. And the fact that it remains intact after Katrina is enough reason to take a walk down this storied street. With every kind of music, from jazz, blues, and rock-and-roll to rhythm and blues, country, Celtic, and Cajun, it's not the quality so much as the sheer variety that's important here.

Many Bourbon Street establishments are open 24 hours. Others open late in the afternoon, when the area starts to come to life. After 8 p.m. the street is blocked off to traffic, and the streets and sidewalks are filled with people.

You may notice that St. Ann Street, about eight blocks off Canal, marks a division on Bourbon Street — it's the unofficial boundary between the straight and gay sections of the area. Although not every bar or person east of St. Ann is gay, and not every bar or person west is straight, you'll likely notice a marked difference in the feel of the areas.

Be careful when exploring: The farther you get away from the river or the farther you go down Bourbon Street (away from Canal), the fewer people will be around and the less safe the area becomes. If you must explore more-deserted sections, keep alert. Ladies, don't carry a purse if you can help it.

Hitting the quarter notes: Some prime French Quarter spots

Locals widely consider the French Quarter to be one large tourist trap. You need a scorecard to distinguish the authentic, character-filled spots, which *do* exist, from the tourist magnets. Following is my subjective list, all of which went through difficult stages of fewer bands and staff due to fewer patrons but are now getting back to normal numbers:

- ✔ Check out the **Funky Pirate** (727 Bourbon St.; ☎ 504-523-1960) for a true Bourbon Street blues experience. One of the area's biggest (literally and figuratively) blues musicians, Big Al Carson, deals out Chicago-style electric blues most nights. His schedule varies; call to find out when he's playing. No cover, but expect a one-drink minimum.

- ✔ **The Hideout** (1207 Decatur St.; ☎ 504-529-7119) can best be described as a safe, friendly approximation of a hole-in-the-wall experience. The place used to house a pretty intimidating gay/biker bar, but these days most everyone, from punks to tourists, is welcome.

- ✔ **Johnny White's Sports Bar** (720 Bourbon St.; ☎ 504-524-4909). Like the sign says, this place never closes, even during the insanity of Katrina, which is now a special (and rare) badge of pride for any establishment. It might have been a regular ol' bar before the hurricane, but now it's practically an historic landmark.

- ✔ **Molly's at the Market** (1107 Decatur St.; ☎ 504-525-5169) draws a strange cross-section of locals. Something of a hangout for local media types (especially on Thursday nights), the pub-crawling legions make this a frequent stop as well. That includes Goth types as well as bohemians in tie-dyes who look like they haven't washed in weeks, and even just regular Joes out for a drink.

- ✔ **Ol'Toone's Saloon** (233 Decatur St.; ☎ 504-529-3422) is a somewhat nondescript bar next to House of Blues on Decatur. A good place to unwind after catching a show next door, it has a pretty good vibe when it fills up. It attracts its fair share of characters and is open 24 hours.

French Quarter Nightlife

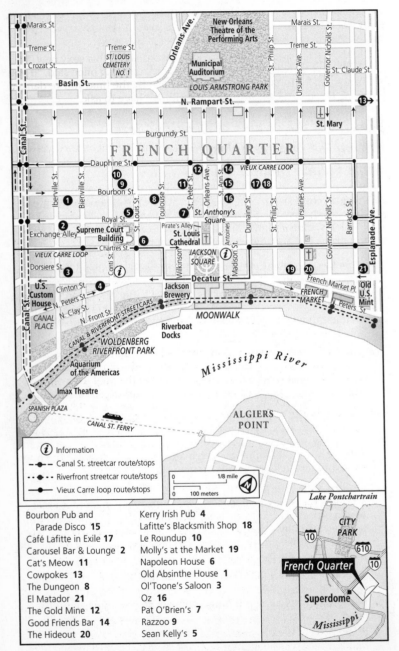

Bourbon Pub and Parade Disco **15**
Café Lafitte in Exile **17**
Carousel Bar & Lounge **2**
Cat's Meow **11**
Cowpokes **13**
The Dungeon **8**
El Matador **21**
The Gold Mine **12**
Good Friends Bar **14**
The Hideout **20**

Kerry Irish Pub **4**
Lafitte's Blacksmith Shop **18**
Le Roundup **10**
Molly's at the Market **19**
Napoleon House **6**
Old Absinthe House **1**
Ol'Toone's Saloon **3**
Oz **16**
Pat O'Brien's **7**
Razzoo **9**
Sean Kelly's **5**

Getting All Jazzed Up

New Orleans is the birthplace of jazz. Some say the genre was born in the brothels of old Storyville (New Orleans's long-gone, but still-legendary, red-light district), where the city's innovative young musicians entertained the clients, who in turn spread the word about this sexy new music. "Just what is jazz?" you ask. As Louis Armstrong once said, "If you got to ask what it is, you'll never get to know." By the time you've danced your way through these clubs, you'll no longer have to ask.

Preserving the strains of Dixieland jazz

Interested in hearing some old-school jazz? Head to one of these venues for a memorable evening of traditional New Orleans jazz and support America's original contribution to world music.

✔ For jazz with a little different slant, try **Fritzel's European Jazz Club** (733 Bourbon St.; ☎ 504-561-0432; www.fritzels.tripod. com). Fritzel's is known for late-night (or early-morning) jam sessions. Musicians who have finished playing their sets at other jazz clubs often come here to take turns running through old-time traditional jazz. An oasis among the sanitized jazz spots in the French Quarter, this place boasts an agreeable German beer-house decor, with a one-drink minimum per set instead of a cover charge. Come here way after midnight, order a German beer, and watch some talented musicians compare notes. Children aren't allowed. Music starts at 9:30 p.m. and runs late.

✔ The sign outside **Maison Bourbon** (641 Bourbon St.; ☎ 504-522-8818) proclaims that the place is "Dedicated to the Preservation of Jazz," which means that Dixieland jazz is the only item on the musical menu. Despite being located on Bourbon Street, this isn't a tourist trap. No children are allowed, so if you're with kids and want them to get a taste of some Dixieland, simply stand outside the bar — you can hear and see everything just fine. Records and CDs are available for purchase. Show times vary; it's open from 2:30 p.m. to 12:15 a.m. Monday through Thursday, and from 3:30 p.m. to 1:15 a.m. Friday through Sunday. Though you won't face a cover charge, a one-drink minimum is enforced.

✔ The **Palm Court Jazz Café** (1204 Decatur St.; ☎ 504-525-0200; www.palmcourtjazz.com), like Preservation Hall, offers old-style jazz played by old-style musicians — but the Palm Court also has air conditioning, food (which can be a little pricey), and drinks. You may want to make reservations. Music is played from 8 to 11 p.m., Wednesday through Sunday. Cover $5 per person at tables; no cover at bar.

✔ **Preservation Hall** (726 St. Peter St.; ☎ 800-785-5772 or 504-522-2841; www.preservationhall.com) is run by a nonprofit group dedicated to the preservation of jazz — and they continue to offer music after preserving their building as well. They reopened in

April 2006 after extensive renovations. Shows start Thursday through Saturday at 8:30 p.m. (doors at 8 p.m.), and usually end around midnight, with 35-minute sets followed by 10-minute breaks. The band makes requests if you make a decent offering, but try not to be the fifth person in a row to request "When the Saints Go Marching In." Keep in mind you'll find minimal seating, no air conditioning, and no food or drinks. Still, you'll almost certainly enjoy yourself, and the kids should love it, too. A selection of tapes and CDs is for sale if you find you can't get enough of the music. Sunday afternoon shows start at 3:30 p.m. (doors at 3 p.m.). Cover $8.

In praise of contemporary jazz

If you have a taste for modern interpretations of jazz, try one of these suggestions:

✔ Jazz Fest–quality music and food from the Brennan family (thanks to the Red Fish Grill right next door) are the twin draws of the **Jazz Parlor** (125 Bourbon St.; ☎ **504-410-1000**), formerly the ambitious Storyville District. Jazz is the order of the day, obviously, and despite the Parlor's prime Bourbon Street real estate, it's the real deal, not watered-down tourist bait. Show times are generally 5, 7:30, and 11 p.m., with a one-drink minimum per person per set.

✔ In comparison with Preservation Hall and the Palm Court, **Snug Harbor** (626 Frenchmen St.; ☎ 504-949-0696; www.snugjazz.com) is more in line with the times. Located in Faubourg Marigny, just outside the French Quarter, this is one of the prime spots for modern jazz in the city. The place enjoys a very good reputation among local musicians and fans. A show at this small, often-crowded spot is shorthand for class. Drinks, sandwiches, and a full dinner service are available. The cover charge varies according to the performer but is usually between $8 and $20. Shows begin nightly at 9 and 11 p.m.

✔ **The Spotted Cat Cocktail Lounge** (623 Frenchmen St.; ☎ 504-943-3887) has been around for a couple years, but it didn't become the slinky hipster place it is now until live music became a regular fixture. Now the sweaty vibe encourages you to quench your thirst with the signature drink, a rum punch chocolate martini. No cover.

✔ **Sweet Lorraine's** (1931 St. Claude Ave., ☎ **504-945-9654**, www.sweetlorrainesjazzclub.com) aims to be a throwback to the days when jazz clubs lined the streets. This establishment offers a program of modern and traditional jazz. It's not in the safest neighborhood, and parking is a bit chancy, so take a cab. The cover varies from $5 to $15. Show times vary but generally start at 10 p.m. and midnight.

Toe-tapping to the top brass

Try the following venues for some live brass-band music and a basic dive-bar atmosphere:

French Quarter Music

Bombay Club **3**
Chris Owens Club **8**
Donna's Bar & Grill **14**
Fritzel's European Jazz Club **12**
Funky Pirate **11**
House of Blues **4**
Jazz Parlor **2**
Jimmy Buffett's Margaritaville Café **15**
Kerry Irish Pub **5**
Maison Bourbon **9**
Palm Court Jazz Café **16**
Preservation Hall **10**

ⓘ Information
–●– Canal St. streetcar route/stops
⋯●⋯ Riverfront streetcar route/stops
—●— Vieux Carre loop route/stops

CLOSED, MAY REOPEN ○
Saenger Theatre **1**

CLOSED PERMANENTLY ●
Funky Butt **13**
O'Flaherty's Irish Channel Pub **7**
Shim-Sham Club and Juke Joint Lounge **6**

✓ **Donna's Bar & Grill** (800 N. Rampart St.; ☎ 504-596-6914) is known as "Brass Band World Headquarters," the only place in town where you can reliably expect to hear brass-band music (picture a cross between marching-band music and jazz) on a regular basis. Only three blocks from Bourbon Street at North Rampart and St. Ann, Donna's has a funky hole-in-the-wall vibe that's relaxed and unpretentious. The crowds often follow bands onto the street for a second-line parade. Because the neighborhood can be dicey, take a cab if you're concerned about safety. Show times are 10 p.m. Thursday through Monday (closed Tues and Wed). The average cover is $5.

Imbibing History

These special spots offer a little bit of history with your liquor; rumor has it that Andrew Jackson patronized one of them. (See Chapter 12 for more on the history of each of these joints.)

✓ Dating from 1772, **Lafitte's Blacksmith Shop** (941 Bourbon St.; ☎ 504-522-9377) is the oldest building in the Quarter and was reportedly the headquarters of the notorious pirate Jean Lafitte. Please try to overlook the poor plastering job on the exterior, which was a very misguided attempt at preservation. Agreeably dark (barely candlelit at night), all types of characters frequent the popular hangout.

✓ Another dark and historic place that seems full of schemes — or maybe it's just the low-key lighting — is the **Napoleon House** (500 Chartres St.; ☎ 504-524-9752). If you're the imperial type, have a drink and muse over what the place would've been like if Napoleon had moved in here, as certain New Orleanians allegedly hoped he would. *Note:* Bar closes at 6 p.m. but hopefully normal evening hours will soon return.

✓ The **Old Absinthe House** (240 Bourbon St.; ☎ 504-523-3181; www.oldabsinthehouse.com) is supposed to be the place where Andrew Jackson and the Lafitte brothers plotted their defense of the city in the Battle of New Orleans. William Makepeace Thackeray, Walt Whitman, and Oscar Wilde are also said to have knocked back a few inside these walls. This place is also said to have been a speakeasy during Prohibition, though when it was closed down in the 1940s, its antique fixtures — including the original marble-topped bar — were regrettably removed.

Keeping Cool: The Hip Spots

The clientele of these spots gives off a certain aura of that indefinable, elusive quality known as "cool." As always, it can be a little difficult to separate the trendsetters from the fashion followers, but they're both here:

Nightly club highlights

Like clockwork, you can count on some legendary music acts (or just great music in general) at certain venues on certain nights of the week. (You should still call to confirm, as schedules change.) For more specific events during your visit, see the *Lagniappe* entertainment directory in the *Times-Picayune* each Friday or the music calendar in *Gambit Weekly* every Tuesday.

Sunday: The popular Cajun "Fais Do Do" at **Tipitina's** (see p. 299) usually starts at 12:30 p.m. ($7 to $12).

Monday: Charmaine Neville and her band play jazz/pop cabaret at **Snug Harbor** (see p. 290) at 8 p.m. and 10 p.m. ($10 to $25). Bob French and Friends put on a smokin' traditional jazz jam at **Ray's Boom Boom Room**, 508 Frenchmen St. (☎ 504-523-5394), at 9 p.m. **Donna's** (see p. 292) on Rampart is usually a great place to be on Monday night.

Tuesday: The funky, electrifying Rebirth Brass Band play to packed crowds at the **Maple Leaf Bar** (see listing on p. 297 and box on p. 298), over near Tulane University, at 10:30 p.m. ($5).

Wednesday: Legendary Walter Wolfman Washington & the Roadmasters play a blend of funk, jazz, and soul at **d.b.a.** (see p. 296) on Frenchmen Street at 10 p.m. (free). Or try live music at the **Carousel Bar** (see p. 304) at the Hotel Monteleone from 9 p.m. to midnight (free, through Saturday night).

Thursday: Celebrity trumpeter Kermit Ruffins and the BBQ Swingers play **Vaughn's** (see p. 303) in the Bywater at 10:30 p.m. ($10). A popular zydeco stomp night at **Mid City Lanes Rock 'n' Bowl** (see p. 300) starts at 8:30 p.m. "Media night" at **Molly's at the Market** in the French Quarter (see p. 287) features local "celebrity bartenders" and big crowds.

Friday: Try free salsa lessons with Freddy Omar and live Latin jazz at **Café Brasil** (see below) at 9:30 p.m.

Saturday: "Bustout Burlesque!" night at **Tipitina's** (see p. 299) features a comic emcee, a jazz band, lots of sexy stripteases (supposedly recreations of old burlesque routines), and more, starting at 10 p.m. ($15). At **Mimi's** (2601 Royal St. at Franklin St. (☎ 504-942-0690), DJ Soul Sister spins a "HUSTLE!" funk dance party ("with your behind in mind") that *Spin* magazine gives 4 stars, free, at 11 p.m.

— *Special thanks to Grace Wilson of www.neworleansonline.com for her contributions.*

✔ **Café Brasil** (2100 Chartres St.; ☎ 504-949-0851) is the epicenter of the Frenchmen Street scene in Faubourg Marigny; no telling what you may find on any given night, including R&B, funk, and even jazz. During Mardi Gras or Jazz Fest it becomes a whirlwind of activity. The scene often spills out into the street (usually out of sheer necessity when the crowd becomes too large for the dance floor). Try to catch trumpeter Kermit Ruffins here as he has been

New Orleans Nightlife and Music

Circle Bar **2**
Contemporary Arts Center **3**
Feelings **24**
The Howlin' Wolf **5**
Le chat noir **13**
Le Petit Theatre du Vieux Carre **8**
Michaul's on St. Charles **12**
Mulate's **7**
NORD Theater **11**
Old Point Bar **23**
Pete Fountain's **9**
Sazerac Bar **15**
Southern Rep Theatre **22**
Vic's Kangaroo Café **10**
Whiskey Bar **14**
Zeitgeist Multi-Disciplinary
　Arts Center **1**

CLOSED, MAY REOPEN ○
Ampersand **17**
Ernie K-Doe's
　Mother-in-Law Lounge **19**
The Lion's Den **18**
Mahalia Jackson Theatre
　of the Performing Arts **20**
Mermaid Lounge **4**
New Orleans Municipal
　Auditorium **21**
Orpheum Theater **16**

CLOSED PERMANENTLY ●
True Brew Coffee House
　and Theater **6**

S. Broad Ave.
S. Dorgenois
S. Rocheblave
S. Johnson
S. Prieur
Seminole
S. Derbigny
S. Roman
Earhart Blvd. (Calliope St)
Erato
BROADMOOR
Martin Luther King Blvd.
Thalia
Clio
Erato
New Orleans Arena
Union Passeng Terminal (Amtra
Simon Bolivar
S. Robertson
Freret
La Salle
S. Liberty
Loyola
S. Saratoga
4th　3rd　2nd　1st
Dryades
Baronne
Carondelet
St. Charles
St. Charles Ave.
Prytania
Jackson Ave.
Magnolia
Thalia
Clio
Erato
Euterpe
Terpsichore
Polymnia
Melpomene
Pontchartrain Expwy.

Constantinople
Peniston
Amelia
Foucher
Delachaise
Louisiana Ave.
Harmony
8th　7th　6th
UPTOWN
Aline
Harmony

GARDEN DISTRICT
Toledano
Pleasant
9th
Washington
Coliseum
Chestnut
Camp
Magazine
Constance
Laurel
Annunciation
Josephine
St. Andrew
St. Mary
Felicity
Camp
Magazine
Constance
Annunciation
BF
90

ⓘ Information
⛴ Ferry Service to
　Algiers Point
•••◆••• Riverfront streetcar
　route/stops
––◆–– St. Charles streetcar
　route/stops
——◆—— Vieux Carre loop
　route/stops
–•◆•– Canal St. streetcar
　route/stops

St. Thomas
Rousseau
Chippewa
■ **New Orleans
General Hospital**
Orange
Richard
Market
Race
Euterpe
Celeste

See also "Uptown Music and Nightlife" map

Mississippi River

0   1/4 mi
0   0.25 km

N. Broad Ave.

(18)

N. Dorgenois

N. Rocheblave

N. Tonti

N. Miro

MID-CITY

N. Galvez

N. Johnson

N. Prieur

N. Roman

Derbigny

Tulane Ave.

(90)
(61)

LaFitte Ave.

Orleans Ave.
St. Ann
Dumaine
St. Phillip
Ursulines Ave.

Bayou Rd.

St. Bernard Ave.

N. Claiborne Ave.

erdome

(10)

(19)

ST. LOUIS
CEMETERY
NO. 2

N. Villere

La Salle St.
Duncan
Plaza

Poydras

**LOUIS
ARMSTRONG
PARK**

(20)

See also "French Quarter Music"
and "French Quarter Nightlife" maps

ST. LOUIS
CEMETERY
NO. 1

Basin St.

(21)

N. Rampart

McShane Pl.

**FAUBOURG
MARIGNY**

erdome

Univ. Pl.

Conti
St. Louis
Toulouse

St. Ann
Dumaine

Burgundy

(17)

(16)

Dauphine

Barracks

Esplanade

Touro

Frenchmen

Elysian Fields Ave.

Ave.
S. Rampart
O'Keefe St.

Gravier

(15)

Iberville
Bienville

Bourbon

Ursulines
Gov. Nichols

**CENTRAL
BUSINESS
DISTRICT**

Union
Perdido

**THE FRENCH
QUARTER**

Royal

Marigny
Mandeville

St. Charles Ave.

(14)

Common

Chartres

Spain

(13)
Lafayette
Square

Poydras

Decatur

(i)

**French
Market**

Chartres St.

Girod

(11)

(22)

Magazine St.

(10)

Tchoupitoulas
Commerce
S. Peters
Fulton

See also
"Faubourg Marigny/Bywater
Music and Nightlife" map

(24)

(5)
(6) (8)
(7)

(9)

Conv. Ctr. Blvd.

**World Trade
Center**

Canal St. Ferry

Morgan

(23)

Lake Pontchartrain

CITY
PARK

ew Orleans
nvention &
tion Center

ALGIERS

Powder
Bounty
Seguin
Bermuda
Pelican

(10)   (610)

The Crescent City
Connection (Toll)

Verret

Area of detail

(10)

Superdome

extra hot post-Katrina. Cover ranges from $5 to $15 when music is playing.

✔ **The Circle Bar** (1032 St. Charles Ave. at Lee Circle; ☎ 504-588-2616) is an enclave of hipness on the lip of the Warehouse District. It's a small, comfortable space, with easy bartenders and a clientele of musicians, workers, and just plain characters. Music runs toward singer-songwriters and local hard-to-define bands whose followings make getting around difficult — as I said, it's a tiny place, but an important one as it is a much-needed gathering place for music lovers.

✔ **The Dungeon** (738 Toulouse St.; ☎ 504-523-5530) may seem more imposing than it is, though it's still more of a habitat for fringe characters than college students or button-down tourists. It's a narrow, two-story hangout with an upstairs dance floor and all sorts of "spooky" décor. A real late-late-night spot, it doesn't open until midnight. Cover is around $3.

✔ **d.b.a.** (618 Frenchmen St.; ☎ 504-942-3731; www.drinkgoodstuff. com) is dedicated to the sale and consumption of quality beer and liquor, as its Web site address makes clear. An offshoot of a popular New York hangout, d.b.a. attracts a diverse mix of status-conscious drinkers to the hot Frenchmen Street restaurant and bar scene. Its spacious, dark wooden interior and extensive beer list are both inviting and comforting. Although it's fairly open, crowds can become hard to navigate during prime weekend hours.

✔ **El Matador** (504 Esplanade Ave.; ☎ 504-586-0790) sits right on Esplanade Avenue at Decatur Street on the site of a former gay/drag bar. Its tiny cabaret-style stage sometimes hosts rock bands. Part of almost every Quarter hipster's nightly itinerary, rock stars and local celebrities make their way here quite often. Cover is $5 to $15 when a live band plays.

✔ **F&M Patio Bar** (4841 Tchoupitoulas St.; ☎ 504-895-6784) is a venerable institution among the college and young working-professional sets. Late night is prime time here, with service-industry types, sorority girls, and on-the-prowl yuppies chatting each other up over a classic rock jukebox. Invariably, some sloshed individual will jump up on the pool table and start dancing, more because it's expected than because it's funny.

✔ The **Sazerac Bar** (in the Fairmont Hotel, 123 Baronne St.; ☎ 504-529-4733) is frequented by young professionals who come to mingle in the very posh atmosphere. This place was featured in the movie *The Pelican Brief* with Julia Roberts. Be sure to try its signature cocktail for which the bar is named (ask the bartender to make it from scratch and not a mix).

✔ The **Whiskey Bar** (201 St. Charles Ave. in the Central Business District/Warehouse District area; ☎ 504-566-7770) promises a New

York–style lounge atmosphere, and the inhabitants delight in dressing up — lots of jackets and short black dresses. The decor is dark and stylish, and the black marble bathrooms are cool. The doormen really give you the New York experience: they look you over before deciding whether to admit you inside.

Hanging Loose: Casual Bars

In their own way, each of these places is fine for just milling around, drinking, talking, and taking in the scenery:

- ✔ **Le Bon Temps Roule** (4801 Magazine St.; ☎ 504-895-8117) lets the good times roll by being all things to all people: a neighborhood joint, a college hangout, and (on weekends) a popular music destination (thanks in no small part to the lack of a cover charge).

- ✔ **Live Bait Bar and Grill** (501 River Rd. in Jefferson; ☎ 504-831-3070) is exactly what it says it is — a bait shop and neighborhood bar rolled into one. Bands (from locals to comeback-trail '80s hard-rock acts) regularly play in a large converted-garage area just off to the side, and older regulars coexist peacefully with drunken college types at the bar. It's a loose, friendly place, even given the fleet of Harleys and other motorcycles often found parked in the vicinity.

- ✔ The **Maple Leaf** (8316 Oak St.; ☎ 504-866-9359) is what a New Orleans club is all about. A small space, it features a hammered tin ceiling, a patio out back, and a good bar. Its reputation is in inverse proportion to its size; the place is almost always packed, with crowds often spilling out into the street. If Beausoleil or the ReBirth Brass Band is playing, you simply have to go. Owner Hank Staples claims he hosted the first concert in New Orleans after Katrina, on September 30, 2005 featuring Walter "Wolfman" Washington. Other clubs and musicians say otherwise, but this concert did have the largest audience and the most media for any show since the storm. Shows usually begin around 10:30 p.m.; cover varies anywhere from $5 to $20. See the "Tuesday night at the maple leaf" box in this section.

- ✔ The **R Bar** (1431 Royal St. in the Faubourg; ☎ 504-948-7499) attracts a mix of Marigny residents, bohemian types, local musicians, and Frenchmen scene stragglers. This place has one of the best vibes in town: slightly sophisticated, but in a low-key, grungy way. The atmosphere is an odd mish-mash of '50s-style decor and stylish neighborhood charm, with a pool table and a couch or two. Owner Jonathan Ferrara got into a little tiff just before Carnival 2006 when he announced that the Société de St. Anne parade would begin at his bar. On the contrary, said the At. Anne krewe, who said the parade has always started in the Bywater, and they deliberately changed their route so as not to go past the bar. Just tells you how seriously New Orleanians take Mardi Gras matters, even post-Katrina.

Tuesday night at the Maple Leaf

The following is an excerpt from a column by Chris Rose that originally appeared in the Times-Picayune *on 9/25/06. For more on the **Maple Leaf**, see p. 297 and read about the **Rebirth Brass Band** at* www.rebirthbrassband.com. *Read the full text of this article at:* http://www.nola.com/rose/t@@hyp/index.ssf?/rose/katrina/rebirth_at_the_maple_leaf.html.

The Tuesday night Rebirth gig at the Maple Leaf has iconographic standing in the lore of New Orleans nightlife, like the Thursday night zydeco stomp at Mid-City Lanes or the Sunday afternoon fais do-do at Tip's.

Something you can count on. No need to consult a schedule.

Long before Katrina, the Rebirth shows at Maple Leaf were where I'd drop in from time to time to remind myself why I live here, why I love here. Why I am here.

For the uninitiated (and if that's you, shouldn't you ask yourself why?) the Rebirth Brass Band is one of the veteran standard bearers of the New Orleans brass-band renaissance and I realize that if you ask me what that means, well . . . I don't know. What is New Orleans brass-band music? Got me. Jazz, I guess, in its basic DNA. Layered with rock influences. Smothered in hip-hop beat and attitude. All rolled together in a scary marching band.

It is an explosion of sound, just drums and horns — who needs anything else, really? — and it is the sound of Mardi Gras, of second-lines, street parades and house parties. Of New Orleans.

The Rebirth Tuesday night gigs have been colossal draws for years, crowded, sweaty, throbbing, disorganized affairs packed with Tulane students, downtown hipsters, stiff-collar types and soul brothers.

It is so energetic, so in the groove, so diverse and so perfect that it almost looks contrived, like if a director wanted to create the quintessential bar scene for a movie, this is what he would make.

But Hollywood could never make this. Not on a Tuesday night. And not in any other town.

It's organic. Sexy. Maybe even mildly dangerous — all that sweat. In the ultimate act of self-absorption, I'm going to quote myself, from a tourist guidebook I wrote several years ago, trying to capture a moment at one of these shows: "Loud. Fast. Free-falling. Funky. You've got ten new friends. The girl in your arms — what's her name? Who cares? Dance. If you saw yourself in a mirror at this instant, you wouldn't recognize yourself. And that can be a good thing."

✔ The **Rivershack Tavern** (3449 River Rd. in Jefferson; ☎ 504-834-4938) is a popular drinking place for a diverse cross-section of locals, from college students to bikers to medical professionals (Ochsner Hospital is just down the road), among others. Located on River Road along the Mississippi River, the Rivershack is renowned as "the home of the tacky ashtrays." You can listen to the jukebox and drink at this unpretentious hangout or enjoy occasional live music (mostly blues and rock). The food is a couple of notches above regular bar food; try the burgers or anything made with alligator.

✔ A very New Orleans kind of place, **St. Joe's Bar** (5535 Magazine St., Uptown; ☎ **504-899-3744**) is a friendly, unpretentious, agreeably dark neighborhood corner bar with intentionally peeled walls and folk-art crosses. Inside, this long, narrow spot has a well-stocked jukebox; outside is a tropical patio that gets crowded on pleasant weekend evenings.

✔ **Tipitina's** (501 Napoleon Ave.; ☎ **504-895-8477** or 504-897-3943; www.tipitinas.com) was, for a long time, *the* New Orleans music club. Posters advertising shows from the club's long history give the place a tangible sense of legacy and atmosphere. Local bands and touring national alternative rock acts play here, and during Jazz Fest the place is a thriving, visceral center of musical activity. If you can't make it out to Cajun Country, on Sunday afternoons this place holds a "Fais Do Do," complete with free food and dance lessons. The surrounding residential neighborhood has improved considerably, but you still may want to take a cab. The Tipitina's Foundation is dedicated to helping musicians rebuild their lives and careers in the Crescent City, and preserving the city's cultural traditions. Shows begin at 10 p.m.; Fais Do Do begins at 5 p.m. Sunday. Cover varies.

✔ **Vic's Kangaroo Café** (636 Tchoupitoulas St.; ☎ **504-524-4329**) is a friendly Warehouse District spot with an Australian theme (the phone number spells 524-GDAY) and a sand volleyball court that caters to the after-work crowd; have a shepherd's pie and wash it down with something from an impressive beer selection. Regulars and visitors alike can have a good old time playing games of darts or pool. Vic's also offers some better-than-average local blues and R&B acts (not your French Quarter tourist-trap variety).

Chilling to Cajun and Zydeco Music

Because Cajun and zydeco (see the sidebar, "AAIIEEE! Cajun and zydeco in two easy steps" in this chapter) originated not in New Orleans but in the swamps and bayous around Lafayette; the genuine article remains out in the country. Still, on any given night you can find a regional heavyweight playing somewhere.

✔ **Michaul's on St. Charles** (840 St. Charles Ave.; ☎ **504-522-5517**) and **Mulate's** (201 Julia St.; ☎ **504-522-1492**) present the tourist version of the Cajun experience, with the requisite wood floors and walls, kitsch, and a whole lot of crawfish. However, both clubs offer Cajun dance lessons (Michaul's are free), and you may even catch a

AAIIEEE! Cajun and zydeco in two easy steps

Although jazz was born in the Crescent City, Cajun and zydeco music originated in the wetlands around Lafayette, which was settled by the Acadians (see Chapter 15). Cajun music and zydeco both started out with Acadian folk music and French ballads, evolving into two distinctive new forms of music native to Louisiana and heavily influenced by the cultural diversity of the American Indian, Scotch-Irish, Spanish, Afro-Caribbean, and German folks who also lived in the bayous and swamps near Lafayette. Although both of these native forms rely on the accordion as a core instrument, Cajun music today generally retains a rustic sound and feel, while zydeco has evolved into a more urbanized sound.

A lively style reminiscent of bluegrass and country music, Cajun dance music is traditionally played on button accordions, scratchy fiddles, triangles, and rub-boards (or *frottoir*). Expect to have a great time dancing to it, but don't try to sing along: Many Cajun songs are still sung in the Acadian dialect of French or with such thick accents that you probably can't understand many of the lyrics.

Zydeco began as Cajun dance music but was flavored more than 150 years by the African, blues, and R&B traditions also enjoyed by the rural Creole population. Zydeco has a faster beat than Cajun, especially because funkier rhythms have been mixed in recently. Old-school zydeco performers rely only on the accordion, drums, and trademark rub-board, but over the last few decades some innovative performers have introduced electric guitars and basses, saxophones, and trumpets as well. Some of the genre's elder statesmen good-naturedly compete for the title "King of Zydeco," which comes with a ceremonial crown.

really good band that's in town for the day. Shows begin at 7 p.m. in both spots; no covers.

✔ **Mid City Lanes Rock 'n' Bowl** (4133 S. Carrollton Ave.; ☎ **504-482-3133,** www.rockandbowl.com), which also houses a bowling alley, took a beating from Katrina and the entire neighborhood was flooded very badly; thankfully they've recovered. Although the neighborhood is dicey, this is one of the most unique experiences in town. Tom Cruise stopped by when filming *Interview with the Vampire,* and numerous rockers, including Mick Jagger, have been known to sneak in when they're here on tour.

Rock-and-Roll All Night

Although New Orleans R&B, as practiced by such legends as Fats Domino — who was thankfully rescued from his Lower Ninth Ward home during Katrina — laid the groundwork for what today people call rock-and-roll, the city isn't well known for its contributions to modern-day rock. Still, it *does* boast a good rock scene, including such well-traveled names as the Radiators and modern rockers Better Than Ezra. Following are some of the clubs where you may catch the Next Big Thing or a national touring act:

- ✔ **Checkpoint Charlie's** (501 Esplanade Ave.; ☎ **504-947-0979**) tends toward rock and R&B and feels like something between a biker bar and a college hangout. A part of the Frenchmen Street strip in the Faubourg Marigny, it doesn't really fit into the bohemian aesthetic of that hip enclave. This place is good to check out young up-and-coming rock acts. Shows begin at 10:30 p.m.; no cover.

- ✔ From its humble beginnings as a suburban bar and venue for local alternative acts, **The Howlin' Wolf** (828 S. Peters St.; ☎ **504-522-9653**; www.howlin-wolf.com) has grown into a Warehouse District landmark and the main competitor with House of Blues (and, to a lesser extent, Tipitina's) for out-of-town acts. The Wolf's staff is among the friendliest in town, while the overall vibe is among the least pretentious and most agreeable in the city. Shows begin at 10 p.m.; cover varies from $5 to $20.

- ✔ **Jimmy's Music Club and Patio Bar** (8200 Willow St.; ☎ **504-861-8200**) is right across the street from Carrollton Station, and on weekend nights you're likely to find a good crowd milling about in the street between the two. Jimmy's used to be a prime spot for local rock bands and touring acts, though its smaller capacity precludes it from competing with Tipitina's, the Howlin' Wolf, or House of Blues. Now, obscure local hard-rock acts are featured plus some local and touring reggae, punk, and ska bands. Shows begin at 10 p.m.; cover varies from $5 to $15.

- ✔ The **Mermaid Lounge** (1100 Constance St. in the Central Business District), against all odds, carved a pretty nice niche for itself booking an eclectic mix of acts. It is temporarily closed due to storm damage.

Drafting a Good Time: Prime Places for Beer Nuts

Here are some key spots with some killer brews:

- ✔ **Carrollton Station** (8140 Willow St.; ☎ **504-865-9190**) is a small, folksy spot that's equal parts neighborhood joint, college hangout, and music venue (on the weekends). Order a draft beer (I recommend anything by Abita), strike up a conversation with the person next to you, and enjoy the gristly parade of New Orleans barflies. The Carrollton Station Foundation is a nonprofit organization created to help musicians recover from Katrina. Occasional cover charge for music on weekends ranges from $5 to $10.

- ✔ **Cooter Brown's Tavern** (509 S. Carrollton Ave., Uptown at the Riverbend; ☎ **504-866-9104**) experienced some structural damage, but reopened within a few months of the storm. It features a

Uptown Nightlife and Music

Carrollton Station **8**
Cooter Brown's Tavern **7**
F&M Patio Bar **2**
Jimmy's Music Club and Patio Bar **9**
Le Bon Temps Roule **3**
Live Bait Bar and Grill **11**
Maple Leaf **10**
Neutral Ground Coffeehouse **5**
Rivershack Tavern **12**
Snake & Jake's Xmas Club Lounge **6**
St. Joe's Bar **4**
Tipitina's **1**

CLOSED, MAY REOPEN ○
Mid City Lanes Rock 'n' Bowl **13**

staggering array of domestic and international beers. You can drink
your way around the world, and if you follow a beer-a-night
itinerary, you'll be in town for a long, long time. This hangout is
popular with college students, as well as older professionals, service-industry types, musicians — you name it, they're here. Pretty
decent bar food is served until reasonably late.

✔ If you want to kick back in an Irish pub, you have some very good
options, such as **Kerry Irish Pub** (331 Decatur St.; ☎ 504-527-5954).
This establishment not only boasts a good variety of beers and
other spirits but also can show you the proper way to pour pints of
Guinness and hard cider. A great spot for throwing darts and shooting pool or for catching some live Irish and alternative folk music.

✔ A new Irish pub, **Sean Kelly's** at 720 St. Louis St.; ☎ 504-525-1406)
opened after Katrina, and it's in the same vibe as the once-popular
O'Flaherty's, which sadly closed after severe hurricane damage.

Digging for Gold: Hard-to-Find Gems

These bars are all located a good way off the beaten path, in distant sections of town or tucked away in residential neighborhoods.

✔ The **Hi-Ho Lounge** (2239 St. Claude Ave., between the Quarter and
Bywater; ☎ 504-947-9344) had a particularly haphazard assortment of mismatched furniture that *Gambit Weekly* once called
"grungedom's living room." Closed due to flooding, let's hope they
recreate the interior exactly as it was.

✔ The **Neutral Ground Coffeehouse** (5110 Danneel St.; ☎ 504-891-3381;
www.neutralground.org) is an amiable throwback to the coffeehouses of the 1960s. Volunteers run it, it has no cover charge (instead,
they pass the hat), and it feels kind of like a college-dorm common
room. Acoustic and folk performers are on hand most nights, and
Sundays feature an open-mic night where anyone can join in.

✔ **Snake & Jake's Xmas Club Lounge** (7612 Oak St.; ☎ 504-861-2802)
appeals to people who like their holiday decor in dark places. Co-
owned by local musician Dave Clements and featuring a jukebox
heavy on soul and R&B, this is the kind of dive where everybody
knows your — and your dog's — name. That's right; pups are welcome, adding to the already unusual mix.

✔ **Vaughn's Lounge** (800 Lesseps St.; ☎ 504-947-5562) is a homey
little place tucked into the residential Bywater neighborhood. It
was closed for awhile in order to repair storm damage, but is now
open. The down-home atmosphere is charming, especially if you're
lucky enough to be here when local trumpet player Kermit Ruffins
(a modern-day Louis Armstrong) is playing (most Thurs nights,
when he's in town); more than likely, he'll be barbecuing on a grill
before the show. Be sure to take a cab; parts of this neighborhood
are rough. Cover is $10 on Thursday nights.

Playing Your Song: Piano Bars

Piano bars are everywhere in New Orleans, popping up from hotel lobbies to tourist magnets such as Pat O'Brien's. Here are just a few of the choicest establishments:

- ✔ The **Bombay Club** (830 Conti St., in the Prince Conti Hotel; ☎ 504-586-0972) offers not only live piano jazz Wednesday through Saturday but also world-famous martinis (often voted best in the city by the readers of *Gambit Weekly*).

- ✔ One of the most popular piano spots in town is the **Carousel Bar & Lounge** (214 Royal St., in the Hotel Montelone; ☎ 504-523-3341). The bar is literally a revolving carousel, so watch your step no matter how little you've had to drink. Catch some great piano music Tuesday through Saturday.

- ✔ **Feelings Café** (2600 Chartres St. at Franklin Ave. in the Faubourg; ☎ 504-945-2222; www.feelingscafe.com) is a friendly, funky, low-key neighborhood restaurant in the Faubourg Marigny. People tend to gather in the classic New Orleans courtyard, unless they're inside singing along with the piano player.

- ✔ **Pat O'Brien's** (718 St. Peter St.; ☎ 504-525-4823; www.patobriens.com) is a popular tourist attraction in the heart of the French Quarter. Despite that (or maybe because of it), it can be a good place to get a look at the teeming masses of humanity. The popularity of "Pat O's" has more to do with savvy marketing, I think, than anything else (though the high-trafficked location, lush patio/courtyard, and flaming fountain probably have something to do with it).

Shaking Your Groove Thing: The Best Dance Clubs

New Orleans features lots of places to go if you just want to shake your moneymaker.

- ✔ At the **Cat's Meow** (701 Bourbon St.; ☎ 504-523-1157; www.catsmeow-neworleans.com), you can listen to popular rock songs all night long or sing them yourself — karaoke is available if you have the guts to make a fool out of yourself. Cover charge is $5 for those under 21; free for those older than 21.

- ✔ **The Gold Mine** (701 Dauphine St.; ☎ 504-586-0745) is a popular spot for college-age kids who congregate here and dance all night long to the latest hits. If that's not your thing, you'd be more comfortable somewhere else. If you stay, try the flaming Dr. Pepper shot. Only open Friday and Saturday nights; $2 cover.

Elizabeth's Restaurant

Faubourg Marigny/Bywater Nightlife and Music

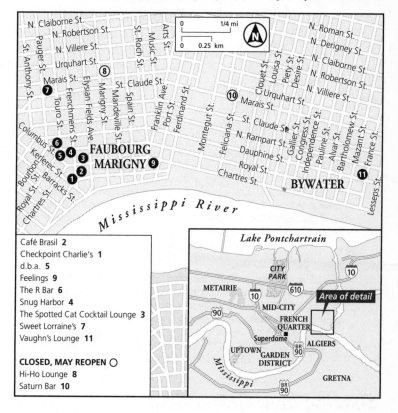

Café Brasil **2**
Checkpoint Charlie's **1**
d.b.a. **5**
Feelings **9**
The R Bar **6**
Snug Harbor **4**
The Spotted Cat Cocktail Lounge **3**
Sweet Lorraine's **7**
Vaughn's Lounge **11**

CLOSED, MAY REOPEN ○
Hi-Ho Lounge **8**
Saturn Bar **10**

✔ **Razzoo** (511 Bourbon St.; ☎ **504-522-5100**) is another popular spot
for the young dancing set; high-energy hits and dance mixes are the
norm here. Mix it up on the dance floor, and then take a breather
out on the patio, where you can watch everyone else dance and
delude yourself into thinking that you don't look nearly as foolish
on the floor as they do.

Stepping Out: Gay and Lesbian Scene

Are you looking for the best gay and lesbian hangouts? Check out the
following:

✔ **Bourbon Pub and Parade Disco** (801 Bourbon St.; ☎ **504-529-
2107**) is one of the largest gay nightclubs in the United States.
Downstairs is the Bourbon Pub, a 24-hour establishment with a
video bar. The disco upstairs opens at 9 p.m.; a $5 to $10 cover is
charged on weekends.

Musical names explained

✔ If you're looking for a Vegas-style revue, the **Chris Owens Club** (500 Bourbon St.; ☎ 504-523-6400; www.chrisowens.com) is it. The ageless, well-proportioned Ms. Owens puts on a high-energy show filled with standards from the worlds of pop, jazz, blues, and country and western. She lives above the club and didn't leave for Katrina. I always knew she was tough, but that says it all. Call for reservations and admission prices. Shows begin at 8:30 p.m. and 10 p.m.

✔ Remember the vintage R&B chestnut "Mother-In-Law"? Before his death in 2001, flamboyant singer Ernie K-Doe turned that song into a career — and later, a nightclub. **Ernie K-Doe's Mother-In-Law Lounge** (1500 N. Claiborne Ave. at Columbus; ☎ 504-947-1078), is where K-Doe held court for years. Please take a cab — the neighborhood is rough. The lounge flooded badly from Katrina, and K-Doe's widow, Antoinette, thought up a most unusual rebuilding fundraiser; she started a mayoral campaign on behalf of her late husband, proclaiming him to be the only qualified candidate. See the box on p. 27, "A music lounge owner returns and rebuilds," for more information.

✔ The local **House of Blues** (225 Decatur St.; ☎ 504-529-BLUE [2583]; www.hob.com/venues/clubvenues/neworleans) doesn't *really* fit here, unless you consider celebrity cofounder Dan Aykroyd's alter ego, Elwood Blues, a big name. But most major touring rock, reggae, and hip-hop acts play here. The restaurant is decent and pricey, with some inventive takes on local fare. Other chains should be this stylish. Shows usually begin at 9 p.m. Cover varies from $10 to $20.

✔ Parrot heads abound at **Jimmy Buffett's Margaritaville Café** (1104 Decatur St.; ☎ 504-592-2565; www.margaritaville.com). Buffett took part in a Katrina fundraising concert, "From the Big Apple to the Big Easy" in September 2005, which was a very welcome gesture (a DVD is available). Otherwise, this chain has contributed to the brand-name takeover of the Quarter, though mostly it's a venue for journeyman local performers, from blues to R&B to reggae and New Orleans roots music. You find music all day long here, with shows generally beginning at 3, 6, and 9 p.m. No cover except for special shows on weekend nights, which start around 10:30 p.m.

✔ Located in flooded Mid-City, **The Lion's Den** (2655 Gravier St.; ☎ 504-822-4693) remains closed. Owner Irma Thomas, the "Soul Queen of New Orleans," has been so busy traveling around the nation to perform and serve as an informal New Orleans music ambassador that she hasn't been given much of a chance to focus on the club's return. Of course, we all hope it will, and soon.

✔ **Pete Fountain** is practically synonymous with New Orleans music. This local boy, once a member of Lawrence Welk's orchestra, lost just about everything when Katrina swept through his home near Bay St. Louis, Mississippi. Fortunately, two of his best clarinets survived and the spry 75-year-old jazzman continues to play select gigs in the Greater New Orleans area. If you get a chance to hear him, don't miss it.

- A legendary spot in the gay community, **Café Lafitte in Exile** (901 Bourbon St.; ☎ **504-522-8397;** www.lafittes.com) was opened by Tom Caplinger, who used to run Lafitte's Blacksmith Shop. Reluctant to leave the original place behind, he brought friends and patrons (including Tennessee Williams) with him when he opened this place. Open 24 hours, this bar is usually crowded.

- If you like everything country, dress head to tow in denim and leather and go to **Cowpokes** (2240 St. Claude Ave.; ☎ **504-947-0505;** www.cowpokesno.com). Please take a cab as this can be an iffy neighborhood. Free line-dance lessons on Tuesdays and Thursdays and karaoke on Wednesdays.

- **Good Friends Bar** (740 Dauphine St.; ☎ **504-566-7191;** www.good friendsbar.com) is a neighborhood type of place with tons of atmosphere and a piano in the corner that invites karaoke-style misuse.

- The 24-hour **LeRoundup** (819 St. Louis St.; ☎ **504-561-8340**) has a friendly atmosphere, attracting the most diverse crowd around. The bar charges occasional small covers for entertainment/revue-type shows.

- The hot dance spot **Oz** (800 Bourbon St.; ☎ **877-599-8200** or 504-592-8200; www.ozneworleans.com) is recognized both locally and nationally as a place to see and be seen. Gambit Weekly ranked it as the city's No. 1 dance club, and Details magazine ranked it as one of the top 50 clubs in the country. If you like to dress up (and by that, I don't mean don a tux), call ahead to inquire about their frequent theme nights. Cover is $3 on Wednesday and Sunday nights; $10, Friday and Saturday nights ($5 discount for gay males).

Part VI
The Part of Tens

The 5th Wave   By Rich Tennant

IN THE ABSENCE OF ANY ALLIGATORS, GRIZZLED CAJUN, "SWAMP RAT" LAFITTE WOULD OFTEN WRESTLE AN IBIS FOR CURIOUS TOURISTS.

In this part . . .

This part is designed to give you some "distilled" information about New Orleans, and I'm using this opportunity to focus on some post-Katrina issues. I start off on a positive note, with a list of the "Ten Classic Experiences You Can Still Have in Post-Katrina New Orleans" (Chapter 18). But it's also important to chronicle the damage the city sustained, so I note "Ten Things We Lost in the Hurricane" (Chapter 19). Finally, I give an opinionated take on "Ten Issues Facing New Orleans Right Now" (Chapter 20). For more information about the hurricane's impact, see Chapter 2.

Chapter 18

Ten Classic Experiences You Can Still Have in Post-Katrina New Orleans

· ·

In This Chapter

▶ Downing decadent drinks (and figuring out the drinking laws)

▶ Rolling the dice on the river

▶ Getting down with ghosts, ghouls, and goblins

· ·

The Big Easy tends to exaggerate your own vices, which I have found to be all too true. Of course, these days, locals are more than willing to give in to temptation to forget their Katrina troubles for a spell. Fortunately, you can get creative and indulge in more than just booze on Bourbon Street. In this chapter, I run down ten irreverent, only-in-New-Orleans experiences that you can still enjoy, from can't-miss music to sinfully indulgent meals.

Gulping Gin from a "Go-Cup"

Barhopping in New Orleans is a marathon undertaking to begin with, but it'd be much longer and less fun without these handy timesaving measures. The city's permissive liquor laws allow bar patrons to leave the premises with their unfinished drink in hand — provided it's poured into a plastic cup, known as a *go-cup*. Drinking in a go-cup lets drinkers leave at their leisure, without having to worry about finishing their drink in a hurry. Don't be holding a go-cup in your hand if the car you're riding in gets pulled over — and I don't have to tell you to forget about driving with one, right? But if you're walking down Bourbon Street — or any street, for that matter — and want to savor your brew (hopefully one locally made; try a Dixie or an Abita) or just stand still for a while to soak up the atmosphere, these cups rule.

Delighting in Drive-Thru Daiquiris

It makes a perverse kind of sense that the city that lets you walk around with liquor in your hand would let you drive around with it, too. I certainly don't advocate drinking and driving, and the city does have — and enforce — an open-container law that prohibits imbibing while behind the wheel. But that said, ordering a daiquiri from the comfort of your car (as you can do at **New Orleans Original Daiquiris,** 3301 Veterans Blvd. in Metairie, ☎ 504-837-8474) is a staple of suburban nightlife and quite the "Am I really getting away with this?" experience for first-timers.

You can also grab daiquiris at walk-up windows throughout the city, including New Orleans Original Daiquiris locations Uptown (8100 St. Charles Ave.) and on Bourbon Street (633 Bourbon). Locations in Mid-City (301 N. Carrollton Ave.) and neighboring suburb Chalmette (8304 Judge Perez Dr.) are closed due to flooding and might not reopen.

Succumbing to a Liuzza's Po' Boy

Thankfully, post-Katrina New Orleans still has countless variations of this popular sandwich. But po' boys from **Liuzza's on Bienville** (1518 N. Lopez St.; ☎ 504-482-9120), a neighborhood hangout within walking distance of the Canal Streetcar, have extra bite. "Rich" and "buttery" don't begin to describe its bang-fist-on-table sensation. I think they taste extra good now because I didn't know if I'd ever taste one again. The restaurant flooded so badly that many locals worried about its fate. But Liuzza's is back and better than ever.

Grooving at the Maple Leaf

Most Tuesday nights when it's not on the road, the ReBirth Brass Band makes the **Maple Leaf** (see Chapter 17) its home for a down-and-dirty whistle-stop tour of modern brass that's become an ingrained local tradition. College students (lots of them), tourists, and all-around music lovers stand shoulder to shoulder in this unassuming nightspot as the band conducts a raucous dance workout. ReBirth is New Orleans's premier purveyor of "modern brass," mixing pop, funk, hip-hop, and gospel elements into the traditional brass-band sound. The band's bawdy grooves and precision swagger are infectious, and a show at the Maple Leaf is nothing short of jubilant musical abandon. See the "Tuesday Night at the Maple Leaf" box on pg. 298.

Trying Your Luck with a Lucky Dog

Popularized by John Kennedy Toole's classic novel, *A Confederacy of Dunces,* these high-cholesterol hot dogs are a junk-food staple in the French Quarter. In fact, distinctive hot dog–shaped Lucky Dog carts (each more than 600 pounds!) are about as common a sight in the Quarter as drunken sailors, even late at night (when they're a godsend for stumbling drunks looking for a quick grease fix). Taste-wise, the mustard-heavy, calorie-laden Dog is far better than your average hot dog. Though each bite brings you closer to cardiac arrest, legions of French Quarter denizens swear that the taste is worth it.

Rolling the Bones

As seen in television and movies, the idea of a riverboat casino holds a certain Mark Twain kind of romance. The reality may not be quite as romantic, but it's an increasingly popular way for locals and tourists to willingly part with large amounts of their cash. Truth be told, you can't see much of the river on a riverboat casino, and not just because it doesn't have windows. Most riverboats are loath to leave their berths (which is a sin in itself). They want customers to be able to come and go at will rather than be stuck, you know, enjoying the sights, sounds, and spray of a riverboat cruise. Still, despite the lack of nautical atmosphere, riverboat casinos (see Chapter 12) combine modern-day avarice with the idyllic sheen of yesteryear — a hard combination to beat. If you really have an urge to roll along the river, forget the floating casinos and come aboard old-fashioned steamboats or paddlewheelers (see Chapter 12) offering dinner, dancing, live music and much more.

Having a Hurricane at Pat O'Brien's

Pat O'Brien's (see Chapter 17) is one of New Orleans's most popular bars, due in no small part to its signature drink, the Hurricane. Named for the glass it comes in (its shape resembles a hurricane lamp), this fruity concoction originated during World War II, when rum was so widely available that liquor distributors pushed it heavily and retailers had to find a way to use it all. The Hurricane is a potent cocktail, but its true popularity likely derives as much from the souvenir glass it comes in — which, in case you're interested, has at least one use after you finish your drink: According to the bar's Web site (www.patobriens.com), a Hurricane glass holds exactly $10 in pennies.

Surrendering to Your Slothful Side

New Orleans's signature phrase is "Let the good times roll" for a reason: The city's atmosphere is perfectly suited for indolent lounging, whiling away the hours in as lazy a fashion as you can muster. From a leisurely breakfast of beignets and café au lait at **Café du Monde** (see Chapter 11) to a relaxed **carriage ride** (see Chapter 12) around the Quarter to an unhurried afternoon sipping a Pimm's Cup at **Napoleon House** (see Chapter 17), you can easily make a day out of doing next to nothing. And an evening, too: Idling at **Lafitte's Blacksmith Shop** or nursing an anisette at **Old Absinthe House** (see Chapter 17) is a perfect way to wind down after a hard day of, well, hardly moving. If you're fortunate enough to be staying at a swanky hotel like the **Hotel Monteleone** or the **Windsor Court** (Chapter 10), all the better — spending a whole day lounging and being pampered without ever leaving the premises is possible (if not necessarily advisable).

Meeting Creatures of the Night

New Orleans enjoys a supernatural reputation, and some establishments (such as the **Hi-Ho Lounge** or **Hotel Provincial**) claim to play host to spirits. But spending the night in a particular hotel or bar, waiting for a ghost to come to you, can be a frustrating endeavor, especially when you can be proactive and track down the specters yourself! Outfits such as **Haunted History Tours** and **Magic Walking Tours** (see Chapter 12) offer a variety of walking tours that are themed around ghosts, vampires, and cemeteries. The Cemetery/Voodoo Tour offered by **Historic New Orleans Walking Tours** (see Chapter 12) allows you to take in the tomb of famed voodoo priestess Marie Laveau and an actual voodoo temple.

Speaking of vampires, New Orleans's own Queen of the Damned, vampire novelist **Anne Rice,** used to allow tours of historical landmark **St. Elizabeth's Orphanage** and her Garden District home at **1239 First Street.** But shockingly, in 2004, Rice sold the last of her New Orleans properties and initially moved to (gasp!) a gated community in suburban Kenner, Louisiana. In 2005, she moved to La Jolla, California, to be closer to her son, novelist Christopher Rice, and then moved again less than one year later to the warmer climate of Rancho Mirage, California. Fans can still get their fill of Rice in New Orleans, including autographed books, first editions, and other rarities at the **Garden District Book Shop** (see Chapter 13). Loyal fans might want to plan their New Orleans trip around the annual "The Vampire Lestat Ball," always held the weekend closest to Halloween. Go to www.lestatsdarkgiftshop.com for tickets and additional info. For late-night options, wander Bourbon Street, where you're sure to run into someone (or something) other worldly before long or descend into **The Dungeon** (see Chapter 17) after midnight.

Suffering Through Saints Games

Yes, Saints games — the way New Orleans's long-suffering football fans have to bear the team's tumultuous ups and downs is indeed a sin. The team once known derisively as "the Aints" perpetually and notoriously fails to capitalize on its momentum; the team's failures are often blamed on the fact that the Superdome is built on a former graveyard (rumors have it that not all the bodies were removed). Still, Saints fans are arguably as tenacious as followers of the Chicago Cubs, and martyrdom is of course alive and well in this predominantly Catholic town. Serving as a shelter of last resort and Katrina's winds and rain took a toll on this modern landmark, but a $186-million renovation put the Superdome (and the Saints) back in business. The opener on September 25, 2006, saw the Saints defeat the Falcons to much fanfare. Even Falcons coach Jim Mora acknowledged the significance of the event: "As tough as it is to lose a game, I'd be lying if I said there isn't a little, little, little piece of me that didn't appreciate what this game meant to this city. It meant a lot" (Associated Press, 9/26/06).

Chapter 19

Ten Things We Lost in the Hurricane

*W*hen I asked one of my friends to help me pare down the list of things we lost to Katrina, she reminded me that it's the little things that we miss the most — a neighbor or friend who moved away and isn't coming back, a grand old tree we'd pass on our way to work, a favorite little corner store or restaurant that closed because of insurance woes. Some things are more nebulous than others. Lacking any kind of a normal, daily routine is hard to take, but that isn't necessarily a "thing" lost.

Much of what we miss was a part of our day-to-day lives rather than part of the tourist experience, so it would be unfair to expect you to "miss" them in the same way we would. I'm going to assume that because you are reading this book and planning a trip to New Orleans, that you do care. New Orleanians do not want to be pitied, but it means a great deal to us when visitors make an effort to understand.

For more information on Katrina and its aftermath, including a list of organizations accepting donations, see Chapter 2.

People

The biggest tragedy of Hurricane Katrina is the loss of family, friends, neighbors and co-workers. Many of them were among the 1,836 victims of the storm, and more than 700 people are still missing more than one year after the storm. Other people survived the hurricane, only to learn that they could not afford to rebuild, or lost their job or faced some form of personal crisis, and moved away out of necessity. For the locals who stayed, myself included, it is difficult to lose so many people in your life over a short period of time and in such dramatic fashion.

Neighborhoods

The Lower Ninth Ward received the most attention from the mainstream media, perhaps because most of its residents were considered an abomination in the United States: poor. But there were many other neighborhoods that suffered complete devastation in the wake of Katrina and the faulty levees. Middle-class, lakeside neighborhoods such as Gentilly, where Mayor Ray Nagin lives, and my neighborhood, Lakeview, were also among the worst flooded areas. To the south, Mid-City, Broadmoor, the Seventh Ward, and Treme took on water from levee breaches at the 17th Street and London Street canals. To the east, all of New Orleans East and parts of Holy Cross were submerged by storm surge. I could name all of the neighborhoods that flooded, but the names would probably be meaningless to you. What's important to remember, especially if you choose to tour any of these damaged areas, is that people — perhaps like you — once lived there and are trying to rebuild that way of life.

Restaurants

More than 80 percent of the city was flooded at one point, so I am genuinely surprised when I hear of another local restaurant that has risen from the ruins. The city's many mom 'n' pop places did not have the benefit of falling back on a corporate parent company and yet, often these independent establishments were the first to come back. However, areas like the West End, the northwestern corner of Lakeview, will not return. A cluster of favorite seafood joints (including 146-year-old Bruning's) were built on pilings, extending into Lake Pontchartrain. They didn't stand a chance against Katrina's winds and storm surge. Of course, even that wouldn't be enough to stop some New Orleanians from coming back, but the Army Corps of Engineers seized the land. That prevented any of these historic businesses from returning and left a huge void in Lakeview. See "Assessing Katrina's Effect on the Dining Scene" in Chapter 11 for more information.

Musicians

You probably remember the search for rock 'n' roll pioneer Fats Domino almost immediately after the storm. A long-time resident of the Lower Ninth Ward, he and his family decided to ride out the storm and were rescued by boat days later. Hundreds of local, less-famous musicians lost musical instruments, master tapes, CDs and more, hindering their ability to ply their trade. Some had to leave the city for better opportunities (in Houston, for example), which has taken a toll on New Orleans' unique music culture. During the first year after Katrina, there were not as many visitors as years past, and club owners fought to stay open despite lack of customers. Please help support New Orleans musicians by attending live shows and/or buying their music (www.louisiana musicfactory.com). See Chapter 17 for club suggestions, and look for a list of music charity organizations in Chapter 2.

Architecture

The **Preservation Resource Center** (☎ 504-581-7032; www.prcno.org), a nonprofit organization dedicated to preserving New Orleans' historic neighborhoods, is on the frontlines of protecting the city's signature housing stock, such as the shotgun house. This has always been a challenge as the population shifted toward the suburbs, leaving behind old houses to decay or be demolished. Due to Katrina, there will be an estimated 15,000 demolitions, some of which will take place in historic districts. In some cases, there is no proposed salvaging of historic materials, such as heart pine flooring, windows, doors, cypress floor joists, fireplace mantels, brackets, pocket doors, and more. Having lost so many historic homes and buildings already, many New Orleanians feel it should be a priority to maintain as much of New Orleans's urban landscape as possible.

Trees

You may not notice if you haven't visited the city before or haven't been back in awhile, but a lot of New Orleans' gorgeous old trees succumbed to wind or water during Katrina. Fortunately, many of the live oaks survived, but magnolias — like the massive 100-year-old tree in front of my house — couldn't handle the brackish waters of the lake, and drowned. They are as much a part of the urban landscape as the residences and buildings, and it's heartbreaking that these old trees that lived for so many years — in some cases, hundreds — died this way.

City Park

At 1,500 acres, City Park (see Chapter 12) is the country's fifth largest urban park. It shelters the largest collection of mature live oaks in the world. Many of these beautiful trees — which have lived for hundreds of years — could not survive the two weeks they spent under three- to eight-feet of brackish water. Once the floodwaters receded, all of the grass, flowers, and bushes had died, and brown muck covered everything. Even now, the park is scarred, dotted with chopped trunks and overgrown grass and foliage because the park lacks the staff and resources to do even basic maintenance. The park is slowly being restored. Log on to www.neworleanscitypark.com for the most recent updates.

Chalmette Battlefield

This park (see Chapter 12) is the site of the historic Battle of New Orleans, where General Andrew Jackson and a ragtag band staged a desperate defense of the city against the British. Tragically, Chalmette was inundated with storm surge pushed up the Mississippi River Gulf Outlet, nicknamed "Mr Go," an underutilized channel dug up by the Army Corps of Engineers. Also on the grounds is the Chalmette National Cemetery. The park remains closed due to extensive damage, and the funds to rehabilitate it may be a long time coming.

St. Charles Streetcar (temporarily)

From aprons to postcards, images of the famous St. Charles Streetcar appear on an array of New Orleans–themed souvenirs (see Chapter 12). More than a year after Katrina, this historic line is still closed, though its cars are temporarily running on the Canal Streetcar line (the new Canal cars flooded). I still catch myself checking for an oncoming streetcar before I drive across the neutral ground. I can't wait to hear that familiar sound of the wheels on the tracks. Check the Transit Authority (www. norta.com/st_charles.php) for more information. They claim streetcars will be up and running by the end of 2007, and that, before then, "If you want to see the attractions on St. Charles Avenue and Carrollton Avenue, take the RTA St. Charles bus, which operates on the same route that the St. Charles streetcars did before Katrina."

Sense of Identity

The sudden loss of its people and culture could lead to another loss: its identity. What is the City of New Orleans without its diverse population and trademark food, music, and subtropical urban landscape? Change can be good in the sense that New Orleans could've used some improvements prior to the storm. However, the recovery process could threaten what makes this city so special if we're not careful; already the French Quarter — once an artist's haven — is seeing rents climb so high that artists can't afford to return. Who will repopulate the new New Orleans?

Chapter 20

Ten Issues Facing New Orleans Right Now

. . . .

In This Chapter

▶ Understanding the city's current dilemmas

▶ Examining crime, unemployment, and education statistics

▶ Getting the author's two cents

. . . .

*I*nitially after the storm, there was a lot of talk about whether New Orleans should rebuild. Now that the recovery process is under way, many other variables such as the economy, health care, insurance, repopulation levels and schools are affecting New Orleanians' ability to rebuild and continue to live there. The following is my personal assessment of the top issues.

Identity

In our eagerness to rebuild the city and our lives, there is a danger of creating a theme park version of New Orleans. Or worse, we could construct a cookie cutter city, one that looks like Anytown, U.S.A. It would help if our government officials at all levels and residents could agree on an overall plan for the city and work together. Unfortunately, I still see stubborn divisiveness among a few key players (see "Names in the News" in Chapter 2) and that will only serve to hurt us and future generations of New Orleanians.

Repopulation

Before Katrina, New Orleans was home to 484,000 residents. As of December 2006, city officials estimated a post-Katrina population of 210,000 or less than half. The city can survive with fewer people, but flooded neighborhoods with only a few inhabitants and limited city services might struggle for survival. Early plans to only rebuild nonflooded areas were quickly forgotten in the face of heated public criticism. Of course, I understand their concerns as I would not appreciate someone telling me that I couldn't rebuild my home, but I recognize the fact that the city as a whole is at stake, and not just my little corner of it. Given that context, I want to do what I can to ensure New Orleans lives on, and I think supporting a citywide recovery plan — whatever sacrifices that entails — is the best way to bring people back or encourage others to move here for the first time.

Crime

Despite the smaller population, the crime rate is nearly equal to what it was before Katrina. Most people who lost everything are working hard to rebuild their lives. Unfortunately, looting and burglaries have become common in areas where people are trying to repair their homes and replace belongings like appliances and furniture. In an infamous story from August 2006, thieves stole $100,000 worth of the Walton Construction concrete-pouring equipment being used to build a Katrina memorial in the storm-battered Lower Ninth Ward. "This takes a lot of guts," said Walton senior vice president Bill Petty. "This is the largest piece of equipment that has even been stolen from Walton" (*Times-Picayune*). Someone in my neighborhood reported that a scavenger stole her carport and gutter, most likely to sell as scrap metal. The National Guard and New Orleans Police Department must gain the upper hand. Crime in the city usually happens at night; if you're traveling long distances after dark, be sure to take a taxi.

Levees

Imagine how locals felt when the Army Corps of Engineers — which admitted that its faulty levee design and implementation led to the levee breaches — was put in charge of repairing them and shoring up the weakened levee system in general. If the necessary federal funds ever come through, the Corps will also be responsible for constructing levees that can withstand a Category 5 storm.

Economy

Business is not exactly booming in Orleans Parish, the county that encompasses New Orleans. A surprising number of companies and mom 'n' pop–type establishments managed to overcome flooding or looting, but could not get insurance. In New Orleans, the number of occupational licenses is down 50 percent, yet neighboring parishes such as Jefferson and St. Tammany (across Lake Pontchartrain) have seen an incredible increase, as New Orleans businesses migrate there. These businesses are understandably attracted to the large, stable populations, reliable city services, and higher ground elevation. So it's especially important to support those businesses that did opt to stay in the city.

Employment

In the months after the storm, thousands of people were laid off because companies were either closing or paring down their staffs in order to stay afloat. One strange sight was fast food companies advertising pay of $15 to $20 an hour and signing bonuses up to $6,000. (Many of their workers evacuated the city and didn't come back until months later or simply didn't return at all.) With the business climate in a state of flux, steady employment remains a major concern unless you work construction or ply a trade involving rebuilding.

Health Care

Before the storm, there were 16 hospitals that served patients throughout the Metro area. Due to flooding or fears of looting, 13 hospitals were temporarily closed for months after the storm. One year later, some hospitals closed permanently due to lack of money, insurance, or both. The **Louisiana Department of Health and Hospitals** (www.dhh.louisiana. gov) estimates that the city lost half of its physicians. Citizens without health insurance, transportation or money will most likely suffer the consequences.

Insurance

Residents and businesses are struggling to maintain their insurance policies or are having a tough time attaining policies post-Katrina. More than a year after the storm, some homeowners are still fighting with their insurance companies over payment for Katrina damage. Many predict that if the state and federal government do not ensure that everyone can be insured, only the wealthiest people will be able to stay.

Schools

New Orleans' public schools were failing miserably well before Katrina, with just a few exceptions located in predominantly white, middle- and upper-class neighborhoods. Many school buildings were destroyed by flood, and teachers and staff were in short supply. Families were forced to enroll their children elsewhere and, in some cases, found better schools in other cities and stayed there. Soon after the storm, the Louisiana state legislature voted to take over the city's public schools.

As of May 2006, only 25 of 117 schools had reopened and the public school system has been largely replaced by a charter system, which is no longer held accountable to the school board or superintendent. Only

20 percent of public school students have returned, compared to 90 percent of private school students. This is a historic opportunity to completely revamp education in the city, but it will require leadership from all levels of government and loyal support from parents and students.

Race and Class

One of the ironies of New Orleans is its social emphasis on race and class, yet prior to Katrina, it was home to one of the most integrated communities in the country. Sure, some neighborhoods were predominantly white or predominantly African-American, but far more neighborhoods were mixed. And wealthy enclaves such as the Garden District and the French Quarter either border (or are just blocks away from) poorer areas and housing projects. Long ago, when its port helped sustain the slave trade, New Orleans also nourished a well-to-do community of Free Persons of Color — the largest in the South, in fact.

But Katrina revealed that there is still a divide, even among African Americans. Mayor Nagin, who was a wealthy (though self-made) African-American businessman before seeking political office, was accused by the African-American community of winning his first election thanks to mostly white support. Yet when he attempted to reach out to the exiled African-American community, he awkwardly called for a "chocolate city" and managed to upset white voters as well. You would think that his re-election was in jeopardy, but Nagin was re-elected. There's a saying that the governor of Louisiana will always be white and the mayor of New Orleans will always be black. I'm not sure that the racial tension in New Orleans will ever go away, especially since many poor African Americans face more challenges and have fewer options in a post-Katrina city than their wealthier white counterparts. Let's hope that the storm will encourage people of all races and classes to present a united front and work together to rebuild this great American city.

You'll find further discussion of race and class post-Katrina in many of the articles and books I recommend in Chapter 2, especially Michael Eric Dyson's provocative *Come Hell or High Water: Hurricane Katrina and the Color of Disaster* (Basic Books, 2006).

Appendix

Quick Concierge

Fast Facts: Post-Katrina New Orleans

AAA

For road service, call ☎ 800-222-4357 or 504-367-4095.

Ambulance

Call ☎ **911** for emergency ambulance service.

American Express

The American Express office (☎ 504-586-8201) is located at 201 St. Charles Ave. in the Central Business District. It's open Monday to Friday from 9 a.m. to 5 p.m. For cardholder services, call ☎ 800-528-4800; for lost or stolen traveler's checks, call ☎ 800-221-7282.

Area Codes

The area code for the greater New Orleans metropolitan area is **504**. The North Shore, the region north of the city across Lake Pontchartrain, which includes Slidell, Covington, and Mandeville, is **985**.

ATMs

Automatic teller machines are as ubiquitous in New Orleans as they likely are in your hometown. The 800 numbers for the major ATM networks are ☎ 800-424-7787 (800-4CIRRUS) for Cirrus and ☎ 800-843-7587 for Plus.

Among the more convenient ATM locations in the French Quarter are the following: corner of Chartres and St. Ann; 400 block of Chartres near K-Paul's restaurant;

corner of Chartres and Toulouse; corner of Royal and Iberville; and 240 Royal St.

Baby sitters

Ask your hotel or call one of the following agencies for sitting services: Accents on Children's Arrangements, ☎ 504-524-1227 or Dependable Kid Care, ☎ 504-486-4001.

Business Hours

On the whole, most shops and stores are open from 10 a.m. to 6 p.m. Banks open at 9 a.m. and close between 3 and 5 p.m.

Camera Repair

Try AAA Camera Repair, 1631 St. Charles Ave. (☎ 504-561-5822).

Convention Center

Ernest M. Morial Convention Center, 900 Convention Center Blvd., New Orleans, LA 70130, ☎ 504-582-3000. Convention Center Boulevard sits at the end of the Warehouse District, on the river between Thalia and Water streets; the Canal Streetcar (formerly Riverfront Streetcar) drops you off at the Convention Center.

Credit Cards

Information numbers for American Express are listed earlier in this section (see "American Express"). MasterCard's general information number is ☎ 800-307-7309. For Visa, call ☎ 800-847-2911.

Customs

To reach the New Orleans office of the U.S. Customs Service, call ☎ 504-670-2206.

Dentists

Contact the New Orleans Dental Association (☎ 504-834-6449; www. nodc.org/noda.htm) to find a reliable dentist near you.

Doctors

If you're in need of a doctor, call one of the following: Orleans Parish Medical Society, ☎ 504-523-2474; Tulane Medical Clinic, ☎ 504-588-5800; or Children's Hospital, ☎ 504-899-9511.

Emergencies

For fire, police, and ambulance call ☎ **911.**

For the Poison Control Center, call ☎ 800-256-9822.

The Travelers Aid Society (846 Baronne St., ☎ 504-525-8726) also renders emergency aid to travelers in need. For help regarding a missing or lost child, call Child Find at ☎ 800-IAM-LOST (426-5678).

If a hurricane threatens, ask your hotel concierge to help you arrange for transportation out of the city. Most hotels post-Katrina no longer allow guests or even their employees to ride out the storm.

Hospitals

Should you become ill during your visit, most major hospitals have staff doctors on call 24 hours a day. However, there are fewer physicians post-Katrina, so after-hours health care may be more limited or require longer waiting periods. If a doctor isn't available in your hotel or guesthouse, call or go to the emergency room at Ochsner Medical Institutions, 1516 Jefferson Hwy. (☎ 504-842-3460).

Hot Lines

YWCA Rape Crisis is ☎ 504-483-8888; Travelers Aid Society is ☎ 504-525-8726; Gamblers Anonymous is ☎ 504-431-7867; Narcotics Anonymous is ☎ 504-899-6262; Alcoholics Anonymous is ☎ 504-779-1178.

Information

The local Tourist Information Center is at 529 St. Ann St., ☎ 504-568-5661 or 504-566-5031). Also see "Where to Get More Information" at the end of this Appendix.

Internet Access

Three of the most convenient cybercafes are Cybercafe @ the CAC, inside the ground floor of the Contemporary Arts Center (900 Camp St.; ☎ 504-523-0990); Royal Access (621 Royal St.; ☎ 504-525-0401); and The Bastille Computer Cafe (605 Toulouse St.; ☎ 504-581-1150). For a comprehensive list of Internet cafes around the globe, visit www.cybercafes.com.

Liquor Laws

The legal drinking age in New Orleans is 21. You can buy liquor most anywhere 24 hours a day, 7 days a week, 365 days a year. All drinks carried on the street must be in plastic cups; bars often provide one of these plastic *go-cups* so that you can transfer your drink as you leave.

Mail

For U.S. Postal Service information and office hours, call ☎ 800-275-8777.

Maps

You can obtain maps at any of the information centers listed in Chapter 10 or at most hotels; www.mapquest.com is a good online resource for destination-specific U.S. maps, providing helpful driving information and hotel, restaurant, and attraction information.

Newspapers and Magazines

To find out what's going on around town, pick up a copy of the *Times-Picayune* (www.nola.com) or *Gambit Weekly* (www.bestofneworleans.com). Both publications' buildings flooded during Katrina, temporarily forcing them to stop publishing hard copy papers. Repairs have since been completed. *Times-Picayune* columnist Chris Rose has written moving accounts of Katrina's long-term effects on locals and is very popular for his plainspoken voice. *OffBeat* (www.offbeat.com) is an extensive monthly guide to the city's evening entertainment, art galleries, and special events; it's available in most hotels. Also refer to the "Where to Get More Information" section at the end of this appendix.

Pharmacies

The Walgreens Drug Store at 4400 S. Claiborne Ave. at Napoleon is the closest one to the French Quarter that offered 24-hour pharmacy service; however, it flooded and remains closed at the time of this writing. Call ☎ 504-891-0976 to ensure it has reopened. Take a cab here at night, or have the hotel send a taxi for your prescription.

Police

For nonemergency situations, call ☎ 504-821-2222. For emergencies, dial ☎ 911.

Radio Stations

Some of the more helpful and/or popular radio stations in the city include WSMB, 1350 AM (sports talk); WWNO, 89.9 FM (National Public Radio, classical); WWOZ, 90.7 FM (New Orleans and Louisiana music; jazz, R&B, and blues); WQUE, 93.3 FM (urban/R&B); and KKND, 106.7 FM (modern rock). If you'd like to hear local news, which still tends to revolve around Katrina-related issues, tune in to talk radio station WWL, 870 AM.

Restrooms

Public restrooms are located at Jax Brewery, Riverwalk Marketplace, Canal Place Shopping Center, Washington Artillery Park, and any of the major hotels.

Safety

Though many areas of New Orleans are perfectly safe, the general rule when visiting any city is to be on your guard all the time. Public transportation is relatively safe, though at night you'd be wise to take a cab if you're traveling to a dimly lit area. The St. Charles and Canal streetcars run 24 hours (though the St. Charles line is still closed temporarily as of this writing), but both run through some iffy neighborhoods, which can change from nice to not-so-nice within a couple of blocks; again, take a cab at night. Always use caution when walking through an unlit area at night. Avoid the Iberville Housing Project located between Basin, N. Claiborne, Iberville, and St. Louis streets, just outside of the French Quarter. You should also avoid St. Louis Cemetery No. 2 near Claiborne on the lake side of the Iberville Housing Project unless you're traveling with a large tour group. Also stay away from the area behind Armstrong Park. Remember: The city looks deceptively safe, and neighborhoods change very quickly.

Smoking

In this regard, New Orleans is like most major U.S. cities and more lenient than many. At most attractions and in most business buildings and shops, smokers should be prepared to stand around outside with all the other smokers. Most local restaurants cater to both smokers and nonsmokers; a relative few (in relation to the rest of the country) prohibit smoking altogether. Ask before you sit down.

Taxes

Louisiana's sales tax is very confusing. In addition to the state and federal taxes, each parish (county) may have additional taxes. To make things more confusing, some items such as unprepared food and some types of drugs are partially exempt, while prescriptions are totally exempt. In general, the total sales tax in New Orleans is 9 percent; it's 8.75 percent in Jefferson Parish.

Taxis

In most tourist areas, you can usually hail a taxi or get one at a taxi stand. If you can't find a taxi, call United Cab at ☎ 504-522-9771. If you have any complaints or left something in a taxi, call the Taxicab Bureau at ☎ 504-565-6272.

Time Zone

New Orleans is in the Central time zone. Daylight saving time is in effect from April through October.

Tipping

For most services — including restaurants and taxis — add 15 to 20 percent to your bill (before taxes). Many restaurants automatically add a 15 to 20 percent gratuity for parties of six or more. If you're just drinking at a bar, tipping 10 to 15 percent is typical. You should give bellhops $1 or $2 per bag, maids $1 per day, coat-check people $1 per garment, and automobile valets $1.

Transit Information

For information about streetcars and buses, call the Regional Transit Authority at ☎ 504-248-3900, or check out its Web site at www.norta.org.

Weather Updates

For the date, time, and temperature as well as a prerecorded weather update, including a daily forecast and marine forecast, call ☎ 504-828-4000. On the Web, visit www.intellicast.com for weather updates on all 50 states and most major U.S. cities, including New Orleans. Another handy site is www.weather.com, the online home of The Weather Channel.

Toll-Free Numbers and Web Sites

Major North American carriers

Air Canada
☎ 888-247-2262
www.aircanada.ca

AirTran Airlines
☎ 800-247-8726
www.airtran.com

America West Airlines
☎ 800-235-9292
www.americawest.com

American Airlines
☎ 800-433-7300
www.aa.com

Continental Airlines
☎ 800-525-0280
www.continental.com

Delta Air Lines
☎ 800-221-1212
www.delta.com

Frontier Airlines
☎ 800-432-1359
www.frontierairlines.com

JetBlue Airlines
☎ 800-538-2583
www.jetblue.com

Northwest Airlines
☎ 800-225-2525
www.nwa.com

Southwest Airlines
☎ 800-435-9792
www.southwest.com

United Airlines
☎ 800-241-6522
www.united.com

US Airways
☎ 800-428-4322
www.usairways.com

Car-rental agencies

Alamo
☎ 800-327-9633
www.goalamo.com

Avis
☎ 800-331-1212
www.avis.com

Budget
☎ 800-527-0700
www.budget.com

Dollar
☎ 800-800-4000
www.dollar.com

Enterprise
☎ 800-325-8007
www.enterprise.com

Hertz
☎ 800-654-3131
www.hertz.com

Major hotel and motel chains

Best Western International
☎ 800-528-1234
www.bestwestern.com

Clarion Hotels
☎ 800-CLARION
www.clarionhotel.com

Comfort Inns
☎ 800-228-5150
www.hotelchoice.com

Courtyard by Marriott
☎ 800-321-2211
www.courtyard.com

Days Inn
☎ 800-325-2525
www.daysinn.com

Doubletree Hotels
☎ 800-222-TREE
www.doubletree.com

Econo Lodges
☎ 800-55-ECONO
www.hotelchoice.com

Fairfield Inn by Marriott
☎ 800-228-2800
www.marriott.com

Hampton Inn
☎ 800-HAMPTON
www.hampton-inn.com

Hilton Hotels
☎ 800-HILTONS
www.hilton.com

Holiday Inn
☎ 800-HOLIDAY
www.basshotels.com

Howard Johnson
☎ 800-654-2000
www.hojo.com

Hyatt Hotels & Resorts
☎ 800-228-9000
www.hyatt.com

ITT Sheraton
☎ 800-325-3535
www.starwood.com

La Quinta Motor Inns
☎ 800-531-5900
www.laquinta.com

Marriott Hotels
☎ 800-228-9290
www.marriott.com

Quality Inns
☎ 800-228-5151
www.hotelchoice.com

Radisson Hotels International
☎ 800-333-3333
www.radisson.com

Ritz-Carlton
☎ 800-241-3333
www.ritzcarlton.com

Ramada Inns
☎ 800-2-RAMADA
www.ramada.com

Sheraton Hotels & Resorts
☎ 800-325-3535
www.sheraton.com

Red Carpet Inns
☎ 800-251-1962
www.reservahost.com

Super 8 Motels
☎ 800-800-8000
www.super8.com

Renaissance
☎ 800-228-9290
www.renaissancehotels.com

Travelodge
☎ 800-255-3050
www.travelodge.com

Residence Inn by Marriott
☎ 800-331-3131
www.marriott.com

Wyndham Hotels and Resorts
☎ 800-822-4200
www.wyndham.com

Where to Get More Information

An excellent source of information is the **New Orleans Metropolitan Convention and Visitors Bureau** (2020 St. Charles Ave., New Orleans, LA 70130; ☎ **800-672-6124** or 504-566-5003; www.nomcvb.com). Staff members are extremely helpful and accessible, and they can give you in-depth information on nearly whatever you seek.

Another good resource is the **New Orleans Multicultural Tourism Network** (1520 Sugar Bowl Dr., New Orleans, LA 70112; ☎ **800-725-5652** or 504-523-5652; www.soulofneworleans.com), which can point you to a number of local minority-owned businesses, from convention-related services (such as audio/visual services) to restaurants and hotels.

Tourist offices

The **Tourist Information Center** is located at 529 St. Ann St. (☎ **504-568-5661** or 504-566-5031). It's operated by the State of Louisiana and is located in the French Quarter in the historic Pontalba Buildings next to Jackson Square. Following is a list of other centrally located information centers:

- ✔ **Canal Street and Convention Center Boulevard** (☎ **504-587-0739**), at the beginning of the 300 block of Canal Street on the downtown side of the street

- ✔ Close to the **World Trade Center** (☎ **504-587-0734**) at 2 Canal St.

- ✔ Near the **Hard Rock Cafe** (☎ **504-587-0740**) on the 400 block of North Peters Street

✔ **Julia Street and Convention Center Boulevard** (walk-up booth)

✔ **Poydras Street and Convention Center Boulevard** (walk-up booth)

✔ **Vieux Carre Police Station** (☎ 504-565-7530), located at 334 Royal St.

City guides

For a more comprehensive and detail-packed peek at New Orleans than you can find in this book, check out *Frommer's New Orleans* by Mary Herczog (Wiley). Frommers.com is an excellent resource, as well, full of travel tips, online booking options, and a daily e-mail newsletter offering bargains and travel advice.

Some of the most indispensable online city and entertainment guides are the following:

✔ ***Ambush*** (www.ambushmag.com) provides excellent information on what's going on. You can also find a paper copy in most gay-friendly establishments.

✔ **Satchmo** (www.satchmo.com) provides a roundup of musical events and resources for wanting information about local musicians. It's especially valuable during Jazz Fest.

✔ **New Orleans CitySearch** (http://neworleans.citysearch.com), part of the extensive CitySearch network of city sites, offers staff picks and background information on food, music, entertainment, and the arts.

✔ **New Orleans Online** (www.neworleansonline.com) allows you to hone in on exactly what you're looking for; click on "Cuisine" to search for a Cajun restaurant in the French Quarter, for example, and peruse a list of available options.

✔ **New Orleans Travel Guide** (www.neworleans.com) allows you to scan restaurant menus, look inside certain hotels, and order free coupon books online. It also has an extensive list of attractions and links to dozens of useful, informative and/or fun New Orleans resources.

Index

SPORTS, FITNESS, PARENTING, RELIGION & SPIRITUALITY

0-7645-5146-9   0-7645-5418-2

Also available:
- Adoption For Dummies
  0-7645-5488-3
- Basketball For Dummies
  0-7645-5248-1
- The Bible For Dummies
  0-7645-5296-1
- Buddhism For Dummies
  0-7645-5359-3
- Catholicism For Dummies
  0-7645-5391-7
- Hockey For Dummies
  0-7645-5228-7

- Judaism For Dummies
  0-7645-5299-6
- Martial Arts For Dummies
  0-7645-5358-5
- Pilates For Dummies
  0-7645-5397-6
- Religion For Dummies
  0-7645-5264-3
- Teaching Kids to Read
  For Dummies
  0-7645-4043-2
- Weight Training For Dummies
  0-7645-5168-X
- Yoga For Dummies
  0-7645-5117-5

TRAVEL

0-7645-5438-7   0-7645-5453-0

Also available:
- Alaska For Dummies
  0-7645-1761-9
- Arizona For Dummies
  0-7645-6938-4
- Cancún and the Yucatán
  For Dummies
  0-7645-2437-2
- Cruise Vacations For Dummies
  0-7645-6941-4
- Europe For Dummies
  0-7645-5456-5
- Ireland For Dummies
  0-7645-5455-7

- Las Vegas For Dummies
  0-7645-5448-4
- London For Dummies
  0-7645-4277-X
- New York City For Dummies
  0-7645-6945-7
- Paris For Dummies
  0-7645-5494-8
- RV Vacations For Dummies
  0-7645-5443-3
- Walt Disney World & Orlando
  For Dummies
  0-7645-6943-0

GRAPHICS, DESIGN & WEB DEVELOPMENT

0-7645-4345-8   0-7645-5589-8

R.C.L.

AOUT 2007

Also available:
- Adobe Acrobat
  For Dummies
  0-7645-3760-1
- Building a Web S
  0-7645-7144-3
- Dreamweaver M
  For Dummies
  0-7645-4342-3
- FrontPage 2003
  0-7645-3882-9
- HTML 4 For Dum
  0-7645-1995-6
- Illustrator cs For
  0-7645-4084-X

NETWORKING, SECURITY, PROGRAMMING & DATABASES

0-7645-6852-3   0-7645-5784-X

Also available:
- A+ Certification For Dummies
  0-7645-4187-0
- Access 2003 All-in-One Desk
  Reference For Dummies
  0-7645-3988-4
- Beginning Programming
  For Dummies
  0-7645-4997-9
- C For Dummies
  0-7645-7068-4
- Firewalls For Dummies
  0-7645-4048-3
- Home Networking For Dummies
  0-7645-42796

- Network Security For Dummies
  0-7645-1679-5
- Networking For Dummies
  0-7645-1677-9
- TCP/IP For Dummies
  0-7645-1760-0
- VBA For Dummies
  0-7645-3989-2
- Wireless All In-One Desk Re
  For Dummies
  0-7645-7496-5
- Wireless Home Networking
  For Dummies
  0-7645-3910-8